W9-BLR-404

The Impact of
European Integration

The Impact of European Integration

Political, Sociological, and Economic Changes

Edited by
George A. Kourvetaris
and
Andreas Moschonas

Westport, Connecticut
London

Library of Congress Cataloging-in-Publication Data

The impact of european integration : political, sociological, and
   economic changes / George A. Kourvetaris, Andreas Moschonas, [co-
   editors].
       p.   cm.
   Includes bibliographical references and index.
   ISBN 0–275–94952–4 (alk. paper).—ISBN 0–275–95356–4 (pbk.)
       1. European Economic Community.   2. European Economic Community
   countries—Politics and government.   3. Europe—Economic
   integration.   4. Europe—Economic integration—Social aspects.
   I. Kourvetaris, George A.   II. Moschonas, Andreas.
   HC241.2.I428   1996
   306.2'094—dc20   95–19347

British Library Cataloguing in Publication Data is available.

Copyright © 1996 by George A. Kourvetaris and Andreas Moschonas

All rights reserved. No portion of this book may be
reproduced, by any process or technique, without the
express written consent of the publisher.

Library of Congress Catalog Card Number: 95–19347
ISBN: 0–275–94952–4
        0–275–95356–4 (pbk.)

First published in 1996

Praeger Publishers, 88 Post Road West, Westport, CT 06881
An imprint of Greenwood Publishing Group, Inc.

Printed in the United States of America

The paper used in this book complies with the
Permanent Paper Standard issued by the National
Information Standards Organization (Z39.48–1984).

10 9 8 7 6 5 4 3 2 1

Contents

Tables

Acknowledgements

This edited volume would not have been possible without the assistance of The College of Liberal Arts and Sciences of Northern Illinois University, Office of Manuscript Services.

The co-editors would like to extend their appreciation to Karen Blaser, Director of Manuscript Services; Dolores Henry (who retired in May of 1995); and Susan Harshman, who diligently worked on the project and helped us to organize it in a comprehensive book form.

In addition, it would be an omission if the co-editors did not extend their deepest appreciation to Sue Barkman, Faculty Secretary of the Sociology Department, who assisted us with multiple correspondence to the many contributors to the volume from European countries and the United States.

In the last analysis, however, the co-editors and authors assume the responsibility for any omissions or shortcomings of the edited volume on European Integration.

The Impact of
European Integration

Introduction

Andreas Moschonas and George A. Kourvetaris

Historically, the idea of European integration goes back to the late Middle Ages and the early Renaissance. According to Tounta-Fergadis (P. 47),[1] the notion of a continental Europe followed two basic ideological trends. The first was characterized by two main subdivisions—one under Latin and German, the second by a European union under an Anglo-Saxon tutelage. The most important advocates of the first view were Pierre Dubois, Emeric Cruce, Sully, de Saint Pierre, Leibnitz, and Kant. The second view was represented by William Penn, Jhon Bellers, and Jeremy Bentham. Due to the continuous wars and conflicts among European peoples, a number of political thinkers and philosophers such as Machiavelli, Hobbes, Locke, and Kant were searching for some political model to bring about order and stability in Europe. At the same time the notion of the nation-state which, was facilitated by the rise of nationalism in the mid-nineteenth century, along with the Napoleonic Wars, contributed to the idea of European union. During the twentieth century similar efforts toward European unification modeled after the United States, the British Empire, and the former Soviet Socialist Republics were made by an Austrian politician, M. Coudenhove-Kallergi, and the French politician Aristide Briand. However, these efforts failed to materialize due to the rise of Nazi totalitarianism and the internal economic problems of most European countries, which led to the outbreak of World War II. Out of these efforts toward a European union, two goals became clear: the need for a European union and the creation of basic institutions and methods by which union could be possible (Tounta-Fergadis, pp. 46-47).

In modern times, the process of European integration has passed through three distinctive stages.[2] The first was the period of the institutional establishment of the so-called European Communities. In 1950 the Frenchmen Jean Monnet and Robert Schuman proposed the formation of the European Coal and Steel Community (ECSC). This was established in 1952 and became the predecessor of the European Economic Community (EEC), established in 1958 together with the European Atomic Energy Community (Euratom). All three were originally composed of six member states: Belgium, France, the Federal Republic of Germany, Italy, Luxembourg, and the Netherlands. This period, which continued throughout the 1960s, was marked by two basic developments: the initial formation and operation of the Common Agricultural Policy (CAP), and the implementation of the common market clauses of the founding treaties centered on the so-called negative integration,[3] implying the removal of the traditional barriers to trade among the member states specified in the treaty.

The second period started in the late 1960s, in the midst of an economic crisis, and continued until the middle of the 1980s. This period was characterized by three additional developments. One was the conclusion of the first enlargement of the Community with the accession in 1973 of three new member states: Denmark, Ireland, and the United Kingdom. Under the political commitment of the community's member states, it was believed that by such an enlargement the old and new members would work together for the materialization of the triptych: completion, deepening, and enlargement. Another development was, in the midst of a growing Euroskepticism, the beginning of a debate on the form of the political union, exemplified by the Tindemans Report, entitled "European Union" (1976),[4] and resulted in the agreement on direct elections for the European Parliament, initially held in 1979. The third development was the commencement during the 1970s of negotiations for the second enlargement of the Community, known as the Mediterranean enlargement, which resulted in the accession of three new members: Greece (1981), Portugal (1986), and Spain (1986).

Finally, the third period began in 1985 with the appointment of the new Commission headed by Jacques Delors. The importance of this period for the future development of the Community has been highlighted by many analysts. Dinan, for example, in his recent book, comments: "In the mid-1980s the European Community underwent an extraordinary transformation. After years of sluggish growth and institutional immobility, the member states concluded the Single European Act (SEA), a major revision of the Treaty of Rome and underpinned the single market (1992) program and "lifted the Community from its stagnant condition to its dynamic phase in the late 1980s." Jacques Delors, who became Commission president in January 1985, is generally credited with the Community's metamorphosis. "Delors is as important to the enterprise today," Stanley Hoffmann wrote at the height of the Community's transformation, "as Jean Monnet was in the 1950s."[5]

The period in question has been marked by three main events. One was the agreement of the member states reached in 1985 on the completion of the internal market by the end of 1992, institutionalized by the Single European Act concluded in 1987. Another was the initiation, immediately thereafter, of a process of broader revisions of the treaties which resulted in the conclusion in 1992 of the agreement on the "European Union," known as the Maastricht Treaty. And the third major event of the period was the agreement reached in 1994 on the third enlargement of the Community with the planned accession on January 1, 1995 of four new member states: Austria, Finland, Norway, and Sweden. (Norwegian voters rejected membership in a referendum.) These recent Community developments have in fact materialized due primarily to the cataclysmic events of 1989 and the great socioeconomic and political transformations which have since then characterized the Eastern European countries and the former Soviet Union.

The present volume has a limited but clear objective. The idea for a book on European integration materialized a few years ago in an effort to focus primarily on the political and sociological aspects of European integration and secondarily on the economic dimension. The editors of this volume felt the need for a "political sociology of European integration," instead of approaching the European Union in the "traditional" way, that is, either as a merely economic entity or as an international organization. In this sense, we share the view expressed at the 1992 Annual Conference of the British Sociological Association by Chris Rootes: "We wanted to bring Europe to the top of the agenda of British sociology because we believed, as we believe still, in the desirability of cross-nationally comparative sociological research, but also because we considered that some of the enthusiasm for European integration was indiscriminate and needed, as a corrective, a stiff dose of critical sociological analysis."[6]

In spite of this clear objective we must acknowledge that in preparing this book we came across three major difficulties as far as the prospective contributors were concerned. First was the realization that there are indeed only a limited number of political sociologists specializing in the European Union. Second, the editors felt that the few people who were identified as EU specialists were at the moment unavailable to contribute scholarly papers for the reader. Third, we not only faced tremendous logistical problems of coordination and communication with those who agreed to contribute chapters for the book but as coeditors ourselves we had to overcome a number of problems due to our living apart from each other. However, we still believe that the present volume does represent a significant contribution to the literature, underlining, at the same time, the obvious: that there is always a social content in any economic or political process, requiring the attention of the researcher and the analyst, and that this is material for critical sociological analysis.

While the focus of the book is on economic and political integration, the contributions cover a broader range of issues on European integration, including institutional, sociocultural, constitutional, administrative, and security. The first article, "The Logic of European Integration," written by Andreas Moschonas, brings to the fore this very point. The author argues that European integration is actually a historical process which stems from the expansionist logic of capitalism. This tendency for capitalism to expand undermines the traditional role of the state, thereby reinforcing a form of institutional organization at the supranational level. However, the crystallization of the European Union's specific form of institutional organization has been possible only under the impact of the historically conditioned cultural and geopolitical peculiarities of Europe. A valuable theory of European integration, therefore, cannot but take into account both these elements, the specific and the general. From this point of view, Moschonas examines critically the conventional theories of European integration and argues instead for a historically and socially conditioned theoretical interpretation of the genesis and evolution of the European Union.

The first step of examining the evolution of the EU is to see the actual synthesis and the real changes occurring in the social and economic structure. In his contribution, Eleftherios N. Botsas argues that the socioeconomic structure of the EU, consisting of the three main economic sectors, agriculture, industry, and services, is being defined by the market mechanism with varying degrees of social control by the national governments. Botsas's analysis reveals the existence of a substantial gap between the North and the South of the Union, or, in other words, between the center and the peripheral areas, in all three economic sectors. In agriculture, the South reflects developing countries more than advanced countries. The manufacturing sector testifies to this dualism as well, in the sense that the North has an advantage in human capital accumulation, while the South specializes in resource-intensive products. Finally, in the service sector the North and the South experience qualitative differences, especially in business services.

These structural differences tend to condition the composition and the dynamism of the capitalist class in the European Union. The issue is analyzed by Otto Holman and Kees Van der Pijl, who argue that capital represents a potentially world-embracing social force, structuring roles and patterns of behavior and consciousness. However, the settings in which a bourgeoisie crystallizes and evolves into a conscious social and political force are concrete. In a historically informed and integrated approach, the authors start their analysis with an elaboration on the postwar corporate-liberal restructuring of capitalist relations in general and bourgeois power in particular. Then, they turn to the rise of global neoliberalism as a restructuring force on existing, predominantly national, power configurations. Finally, they concentrate on the most influential transnational business lobby, the European Round Table of Industrialists (ERT), and its role as a policy-shaping group. The authors argue that this group has been playing a substantial role in cementing a certain degree of cohesion among the leading social forces in Europe.

Also of great importance, however, has been the role played by the petty bourgeoisie. Antigone Lyberaki and Vassilis Pesmazoglou examine only a segment of this social stratum, the small and medium-sized entrepreneurs of the industrial sector, underlining the position that the analysis of this group must be placed within broader macroeconomic trends. The objective here is to examine the variety of ideas and policy prescriptions associated with the persistence and proliferation of small and medium-sized enterprises, both as a response to the recession and as a means of overcoming it. Having presented the most influential contemporary theoretical framework for small and medium-sized enterprises, the authors then examine the evidence at hand, dealing more specifically with issues concerning employment generation, remuneration, and conditions of work, as well as the functioning of industrial districts. Their argument is that the EU context offers some interesting insights concerning the policy issues involved in the support of smaller establishments. However, the authors believe that small and medium-sized enterprises within the European Union will face some formidable problems, including adjustment to and competition with larger industrial firms, business conglomerates, and multinationals.

The significance of the petty bourgeoisie can also be found in the agricultural sector of the European Union. Napoleon Maraveyas examines this by arguing that significant differences among the agricultural strata, and the structures of agriculture of all the member countries, still exist in the EU. The author attributes this multiplicity to the different social, political, and historical developments and to the natural and climatic characteristics of these countries. The analysis centers first on the agricultural inequalities and differences among the EU member states. Then the author examines the mechanisms and the reforms made to the CAP (Common Agricultural Policy) so as to clarify the contradictions involved in the articulation of the interests of the European farmers, as expressed through the European agricultural organizations. These contradictions have contributed to the obvious, that is, the perpetuation of the social inequalities between regions and member countries. As Maraveyas states, after three decades of the application of the CAP, the fact remains that there has not been a substantial convergence of the structures of agriculture among the member countries.

Social inequalities also exist among the Union's urban working class, a substantial part of which consists of foreign or "third world" nationals. Patrick R. Ireland examines the obstacles these foreign-born nationals experience in trying to participate in the European Union, arguing that European integration has indeed had a political effect on immigrant communities, in the sense that they are generating new, European-level forms of organization and lines of solidarity. However, the fact remains that foreign-origin populations, even more than indigenous Europeans, have run into barriers when trying to participate in the EU policy-making process.

The social multiplicity involved also affects the attitudes of people toward European integration. Andreas G. Kourvetaris and George A. Kourvetaris examine the cultural and ethnic dimensions of this issue, using data from interviews with representatives and delegates from EU countries and published material. The authors argue that while economic and, to some extent, political integration has been the major focus of European Union, cultural and ethnic issues, such as assimilation, language, nationalism, and similar ideas, have not been resolved by most Europeans. The authors conclude that while most Europeans share certain values, they identify themselves first as members of distinct nationalities and second as Europeans. The opposite, the authors observe, is characteristic in the United States. The authors believe while the movement toward economic and political integration will bring Europeans closer, only time will reveal the extent to which ethnic and cultural integration will take place.

A question which has extensively been analyzed in the European Union is the way social interests are articulated and expressed.[7] The article by Wolfgang Streeck and Philippe C. Schmitter elaborates on this theme from a specific angle: the authors examine the processes of corporatism and pluralist interest articulation, arguing that the EU setting helps the development of the latter. The reason for this is that, in the EU organized labor not only has been underorganized but there also has never been a real possibility of a mutually organizing interaction effect between labor and the two other major players in the political economy—capital and the state. This means that in the EU there is no mechanism in sight able to rationalize the political system and establish corporatist monopolies of representation.

Social interests are also expressed at the political level through political parties. The history and morphology of the EU political parties are analyzed by Karl Magnus Johansson. His analysis sheds light on the nature of transnational party cooperation within the European Union and the nexus between political parties, national and transnational, and the integration process. The argument is that the party federations in general and the political groups in particular are undergoing constant alignments and mergers. The author believes that in order to understand the nature of European political parties, one has to understand the nature of national and domestic politics. Moreover, he argues that the emerging European parties are not mass parties, and that they have not been successful as mobilizers of public opinion. Instead, they resemble the American parties in that they are active above all in regard to elections and work as channels for competing elites.

European political parties articulate and express social and political interests mainly within the institutionalized processes of the European Parliament (EP). The origin, evolution, functions, and powers of this institution are examined by Juliet Lodge. She argues that the role and functions of the EP, and with them those of its political party groups, have changed dramatically since the end of the 1970s, when the first Euro-elections were held. In fact, the symbiotic relationship between the parties and the EP has become increasingly significant, and will be one of the main features of institutional development during the 1990s. The Maastrict Treaty provisions have indeed strengthened the role of the EP in the Union's institutional structure. And as Lodge states, small incremental changes have potentially large implications for the exercise of influence and authority by the EC's increasingly bicameral legislature: the Council and the European Parliament. Despite its significance for the European Union, the author believes the very existence of the European Parliament creates anxiety among member nation-states. She concludes with an optimistic note, namely that the role of the European Parliament will expand and eventually transform Europe into a federal and liberal democratic polity.

The Maastricht Treaty has also changed the relationship between EU institutions and national states, with the institutionalization of the Commission of the Regions. "European Union and Local Government," by Andreas Moschonas, approaches this new relationship in the light of the challenges posed by the processes of integration and internationalization. The interesting point raised by the author is that a clear understanding of the institutional changes under way requires an examination of the structural transformations happening in the European economies and societies in an era of integration and internationalization. The main argument is that the rationale for the activation of the local-regional authorities in the era of economic crisis and restructuring lies in the need to foster the development of the endogenous forces of the regions. Thus the regionalization of Europe, institutionalized with the Maastrict Treaty, is a direct response to these socioeconomic and political imperatives.

This discussion brings us to a broader debate on European integration and the challenge for political union. The chapter by Gianni Bonvicini presents an overview of the historical process which led to the European Union arrangements. Bonvicini concentrates on the nature and process of European integration by looking at the integration requisites. Specifically, he analyzes the Maastricht Treaty and the decline of public support which undermines the Single European Act of 1986. He examines the reasons for the collapse of public support and provides possible remedies for the process of integration. More specifically, the author puts emphasis on the practical effects and the ad hoc experiences drawn from the application of certain policies and decision-making instruments to the building of Europe. Two scenarios are presented for the future: One is the consolidation of the Maastricht arrangements, and the other is the quick and sharp revision of Maastricht. The author's conclusion is that the future of Europe will be the result of an ad hoc combination of different criteria, such as a mix of institutional procedures, the application of the principle of subsidiarity, and the public perception of the guarantees provided by the participation in the process of integration.

The process toward institutional construction and political union does not take place within definite external boundaries, for the European Union still faces the question of enlargement. The limits of the EU in the context of enlargement is a theme examined by Nicholas V. Gianaris. The author argues that, though there are deeply rooted cultural and ethnic differences, and many doubts and quarrels may appear in the process of enlargement, the momentum should remain irreversible. This is because, for the EU to achieve its main goals, that is, "peace and the refusal to decline," it should be enlarged to an ultimate membership of all the European nations. Enlargement, the author argues, will depend on the success of European integration. His major thesis is that a gradual enlargement of the EU will create more trade, which will lead to sociopolitical stability and development.

The relationship between enlargement and European security, and civil-military issues in general, are further discussed by Kostas Messas. The author believes that European integration has given its institutions valuable experience in building a framework within which nationalist aspirations are curtailed. Thus the European Union must consider accepting some Eastern European countries interested in joining. Furthermore, the author argues that Europe needs a comprehensive framework of security and stability for European unification to be realized. An achievement of this magnitude can only be accomplished through political, economic, and military cooperation among the major actors in the region.

In conclusion, it should be stated that the contributions in this volume are not all on themes originally planned, and thus the overall cohesion is not as comprehensive as the editors would like it to be. There is, however, an obvious pluralism in this volume in terms of diversity of views expressed and the various approaches adopted. There is also a conscious effort to employ social and political analysis in the examination of key issues of European integration. Whether the coeditors and various contributors succeeded in bringing a number of important issues on European integration into one volume will be judged by the readers.

NOTES

1. Arete Tounta-Fergadis, 1987, "E exélixe tis idéas tis evropaikís enopoieseos" [The Evolution of the Idea of European Integration], *Sýchrona Thémata* [Contemporary Themes], Vol. 10, No. 30, May 1987, pp. 42-48.

2. Cf. Desmond Dinan, *Ever Closer Union? An Introduction to the European Community* (London: The Macmillan Press, 1994), especially Part I, for a good introductory discussion on these points.

3. John Pinder, "Positive Integration and Negative Integration: Some Problems of Economic Union in the EEC," in M. Hodges (ed.), *European Integration* (Harmondsworth: Penguin Books, 1972), pp. 124-50.

4. See "European Union," report by Leo Tindemans to the European Council, *Bulletin of the European Communities*, supplement 1/76. For a further analysis, see J. Vandamme, "The Tindemans Report 1975-1976," in R. Pryce (ed.), *The Dynamics of European Union* (London: Groom Helm, 1987), pp. 149-73.

5. Dinan, *Ever Closer Union?*, p. 129.

6. Chris Rootes and Howard David (eds.), *Social Change and Political Transformation* (London: UCL Press, 1994), p. 1.

7. Cf. J. N. Garden, *Effective Lobbying in the European Community* (Deventer: Kluwer Law and Taxation Publishers, 1991); J. Greenwood, J. R. Grote, and K. Ronit, *Organized Interests and the European Community* (London: Sage, 1992); and S. Mazey and J. J. Richardson, *Lobbying in the European Community* (Oxford: Oxford University Press, 1993).

1

The Logic of European Integration

Andreas Moschonas

European integration is interpreted here as a historical process wherein the expansionist logic embodied in the capitalist mode of production tends to disturb the balance between institutional "form" and material "content," thus reinforcing some form of institutional organization at a higher level. However, the crystallization of the European Union's specific form of institutional organization has been possible only under the impact of the historically conditioned cultural and geopolitical peculiarities of Europe.[1]

In this sense the logic of European integration, as exemplified through the various theories of integration, is presented here in association with an analysis of those very European peculiarities. Thus, in what follows, the first section deals with the historical conjuncture, the second section examines the conventional theory of integration, the third section is devoted to an analysis of the Marxist theory of integration, and the final section presents some conclusions.

THE HISTORICAL CONJUNCTURE

It is well known that World War II was mainly a European war, and its impact upon the whole fabric of the European nations was enormous: physical destruction, the paralysis of the transport system, the atrophy of governments, the ruin of the currency, and galloping price rises all combined to bring the 1946 national incomes and outputs well below the levels of prewar years. For example, France's gross domestic product in 1946 was a little under 50 percent of prewar activity; Italy's stood at 61 percent of the prewar figure; the Netherlands' was at 74 percent; and Germany's national income and output in 1946 were as low as 29 percent of those of 1938. It was not until 1948 that most of the European countries were able to approach the prewar levels of output and income.[2]

Moreover, the sociopolitical consequences of the war were also felt throughout Europe. In every European country the working classes as well as fractions of the property-owning classes became discontented with existing socioeconomic and political institutions and thus more receptive to new ideas promising major or even radical transformations. In Eastern Europe the prewar ruling classes were gradually replaced by popular forces, while in most of the Western European countries the challenge posed by the rising and radicalized working classes was obvious. For example, Britain began its recovery program with a Labour government committed to nationalizations and socioeconomic planning; France and Italy could not function without the Left's consent; and Greece had to fight an open class struggle in a bloody civil war.[3]

The most dramatic change, however, was the division of the European continent into two parts and its subsequent demotion in the sphere of international affairs: Europe thus became, as Galtung put it, "not only bicentric, but bicentric with one center in Washington and one in Moscow: in other words, with centers located outside itself."[4] In this sense European developments were necessarily conditioned by the global politico-strategic considerations of the two superpowers, thus losing, to a great extent, their autonomous impulse.

The Soviet presence in and hegemony over the Eastern European countries was the result, not only of past European and Soviet experiences, but also of the emerging balance of power in the world. Because of past experiences, including those of the last world war, the Soviet Union made regional security a high priority in its postwar foreign policy objectives, while the fulfillment of its new role as a rising superpower in world affairs required some international recognition by the Western powers. In the immediate postwar years the Soviet leadership thought that the achievement of these two objectives required a measure of Soviet influence in the Eastern European region, and this for obvious reasons. Historically, the instability of the regimes of the Eastern European countries, the subordination of those regimes to the interests of the major European powers, and their hostility to the Soviet Union, all combined to make the Soviet Union's security a correlate of the fate of Eastern Europe—hence the rationale of Soviet hegemony over Eastern Europe. Through this hegemony the Soviet Union expected to achieve also some sort of status, or international recognition, by making clear, even before the end of the war, that major decisions of European and world politics could no longer be taken without its consent. To the extent therefore, that the Western powers, especially the United States, were prepared to challenge the Soviet Union's presence in Eastern Europe, thus undermining its security objective, and to deny its international status, the latter seemed to have no other choice but to become uncooperative with the Western powers, at times aggressive (as the Berlin incident indicates), and very often tough in exercising its hegemony over Eastern Europe.[5]

On the other side of the sociopolitical polarity, the Soviet presence in Eastern Europe was *perceived* by the Western governments as being a potential or even a real *threat*[6] to the very survival of the Western world. This interpretation gave rise to the escalation of the psychological tension and the ideological conflict between East and West and reinforced the need for the reconstruction and reorganization of the Western European region. The objective then was to strengthen and unite the Western world, under the hegemony of the United States, in order to "contain" the alleged expansion of communism. On the ideological plane, the Truman Doctrine,[7] announced on March 12, 1947, promised "to support free peoples" who were resisting "attempted subjugation by armed minorities or by outside pressures," while the Marshall Plan, announced on June 5, 1947, was intended to promote "the survival of a working economy in the world so as to permit the emergence of political and social conditions in which free institutions can exist."[8]

Marshall's globalization of the economy was dependent on the recovery and growth of the European economies. This was because the American economy, which was under strain at the end of World War II because of surpluses of goods and capital, went through its first postwar recession in 1945-46, with a substantial decline in industrial production and a subsequent rise in unemployment, followed by a second recession in 1948-49. Faced with such problems, the U.S. administration thought that European reconstruction, with American capital, would help the Europeans to overcome their balance of payments problems, provide profitable outlets for U.S. capital, and open new markets for U.S. goods.[9]

The assistance offered through the Marshall Plan was not unconditional: it presupposed that the governments of the recipient countries would cooperate[10] among themselves and would agree on the specific plans necessary for the reconstruction of Europe. The purpose of this cooperation was to facilitate the realization of the central economic goals of the Marshall Plan which, as Block states, included "the restoration of multilateralism, price stability, and the recovery of production."[11] These goals were in fact interrelated and entailed fundamental changes in the organization of the European economies so as to generate high levels of new investment through an expanded inflow of U.S. capital, labor discipline with the aim of curtailing the demands of the Left for expanded social services and higher standards of living, thereby fostering the accumulation of capital, and restoration of European competitiveness as the necessary requirement for the acceptance by the Europeans of a multilateral world economy operating under U.S. hegemony.[12] These capitalist-oriented preconditions forced the Soviet Union, at the Paris discussions held in 1947, to declare its unwillingness to participate in the plan, requesting instead that the assistance be given on a bilateral basis and that the donor country, the United States, respect the recipient country's national sovereignty, that is, its right to employ the assistance so as to construct its own socioeconomic and political institutions.[13] This disagreement reinforced a real split between East and West: while the Soviet Union, exercising its hegemony over the Eastern European countries, managed to block their participation in the Plan, the

Western European countries[14] came together and formed in 1948 the so called Organization for European Economic Cooperation (OEEC).

The OEEC, set up to administer the Marshall Plan, reflected the postwar economic thinking which had provided the justification for greater state intervention into the economy.[15] In keeping with this economic climate, the European governments participating in the OEEC declared their determination "to make the fullest collective use of their individual capacities and potentialities" in order to "increase their production, develop and modernize their industrial and agricultural equipment, expand their commerce, reduce progressively barriers to trade . . . promote full employment and restore or maintain the stability of their economies. . . ."[16] In essence, this declaration entailed a policy designed to enhance the twin goals of economic growth and full employment.[17] The underlying assumption was that the pursuit of this objective through a deliberate political action (state intervention) would, automatically, not only cure the various economic maladies but also increase the confidence of the people in their institutions. None of the participating countries seemed to question the "correctness" of this basic assumption; their disagreements centered on other matters, such as the degree of trade liberalization and the political form the OEEC was to take. On the first question, the countries with open and comparatively more productive economies (Britain and the United States) were in favor of global liberalization, while the continental countries, especially France and Italy, being in an economically weaker position, preferred regionalism and a slow reduction of tariffs. Similarly, on the institutional issue, the British, supported by the Scandinavians, wanted the OEEC to be a traditional intergovernmental body, while the continental countries were in favor of some form of supranationalism.[18] The reasons which explain these positions are related to both domestic and international factors.

On the continental side, France and Italy, which seem to represent here the decisive cases owing to the strong position of the Left, displayed certain political similarities as they began their economic and political reconstruction following the end of the war. The first postwar election in both countries indicated clearly the willingness of the electorate to strengthen the forces of the Left in an attempt to facilitate social transformation. In Italy the first postwar general election, held on June 2, 1946, gave the Christian Democrats about 35 percent of the popular vote and 207 seats in parliament out of a total of 556, the Socialists almost 21 percent and 115 seats, and the Communists roughly 19 percent and 104 seats. These three parties assumed the responsibility of governing the country. Similarly, France's first national election after the war, held on October 21, 1945, for a Constituent Assembly, returned the Communists with 26.2 percent of the popular vote and 160 seats out of 583, the Socialists with 23.4 percent and 146 seats, and the Christian Democrats (MRP) with 23.9 percent and 152 seats. In the following election for the second Constituent Assembly, held on June 2, 1946, the Christian Democrats got 28.2 percent of the popular vote, the Communists 25.9 percent, and the Socialists 21.1 percent.

In the legislative election, held on November 10, 1946, the Communists received 28.2 percent of the popular vote, the Christian Democrats 25.9 percent, and the Socialists 17.8 percent; these three parties assumed the responsibility of government.

Therefore, in this political conjuncture, the removal of the Left from the government could not but intensify political antagonisms, weaken the position of the government, and thus increase the necessity for the adoption of authoritarian measures at home and the cultivation of political cooperation at the European level, called in EEC parlance "European solidarity." This removal, partial in France (Communists only) and total in Italy (Communists and Socialists), came in May 1947, just two months after the announcement of the Truman Doctrine, and symbolized the political commitment of the governments of these two countries to the Western cause in the then emerging Cold War.[19]

These two historical cases, themselves instructive because of the intensity of their sociopolitical conflicts, though not representing the totality of western continental Europe, seem nevertheless to suggest that the European orientation of the capitalist class of the European countries did reflect domestic realities and pressures. Apart from these domestic factors, however, the French desire for supranationalism, at the OEEC in particular, also contained an external component: France's policy toward Germany immediately after the war was based on the axiom that the weakness of Germany was the strength of France.[20] However, when France realized that her policy of keeping Germany very weak and totally divided was getting little support from her allies,[21] she then decided to exercise some kind of control over Germany by incorporating the latter into European institutions vested with supranational powers and properly controlled by France herself. At the Paris meeting, which discussed the formation of the OEEC, the participating countries did declare that "the German economy should be integrated in the economy of Europe," implying by this that future German governments would have to participate in the OEEC and in other European institutions.[22]

Britain's position concerning the form of the European institutions, on the other hand, reflected her hitherto existing status in the world as a great power. In the postwar reality, however, British governments thought that the preservation of their country's strength and independence required the cultivation of three overlapping circles of relationships,[23] namely the relationships with the United States, the Commonwealth, and Europe, the simultaneous functioning of which presupposed the adoption of the traditional intergovernmental form of association. The necessity for this intergovernmental strategy was further reinforced by two other factors: the British political tradition regarding the supremacy of Parliament, itself perceived as the guardian of national sovereignty, and the political climate of the time expressed by the Labour government, which was favorable to nationalizations and economic planning, the achievement of which seemed to suggest that the progressive forces of Britain ought not to establish close associations with the conservative ruling classes of the continent.[24]

Finally the British position prevailed, as a result perhaps of Britain's relative strength at the time, and the OEEC was organized as an intergovernmental body, that is, a body which was under the control of a ministerial council operating on a unanimity basis.[25] The U.S. government could easily have promoted, because of its hegemonic status, some form of supranational organization, but it did not try to impose such a solution, for the U.S. administration seemed to be more interested in establishing some form of European cooperation, in order to strengthen the European security front and also to facilitate economic reconstruction and trade liberalization, than in fostering the United States of Europe advocated by the European visionaries and federalists. The latter were greatly displeased with the American performance, and cried publicly: "It is to be regretted that the Americans, on this score, were duped by Great Britain in one of the greatest deceptions in modern European history," with the result that "instead of a political union we have witnessed the maintenance and the strengthening of the national particularisms, vaguely disguised in European terms," which "for some time have deceived both American and European public opinion."[26]

For the convinced Europeans, like Spinelli, political union was the ultimate goal which must be achieved through direct political action and institutional engineering. This "ideal" goal, properly loaded with metaphysical nuances, encompasses the notion of the "European Idea," a notion which allegedly reflects the existence of a common civilization, a community of interest, and a common destiny for all the European peoples.[27] Over time its real meaning has been adapted to historical circumstances. In earlier times, for example, the notion of the European Idea was used to describe the imaginary picture of a United Christian Europe, while later the same notion was used to describe a politically united Europe, perhaps a European federal union of some kind. In recent times it was a European aristocrat, Coudenhove-Kalergi, who tried to strengthen the consciousness of the European peoples with his Pan-European Idea. He believed that the European continent was burdened with the solution of two burning problems, namely: the European problem produced by the division between sovereign states and the social problem produced by the division between social classes, and that the solution to the former problem (which implied political union) was a precondition for overcoming or controlling the social problem. It was also a precondition for overcoming the external threats posed by "American competition and Russian expansionism."[28]

The perception of a threat and the need for security was also in the mind of Winston Churchill when he expressed his views in 1946 before an audience at the University of Zurich.[29] His call was for the creation of a kind of United States of Europe, which was supposed to function as a regional organization of the United Nations. Churchill's main objective here was not the federal reconstruction of Europe but rather the creation of a European group, through some kind of political cooperation, which would minimize or even eliminate conflicts between rival European states, especially conflicts between Germany and France, and would thus serve as a "coherent natural grouping" in the new balance of power which, under the impact of the war, had become international. Actually, what Churchill wanted was to globalize the hitherto European balance of power system in order to create a role not so much for the European states as for Britain itself: in this sense Britain, along with the Commonwealth, seemed to represent a "coherent natural grouping" which could and should participate in the global balance of power together with other "natural groupings" such as the United States and the Soviet Union. Thus the European grouping was needed to facilitate the smooth functioning of the Churchillian balance of power and to strengthen the British position in its dealings with the emerging superpowers. In this imaginary world the British dilemma was obvious: while, in the Churchillian syllogism, a minimum European cooperation seemed to be necessary for the functioning of the new international system, a real European union was undesirable, for it would have increased the collective power of the European states, thus undermining the British position in the world—after all, a possible continental union had been Britain's traditional fear.[30]

In this context, one has to appreciate de Gaulle's reservations about Britain's true commitment to Europe, and also the criticisms of the European federalists arguing that Churchill decided to play the role of the guardian of the European movement in order to make sure that real union would never be achieved.[31] At the Hague Congress held in 1948, the European federalists, for their part, requested reconciliation and reconstruction, and called for the creation of an economic and political union in order to assure security and social progress:[32] The creation of the Council of Europe in 1949 and its organization along intergovernmental lines once again made visible the split between the British, who favored intergovernmentalism, and the Europeans of the continent, who were seeking some kind of supranational authority. As a result, the latter became convinced that the political union of Europe had to be pursued outside the Council of Europe, though they disagreed among themselves as to the appropriate method to be followed: should European union be the result of a deliberate political action of institutional engineering (federalists), or could that union be the result of a gradual and incremental change (functionalists)? In either case, the feasibility of realizing the union was not questioned, and the climate seemed to be ripe for some decisive action which could lead to what came to be called the "European Community." The term "European Community" describes collectively: (i) the European Coal and Steel Community (ECSC), established by the Treaty of Paris, signed on April 19, 1951 and put into effect on July 25 1952; (ii) the European Atomic Energy Community (Euratom); and (iii) the European Economic Community (EEC), established (as was Euratom) by the Treaty of Rome, signed on March 25, 1957 and put into effect on January 1, 1958.

These being the peculiarities of the historical conjuncture, the question now arises: what does theory tell us about the establishment of these communities in particular and the historical process of European integration in general?

CONVENTIONAL THEORY OF INTEGRATION

The process of European integration, crystallized in the midst of the Cold War, became for some analysts a phenomenon susceptible to conceptualizations drawn from the analytical categories of the conventional theory of international relations, a theory whereby issues of peace and security, pursued through diplomatic-strategic means, are thought to dominate the actions of the personified national states as they compete among themselves for the enhancement of the "national interest" defined in terms of the power of the power elites. Seen from this analytical angle, because the nation is "an institution of decision, of action, of ambition which expresses and serves only the national interest," there is "no European reality other than our nations and the states which are their expression," implying that "to build Europe, there is no solution other than cooperation between nations."[33] However, this very cooperation, reinforced further by a common perception of an external threat, could lead to the formation of a "pluralist security-community" (a military alliance) which, under conditions of compatible sociopolitical values, similar socioeconomic systems, and high interdependence, might be upgraded to an "amalgamated security-community," implying a "community" which possesses one supreme decision-making center.[34] Once this stage is reached, then the analyst of integration automatically enters the realm of the conventional theories on federal political systems, theories which, in their legalistic-institutional currents, make pronouncements about the division of formal powers between the supranational institutions and the institutions of the participating national states.[35] In their sociological-functional currents, on the other hand, these theories make pronouncements and conceptualizations about the background conditions supposedly conducive to the initiation of the process of federalizing a political community and the maintenance of the established institutional arrangement. History is perceived here as an "assembly-line process" which allegedly advances through a multiplicity of causal factors properly manipulated by the political elites, be they in the form of Deutsch's "core areas" or Etzioni's "elite-units," up to the takeoff point: then development-integration becomes a self-reinforcing process.[36]

In the language of functionalism, this allegedly evolutionary dynamic was conceptualized by some analysts in terms of an observed discrepancy between the particularistic nature of the national states and the internationalizing tendencies of the national economies, tendencies thought destined to produce "common needs" among the affected nations the satisfaction of which could not but make imperative the introduction of structural adaptations so as to link authority to a specific activity. The underlying assumptions in this formula are as follows: that there is noncontroversiality surrounding the venture itself as a result of the alleged autonomy of functions, allowing the separation of all political problems from the economic and social ones and from each other, and sustaining the "virtue of technical self-determination" whereby the functional dimensions determine themselves and the appropriate administrative organs; that men, being by "nature" not only good, rational, devoted to the common good, and maximizers of utilities, tend inherently to focus their loyalties on those institutions which gratify their basic needs, thereby reinforcing an ethos of cooperation; that habits of cooperation, learned by the expert and the manager in one sphere of activity, are destined to follow the logic of ramification, expansibility, transferability, spillover, or accumulation until all social, economic, and political spheres of activity are captures.[37]

This basic formula was slightly modified by the neofunctionalists with the introduction into it of a tone of politics so as to firmly uphold the true utilitarian calculus embodied in the so-called interest theory of politics, in which all political action is purposively linked with individual or group perception of interest, and thus cooperation among groups can only be the result of convergences of separate perceptions of interest. In this new formula, political development or integration is conceptualized on the grounds of an institutionalized pattern of interest politics, played out within existing political institutions, a conceptualization which entails for the European Union the adoption by its supranational institutions (especially the Commission) of a strategy of "informal coaptation" or gradual politicization of the elites of the various interest groups with the aim of refocusing their loyalties away from national governments toward the institutions of the Union. The warrant for the success of this task lies in the functionalist logic of spillover, which postulates a gradual accumulation of political power at the supranational level as the national states are forced to commit the self-willed sacrifice and transfer "authority-legitimacy" because "policies made pursuant to an initial task and grant of power can be made real only if the task itself is expanded."[38] When the European experiments began in the 1960s to show signs of unmanageable stress, the neofunctionalists abandoned the alleged automaticity of the expansive logic of integration and decided instead to pay attention to external disturbances, to strengthen the voluntaristic elements of their conceptualizations, and thus to cast their formula in probabilistic terms through the notion of "cultivated spillover" whereby "problems are deliberately linked together into package deals not on the basis of technological necessity but on the basis of political and ideological projections and political possibilities."[39]

This relaxation of the teleological assumptions of neofunctionalism was further reinforced in the 1970s by the crisis of capitalism, which prompted Haas, the founder of neofunctionalism, to proclaim the obsolescence of regional integration theory by arguing that "the logic of incrementalism and regional self-containment no longer holds for certain activities of the European Community" because, under the impact of perceived interdependencies, the European Community has now found itself in turbulent fields where "confusion dominates discussion and negotiation."[40] As a result, theorizing shifted from regional integration to global interdependencies conceptualized by some analysts in terms of international regime changes on the basis of institutionalized patterns of interest politics taking the form of international (instead of national) pluralism: thus, what actually changed in the transition was the level of analysis and the designation of actors, not the theoretical presuppositions.[41]

MARXIST THEORY OF INTEGRATION

In an effort to formulate an alternative theoretical paradigm Peter Cocks has argued that "orthodox integration literature is fundamentally ahistorical," for "it fails to give an adequate account of the roots of modern European integration."[42] Having taken history in a materialistic conception, where the human essence is nothing but the ensemble of social relationships conditioned by specific modes of production, Cocks argues that European integration has "evolved as a policy response to certain problems endemic to the growth of capitalism," and "conceive[s] successful political integration in Europe since the sixteenth century as a method of state-building at the national and international level."[43]

This position seems to be in accord with Perry Andreson's views on the emergence of the absolutist state in the West: he argues that, in the course of the sixteenth century, the absolutist state and the Roman law it embodied were the most powerful political and ideological weapons conducive to "territorial integration and administrative centralism" aimed at performing "certain partial functions in the primitive accumulation necessary for the eventual triumph of the capitalist mode of production itself."[44] In seeking to understand the "present as history," Cocks examines the relationship between the state and the imperatives of capital accumulation in relation to three historical instances, namely, the unique case of Britain in early capitalism, when competition between capitalist countries was not yet a factor hindering the expansionary impulses endemic to capital; the case of Germany and Italy in conditions of delayed industrialization in the nineteenth century, in which interimperialist rivalry was a crucial factor; and the European case of mature capitalism, in which capital concentration and centralization has acquired international dimensions.

In the case of Britain, says Cocks, the interplay was between imperialist expansion, fostered by the emerging bourgeoisie and the state, and national unification, in the sense that the relative prosperity brought home by the external expansion and the resultant international accumulation of capital tended to reinforce national unification by strengthening the legitimation of the very institutions which had themselves facilitated the imperialist expansion.[45] In contrast to this example in conditions of delayed industrialization, the interplay was between interimperialist competition and national unification, in the sense that the legitimation of the expanding role of the national state through national unification was reinforced by the need to facilitate rapid development of the productive forces and high levels of capital accumulation within the boundaries of the national economy so that the domestic bourgeoisie and the state could successfully face the challenge posed by the external competition: nationalism thus became the official ideology necessary for the legitimation of the state's actions.[46] This very institutionalization of bourgeois nationalism reflected the relative weakness of the capitalist class in the international division of labor and in the domestic constellation of social classes and class struggles, and the low degree of socioeconomic integration of the world capitalist economy coupled with good prospects for capitalistic development and thus capital accumulation within the national economy. In contrast, when the integration of international capitalism is high (as is the case in mature capitalism) and the prospects for capitalistic development within the national economy are very poor, then the weakness of the capitalist class tends to reinforce the negation of bourgeois nationalism and the celebration of its opposite, supranationalism and cosmopolitanism, as the Greek case indicates.[47]

This reasoning implies that in the case of mature capitalism,[48] the inner logic of territorial (European) integration stems from the internationalization of capital, reinforced by the expansionary impulses endemic to capitalism, and the concomitant inability of the capitalist class to maintain political and ideological hegemony at the level of the national state, implying legitimation of the institutions which foster the accumulation of capital and the realization of surplus value.[49] Reference to the historical reality of the European Community may suffice to make this position clear. The Spaak Report, which represented the first blueprint for the EEC, indicated that the fusion of the separate markets of the member states was "an absolute necessity" in order to remove the obstacles to trade, thereby facilitating the expansion of trade and capital, and to provide an institutional framework for the legitimation of the monopolistic tendencies of the national economies.[50] The underlying idea was that *de facto* monopolies within the member states were destined to "disappear" as soon as they were placed in the context of the enlarged market.[51]

This metamorphosis implied that the role of the national state had to change accordingly: instead of taking steps against the creation of national monopolies, which by their very nature tend to discredit the capitalist system, the member states are now expected to introduce measures fostering the development of big industries so that they can meet the competition in the enlarged market. Thus the survival of big (monopolistic) industries becomes *de jure* a "national goal."[52] But it has been a "supranational goal" as well, because the survival of Union industry in the competition of the international market calls for the acceptance of industrial concentration.[53] In this context, the national governments and the institutions of the European Union are faced with a real dilemma which forces them to waver between their ideological pretensions and the realities of the European economies. Put differently, they are confronted with the dilemma which calls for the reconciliation of the exigencies of two contradictory aims, namely, the achievement of economies of scale, which renders necessary the acceptance of capital concentration, and the respect for the liberal ideology which requires the maintenance of fair competition.[54] The solution to this dilemma can only be the observance of the rules of competition amongst mainly monopolistic or oligopolistic establishments.[55]

From a theoretical angle, the trend toward capital concentration may take one of the following three forms or a combination of them: first, the form of "national" concentration, which implies the fusion of existing national enterprises; second, the form of "supranational" concentration through a process assumed to lead to the creation of a new entity, called the "European company," which is supposed to represent the motor for the transcendence of the nation-state; and third, the form of "international" concentration under the force of the logic of an internationalized and internalized reproduction of capital which entails in the European context the fusion of European capital with foreign capital or rather the absorption of national companies by the American multinationals.[56]

Although all these forms of concentration stem from the same logic of capital, that is, from the expansionary impulses endemic to capitalism, the primacy assigned to one or the other form of capital concentration tends to condition the *conception* of the relationship between the process of capital accumulation, the constellation/articulation of social classes and class struggles, and the state. On this, there have been three currents of interpretation, all within the Marxist problematic.

In the first instance some Marxists postulate, in accordance with the classical Marxist-Leninist position, that the rapid development of the productive forces, under the impetus of the scientific and technological revolution characteristic of mature capitalism, tends to reinforce capital concentration and centralization in the advanced form of (national) monopolies and thus to facilitate the fusion of these monopolies with the national state, thereby producing the collective organ called "state-monopoly capitalism."[57] This conceptualization implies that the prime contradiction in the corresponding sociopolitical conjuncture cannot but be the classical antithesis between exploiters and exploited, taking the form of a singular polarization between big monopolies and the rest of the society, and that the big bourgeoisie, by its being based on "national" monopolies, tends to consolidate the national state, thereby confining European integration to the conventional intergovernmental form. As Kirsanov put it, because "the merging of the gigantic strength of the monopolies with the gigantic strength of the state" has produced a "single mechanism," that of "state-monopoly capitalism," European integration can only be "an organization promoting inter-state economic cooperation."[58] This in turn seems to provide the *raison d'être* for both the late bourgeois nationalism *à la* de Gaulle's and the tactical nationalism embodied in the political programs of the Western European orthodox communist parties.[59]

Secondly, with a significant relaxation of the political postulates of "state monopoly capitalism," but still in the spirit of the classical Marxist (Leninist) position, others hold that the advanced development of the productive forces, again under the impetus of the scientific and technological revolution characteristic of mature capitalism, tends to reinforce capital concentration and centralization within and beyond the boundaries of the national economy: this endemic tendency toward the "supranationalization" of capital is assumed to reinforce in its turn the formation of a supranational institutional structure, thereby undermining the position of the national state.[60] This metamorphosis of institutions becomes necessary in order to help the European Union become a great power able to face interimperialist rivalry, thought to be now crystallized in the form of a triangular relationship with the United States and Japan.[61] The material base of this "new power" is assumed to be the amalgamation of the hitherto national capitals at best or the European coalition of the national coalitions of capital at worst.[62]

In either case, this supranational logic entails the crystallization of the unity of the capitalist class at the supranational level in the form of a "European bourgeoisie" and the concomitant appearance of the simple polarization, postulated by "state-monopoly capitalism," between the supranational monopolies ("European capital") and the "European proletariat."[63] The "European proletariat," without abandoning the efforts to exploit "favorable opportunities for a socialist breakthrough whenever they occur in one country,"[64] must nevertheless be educated "towards an internationalization of the class struggle, which results from the growing trend towards an internationalization of capital;"[65] while the "European bourgeoisie" is destined to cultivate its unity in order to face both the domestic pressures of the working class and the external challenges of international capital. This last aspect was also stressed by the former president of the Commission of the European Community, Francois-Xavier Ortoli, in his call for "unity" and "independence" in which he argued that an "independent Europe is a Europe that is able on its own to take those great decisions that shape its destiny," a task which presupposes that the European Union "is sufficiently aware of its own identity and possesses enough material resources and economic power to make the transition from talk to decision making."[66]

Finally, others, starting from the concept of capital accumulation on a world scale, argue that the internationalization of capital, a process characteristic of and dominant in mature capitalism, places the European specificity in the context of the capitalist totality in which internationalized capital establishes its dominance in the "imperialist chain" through penetration and induced reproduction.[67] By pushing this logic to its limits, one is able to visualize a polarization and a fundamental cleavage between a dominant and a dominated entity, that is, between a center and its periphery. In this heuristic-sensitizing schema, the European Union is assumed to lie somewhere between the two extremes, for two main reasons: first, because the advanced capitalist countries of Europe themselves constitute centers of capital accumulation, and second, because these very capitalist/imperialist countries possess *ipso facto* a position of dominance over other countries in the imperialist chain in particular and in the chain of international accumulation of capital in general.[68] The inference from these two factors is that the European capitalist/imperialist countries and thus the European Union itself tend to acquire a "relative autonomy" in the imperialist chain, an autonomy whose content and form become a correlate of the process of capital accumulation in a changing international division of labor.

This means that the strengthening of this "relative autonomy" presupposes an expansionary drive on the part of "European capital," be it "supranational" or "national," a drive which depends on the cohesion of the national or supranational institutions and their ability to legitimate the process of capital accumulation and the realization of surplus value. On this very "cohesion" of the institutions, it is postulated that the European Union and the corresponding national states, being themselves penetrated entities, inherently evolve along contradictory paths which include both integration and fragmentation, articulation and disarticulation.[69] The reason for this is that the internationalization of capital tends to reinforce a disfunction between national economies and national capitalisms, thereby preparing the ground for the emergence of a triangular relationship between national or international capital, the national economy, and the state.[70] This very sociopolitical heterogeneity, reinforced by the logic of the internationalization of capital, precludes the two possibilities mentioned above, namely, the possibility of the national state being the instrument of the big bourgeoisie, postulated by "state-monopoly capitalism";[71] and the possibility of the national state being replaced by a supranational one, postulated by the conceptualizations of the Europeanization of capital and the concomitant formation of a supranational political structure.[72]

In short, the inference from this logic of the international accumulation of capital is that supranationalism and the Europeanization of capital become theoretically possible outcomes, not in spite of, but because of the imperatives of classical imperialism, embodied in the notion of "state-monopoly capitalism," which postulates the crystallization of interimperialist rivalries between national (supranational) states themselves enhancing the interests of national (supranational) capitals. In reality, however, the classical "state-centered" notion of imperialism coexists in late capitalism with the internationalization of capital which renders problematic the full development of European supranationalism. This coexistence of tendencies, militating against singular explanations, entails on the level of abstraction of the world capitalist economy the conceptualization of an analytical space of possibilities defined by the imperatives of the classical "state-centered" conception of imperialism,[73] and the modern imperialism of the international accumulation of capital, the latter representing the dominant tendency in late capitalism.[74]

Moreover, on the level of abstraction of class configurations and class struggles, the aforementioned theoretical position of modern imperialism and the internationalization of capital tends to put emphasis on the characteristics of the various fractions of the capitalist class, crystallized as class configurations of the power bloc, to the virtual exclusion of the actual class struggle between antagonistic social classes; while the theoretical position of classical imperialism, reflected in the notion of "state-monopoly capitalism," tends to put emphasis on patterns of exploitation and class struggle to the virtual exclusion of the characteristics of and the rivalries among the various fractions of the capitalist class. We would argue that class configurations and class struggles actually evolve within a material reality and an analytical space of possibilities historically constituted and socially mediated through the interclass cohesion or rivalry among fractions of capital as the *secondary* contradiction in capitalism, and the relations of exploitation and struggle between exploiters and exploited, capitalists and workers, as the *fundamental* contradiction in capitalism. For, as Robert Brenner put it, "The historical evolution or emergence of any given class structure is not comprehensible as the mere product of ruling-class choice and imposition," but rather "represents the outcome of class conflicts through which the direct producers have, to a greater or lesser extent, succeeded in restricting the form and extent of ruling-class access to surplus labor."[75]

This very perception lies, in Leo Panitch's words, "at the theoretical core of Marxism," as is illustrated by Marx's statement that "the specific economic form, in which unpaid surplus-labor is pumped out of the direct producers, determines the relationship of rulers and ruled" and "reveals the innermost secret, the hidden basis of the entire social structure."[76] This appropriation of surplus value from labor power, a process endemic to capitalism, entails in fact the production and reproduction of the capital-relation itself—the reproduction of the capitalist and the wage laborer, whose contradictory social relation can crystallize only at the political level where social classes are formed.[77] This in turn means that the capitalist state, whether national or supranational, being the guarantor of the "collective" capitalist interest, must act in such a manner as to legitimate the capital-relation itself and thus enhance the appropriation of surplus value. In this sense, we would argue that the crucial political contradiction characteristic of the process of European integration centers on the imperatives of the accumulation of capital and the realization of surplus value on the one hand, and the legitimation of the institutions within which these forces operate on the other.

This crucial contradiction historically takes the form of what might be called a "functional discrepancy" between capital accumulation and political legitimation, a discrepancy which implies that the state, whether national or supranational, may at some historical juncture be forced into a position in which it could effectively discharge its obligations only by suspending either its liberal democratic principles or the private character of capital accumulation.[78] This dilemma appears along with a "structural fragmentation" reinforced by the imperatives of capital accumulation and the law of uneven development, which tend to produce and reproduce economic divergences and spatial structures in the form of regional disparities,[79] and a "social discrepancy" reinforced by the multiform nature of the appropriation of surplus value from labor, which tends to produce and reproduce divisions within the working class through devaluation of labor power and on the basis of skill, wage mechanisms, and ethnicity.[80] In late capitalism, although the devaluation of labor power through dequalification tends to enhance the proletarianization of the new middle class,[81] the reproduction of the divisions within the working class tends to become a means suitable for the perpetuation and thus legitimation of the institutions which sustain the process of capital accumulation and the realization of surplus value.[82]

This is best exemplified by the migratory movement and the associated mechanism characteristic of late capitalism in Western Europe whereby the institutionalized system of discrimination or the inevitably slow process of social adjustment helps to perpetuate the division of the working class, while on the other hand migrant labor itself, being a reserve army in constant motion, fosters capital accumulation by reinforcing "the full employment of the indigenous labor power in times of high conjuncture" at relatively low levels of wages and "social peace" by its being a condition of "reduced unemployment in times of low conjuncture."[83] At the same time, migrant labor works as a "safety valve" for the countries of origin by mitigating their pressures of unemployment in times of low conjuncture, thereby averting the explosion of social disturbances, and by making a contribution to the correction of the external balance of payments through the remittances of emigrants.[84]

In short, these are tendencies endemic in the process of international accumulation of capital and the law of uneven development which in themselves reinforce a "political discrepancy" between the crystallization of the collective capitalist interest at the European level and that of the collective interest of the working class. This discrepancy implies that the unity and cohesion of the working class at the European level tends to lag behind that of the capitalist class because the imperatives of the international social division of labor, which reproduce divisions among the working class, and the specificities of each country become factors conducive to the crystallization of the collective interest of the working class at the national instead of the supranational level.[85] This centrality of the national state is further reinforced by the fact that, because the collective interest of the working class is realized only through the transformation and transcendence of existing institutions, the orientation of the working class depends on the relative power and the significance of the institutions to be transformed.[86]

In this sense, the very weakness of the supranational institutions is the consequence of the persistence of the national states and the cause for the perpetuation of these states, institutions which become *ipso facto* the epicenters of the class struggle.[87] This endemic tendency, coupled with the exigencies of the international accumulation of capital, forces the capitalist class to waver at the political level between national loyalty and supranationalism, between the consolidation of the collective capitalist interest of individual national states and the enhancement of the collective interest of the European Union, both of which are part and parcel of the collective capitalist interest of the West as a whole. In the final analysis, the preservation of the collective capitalist interest, whether "national," "supranational" or "international," entails in fact the legitimation of the institutions which themselves foster capital accumulation and the realization of relative surplus value.

CONCLUSIONS

We have argued that the logic of European integration stems from the objective realities associated with the industrial European societies. Specifically, the tendency toward the internationalization of the process of production and exchange, manifested in all Western European societies, has reinforced a form of political organization at the regional/supranational level. In theory, the organization so established could vary from a simple intergovernmental form to a truly supranational form. In practice, however, the specific form of political organization crystallized through the historical process of European integration has greatly been conditioned by the peculiarities of the historical conjuncture.

These historical peculiarities have been twofold, domestic and external to the Western European societies. On the external side, the most dramatic change that occurred in Europe after World War II was the division of the European continent into two parts, Western and Eastern, and its subsequent demotion in the sphere of international affairs. In this sense European developments were necessarily conditioned by the global politico-strategic consideration of the then two superpowers, thus losing to a great extent their autonomous impulse. The formation of the European Communities was a reflection of these external factors and represented an effort on the part of the Western European governments concerned to create a new economic and political entity able to face the great powers of the time. On these grounds one could argue that the external factors tended to create conditions conducive to a trans-class political legitimization of the process of European integration.

On the domestic side, on the other hand, the peculiarities of the historical conjuncture centered on the challenge posed to the power of the ruling classes in most of the Western European countries by the rising and radicalized working classes. This crisis of hegemony, associated with the increasing internationalization of the European economies, reinforced the process of European integration and the establishment of the European Union institutions. On these grounds one could argue that the domestic factors tended (especially during the initial period of European Union construction) to reinforce a class-based political legitimization of the process of European integration: at least initially, political support for

European integration stemmed primarily from the ruling groupings of the time, the conservatives and the Christian democrats.

The conventional theory of European integration has been a response to both political and economic considerations. On the political side the urgent need was posed by the historical conjuncture. For peace and security in the Western European region, associated with the claim for the existence of a common European heritage, reinforced the quest for political engineering at the European level along the lines of the traditional theories of federalism. Similarly, on the economic side the historical tendency toward the internationalization of the European economies tended to produce areas for cooperation at the regional level, theorized along the lines of functionalism and neofunctionalism. What conventional theory has produced so far is a body of literature centered mainly on how the European Union functions, or is supposed to function, being a decision-making mechanism. This positive aspect, however, has been circumscribed by the fact that the conventional theory of European integration, being ahistorical, has failed to explain the logic and the roots of modern European integration.

The Marxist theory of European integration responds positively to this weakness by examining European integration as a historical process rooted in the very logic of the capitalist mode of production. This means that European integration, seen as a method of political institution building at the supranational level, stems from the internationalization of capital and the concomitant inability of the capitalist class to maintain political and ideological hegemony at the level of the national state. The weakness of this theory is that it places much emphasis on the economy, thereby incorporating the element of economic reductionism, and has a high level of abstraction, being essentially a macro-theory, thus failing to examine properly political processes at the level of microanalysis.

The discussion so far has shown that there is a need for theoretical work to be done if we really want to understand the logic of political integration and the historical process of European integration in general. I would suggest two directions, both within the Marxist problematic, that one could follow in order to improve the analytical tools for understanding European political integration.

First, the economic reductionism inherent in the Marxist theory could be *mitigated* by putting emphasis on the "relative autonomy" of the political as theorized in contemporary analyses of the state.[88] The works on integration by P. Cocks[89] and S. Holland,[90] for example, seem to move in that direction, though much more theoretical work must still be done in order to formulate a coherent analytical framework suitable for understanding European political integration within both the general and the microlevel analysis.[91]

Second, the economic reductionism of the Marxist theory could be *surpassed* by putting emphasis on the "analytical autonomy" of the political as theorized recently in Mouselis's work.[92] The idea is to construct a theoretical framework based on concepts (such as the mode of domination as opposed to the

Marxist concept of the mode of production) which will describe the noneconomic institutional spheres without direct reference to the economy, and thus avoid economic reductionism, without, however, falling into a kind of "water-and airtight" separation of the political from the economic sphere as is the case with neoclassical economics and non-Marxist political theory. This approach, apart from the epistemological questions one might have with it, could help in the construction of an analytical framework of a heuristic value—able to facilitate a synthesis of the Marxist with the conventional theory of European integration, and thus suitable for understanding European political integration at both the general and the specific level of analysis.

In both directions, the questions have just been raised, and the challenge is in front of us!

NOTES

Theories of economic integration are not examined in this chapter. For a general reading on this see, for example, J. Viner, *The Customs Union Issue* (New York: Carnegie Endowment for International Peace, 1950); J. Meade, *The Theory of Customs Union* (Amsterdam: North-Holland Publishing Company, 1955); Tibor Scitovsky, *Economic Theory and Western European Integration* (Stanford, CA: Stanford University Press 1958); B. Balassa, *The Theory of Economic Integration* (Homewood, IL, 1961); Paul Streeten, *Economic Integration: Aspects and Problems*, (Leyden: A.W. Sythoff, 1964); and Jacques Pelkamns, "Economic Theories of Integration Revisited," *Journal of Common Market Studies*, Vol. 18, No. 4, June 1980.

1. Cf. Andreas Moschonas, *A Disputed Partnership: The Political Debate on the Greek Accession to the European Community*, Ph.D. Thesis, Queen's University at Kingston, Canada 1982, Chapter II.

2. See M. M. Postan, *An Economic History of Western Europe, 1945–1964* (London: Methuen and Co., 1967), pp. 12–13.

3. Cf. Fernando Claudin, *The Communist Movement: From Comintern to Cominform* (London: Penguin Books, 1975), Chapter 5; and Wolfgang Abendroth, *A Short History of the European Working Class* (London: N.L.B., 1978), Chapter 7 and Postscript.

4. Johan Galtung, *The European Community: A Superpower in the Making* (London: George Allen and Unwin, 1973), p. 15.

5. For an analysis of the postwar Soviet objectives in Europe, see Roger Morgan, *West European Politics since 1945: The Shaping of the European Community* (London: B. T. Batsford, 1972), pp. 11-14.

6. For an analysis of the notion of "perceived threat," see Raymond Cohen, *Threat Perception in International Crisis* (Madison: University of Wisconsin Press, 1979).

7. Though the immediate objective of the Truman Doctrine was to help Greece and Turkey, its implications were broader in scope as far as the "containment" of communism was concerned. For a detailed analysis of the Truman Doctrine, see Richard Mayne, *The Recovery of Europe: From Devastation to Unity* (London: Weidenfeld and Nicolson, 1970), Chapter 5. For its ideological implications and for an analysis of the issue of

"containment," see "The Sources of Soviet Conduct," *Foreign Affairs*, Vol. 25, No. 4, July 1947.

8. Quoted from Marshall's speech at Harvard University cited in Richard Vaughan (ed.), *Post-War Integration in Europe* (London: Edward Arnold, 1976), pp. 22–24.

9. For an analysis along these lines, see Fred J. Block, *The Origins of International Economic Disorder* (Berkeley: University of California Press, 1977), Chapter 4; and Ernest Mandel, *Europe vs. America: Contradictions of Imperialism* (New York: Monthly Review Press, 1970).

10. Marshall explained in his statement, indicated above (note 8), that "there must be some agreement among the countries of Europe as to the requirements of the situation and the part those countries themselves will take in order to give proper effect to whatever action might be undertaken by" the U.S. government.

11. Block, op. cit. (note 9), p. 89.

12. Ibid., pp. 86–92. Cf. David P. Calleo and Benjamin M. Rowland, *America and the World Political Economy: Atlantic Dreams and National Realities* (Bloomington: Indiana University Press, 1973), p. 39.

13. At a Paris meeting the Soviet foreign minister, Molotov, stated that "questions of internal economy were a matter concerning the sovereignty of the peoples themselves, and that other countries should not interfere in such questions. Only on this basis can relations between countries develop normally." Quoted in Mayne, op. cit. (note 7), p. 110.

14. Namely, Austria, Belgium, Denmark, France, Greece, Ireland, Iceland, Italy, Luxembourg, Norway, the Netherlands, Portugal, the U.K., Switzerland, Turkey, and West Germany represented by the commanders in Chief of the French, the British, and the American zones of occupation. In 1961, with the participation of Canada and the United States, the OEEC was transformed into the Organization for Economic Cooperation and Development (OECD), whose main functions are economic policy coordination, aid to developing countries, and the expansion of world trade. For an analysis of both organizations, see Political and Economic Planning, *European Unity: A Survey of the European Organizations* (London: George Allen and Unwin, 1968), Chapters 3 and 12.

15. This "intervention" signifies the function of the capitalist state in channeling and containing the class struggle so as to promote the accumulation of capital. Following the capitalist crisis of the 1930s, Keynes managed to make respectable among the capitalist class this very role of the "interventionist state" by arguing that capitalist governments are required, in order to maintain effective demand in general, to undertake "the task of adjusting to one another the propensity to consume and the inducement to invest," but that everything else is best left to "the free play of economic forces." For a synoptic analysis of the "Keynesian Revolution," see Joan Robinson, *Economic Philosophy* (London: Penguin Books, 1962), Chapter 4.

16. See the Convention for European Economic Cooperation, Paris, April 16, 1948, cited in Vaughan, op. cit. (note 8), pp. 30–35.

17. According to Postan (op. cit., note 2, p. 25), in the postwar era "in all European countries economic growth became a universal creed and a common expectation to which governments were expected to conform. To this extent economic growth was the product of economic growthmanship." Apart from the "creed" itself, however, in actual practice individual governments, responding to domestic sociopolitical realities, were forced to make trade-offs between the policy of economic growth (given priority by the United

States and Canada), the commitment to full employment (given priority by Sweden, Britain, and Australia), and the policy of monetary deflation (given priority by West Germany, Japan, Italy, and France) to stabilize the economy and demobilize a militant working–class challenge. For a forceful analysis, see Nixon Apple, "The Rise and Fall of Full Employment Capitalism," *Studies in Political Economy*, No. 4, Autumn 1980.

18. On these issues, see Mayne, op. cit. (note 7), pp. 125–27; Morgan, op. cit. (note 5), p. 81; and Dennis Swann, *The Economics of the Common Market* (London: Penguin Books, 1975), pp. 17–18.

19. For a synoptic analysis of postwar developments in France and Italy, see Morgan, op. cit. (note 5), Chapters 2 and 4. See also Antonio Gambino, *Storia del dopoguerra*, 2nd ed., Vol. II (Roma–Bari: Laterza, 1978), pp. 301–9, for an analysis of the relationship between Washington and the De Gasperi government.

20. See Frank Roy Willis, *France, Germany, and the New Europe 1945–1967* (Stanford, CA: Stanford University Press, 1968), p. 81.

21. See Morgan, op. cit. (note 5), pp. 47–48.

22. Ibid., p. 56.

23. This was the so-called Churchillian concept of British influence. See Roy Pryce, *The Politics of the European Community* (London: Butterworths, 1973), p. 3.

24. All these issues were extensively discussed following Schuman's proposal. See William Diebold, *The Schuman Plan: A Study in Economic Cooperation 1950–1959* (New York: Frederick A. Praeger, 1959), pp. 48–60. For the Labour Party's foreign policy, see John Roper, "The Labor Party and British Foreign Policy," in Werner J. Feld (ed.), *The Foreign Policies of West European Socialist Parties* (New York: Praeger Publishers, 1978), pp. 9–16; and Michael A. Wheaton, "The Labor Party and Europe 1950–71," in Ghita Ionescu (ed.), *The New Politics of European Integration* (London: The Macmillan Press, 1972), pp. 80–97.

25. See Swann, op. cit. (note 18), pp. 15–18.

26. Altiero Spinelli, "The Growth of the European Movement since the Second World War," in Michael Hodges (ed.), *European Integration* (London: Penguin Books, 1972), p. 59.

27. In this connection, see Mayne, op. cit. (note 7), Chapter 8. For a detailed analysis of the "European Idea," see Lord Gladwyn, *The European Idea* (London: Weidenfeld and Nicolson, 1966).

28. See Count Coudenhove-Kalergi, *An Idea Conquers the World* (London: Hutchinson, 1953), p. 93 and passim. During the interwar period the European question was also raised, for security reasons, by Briand, the then French minister of foreign affairs, who produced a memorandum on the organization of a system of European federal union. See Vaughan, op. cit. (note 8), pp. 11–12; and René Albrecht-Carrié, *One Europe: The Historical Background of European Unity* (New York: Doubleday and Company, 1965), pp. 223–25.

29. See S. Patijn (ed.), *Landmarks in European Unity: 22 Texts on European Integration* (Leyden: A. W. Sijthoff, 1970), pp. 27–35. Cf. note 6, above.

30. See Spinelli, op. cit. (note 26), p. 58; and Coudenhove-Kalergi, op. cit. (note 28), pp. 114, 307.

31. See Spinelli, op. cit. (note 26), p. 58.

32. See Patijn, op. cit. (note 29), pp. 37–41; Political and Economic Planning, op. cit. (note 14), pp. 27–29; and Coudenhove-Kalergi, op. cit. (note 28), p. 288.

33. Charles de Gaulle's statement quoted in J. Bodenheimer, *Political Union: A Microcosm of European Politics, 1960-1966* (Leyden: A. M. Sijthoff, 1967), p. 41; and in L. Tsoukalis, *The Politics and Economics of European Monetary Integration* (London: George Allen and Unwin, 1977), p. 28. Works in line with this conventional (realist) position include: Stanley Hoffmann, "Obstinate or Obsolete? The Fate of the Nation-State and the Case of Western Europe," *Daedalus*, Vol. 95, No. 3, Summer 1966; "Discord and Community: The North Atlantic Area as a Partial International System," in F.O. Wilcox and H. F. Haviland (eds.), *The Atlantic Community* (New York: Frederick A. Praeger, 1963), pp. 3-31; "De Gaulle, Europe and the Atlantic Alliance," *International Organization*, Vol. 18, No. 1, Winter 1964; "The European Process at Atlantic Crosspurposes," *Journal of Common Market Studies*, Vol. 3, No. 2, 1965; and Raymond Aron, "Old Nations, New Europe," in S. R. Graubard (ed.), *A New Europe?* (Boston: The Riverside Press, 1964), pp. 38-61. For a synthesis and critique, see Charles Pentland, *International Theory and European Integration* (London: Faber and Faber, 1973), Ch. 2.

34. Cf. Karl W. Deutsch et al., *Political Community and the North Atlantic Area: International Organization in the Light of Historical Experience* (Princeton, NJ: Princeton University Press, 1957).

35. Cf. Peter Hay, *Federalism and Supranational Organizations: Patterns for New Legal Structures* (Urbana: University of Illinois Press, 1966). For a standard textbook, see K. C. Wheare, *Federal Government*, 4th ed. (London: Oxford University Press, 1963).

36. Cf. Deutsch, op. cit. (note 34); Amitai Etzioni, *Political Unification: A Comparative Study of Leaders and Forces* (New York: Holt, Rinehart and Winston, 1965); Donald J. Puchala, "Of Blind Men, Elephants and International Integration," *Journal of Common Market Studies*, Vol. 10, No. 3, 1972, pp. 267-84; John Pinder, "Integrating Divergent Economies: The Extranational Method," *International Affairs*, Vol. 55, No. 4, October 1979, pp. 546-59; Pentland, op. cit. (note 33), Chapter 5; and Murray Forsyth, "The Political Objectives of European Integration," *International Affairs*, Vol. 43, No. 3, 1967, pp. 483-97. The notion of "takeoff," borrowed from aerodynamics, was transformed into a key concept of development by W. W. Rostow, "The Take-off into Self-Sustained Growth," *The Economic Journal*, Vol. LXVI, March 1956; and *The Stages of Economic Growth: A Non-Communist Manifesto* (Cambridge: Cambridge University Press, 1960). Since then, the "takeoff" became a "self-sustained" concept in the field of political development. Cf. A. F. K. Organski, *The Stages of Political Development* (New York: Alfred A. Knopf, 1965); Deutsch et al., op. cit. (note 34), pp. 83-85; and Etzioni, ibid., pp. 51-55. For a forceful critique on Rostow's ideas, see P. A. Baran and E. J. Hobsbawm, "The Stages of Economic Growth," *Kyklos*, Vol. 14, 1961.

37. The representative work of functionalism is that of David Mitrany, *A Working Peace System* (Chicago: Quadrangle Books, 1966), first published in 1943. For an analysis and critique, see Ernst B. Haas, *Beyond the Nation-State: Functionalism and International Organization* (Stanford, CA: Stanford University Press, 1964), esp. Part I; Pentland, op. cit. (note 33), Chapter 3; and Reginald J. Harrison, *Europe in Question: Theories of Regional and International Integration* (London: George Allen and Unwin, 1974), Chapters 2, 5. Cf. James Patrick Sewell, *Functionalism and World Politics* (Princeton, NJ: Princeton University Press, 1966); and Talcott Parsons, *The Social System* (New York: The Free Press, 1951), esp. Chapter 4.

38. Ernst B. Haas, "International Integration: The European and the Universal Process," *International Organization*, Vol. 15, 1961, p. 368. Neofunctionalism came into being as certain pluralist analysts attempted to explain the phenomenon called European integration. The most representative works are those of Ernst B. Haas, *The Uniting of Europe: Political, Social, and Economic Forces, 1950–1957* (Stanford, CA: Stanford University Press, 1958); *Beyond the Nation–State*, op. cit. (note 37); and Leon N. Lindberg, *The Political Dynamics of European Economic Integration* (Stanford, CA: Stanford University Press, 1963). For an analysis of neofunctionalism, see Pentland, op. cit. (note 33), Chapter 4; and Harrison, op. cit. (note 37), esp. Chapters 4, 5.

39. J. S. Ney, "Comparing Common Markets: A Revised Neo–Functionalist Model," in Leon N. Lindberg and Stuart A. Scheingold (eds.), *Regional Integration: Theory and Research* (Cambridge, MA: Harvard University Press, 1971), p. 202. This publication represented an assessment of neofunctionalism by its founders and some other analysts and was initially published as a special issue of *International Organization*, Vol. 24, No. 4, Autumn 1970. See also Philippe C. Schmitter, "Three Neo–Functional Hypotheses about International Integration," *International Organization*, Vol. 23, Winter 1969; Ronn D. Kaiser, "Toward the Copernican Phase of Regional Integration Theory," *Journal of Common Market Studies*, Vol. 10, No. 2, 1972; D. J. Puchala, "Of Blind Men. . . ," op. cit. (note 36); and J. Lodge, "Loyalty and the EEC: The Limitations of the Functionalist Approach," *Political Studies*, Vol. 26, 1978. For a recent reappraisal, see Jeppe Tranholm-Mikkelsen, "Neo–functionalism: Obstinate or Obsolete? A Reappraisal in the Light of the New Dynamism of the EC," *Millennium*, Vol. 20, No. 1, 1991; and D. Mutimer, "1992 and the Political Integration of Europe. Neofunctionalism Reconsidered," *Revue d' Integration Européene*, Vol. 13 (1), 1989.

40. Ernst B. Haas, "Turbulent Fields and the Theory of Regional Integration," *International Organization*, Vol. 30, No. 2, Spring 1976, p. 178. This article is a shorter version of his *Obsolescence of Regional Integration Theory* (Berkeley: Institute of International Studies, University of California, 1975). Haas envisages a new institutional structure for the European Community, called "asymmetrical overlap," which implies that "there will be no European federation, no political union of even the confederal type, and no economic and monetary union which looks like the federal governance of the customs union," and also states that "no component of the system will ever be characterized by full reciprocal patterns of interdependence with components outside the system," Ibid., pp. 207–8. To Nau, this marks the end of neofunctionalism, for "No action is possible without priorities, and no explanation is possible without assumptions. What we have lost, most unfortunately, in the transition from integration to interdependence theories is the hierarchy of issues, interests, and institutions that guided earlier integration studies." Henry R. Nau, "From Integration to Interdependence: Gains, Losses, and Continuing Gaps," *International Organization*, Vol. 33, No. 1, Winter 1979, p. 144.

41. The central work in this connection is that of Robert O. Keohane and Joseph S. Nye, *Power and Interdependence: World Politics in Transition* (Boston: Little, Brown, 1977). The authors build on their previous works, *Transnational Relations and World Politics* (Cambridge, MA: Harvard University Press, 1972), and "International Interdependence and Integration," in Fred I. Greenstein and Nelson W. Polsby (eds.), *International Politics, Handbook of Political Science*, Vol. 8 (Reading, MA: Addison–Wesley, 1975), pp. 363–414. Cf. Kal J. Holsti, "A New International Politics? Diplomacy and Complex Interdependence," *International Organization*, Vol. 32, No. 2,

Spring 1978; Nau, op. cit. (note 40); Haas, op. cit. (note 40); and Haas' "Is There a Hole in the Whole? Knowledge, Technology, Interdependence, and the Construction of International Regimes," *International Organization*, Vol. 29, No. 3, Summer 1975. See also S. P. Krasner (ed.), *International Regimes* (Ithaca, NY: Cornell University Press, 1983).

42. Peter Cocks, "Towards a Marxist Theory of European Integration," *International Organization*, Vol. 34, No. 1, Winter 1980. Quote at p. 1. Deutsch, op. cit. (note 34), and his *Nationalism and Social Communication* (Cambridge, MA: MIT Press, 1966), do deal with history, but, as Cocks states (p. 2), "These works are historical only in the sense that he and his co-workers have used history as a data bank to provide generalizations applicable irrespective of space or time about the necessary conditions for integration," thus failing to explain "the dynamic that connects or disconnects past and present cases of unification."

43. Ibid., p. 4.   This is because the capitalist state must perform two critical functions: "provision of the political infrastructure for the expansion of productive forces in protocapitalist and capitalist societies; and an appropriate means for legitimating the power necessary to maintain the social relations integral to these societies." Ibid., p. 4.

44. Perry Andreson, *Lineages of the Absolutist State* (London: New Left Books, 1974), Part I, Chapters 1 and 2. Quote at pp. 28, 40. Cf. Immanuel Wallerstein, *The Modern World-System: Capitalist Agriculture and the Origins of the European World-Economy in the Sixteenth Century* (New York: Academic Press, 1974). For an analysis of the various theoretical positions on the national question and the state, see Gilles Bourque, *L'Etat capitaliste et la question nationale* (Montréal: Les Presses de l'Université de Montréal, 1977); and Michael Lowry, "Marxism and the National question," in Robin Blackburn (ed.), *Revolution and Class Struggle: A Reader in Marxist Politics* (Glasgow: Fontant, 1977), pp. 136-60.

45. Cocks, op. cit. (note 42), pp. 15-21.

46. Ibid., pp. 21-24. In general, Cocks argues (p. 17) that the distinct patterns of national unification were "determined by the relative strength of socioeconomic classes within the state and by the particular country's relationship to the international system." An instructive theoretical position on this domestic factor was presented by Otto Bauer with his analysis of the German case, in which he examined the national question (unification) in relation to the then persisting unequal development manifested in differences between industry and agriculture, and within the industrial sector between heavy industry and light industry. In this configuration of classes, nationalism and strong central states were the means suitable to foster domestic development through the elimination of barriers to trade. This historical case resembles the modern process of European integration in which the interests of big capital, pushing for the enlargement of the market through the elimination of all economic barriers, had to be accommodated with those of the backward industrial sectors and of agriculture. On Bauer's theoretical position, see Bourque, op. cit. (note 44), pp. 244-47. For a broader discussion, see Ephrain Nimni, "Marxist Theories of Nationalism, the Great Historical Failure," *Capital & Class*, No. 25, Spring 1985.

47. Cf. Moschonas, op. cit. (note 1), especially Chapters 4 and 5.

48. The notion "mature capitalism," used interchangeably with "modern" or "advanced" or "late" capitalism, implies that the high stage of development of the productive forces and the concomitant concentration and centralization of capital on a national and international scale have produced an articulated system of relations of

production and exchange between capitalist countries, thereby forming a capitalist world economy. See Ernest Mandel, *Late Capitalism* (London: Verso Edition, 1978), pp. 48–49, 310–11.

49. Cocks, op. cit. (note 42), pp. 24–35. Cf. Robin Murray, "The Internationalization of Capital and the Nation State," *New Left Review*, No. 67, May–June 1971, reprinted in Hugo Radice (ed.), *International Firms and Modern Imperialism* (London: Penguin Books, 1975), pp. 107–34; Ernest Mandel, "International Capitalism and 'Supranationality,'" in Hugo Radice (ed.), *Ibid.*, pp. 143–57; Nicos Poulantzas, "Internationalization of Capitalist Relations and the Nation-State," *Economy and Society*, Vol. 3, No. 2, 1974, reproduced in his *Classes in Contemporary Capitalism* (London: Version Edition, 1978), part I; and Sol Picciotto "The Internationalization of the State," *Capital & Class*, No. 43, Spring 1991.

50. Richard Mayne, "Economic Integration in the New Europe: A Statistical Approach," *Daedalus*, Vol. 93, No. 1, Winter 1964. Quote at p. 113.

51. As the Spaak Report states, the "fusion of markets opens large outlets for the use of the most modern techniques. . . . But above all, in many branches of industry, national markets offer the opportunity of attaining optimum dimensions only to firms which enjoy a de facto monopoly. The strength of a large market is its ability to reconcile mass production with the absence of monopoly" Ibid., p. 113. See also Cocks, op. cit. (note 42), p. 29.

52. "Continental governments . . . were encouraging or obliging large industrial enterprises to become instruments of national policy. Mergers and acquisitions were announced in every continental nation, and in some industrial sectors they left in operation only one or two large 'national champion' enterprises." Lawrence G. Franko, *The European Multinationals: A Renewed Challenge to American and British Big Business* (London: Harper and Row Publishers, 1976), p. 2.

53. "The Rome Treaty forbids cartels, but the European Economic Commission, in the course of applying the provisions of the Treaty, has chosen to distinguish between good agreements and bad ones. In the early period of the Common Market a number of agreements between national firms were made in the interests of nationalization. One company would make this product, and the other that." C. P. Kindleberger, "European Integration and the International Corporation," in Courtney C. Brown (ed.), *World Business* (New York: Macmillan Company, 1970), p. 106.

54. For an elaboration on these points, see Cocks, op. cit. (note 42), p. 29; Stuart Holland, *The Socialist Challenge* (London: Quartet Books, 1975), p. 317; Dennis Swann, "Cartels and Concentrations—Issues and Progress," in G. R. Denton (ed.), *Economic Integration in Europe* (London: Weidenfeld and Nicolson, 1971), pp. 171–72 and 188–89; and Z. Kamecki, "Comments of an Eastern Devil's Advocate on L. Morissens," in E. S. Kirshen (ed.), *Economic Policies Compared*, Vol. 2, (Amsterdam: North-Holland Publishing Company, 1975), pp. 316–20.

55. For an analysis of economic tendencies and unequal competition, see Stuart Holland, *Capital Versus the Regions* (London: The Macmillan Press, 1976), esp. Chapter 5; his "Mesoeconomics, Multinational Capital and Regional Inequality," in Roger Lee and P. E. Ogden (eds.), *Economy and Society in the EEC* (London: Saxon House, 1976); and Franco Archibugi, J. Delors and S. Holland, "The International Crisis," in Stuart Holland (ed.), *Beyond Capitalist Planning* (Oxford: Basil Blackwell, 1978). For a critical Marxist analysis of the related concepts of integration and spatial structure, see Roger Lee, "Integration, Spatial Structure and the Capitalist Mode of Production in the

EEC," in Roger Lee and P. E. Ogden (eds.), *Ibid.*, pp. 11–37. The trend toward concentration and centralization has been reported by several studies. See, for instance, Franko,op. cit. (note 52), esp. Chapter 1; Kenneth D. George and T. S. Ward, *The Structure of Industry in the EEC* (Cambridge: Cambridge University Press, 1975); Sam Aaronovitch and Malcolm C. Sawyer, *Big Business: Theoretical and Empirical Aspects of Concentration and Mergers in the United Kingdom* (New York: Holmes and Meier Publishers, 1975); Rich Kronish, "Crisis in the West European Automobile Industry," *Monthly Review*, Vol. 31, No. 4, September 1979; and Alex P. Jacquemin and Michel Cardon de Lichtbuer, "Size Structure, Stability and Performance of the Largest British and EEC Firms," *European Economic Review*, Vol. 4, 1973. Cf. Alex P. Jacquemin and Anne–Marie Kumps, "Changes in the Size and Structure of the Largest European Firms: An Entropy Measure," *Journal of Industrial Economics*, Vol. 20, No. 1, November 1971; and Dennis Swann and D. L. Mclachlan, *Concentration or Competition?—A European Dilemma* (London: Chatham House, 1967).

56. Cf. A. Kirsanov, *The USA and Western Europe: Economic Relations after World War II* (Moscow: Progress Publishers, 1975), Chapter 7; Ernest Mandel, *Europe vs. America: Contradictions of Imperialism* (New York and London: Monthly Review Press, 1970); Nicos Poulantzas, *Classes in Contemporary Capitalism*, op. cit. (note 49), Part I; and John Holloway, "Some Issues Raised by Marxist Analyses of European Integration," *Bulletin of the Conference of Socialist Economists*, March 1976.

57. See Kirsanov, op. cit. (note 56), pp. 181–91. Cf. Holloway, op. cit. (note 56), pp. 8–11.

58. Kirsanov, *The USA and Western Europe: Economic Relations after World War II*, pp. 190–91.

59. Cf. Louis Althusser, "What Must Change in the Party," *New Left Review*, No. 109, May–June 1978; and Heinz Timmermann, "The Eurocommunists and the West," *Problems of Communism*, Vol. 28, May–June 1979.

60. See Ernest Mandel, "International Capitalism and 'Supranationality,'" op. cit. (note 49); *Europe vs. America*, op. cit. (note 56), esp. Chapter 5; and *Late Capitalism*, op. cit. (note 48), Chapter 10. Cf. Holloway, op. cit. (note 56), pp. 1–5; Santiago Carrillo, *Eurocommunism and the State* (Westport, CT: Lawrence Hill and Co.. 1978), Chapter 1, pp. 45–48, 105–9; Donald Sassoon, "The Italian Communist Party's European Strategy," *Political Quarterly*, Vol. 47, No. 3, 1976, esp. pp. 260–63.

61. Cf. Mandel, *Late Capitalism*, op. cit. (note 48), pp. 326–42; Carrillo, op. cit. (note 60), pp. 105–9; Sassoon, op. cit. (note 60), p. 264; Holloway, op. cit. (note 56), pp. 3–4. Mandel qualifies this "supranational logic" with two exceptions: (i) the occurrence of a major economic crisis which may undermine the whole process of integration by giving rise to national protectionism; and/or (ii) the retardation, through deliberate national action, of the process of capital concentration at the European level. This latter development seems to be irrational for Mandel because the nationalist de Gaulle "by opposing amalgamation between French, German and Italian industrialists . . . only prepares the ground for them to be swallowed up by the Americans!" Mandel, "International Capitalism and 'Supranationality,'" op. cit. (note 49), p. 150. De Gaulle's behavior is labelled "irrationality" because Mandel precludes the possibility of unequal partnership among the various coalitions of European capital, coalitions which in his view represent the "fusion of capital without the predominance of any particular group of national capitalists." *Late Capitalism*, op. cit. (note 48), p. 326. Yet the fact remains that de Gaulle's nationalism sprang not only from his

glorification of the French nation but also from the very economic weakness of that nation, that is, the relative backwardness of the French economy during the early period of European integration. See Gianni Simoni, "West Germany in the Common Market," *International Socialist Journal*, Vol. 3, No. 15, July 1966; Holland, *The Socialist Challenge*, op. cit. (note 54), pp. 328–29; and Poulantzas, op. cit. (note 49), pp. 67–68.

62. "The growth of capital interpenetration inside the Common Market, the appearance of large amalgamated banking and industrial units which are not mainly the property of any national capitalist class, represent the material infra-structure for the emergence of supranational state-power organs in the Common Market," Mandel, "International Capitalism . . . ," op. cit. (note 49), p. 147. Cf. Holloway, op. cit. (note 56), pp. 3–5.

63. Cf. Mandel, *Europe vs. America*, op. cit. (note 56), Chapter 10; Carrillo, op. cit. (note 60), pp. 24–25, 46–48, 103–5; Sassoon, op. cit. (note 60), pp. 262–65, 269, 271–75.

64. Mandel, "International Capitalism . . . ," op. cit. (note 49), p. 155.

65. Ibid., p. 156. "This implies among other things a study of the possibilities for setting up international trade-unions where they face a single international company and fighting for an international collective contract, which would prevent the employers from exploiting international wage differentials." Cf. Carrillo, op. cit. (note 60), pp. 103–5; and Sassoon, op. cit. (note 60), p. 263. Here it is postulated that there is a threshold in internationalism which implies that a struggle on the national level is objectively possible "as long as international capital amalgamation, international economic integration and growth of supranational powers have not reached the point where it is no more possible to break the stranglehold of private property and the bourgeois state over that country's resources on a national scale." Mandel, "International Capitalism . . . ," op. cit. (note 49), p. 156. Even so, this leaves unresolved the question of how to identify the "threshold of internationalism" and how to judge whether or not it is possible for the class struggle to become international in the face of the sociopolitical specificities of the national state and the structural constraints posed by the logic of the international accumulation of capital.

66. Address to the European Parliament on February 10, 1976, *Ninth General Report on the Activities of the European Community*, Brussels, 1976, p. XI. In his previous address (1975), in an attempt to instill a kind of "supranational nationalism," Ortoli stated clearly that "Europe's real problem is independence, control of its own destiny," and added: "The centers of political and financial power have shifted. Our dependence is physical, as the embargo showed us, but it is more than that. It is economic, since our structures have undergone a radical transformation. It is monetary, since we discovered overnight that we can only pay our bills by a transfer of resources, of the fruits of our labor. Borrowing, a hazardous process in itself, can only postpone the evil day. These are hard facts to face." *Eighth General Report on the Activities of the European Community*, Brussels, 1975, p. X.

67. The most articulated statement of this theoretical position is that of Nicos Poulantzas, *Classes in Contemporary Capitalism*, op. cit. (note 49), part I. As he put it, "The imperialist chain is itself characterized by uneven development; each link of this chain reflects the chain as a whole in the specificity of its own social formation. . . . The process of imperialist domination and dependence henceforth take the form of the reproduction, within the dominated social formations themselves, and in the forms

specific to each of them, of the relation of domination which binds them to the imperialist metropolises." *Ibid.*, pp. 42, 43.

68. Ibid., pp. 47–48.

69. Ibid., pp. 70–84. Cf. Etienne Balibar, "Es Gibt Staat in Europa: Racism and Politics in Europe Today," *New Lift Review*, No. 185, March/April 1991; and Anthony D. Smith, "National Identity and the Idea of European Unity," *International Affairs*, Vol. 68, No. 1, January 1992.

70. Cf. Poulantzas, op. cit. (note 49), pp. 70–78. Here Poulantzas conceptualizes "the class configuration of the power bloc, the specific alliance of the politically dominant classes and class fractions, in the imperialist metropolises." Ibid., p. 75. Holloway (op. cit., note 56, pp. 7, 18) agrees with Poulantzas's conceptualization but criticizes him on the ground that he makes the disjunction between "national economies" and "national capitalisms" too complete, thereby eliminating entirely the existence of "national capital." I agree with Holloway that a mixture of the two must actually exist because, as Poulantzas himself stated, the European capitalist/imperialist countries themselves constitute centers of capital accumulation.

71. In contrast, "The national state . . . intervenes, in its role as organizer of hegemony, in a domestic field already structured by inter-imperialist contradictions, and in which contradictions between the dominant fractions within its social formation are already internationalized." Poulantzas, op. cit. (note 49), pp. 74–75.

72. "What we are faced with is not the emergence of a new state over and above the nations, but rather with ruptures of the national unity underlying the existing national states; this is the very important contemporary phenomenon of regionalism, . . . which demonstrates that the internationalization of capital is leading more towards a fragmentation of the nation, such as it is historically constituted, than to a supranationalization of the state." Ibid., p. 80.

73. Cf. V. I. Lenin, *Imperialism: The Highest Stage of Capitalism* (New York: International Publishers, 1972, first published in 1917).

74. Cf. Poulantzas, op. cit. (note 49), pp. 42–50; and Samir Amin, *Accumulation on a World Scale: A Critique of the Theory of Underdevelopment* (New York and London: Monthly Review Press, 1974).

75. Robert Brenner, "The Origins of Capitalist Development: A Critique of Neo-Smithian Marxism," *New Left Review*, No. 104, July–August 1977. Quote at pp. 59–60.

76. Karl Marx, *Capital*, Vol. III (Moscow, 1959), p. 772, quoted in Leo Panitch, "Dependency and Class in Canadian Political Economy," *Studies in Political Economy*, No. 6, Autumn 1981. Quote at p. 13. In the quotation from Marx, the word "determines" should rather read "conditions" because the relationship between the state and civil society is contradictory, that is, dialectical.

77. Cf. Poulantzas, op. cit. (note 49), pp. 13–35; Adam Przeworski, "Proletariat into a Class: The Process of Class Formation from Karl Kautsky's The Class Struggle to Recent Controversies," *Politics and Society*, Vol. 7, No. 4, 1977; Erik Olin Wright, "Varieties of Marxist Conceptions of Class Structure," *Politics and Society*, Vol. 9, No. 3, 1980; G. Carchedi, "Reproduction of Social Classes at the Level of Production Relations," *Economy and Society*, Vol. 4, No. 4, November 1975.

78. See Claus Offe, "Notes on the Future of European Socialism and the State," *Kapitalistate*, No. 7, 1978; Alan Wolfe, "Capitalism Shows Its Face: Giving Up on Democracy," in Holly Sklar (ed.), *Trilateralism: The Trilateral Commission and Elite*

Planning for World Management (Montreal: Black Rose Books, 1980), pp. 295–307; and William Tabb, "Social Democracy and Authoritarianism: Two Faces of Trilateralism toward Labor," in H. Sklar (ed.), *Ibid.*, pp. 308–23. Cf. M. Crozier, S. P. Huntington, J. Watanuki, *The Crisis of Democracy: Report on the Governability of Democracies to the Trilateral Commission* (New York: New York University Press, 1975).

79. Cf. Roger Lee, "Integration, Spatial Structure and the Capitalist Mode of Production in the EEC," op. cit. (note 55); and Michael Hodges, "The Legacy of the Treaty of Rome: A Community of Equals?" *The World Today*, June 1979.

80. Carchedi identifies two types of devaluation of labor power, one which is due to the increased productivity in the sectors of the economy producing wage goods, and the other which is due to the fact that some laborers are forced to fill positions with a lower skill level required; this produces so-called "devaluation through dequalification." See Carchedi, "Reproduction of Social Classes at the Level of Production Relations," op. cit. (note 77), pp. 377–92. Cf. Poulantzas, op. cit. (note 49), pp. 58–64. For the impact of new technologies on social organization see, for instance, André Gorz, "The New Agenda," *New Left Review*, No. 184, November/December 1990.

81. Cf. Carchedi, "Reproduction of Social Classes . . . ," op. cit. (note 77), pp. 384–404.

82. Cf. Cocks, op. cit. (note 42), pp. 30–32; Poulantzas, op. cit. (note 49), pp. 78–79.

83. Guglielmo Carchedi, "Authority and Foreign Labor: Some Notes on a Late Capitalist Form of Capital Accumulation and State Intervention," *Studies in Political Economy*, No. 2, Autumn 1979; Marios Nikolinakos, "Notes towards a General Theory of Migration in Late Capitalism," *Race and Class*, Vol. 17, No. 1, July 1975.

84. On these general questions, see the sources cited in note 83 above and Cocks, op. cit. (note 42), pp. 30–32; Manuel Castells, "Immigrant Workers and Class Struggles in Advanced Capitalism: The Western European Experience," *Politics and Society*, Vol. 5, No. 1, 1975; R. Rifflet, "Employment Policy Prospects in the European Communities," *International Labor Review*, Vol. 113, No. 2, March–April 1976.

85. Cf. Poulantzas, op. cit. (note 49), pp. 78–79. Cocks, op. cit. (note 42), pp. 30–32. On the continuing importance of the nation-state, see Sam Pooley, "The State Rules, OK? The Continuing Political Economy of Nation-States," *Capital & Class*, No. 43, Spring 1991.

86. Cf. Castells, op. cit. (note 84), pp. 65–66. This seems to explain why the formation of European "pressure groups" has not been followed by a transfer of allegiance from the national state to the supranational institutions, as postulated by neofunctionalism. On the neofunctionalist puzzle, see Marguerite Bouvard, *Labor Movements in the Common Market Countries: The Growth of a European Pressure Group* (New York: Praeger Publishers, 1972); and Juliet Lodge, "Loyalty and the EEC: The Limitations of the Functionalist Approach," *Political Studies*, Vol. 26 (1978).

87. This tendency, coupled with the increasing socioeconomic role of the national state, forces capital, whether "national" or "supranational," to support the national state in order to maintain its position of dominance over the working class. See Holloway, op. cit (note 56), p. 11; Cocks, op. cit. (note 42), pp. 32, 39; Donald J. Puchala, "Domestic Politics and Regional Harmonization in the European Communities," *World Politics*, Vol. 27, No. 4, July 1975. On the growth of public expenditure in the EEC countries, see Lees, op. cit. (note 55), pp. 14–18.

88. See, for example, Ralph Miliband, *The State in Capitalist Society* (London: Weidenfeld and Nicholson, 1969) and Nicos Poulantzas, *Political Power and Social Classes* (London: NLB, 1973).

89. P. Cocks, "Towards a Marxist Theory of European Integration," op. cit. (note 42).

90. Stuart Holland, *Uncommon Market: Capital, Class and Power in the European Community* (London: The Macmillan Press, 1980).

91. Theoretical insights one could also get from Göran Therborn, *What Does the Ruling Class Do When It Rules?* (London: NLB, 1978).

92. Nicos Mouzelis, *Post-Marxist Alternatives: The Construction of Social Orders* (London: Macmillan, 1990).

2

The Socioeconomic Structure of The European Union

Eleftherios N. Botsas

Socioeconomic structure is usually defined in terms of social arrangements with respect to ownership and control of the productive resources, and their allocation in the production of goods and services. The dominant arrangement in the European Union (EU) is that of the market mechanism with varying degrees of social control by the national governments. The degree of control varies according to divergence between private and social costs and benefits as well as the aims of the authorities to achieve certain social goals with respect to education, health, income distribution, and work environment. However, the Single European Act and the Maastricht Treaty attempt to reduce, if not eliminate, national differences in fundamental policies that are viewed as common interest to the Union although there are vast differences in the social and economic structures of the members.

The original Six had very similar economic structures. The first enlargement added two similar countries—Denmark and the United Kingdom—and one dissimilar country, Ireland. The second and third enlargements added three peripheral countries. Thus the Union's structure became more diverse while undergoing more intensive integration.

A complete treatment of the arrangements and the search for an optimum structure that will move the Union to the frontiers of social welfare is beyond the scope of this chapter, which is limited to an examination of the basic structures of the economies by looking into the three main economic sectors: agriculture, industry, and services. The sectoral differences among the members have been determined by varied historical experiences and resource endowments, but the trend of economic history has been one of shifts from agriculture to industry to services.

THE SECTORS OF THE ECONOMY

Agriculture

Table 2.1 shows the general statistical characteristics of the Union while Table 2.2 presents the agricultural structure. It is a matter of historical and statistical record that the poorer a country is, the greater the share of agriculture in both employment of labor and contribution to income. High rates of employment in the agricultural sector can be the result of low per worker productivity in the sector that produces foodstuffs, the absence of employment opportunities in the industrial sector, or protection of agriculture from international competition. As productivity in the agricultural sector increases, the same size of population can be fed with fewer workers. Labor is freed to be employed in the rest of the economy, usually the manufacturing sector. The decline in the relative role of agriculture has been correlated with economic development in all advanced countries. For example, in Britain the contribution of agriculture to national income was over 20 percent in the 1860s, while it is only 2 percent today.

It is clear that Portugal, Ireland, Spain, and, especially, Greece have high rates of labor still working in the agricultural sector. They are also the countries that have high percentages of GDP originating in agriculture. This is the by-product of low levels of industrialization as well as low productivity per worker in the agricultural sector. As can be seen, the per capita GDP is inversely related to the proportion of labor force employed in agriculture. Greece's share (3.8 percent) in the value of final agricultural product of the Union (excluding Portugal) is about equal to Denmark's (3.5 percent), but Greece employs over four times Denmark's relative labor force (European Community Commission, 1989: 10). Arable land per worker in agriculture, and investment in agriculture in order to overcome the land constraint, can explain most of these disparities in relative productivity.

The agricultural structure varies dramatically among the Union members (see Table 2.2). Greece and Portugal have very small farms which vent the introduction of mechanization and economies of scale. Only 3 percent of the Greek farms are larger than 40 hectares, compared with 60 percent in Denmark, 82 percent in the United Kingdom, 52 percent in France, 77 percent in the Netherlands, and 54 percent in Belgium (International Monetary Fund, 1988: 35). The average size of a Greek farm was one-third of the average EC-10 and only 8 percent of the average of the UK's. The inclusion of Portugal and Spain reduced the average size for the Union from 17.4 to 8.9 hectares. Thus agriculture in the periphery tends to be subsistence agriculture rather than agro-business. It is highly labor intensive-and inefficient. One would expect labor to move to other sectors, but the more backward an economy is, the fewer the job alternatives are. In the absence of alternative employment opportunities in

Table 2.1
General Statistical Characteristics of the Union

| | Labor Distribution | | | Share in GDP (1983–87) | | | GDP* | Compensation** | | S. Sec.*** |
	Agriculture	Industry	Service	Agriculture	Industry	Service	US$ 1990	1990	US$ 1988 %GDP
Belgium	2.8	28.5	68.7	2.4	32.8	64.8	19,303	128	28.7
Denmark	5.7	27.4	66.9	5.6	28.6	65.7	25,150	121	28.5
France	6.4	30.1	63.5	3.8	30.6	65.5	21,105	103	28.3
Germany	3.7	39.8	56.5	1.8	40.8	57.4	23,536	146	28.1
Greece	25.3	27.5	47.1	16.6	29.2	54.2	6,505	46	22.6
Ireland	15.1	28.4	56.5	11.2	37.2	51.6	12,131	80	22.9
Italy	9.3	32.4	58.2	4.5	34.6	60.9	18,921	111	26.6
Luxembourg	3.3	31.5	65.2	2.6	37.7	59.5	22,895		30.7
Netherlands	4.7	26.5	68.8	4.2	32.3	63.6	18,579	123	17
Portugal	19.0	35.3	45.7	8.9	38.3	52.8	6,085	25	17.7
Spain	13.0	32.9	54.0	6.1	37.8	56.1	12,609	79	23.6
UK	2.1	29.4	68.4	1.9	39.5	58.5	16,985	84	24.9
EC12:1990	6.6			2.4				115	

* At current prices and current exchange rates
** Compensation in manufacturing index (U.S. 100)
*** S. Sec. = Social security expenditures

Sources: Shares in GDP computed by the author from the World Bank, *World Tables*; rest OECD, *Economic Surveys*;
    U.S. Bureau of Labor Statistics, *International Comparisons of Hourly Costs in Manufacturing*;
    European Community Commission, *A Community of Twelve: Key Figures*, 1991.

Table 2.2
The Structure of EC Agriculture, 1986

	Size[#]	(L/w)[a]	Expend[b]	Share in EC
Belgium	14.1	13.7	21.3	3.2
Denmark	30.7	15.9	23.5	3.5
France	27.0	20.5	20.5	24.7
Germany[c]	16.0	8.9	17.0	15.2
Greece	4.3	5.6	39.9	3.8
Ireland	22.7	33.8	43.2	2.0
Italy	5.6	7.8	28.7	17.9
Luxembourg	28.6	19.7	23.3	0.1
Netherlands	14.9	8.2	19.1	7.6
Portugal	4.3	5.1	38.6	-----
Spain	12.9	15.6	27.2	11.3
UK	65.1	30.1	18.9	10.6
EC-12	8.9	12.8	21.9	100.0

[#]Average farm size in hectares
[a]Hectares per farm worker
[b]Percentage of final consumer expenditures on food, tobacco, and beverages
[c]Former Federal Republic only

Source: European Community Commission, *A Common Agricultural Policy for the 1990s.*

the rural sector, people either migrate to the urban centers or, if they wish to serve a "way of life," depend on government and EU subsidies.   Internal migration has created more problems than it has solved in Greece.

On the overall level of agricultural ownership in the Union, "About 80% of all farm production is now in the hands of only 20% of all farmers" (European Community Commission, 1989: 57), and the average real farm income "in 1988 was below the level of the mid-1970s" (European Community Commission, 1989: 54).   The big landholdings are to be found in the North, not in Greece and Portugal.   It is in the nature and structure of agriculture that, in the absence of intervention, incomes and prices fluctuate widely.   The supply cannot be planned accurately, and price and income elasticities tend to be very low. However, the problem of many small farmers struggling to make a living is not limited to the Union.

Cereals and fruits and vegetables are the only food items wherein Greece is self-sufficient and a net exporter.   In meat and dairy products, which are characterized by higher income elasticities, Greece has very little domestic production.   Denmark, the Netherlands, and Ireland have high ratios of production to consumption in these items, producing more than 300 percent of domestic consumption in many cases (International Monetary Fund, 1988: 29). These are the items that are heavily subsidized by the EU's Common Agricultural Policy (CAP). It is a universal phenomenon that low-income people spend a higher percentage of their income on food items. As income rises, the overall proportion spent on food falls, and a reallocation within the food category takes place away from "low-quality" items (bread) and in favor of high-quality items such as meat and dairy products. Since CAP policies have served high food prices in the EU, these policies work as transfers of income from the poor to the rich of the Union.

Critics of the CAP have argued that high EU subsidies to the agricultural sector vent that reallocation of resources away from agriculture. However, the CAP has had limited benefits for the Mediterranean products of Greece, Portugal, and Spain. Its heavy support had been for cereals, meat, and especially dairy products (European Community Commission, 1989: 52). It is only recently that a reallocation of expenditures has taken place, and the distortion of resource allocation must be due more to the national policies than the supranational CAP. Since agriculture is the primary sector of economic development, it has exercised disproportionate political power in the course of development of all advanced economies. It is considered the backbone of social continuity.

Agriculture plays different roles in the EU economies, but the aims of the CAP are the same for all of them. Article 39 of the Treaty of Rome sets out the objectives of the CAP in terms of the availability of supplies, fair standards of living of farmers and consumers, and price stability (Hitiris, 1991: 168). While the Treaty envisioned all other sectors of the economy to be governed by market forces, agriculture was exempted. Among the reasons for such an exemption one can cite the continued portion of the original Six as net importers of foodstuffs, the political strength of the agricultural sector, and the special concern that all societies show for food security. Although food security is an ill-defined concept, its perceived threat has been with us at least since Malthus's time. The late 1940s and early 1950s were characterized by world food shortages and rising relative food prices. Although these were transitory phases, the fear of food shortages persists even in the presence of an abundance of foodstuffs beyond possible consumption.

The 1992–93 French farm demonstrations against the EU-U.S. agreement to proceed with the discussions on trade liberalization under the auspices of the General Agreement on Tariffs and Trade (GATT) arose from the fact that the CAP had produced surpluses that could not be sustained in the future. France is Europe's main agricultural power, but its farming population declined from about five million in 1955 to about one million in 1990. However, rural decline cannot be vented in France or anywhere else. That is the process of economic growth, and the political distribution of domestic powers follows the redistribution of economic powers, although with a time lag.

Industry

The Cecchini Report (1988: 50) found that six sectors of manufacturing (telecommunications, motors, building products, foodstuffs, textiles and clothing, and pharmaceuticals) resented 43 percent of the Union's industrial output. Fragmentation of the market vented significant investment in research and development, exploitation of economies of scale, and learning experience, since learning the business environment in one country is often location specific and firm specific. Transferability of learning is possible, but it requires integration and rationalization of activities that the fragmented policies of the past could not accommodate.

There are additional problems in EU manufacturing, the most important of which are labor cost and technological change. The Union is perceived as a "welfare state" with high compensation and generous benefits. To some extent, this is borne out by the data. Table 2.1 shows that the Union's compensation cost was 15 percent higher than that of the United States, with Germany's being 46 percent higher. Moreover, during the period 1979–90 the annual rates of growth of per employee compensation and the unit labor cost in the business sector (not only manufacturing), were higher than those of the United States in all EU countries except Germany and the Netherlands. Compared with the rates of the period 1973–79, the Union made progress in the 1980s, but not enough to offset its competitive disadvantage.

Looking at wages and compensation in manufacturing, the composite for the Union shows a loss in competitive position. This labor cost disadvantage could be offset by growth in productivity, and productivity, in turn, would reduce the unit labor cost. This has not happened. The appreciation of the U.S. dollar between 1981 and 1986 gave the Union a cost advantage in the international market for manufactured goods. This advantage disappeared in 1987. Although Greece and Portugal are still far behind the rest of the Union in labor compensation, low productivity makes their manufactured goods uncompetitive.

Because of the heavy industrialization of the Union's North, we tend to think of Europe as an industrial economic space. For example, in 1991 the Union accounted for 33 percent of the world production of motor vehicles, but only Spain was an important producer in the South. Yet, international organizations such as the International Monetary Fund, the World Bank, and the United Nations classify the Twelve as industrial countries. This is not the case, however, for the whole of the Union. Economically, it is a dualistic economic space with a center (the North) and a periphery (the South), as shown in Table 2.1. In addition to the overall distribution of labor and origin of GDP, one can see the dualism of the economies through an analysis of their international specialization. The North specializes in differentiated products that are human-capital intensive and the South in labor-intensive products and services. Trade among the center countries tends to be intra-industry trade arising from economies of scale and product differentiation, while trade between the North and South tends to be interindustry trade, arising from relative factor endowments that may not create dynamic growth.

Damien Neven (1990: 14) attempted to find similarities in trade structure among the Twelve by clustering them. When he created two clusters, Greece and Portugal split from the rest of the Union. With three clusters, Greece was alone; Italy, Spain, and Portugal formed an intermediate group; and the rest of the Union formed the core. A more refined approach would be to cluster the Twelve according to high technology, in which case Germany, France, and the United Kingdom would be separated from the rest.

Orthodox trade theory would dict that the periphery stands to gain proportionately more from the single market than the center because the periphery's economies are relatively small, the factor endowments differ significantly from those of the center (while they tend to be similar among the countries of the center), the industry of the center is already integrated, and complete integration will permit exploitation of economies of scale. Neven (1990: 2) found that "the effect will be much stronger in the South" because the North's labor-intensive industries are important for the periphery, but the human capital advantage of the center is very small in the periphery. Richard Portes (1991: 39) also argues that the EU South lacks human capital. Because of these differences, Neven (1990: 44) concluded that "the main beneficiaries of the 92 programme are however likely to be the Southern European countries." Yet, since Greece's accession, the EU has penetrated the Greek market, but Greece has failed to penetrate the EU market.

There are certain problems with the above reasoning. First, if Greece and Portugal are economically behind because they have specialized in traditionally labor-intensive products, should they continue that kind of specialization? The growth in demand is to be found in differentiated manufactured goods, not in labor-intensive goods in which Greece has no comparative advantage. Michael Gasiorek et al. (1991: 20) found that "in no country does manual labour experience an increase in demand relative to other factors." Not surprising is the authors' finding (Gasiorek et al.: 28) that "the demand for skilled labour increases relative to the demand for unskilled labour." This is a universal phenomenon. Many of the tasks of unskilled labor can be performed by simple machines.

Paul Krugman and Anthony Venables (1990: 74) have argued that there is "a fundamental ambiguity in the effects of Europe 1992 on the relative competitiveness of manufacturing in the peripheral nations." This arises from the relatively lower wages in the periphery that could attract manufacturing activities versus its location away from the center. It is possible that further de-industrialization of the periphery will take place before wages become critical in the location of industry and reverse the trend. Manufacturing is characterized by economies of scale, and the peripheral economies are too small to exploit such economies.

Commenting on this, André Sapir (1990: 76) argued that "infrastructure and human capital are more important factors in determining whether a country will expand or shrink its manufacturing sector." He gives Korea as an example of bad location but high degree of manufacturing activity. He concludes that "neither Greece nor Portugal will remain in the periphery if they succeed, like Spain, in building a sufficient infrastructure" (Sapir, 1990: 77). The author agrees with Sapir on infrastructure, but he fails to see that Greece's location is not only a distance problem; it is also burdened by the "neighborhood effect," that is, the constant need to be on the defense against eastern and northern neighbors. No other EU country faces similar problems from neighbors. Indeed, no other NATO country bears the defense burden that Greece does, and the heavy defense burden has deprived the economy of investment in productive physical capital.

We have certain measurability problems when we talk about human capital. Formal education is one dimension; on-the-job training is another. There is also a qualitative problem that cannot be ascertained with any degree of accuracy except in the consumers' demand for quality products and services. Realizing that the definition of scientists and technicians is likely to vary from one country to the next, we can still proceed with the available data. Whether one looks at formal schooling years or the supply of scientists and technicians per population, Greece is above Spain and closer to Italy (the middle) than to Portugal (United Nations Development Programme, 1992: 190). Lack of physical rather than human capital investment has distorted Greece's production mode.

There are certain "soft" industries that have performed well under EU protection but face competition from the newly industrialized countries (NICs) and Central Europe. One of these industries is textiles and clothing. In Italy, in 1990 it contributed 4.7 percent to GDP and 6.1 percent to employment. Textiles alone account for the following percentage shares of GDP: Belgium 1.8, France 1.3, Netherlands (textiles and leather) 0.7, Portugal (textiles, leather, and clothing) 7.7, and Greece 3.1 (Organization for Economic Cooperation and Development, *Economic Surveys*). Thus for Italy, Greece, and Portugal, this is an important sector that is likely to raise many issues with respect to EU liberalization toward the NICs and Central Europe, although Italy tends to specialize in higher-quality clothing rather than textile production. Since all countries of the Union face unemployment problems in the labor-intensive sectors, liberalization of trade policies is likely to be resisted by labor.

The size of the national markets should be irrelevant in a truly unified Union, but the EU is far from being unified. In Greece, the manufacturing establishments are too small to exploit any economies of scale. The 1984 census found that 94 percent of the manufacturing establishments were employing fewer than ten persons, and the manufacturing sector accounted for 19 percent of the labor force (NSSG 1987: 228). In Belgium, in 1990, establishments in the whole economy employing fewer than ten persons accounted for only 16 percent, in Luxembourg 14 percent, and in France 24 percent of the total employment(Organization for Economic Cooperation and Development, *Economic Surveys*). It is a well-established fact that European firms are smaller than their US or Japanese counterparts. Unilever is the only EU corporation among the twenty largest manufacturing corporations in the world (UN Center on Transnational Corporations, 1988). European corporations tend to be small, and, like farm size, corporate size tends to be still smaller in Greece and Portugal.

Turning to the Union as a whole, we know that it has fallen behind the United States and Japan in high-technology production, especially in the fast-growing sectors of computers, software, and general information technology. Harrop (1989: 95) argues that "the main problem for the EC is not so much technology *per se* but the managerial gap commercially in applying this technology," while Juliet Lodge (1989: 87) argues that "the EC lacks an industrial policy but has the economic instruments through which industrial aims may be pursued." I fail to see the economic instruments at the Union level. One has to remember that the EU's budget is very limited, only 1.2 percent of the EU GDP, with over one-half of it allocated to the CAP. Historically, the philosophy of the EU has been one of competition, not of industrial policy. Moreover, up to the 1992 program, the EU was simply the sum total of its member countries. That is why the Single European Act (SEA), by attempting to achieve rationalization of production and economies of scale, offers a much greater scope to innovative firms. Mergers and acquisitions increased dramatically in the closing years of the 1980s.

In semiconductors, a strategic part of information technology, Europe's share fell far behind. Kenneth Flamm (1990: 263) argues that "although European companies manufacture only a little over 12 percent of the world's semiconductor output, recent mergers have concentrated that production in just three firms." This concentration is still too weak to compete with the Japanese and U.S. giants in the field. The EU Directorate-General XIII (European Community Commission, 1992: 8) estimated that in 1989 Europe accounted for only 10 percent of the world's output and 17 percent of the world's use of semiconductors. Europe's spending on R & D in information technology was only 18 percent of the world's expenditure, while the United States and Japan accounted for 55 percent and 27 percent, respectively (European Community Commission, 1992). The Union has the resources to be a leader in high technology, but fragmentation of effort among the Twelve cannot produce leadership.

Services

The service sector is very heterogeneous. It includes personal services (maids, beauticians, physicians, attorneys) and business services—high-technology services such as data processing as well as low-technology services such as retail trading. Moreover, the basic characteristic of services is that they are location bound. Production and consumption are simultaneous activities: the production and consumption of a haircut occur at the same time and place. Therefore, they do not move from one location to another unless the provider or the consumer of the service moves. This location limitation is one of the explanations of high rates of growth in foreign direct investment in the service sector of the developed economies. Furthermore, within categories of services you have part of it as a commodity and another part as service. For example, a computer is a commodity, but the transmission of information is a service. In general terms, economic growth entails the fall of agriculture as a market for employment and a source of GDP, and the rise of the industrial sector. At high levels of economic development, the demand for services rises disproportionately.

The Union's profile given in Table 2.1 shows high concentration in services in all member countries. This concentration may be higher under the existing country policies than it would be under conditions of free markets. Public utilities are under the protection and control of national governments. In the absence of the profit motive, there is a tendency to overstaff for political or social purposes. That is why public-sector employees resist privatization. The United Kingdom went through this adjustment in the 1980s, and Greece and Italy are facing these problems in the early 1990s.

There are also qualitative differences in services among the members, especially between the North and the South, that cannot be quantified. Moreover, ownership of the providers of business services that enter the balance of payments may be outside the Union. In electronic data processing, accounting, management consulting, and hotel-chain ownership, the United States is the major player along with the United Kingdom, while France and Germany make a significant showing in international statistics (UN Center on Transnational Corporations, 1990).

While the rates of growth in overall employment in the period 1979-86 varied between –4 percent in Belgium and +10 percent in the Netherlands, during the same period professional employment in the business services sector (exclusive of banking and finance) increased by the following percentages: Netherlands 37.8, Belgium 29.8, Germany 26 and France 25.4 (UN Center on Transnational Corporations, 1990: 143). Unfortunately, there is lack of detailed data on all EU members for the distinction between business and nonbusiness services.

The Union is a strong exporter of tourist services, accounting for over 50 percent of the world exports. Spain, Italy, France, the United Kingdom, Germany, Belgium-Luxembourg, the Netherlands, and Greece are important players in this service, accounting (individually) for anywhere from 2 percent to 10 percent of world exports (UN Center on Transnational Corporations, 1990: 90). The free movement of people within the Union is likely to increase the importance of this service in employment and GDP, as well as to reduce the cultural distance among Europeans. However, it must be remembered that travel is highly sensitive to income, and economic slowdowns affect travel more than they affect the demand for commodities.

The business services sector (especially transportation and finance) is still regulated by national governments. However, harmonization under the Single European Market will consolidate this sector mostly in favor of business entities of the North. Economies of scale, capital investment, technological change, and standardization will create a more integrated market in these services. On the other hand, the professional and personal services sector is likely to remain fragmented. For example, an Italian attorney is free to practice law before a Greek court, but language is likely to impose constraints on the practicability of such legal harmonizations. In addition to the language distance there is a cultural distance in services. This distance depends on the degree of cultural dissimilarity among the EU members. Although we tend to think of the Union as one, cultural norms of services vary between countries as well as regions of the same country.

It is sometimes argued that it is manufacturing activities, not services, that provide for increasing standards of living. That is true for personal services that embody low levels of investment in human capital (servants and fast-food workers), but it is not true for services that require high skills, and the Union has high levels of skills, with a mean of 9.8 years of schooling for the population of twenty-five years old and older versus 10.0 for all developed countries (United Nations Development Programme, 1992: 190). Of course, this varies between the North and the South. Portugal has only 6 years, Spain 6.8, Greece 6.9, and Ireland 8.7, compared with 11.6 years in France. Italy, with a median of only 7.3 years of schooling, has had no problems in achieving high rates of economic growth.

The United Nations Development Programme has ranked 160 countries according to a complex index of human development (United Nations Development Programme, 1992: 120). According to this classification, the Union countries have been ranked between eighth in the world (France) and thirty-ninth (Portugal). It is obvious that the Union has a high ranking on human development, and such a profile of human development affects all sectors of the society—economic, political, and cultural. However, even in this case we observe that the Union clusters around three classes: France, the Netherlands, the United Kingdom, Germany, and Denmark cluster together between eighth and thirteenth; Luxembourg, Italy, Ireland, Spain, and Greece form a different group, ranking between nineteenth and twenty-sixth; Portugal, with a rank of thirty-nine, is far removed from the rest of the Union.

Trends and Contradictions

The EU has moved from the euphoria of the 1960s, to the pessimism of "Eurosclerosis" of the late 1970s and early 1980s, to the euphoria of the 1992 Program and the Maastricht Treaty. The negative Danish vote of 1992 and the financial crises of 1992–93 introduced some sobering facts that Maastricht did not anticipate. The willingness and ability of the members to forgo sovereignty over exchange rates came under suspicion. The Union is more likely to move in a two-tier mode than the Economic and Monetary Union heralded to be completed at the latest by January 1, 1999. The "one market, one money" pursuit cannot be achieved by the deadlines set by Maastricht.

The progress made in the 1980s justified the euphoria about complete monetary and fiscal union. With the exception of Greece and Portugal, inflation rates converged and moved to lower levels. The average consumer price index growth for the Union fell from 10.6 percent per year in 1975–84 to 4.4 percent in 1992 (International Monetary Fund, 1993). However, unemployment has remained high (over 10 percent) and structural problems are far from being solved.

We know that the Union is a multiethnic and multicultural entity endowed with different resources and often differing aims, but united in the pursuit of an age-old dream of achieving unification, economic prosperity, and protection of civil and economic rights. It is in the field of economic rights that the literature has assigned the designation "European model," and there has been a business cycle in what this model is. The forces released by the SEA attempt to achieve a Europe with a "human face," social and economic cohesion, as well as a highly competitive Europe that moves to the frontiers of technology. The catching up process of the 1950s and 1960s was successful, but catching up does not move an economy to the frontier of an ever changing world. Yet there is a dilemma here because the Commission tries to promote competition, while technology requires a high degree of market power, and market power is associated with economic concentration. In its decision to approve the joint venture between Philips Electronics, Thomson-CSF, and Société d'Applications Générals in May 1993, the Commission signaled its support for companies of "strategic importance" to the Twelve (*Wall Street Journal*, May 3, 1993: A7).

Although national policies of the Twelve in respect to social security differ in details, we can say that all have certain common characteristics that have given rise to the model as social engineering. As Table 2.1 has shown, social security expenditures, expressed as percent of the gross domestic product, are high. On the average, they are twice as high as in the United States. Moreover, the table shows that it is a privilege of the rich to be generous. The EU attempts to achieve efficiency and social equity. There is a well-established fundamental principle that a trade-off exists between economic efficiency and equity. The pursuit of equity, or social security, introduces rigidities that affect the behavior of the economic agents. The most important rigidity is to be found in labor markets where social benefits reduce incentives to work. The UN Economic Commission for Europe (1991: 199) found that

Most of the countries of the European Community exhibit the worst of all worlds: high levels of union coverage but (with the exception of Denmark) at best only modest level of employer and union co-ordination. In most cases benefits last for a reasonably long time (in several cases indefinitely) and, with the exception of Germany, expenditures on active labor market policy are minimal.

Can the EU achieve its economic aims without reducing the level of social benefits which the EU citizens are accustomed to? Experience and economics argue against it. In the world of the 1990s, with downsizing of corporations in all developed countries, it is not feasible to sustain the level of social expenditures and achieve the efficiencies of the 1992 Program.

In order to improve resource allocation across the EU, free mobility of the factors of production is necessary. There are two contradictory aspects to this. The South cannot compete with the more efficient North unless capital moves from the North to the South, or labor moves from the South to the North, or both mobilities take place. There is no controversy with capital mobility, but it has been feared that labor mobility would create "social dumping." Labor, in the center, is concerned that it will not be able to compete with the low-wage periphery. The trend is, of course, in the opposite direction. Unit labor cost in Greece and Portugal increased by more than twice the rates of increase in the center in the 1980s. The fear that free mobility of labor may create migratory inflows that will lower the center's wages is not supported by the record. Moreover, the possibility of unskilled labor migration has existed for decades in the Union without massive labor mobility. As Table 2.1 shows, wages and fringe benefits are lower in the South than in the North, without emigration. On the other hand, since the center is the magnet for investment, in a world of free capital mobility capital could move from the periphery to the center. In such a case, skilled labor would follow capital and the periphery would fall further behind.

The Maastricht Treaty restructures the fiscal policies of the states and, therefore, curtails the power of the state to encourage perpetuation of the "social contract" by requiring reductions in public expenditures. This reverses the upward trend in public consumption that affects the behavior of the labor markets. In addition, the Treaty sets quantitative criteria for the Union: inflation, long-term interest rates on public bonds, budgetary deficits not to exceed 3 percent of GDP, public debt not to exceed 60 percent of GDP, and irrevocably fixed exchange rates. The ratios of gross debt to GDP in 1992 were as follows: Belgium 121, Greece 108, Ireland 96, and Italy 115 (International Monetary Funding, 1993: 40). These ratios cannot be reduced in such a short period of time without causing massive unemployment.

Creating a single market out of diverse economies redistributes costs and benefits across the member states in unequal terms. There are two tendencies sent. One is toward convergence and one toward divergence. Because of the large gap between the North and South, there is a danger of a cumulative movement away from equilibrium. This can be vented only by massive investment in the South. Otherwise, the EU has to develop a preferential treatment for the South.

Can there be a single market without a monetary union? The most likely answer is no. Independent monetary policies in an otherwise integrated market have spillover effects that can reduce the single market benefits. Does it follow that fiscal policies have to be centralized, too? Tommaso Padoa-Scioppa (1992) argues no, with qualifications. This chapter argues yes, because of the possibility of further retardation of the periphery and the need for industrial policies with respect to R & D. The structural funds need more revenues to overcome the difficulties of the periphery, and this requires greater centralization of fiscal policies. Otherwise, the dream of political unification will remain a dream. It has to be remembered that irrevocably fixed exchange rates create, *de facto*, one money. However, there are *country specific* shocks that, in the absence of exchange rate variability, will require a redistribution of income that only a central authority can achieve. Gary Marks (1992: 194) argues that the growth of the structural funds can be explained as a "bribe" paid by the North to gain the South's assent to integration. There are two problems with this reasoning: the funds are still small, and after EMU (European Monetary Union) there will be no need for the South's assent.

SUMMARY

An analysis of the three main sectors of the EU reveals that the gap between the North and the South is substantial. In agriculture, the South reflects developing countries more than advanced countries. Whether one looks at employment or per capita GDP, the picture is that the South, especially Greece and Portugal, has a long way to go before it can catch up with the North. The manufacturing sector also testifies to the dualism of the EU. Contribution to GDP and specialization indicate that the North has an advantage in human capital accumulation, while the South specializes in resource-intensive products. The wisdom of such specialization is questionable. The service sector, in gross terms, shows no dualism. However, the qualitative differences between the North and the South must be substantial, especially in the business services. In terms of social security, there is also a big gap between the North and the South that affects investment in human capital. The North is likely to experience a fall in social expenditures as percent of GDP. Finally, the demands of high technology require a much stronger effort. Fragmentation does not lead to the frontiers of technological change.

REFERENCES

Cecchini, Paolo. 1988. *1992: The European Challenge*. Hants, U.K.: Wildwood Press.
European Community Commission. 1989. *A Common Agricultural Policy for the 1990s*. Luxembourg.
———. 1991. *A Community of Twelve: Key Figures*. Luxembourg.
———. 1992. *Information and Communications Technologies in Europe*. Luxembourg
Flamm, Kenneth. 1990. "Semiconductors." In Gary Hufbauer (ed.), *Europe 1992: An American Perspective*, pp. 225-92. Washington, DC: The Brookings Institution.
Gasiorek, Michael et al. 1991. "Completing the Internal Market in the EC: Factor Demand and Comparative Advantage." In Alan Winters and Anthony Venables, *European Integration: Trade and Industry*. New York: Cambridge University Press.
Harrop, Jeffrey. 1989. *The Political Economy of Integration in the European Community*. Brookfield, VT: Gower Publishing Company.
Hitiris, T. 1991. *European Community Economics*. New York: St. Martin's Press.
International Monetary Fund. 1993. *World Economic Outlook*.
———. 1988. *The Common Agricultural Policy of the European Community: Principles and Consequences*. Washington, DC.
Krugman, Paul and Anthony Venables. 1990. "Integration and Competitiveness of the Peripheral Industry." In Christopher Bliss and Jorge Braga de Macedo (eds.), *Unity With Diversity in the European Economy*. New York: Cambridge University Press.
Lodge, Juliet, ed. 1989. *The European Community and the Challenge of the Future*. New York: St. Martin's Press.
Marks, Gary. 1992. "Structural Policy in the European Community." In Alberta Sbragia (ed.), *Euro-Politics*, pp. 191-224. Washington, DC: The Brookings Institution.
Neven, Damien. 1990. *EEC Integration Towards 1992: Some Distributional Aspects*. Working Papers No. 90/23/EP/SM Fontainebleau, France.
NSSG: National Statistical Service of Greece. 1987. *Statistical Yearbook of Greece*.
Organization for Economic Cooperation and Development. *Economic Surveys*.
———. 1992. *Economic Outlook*.
Padoa-Scioppa, Tommaso. 1992. "Key Questions on Economic and Monetary Union." In William Adams (ed.), *Singular Europe*, pp. 55-68. Ann Arbor: University of Michigan Press.
Portes, Richard. 1991. "The European Community and Eastern Europe." In Tommaso Padoa-Schioppa (ed.), *Europe after 1992: Three Essays*, pp. 5-16. Essays in International Finance, No. 182, May. Princeton, NJ: Princeton University Press.
Sapir, André. 1990. "Discussion." In Christopher Bliss and Jorge Braga de Macedo (eds.), *Unity with Diversity in the European Economy*. New York: Cambridge University Press.
UN Center on Transnational Corporations. 1988. *Transnational Corporations in World Development: Trends and Prospects*. New York.
———. 1990. *Transnational Corporations, Services and the Uruguay Round*. New York.
———. 1992. *World Investment Report: Transnational Corporations as Engines of Growth*. New York.
United Nations Development Programme. 1992. *Human Development Report*. New York: Oxford University Press.

UN Economic Commission for Europe. 1991. *Economic Survey of Europe: 1990–1991*. New York.
United States Bureau of Labor Statistics. 1991. *International Comparisons of Hourly Compensation Costs in Manufacturing, 1975–1990*. Washington, DC: Government Printing Office.
Wall Street Journal. 1993. "EC Commission Gives the Green Light to Two Ventures and Two Acquisitions." May 3, 1993, p. A7.
World Bank. *World Tables*.

3

The Capitalist Class in The European Union

Otto Holman and Kees van der Pijl

In avoiding transhistorical conceptions of reality, classes are seen in this chapter as social forces whose cohesion derives from the role played in a mode of production, and in a historical sequence of modes of production; and whose ascension at a particular moment in "world time"[1] is geographically confined. Thus, the capitalist class or bourgeoisie has always been the entrepreneurial, property-owning stratum in a mode of production based on private enterprise and wage labor, the capitalist mode of production. Its historical emancipation, as a class, was critically determined, however, by whether (in the course of the consecutive stages of the capitalist mode of production) the bourgeoisie was the ascendant class mobilizing society behind a liberal project in a feudal or absolutist context; whether it redeployed in a defensive configuration with the conservative, landowning class in a context of partially developed, monopolistic capitalism or whether it again developed autonomously on the basis of a class compromise with the workers rooted in productivity growth and rising real wages (the postwar adoption of Fordist production methods).

Capital represents a potentially world-embracing social force, structuring roles and patterns of behavior and consciousness which are sanctioned in the action of the particular capitals on each other—competition. But the settings in which a bourgeoisie crystallizes and evolves into a conscious social and political force are concrete, and hence, *discrete*. Within Western Europe, or even within the distinct countries making up the subcontinent, the relative weight of the bourgeoisie varied at any given time, and its common orientation at the national plane, with respect to directing or influencing the action of the state, likewise cannot be generalized. We are accordingly faced with a situation in which from very diverse vantage points, concrete entrepreneurial groups adopt bourgeois orientations, and these orientations converge on common patterns tending toward concrete unification on a world scale. Hegel, in his day, thought that the basis for unification was preordained in the rationality of the universe, but as Gramsci wrote, "What the idealists call 'spirit' is not a point of departure but a point of arrival, it is the *ensemble* of superstructures moving towards concrete and objectively universal unification and it is not a unitary presupposition" (Gramsci, 1971: 446).

In Europe and elsewhere, states articulate the different bourgeoisies and the overarching context in which they operate, that of capital. In this sense, integration has more often been defined with reference to states than to classes. However, the relationship between the bourgeoisie and the state, and hence, its attitude to integration, is likewise a component part of its class outlook and is intimately related to the sequence of bourgeois postures enumerated above. Thus, the first bourgeoisie to force the hand of the aristocratic classes in guiding state action, the English bourgeoisie, was also able, by its domination of the world market, to tie the working class in with its internationalism. Britain, therefore, largely skipped the subsequent defensive redeployment in the monopolistic stage of capitalism (the era of imperialism). The state in England was stripped of its aristocratic and absolutist antecedents except for appearances. Society, *civil society* in the sense of those enjoying full citizenship and property, could develop a degree of self-regulation once a state of law allowing the legal settlement of disputes "between citizens" was firmly established.

On the continent, by contrast, the bourgeoisie was much less capable of taking on the aristocracy or the absolutist state, which to different degrees were indispensable props in sustaining the integrity of society against British commercial competition or against the aspiring working class. Here, a tradition of a strong, centralizing state was established, which resisted the transition to self-regulation, and hence, constrained the growth of a bourgeoisie. Even in modern France, this tradition has perpetuated an etatism ill adjusted to support the growth of a bourgeoisie strong enough to engage in international competition. As Cohen-Tanugi (1987: 6) writes:

Meant originally to accompany the development of civil society, state tutelage often ends up by constituting an obstacle to that development. Even disregarding authoritarian regimes, a tentacular state most often represents a weak society, if only for the "crowding out" effect operative between the one and the other. In the case of France, it is clear that the channeling of elites through the system of the prestigious schools, the economic-financial drainage of resources realised by fiscal and para-fiscal means, as well as the statisation of society, permanently effectuate a gigantic transfer of human and material resources and responsibilities from society to the state, which, enriching the latter to the point of saturation, necessarily impoverish the former.

European integration has served to partially overcome the incompatibilities between these different traditions. It has created a space in which the bourgeoisies of the different countries have been able to develop toward a common position irrespective of the various national settings. Integration must accordingly be understood, not in the usual sense of states merging into a superstate, but as a process of creating a common civil society forcing close cooperation on the states involved, without suspending their independent legal existence. In the "Post-Hobbesian order," Schmitter writes (1991: 13),

there is no single identifiable sovereign—just a multitude of authorities at different levels of aggregation, territorial or functional, with ambiguous or shared *compétences* at the head of overlapping and diverse organizational hierarchies. Policies are not definitively enunciated and vertically administered; they are constantly negotiated and indirectly implemented. Moreover, there are several centers with differing degrees of coercive power and not all of them are public or governmental. . . . In all cases, it becomes increasingly difficult to differentiate between public and private institutions, the State and the Civil Society.

Such is Schmitter's characterization of developments in the European Union (then the European Community) during the 1980s. And indeed, the material underpinning of these developments, their institutional features, and ideological legitimation all indicate "an emergent and novel form of political domination." The coming into existence of a "European" bourgeoisie has to be understood in this context. It is the ensemble of concrete bourgeois groups adopting a European frame of reference from which to approach the further unification toward a global pattern, a pattern dictated by the global circuits of capital in money or commodity form.[2]

Although Ideas about the United States of Europe circulated from the late nineteenth century on (building on medieval notions of Catholic Europe), the usurpation of the European Idea by German Nazism demonstrated the incapacity of the continental European bourgeoisies to integrate among themselves. During and after the World War II, intensive bargaining among exiled European governments in London charted the future of an integrated Western Europe as part of an Atlantic post-war order. The Marshall Plan subsequently tied European reconstruction into this order, and more particularly, served as the framework for the Atlantic extrapolation of the synthesis between liberalism and state intervention, or *corporate liberalism*, wrought in the New Deal on the basis of a new mode of accumulation, Fordism.

Corporate liberalism served as the frame of reference for postwar European integration. It expressed the tendency in the actual configuration of social forces and the hegemonic project at work in it. Such a frame we will term a comprehensive concept of control. The greater part of the EU (then EC) experience was informed by the Keynesian/Fordist format of this corporate liberal concept. However, in the 1980s class relations were restructured to a *neoliberal* concept, and integration was affected by this restructuring as well. At stake here is the transformation of an *inter*national historic bloc in the context of Atlantic Fordism and a U.S.-centered hegemonic world order to an emergent *trans*national historic bloc[3] in the context of global neoliberalism. The ascension of a "European" bourgeoisie is a concomitant to this process of transnational class formation, which in turn is structured by comprehensive concepts of control.

In the remainder of this chapter we will amplify on this integrated approach. In the next section we will start with an elaboration on the postwar corporate-liberal restructuring of capitalist relations in general, and bourgeois power in particular. We will then turn to the rise of global neoliberalism as a restructuring force on existing, predominantly national power configurations. The enhanced transnationalization of capital and the so-called internationalization of the state are the primary factors in explaining the policy convergence in Western Europe in the early 1980s, and the subsequent relaunch of European integration. Finally, we will concentrate on the most influential transnational business lobby—the European Round Table of Industrialists (ERT)—and its role as a policy-shaping group. It is our belief that the initiating role of the ERT with respect to the Europe '92 project and its subsequent role in the so-called extended relaunch (Maastricht and beyond) point at an emergent and novel form of bourgeois domination at the European level, fundamentally different from existing business lobbies like the European Confederation of National Employers' Federations (UNICE). This latter association was founded in 1958 to canvass and influence EU (then EEC) institutions. Its high degree of institutional fragmentation and the heterogeneous business interests it represents have prevented UNICE from becoming the institutional framework of an emergent capitalist class in the EU. For this reason, we will focus on the less wellknown but highly influential ERT and its role in cementing a certain degree of cohesion among the leading social forces in Europe.[4]

THE BOURGEOISIE IN CORPORATE LIBERAL EUROPE

The infrastructure of bourgeois power is composed of a labor process, embedded in a complex of market (circulation) relations, a structure of profit distribution, and a particular relation to the state. These four aspects may be conveniently taken as coordinates of the formation of the European bourgeoisie. We will take the first two to structure our argument in this section, and turn to profit distribution and the relationship with the state in the next.

First, the *labor process*. The exploitation of living labor power forms the basis of the existence of any concrete bourgeoisie. In the United States, the retooling of industry toward mass production of consumer durables transpired in the course of the 1920s and 1930s, marginalizing craft industry. But in Western Europe, the introduction of the assembly line in car production, and the necessary restructuring of steel production toward the production of flat rolled steel, was begun only tentatively before the war. As David Landes put it, in (relatively advanced) Britain, industrial firms "were caught in a vicious circle: output was not big or uniform enough to warrant heavy outlays for specialized precision equipment and a reorganization of plant layout; yet this was the only way to achieve the lower costs and prices that would yield increased demand and justify longer production runs" (Landes, 1972: 315).

World War II swept away those structures resisting the restructuring of industry, such as the international steel cartel, which by its restrictive practices had kept steel prices at a prohibitive level. Two years after the war, the Marshall Plan synchronized, under American auspices, the reorientation of economic policies in Europe toward a corporate liberal format. Continuous wide-strip mills using American technology developed in the late 1920s were now shipped to Europe to provide the steel industry with the means to produce cheap flat steel for automobile assembly and other uses.

The new equipment required a process of centralization of capital, which in Britain (where three mills were operating or under construction in 1953), took the form of the nationalization of the steel industry (Overbeek, 1980). France saw a regrouping of, on the one hand, the older liberal steel magnates around SOLLAC, and, on the other, a technocratic, state-monopolistic group around USINOR, both established in 1948 (Freyssenet and Imbert, 1975). In West Germany, August-Thyssen-Hütte, the biggest of the successor companies of the wartime Vereinigte Stahlwerke, expanded the prewar mill constructed with U.S. technology (Hexner, 1943: 207n; data on steel mills in ECE, 1953: 18). Other West German firms (Krupp and Hoesch), like two Belgian, one Luxembourgian, one Italian, one Dutch, one Austrian, and another French firm, at the time operated or were constructing semicontinuous or so-called Steckel mills.

Given the prospect of rapidly expanding flat steel production (also in light of war requirements) and the threat of a resurrection of the international steel cartel, the U.S. Marshall Plan authorities supported the French Schuman Plan of 1950 to create a European Coal and Steel Community (ECSC), meant to supplant the occupation regime of the Ruhr steel industry. Paul Hoffman, himself an automobile executive and head of the Marshall Plan's European Cooperation Administration, explained the ECSC to U.S. senators as a means to keep down steel prices and allow automobile production to take off. "Henry Ford introduced us to that new principle, and when he did so, he started a revolution that we are still benefiting by, and I think the Schuman Plan may have that result in Europe," Hoffman stated (*SFRC* II: 548).

While parallel processes of restructuring (notably, the introduction of petrochemical industry) reshaped European industry in the same period, the orientation toward a future Fordist mode of accumulation constituted the central axis of the realignment of the bourgeoisie in the decades ahead. The ECSC, in conjunction with the trade and payments liberalization projected by the OEEC (Organization for European Economic Cooperation) and the European Payments Union, respectively, prevented the bourgeoisie associated with prewar accumulation patterns from taking recourse to national states to uphold their accumulation conditions. Especially once the establishment of the EEC (European Economic Community) and Euratom and the revamping of OEEC to OECD (Organization for Economic Cooperation and Development) in 1957 and 1960, respectively, added the element of synchronizing economic policies to the integration process, the corporate liberal pattern became hegemonic, and the strongest among European capitals, operating the most advanced production processes, could set their sights on direct world market competition.

The profile of the corporate liberal bourgeoisie in Europe as a consequence of the restructuring to Fordism tended toward a technocratic and managerial pattern. This takes us to the second aspect of the differentiation of the capitalist class, *circulation relations*. In addition to the differentiations engendered by the introduction of new labor processes (which we can summarize as separating a forward-looking, internationally oriented bourgeoisie associated with the Fordist mode of accumulation in the framework created by European integration, from the less dynamic bourgeoisie confined to its national settings) the *functional differentiations* between industrial, bank, and commercial capital have to be added to the picture.

Capital cannot circulate and accumulate without assuming the consecutive forms of money (as investment funds), commodities arranged for a productive process (means of production and labor power), and the commodities produced for a market, sold for money. But the degree to which the bourgeoisie associated with the actual transformations has been able to function relatively autonomously, and the resulting hierarchy between the different functional circuits, have varied greatly in different periods. As with class as such, the fractioning of classes can only be understood in a historical perspective.

In early twentieth century capitalism, international financiers largely directed the organization of production of the then prominent industries such as steel. Textiles and food production followed the orientation of large commercial and transport companies. In the crisis of the 1930s, the financiers and the stock markets supplying them with rentiers' savings were put under a Keynesian regime—whether by nationalizing the banks or regulating their activities, by fiscal means or direct supervision. A demand-managed economy required, according to Keynes's own prescription, the "euthanasia of the rentier." After the war, decolonization (the successive waves of which coincided with the efforts launched from the United States during the Marshall and the Kennedy period to modernize and liberalize the economies of Europe), and in West Germany, money reform, contributed decisively to weeding out the rentier element from the class structure for several decades.

Although independent finance and commerce revived under the Marshall Plan, the industrial bourgeoisie, related management, and technocracy, including the state equivalents in nationalized industry and in planning bodies, as well as the employers in the collective bargaining structures with the trade unions, occupied the commanding heights in corporate liberal Europe at least until the mid 1960s. Having said this, we must specify the picture for the different countries.

In France, the technocratic tradition dating back to the 1930s and reinforced and democratized by the nationalizations upon the country's liberation from German occupation faced a Malthusian tradition prevalent among relatively small family firms, grouped together in a multitude of cartel agreements. The technocratic "state bourgeoisie" in its different guises (Granou, 1977), headed by men like Jean Monnet, Pierre Uri, and Robert Marjolin, and supported by the Jewish banking houses (Rothschild, Lazard Frères), shaped the architecture of, first, French modernization and planning; secondly, European integration; and thirdly, Euro-Atlantic integration on equal terms. De Gaulle and Pompidou, and in a different political lineage, Mendès-France and Mitterrand, shared the modernizing attitude with the state bourgeoisie.

In a context shaped largely by the action of these forces, the strongest of the older, liberal bourgeoisie and financial aristocracy could redeploy from terrain lost in Indochina, North Africa, and Eastern Europe to metropolitan France and the Euro-American market. Great business family names such as Schneider and De Wendel, as well as the Suez and Indochine financial empires, took part in this postcolonial repatriation. They were represented in politics, notably, by Valéry Giscard d'Estaing. Once the groundwork for economic development in an international context (European, worldwide) was laid, and decolonization was completed, it was Giscard who unified behind himself the traditional upper crust of the French ruling class, "the most traditional Catholic (practising) Parisian fractions of the bourgeoisie with the closest links to the top levels of industry, banking and commerce" (Marceau 1989: 52; for the overall picture, see van der Pijl, 1984).

While in France the modernization of industry to overcome Malthusian lethargy created a positive and technocratic orientation toward the state and to European institutions, in West Germany world market strategy was presented in "liberal" and antietatist terms in light of the experience with Nazism. Ludwig Erhard, who alongside the conservative Adenauer (a proponent of Catholic Europe) represented the ambitions of the West German bourgeoisie, placed European integration directly in the perspective of a world market strategy. "The best form of European integration that I can imagine," he wrote, "does not rest on the creation of new offices and forms of administration or expanding bureaucracies, but rests first of all on the reestablishment of a free international order, which is expressed best and completely by the free convertibility of currencies. Convertibility of currency self-evidently includes full freedom and the free flow of commodities, services, and capital" (Erhard, 1962: 167).

The superiority of German capital, notably in the production of means of production (machine tools, heavy equipment) by itself preordained a world market strategy. But the historical presence of backward and conservative elements in the social structure, epitomized by the Junker class, and weaker sectors such as the Ruhr iron and steel complex, twice in this century forced Germany to resort to force of arms to secure its expansion in a world already divided. European integration held out the prospect of a peaceful reorganization of the European basis for a renewed attempt to establish a direct presence in the world market. Erhard and after him, Willy Brandt, were the standard-bearers of this orientation. Paradoxically, during Brandt's chancellorship, the "managerial elite of the Federal Republic began its move into the Bonn power apparatus" (Simon, 1976: 171). This reflected the trend toward concentration of capital, urbanization, and the liquidation of the Prussian Junker stratum. Under Brandt, West Germany realized a break with the Cold War order and charted an independent course of peaceful penetration of Eastern Europe.

The traditional proximity of the German bourgeoisie to the state and the conservative aristocracy, was replaced in the process by an orientation toward the middle strata and compromise with the trade unions. Parallel to this, lawyers were replaced in management functions by engineers and natural scientists (Spohn and Bodemann, 1989: 93). This reinforced the marked *productive* orientation of the German bourgeoisie, to which we will come back below.

West Germany, thus, could become the powerhouse of the European economy, "a centre of innovation and modernisation in the world market" initiating product and technology cycles of its own (Schlupp, 1979: 17). Neighboring countries were either historically interlocked with this powerhouse, such as the Netherlands and Scandinavia, or sought to catch up by modernizing strategies of a state sector trying to offset the negative balance by sectoral strategies. This was the case in France and also in Italy. European integration was very much an attempt by the French state bourgeoisie to force its specific pattern of state-monitored modernization on West Germany (as long as the Cold War constrained German ambitions); while for the West German ruling class, it offered an opportunity to organize a European base for a renewed and this time, perhaps peaceful, attempt at a world market strategy.

Under the conditions of the successive shocks of domestic and international crisis (1968, 1973), the postwar hierarchy of national states connected into the comprehensive Euro-Atlantic structure began to disintegrate. The industrial crisis of the 1970s led to widespread, and mutually reinforcing, renationalization of economic policies in the EU (then EC) member states. In order to protect their industries, national governments, still committed to corporate liberalism, resorted to a range of instruments like subsidies, socialization of private losses, and public contracting. European integration thus entered a phase of so-called Eurosclerosis lasting until 1984. Despite geographical and institutional extension (the entrance of England, Denmark, and Ireland in 1973; the application for membership of Greece in 1975, and of Spain and Portugal in 1977; the creation of the European Monetary System in 1978; the first direct elections to the European Parliament in 1979; the accession of Greece in 1981, and of Spain and Portugal in 1986), this period was characterized by the stagnation of *economic* integration, or even disintegration. Lacking the legal means, the Union's institutions were unable to counteract the surge of state interventionism at the member state level. The sole exception concerned the steel industry. In 1980, exercising for the first time its authority under the ECSC Treaty to set minimum prices and to impose production quotas, the European Commission through the Commissioner for Industry, Etienne Davignon, implemented Union-wide measures to regulate the steel sector (Grahl and Teague, 1990: 148).

Only when the neoliberal restructuring forced "competitive austerity" on national governments, a shift to "Europhoria"—the relaunch of market integration through the Commission's White Paper (1985) and the signing of the Single European Act (1986)—gave new impetus to the synchronization of the positions of the national bourgeoisies in Europe.

THE EUROPEAN BOURGEOISIE UNDER NEOLIBERALISM

While the mainstream bourgeoisie in Western Europe still was oriented to a reformist response to the manifold challenges facing it and sought to disentangle itself from the Cold War status quo by relying on unorthodox, often social democratic governments, two parallel developments began to reshape the setting in which the capitalist class found itself in Europe. These were the liberalization of independent finance from Keynesian controls from the late 1960s on and the subsequent reorganization of state functions in the light of enhanced transnationalization of capital. These two departures from the benevolent "equilibrium of compromises" on which postwar Atlantic and European corporate liberal capitalism had rested replaced the socially protective, interventionist state/society complex of the 1950s and 1960s by a Lockean configuration in which the state left society to its own workings except for a vigilant police system. We can discuss these developments conveniently under the heading of our last two dimensions of bourgeois class formation: profit distribution and the relationship to the state.

First, profit distribution. The need to restructure capital, which became apparent in the second half of the 1960s and which interacted with the demise of the U.S.-led Cold War and neocolonial order, involved the liberalization of bank capital from Keynesian constraints imposed in the 1930s. In 1966, French rules concerning the separation of bank functions (commercial, and investment, etc.) were rescinded; German banks, which after brief episodes of nationalization (in the 1930s) and deconcentration (after 1945), had restored their strong positions in the industrial and commercial sphere by direct and proxy holdings, were likewise given greater freedom in the credit sphere in 1967. In 1971 British banks were allowed to become investors in industry. Amid competitive devaluation and inflation set in motion by the dismantling, under President Nixon, of the gold-dollar standard in 1971, bankers looked forward to a new era of opportunity, "which," as one of them put it, "is bringing us back to the times of the London Merchant Bankers" (quoted in van der Pijl, 1984: 263-64).

Parallel to the resurgence of bank capital and the thriving of new offshore lending centers such as the London Eurodollar market, a resurrection of a forgotten species, the rentier, took place in this period. Under the aegis of what was dubbed a "Revenge of the Rentier" with reference to Keynes's prescription for euthanasia in 1936 (Morris, 1982: 30-31), bankers and rentiers became more prominent in the bourgeoisie throughout metropolitan capitalism. This prominence had a profound effect on the general class consciousness of the ruling class and on articulate opinion in society at large, as the crisis of corporate liberalism and its "equilibrium of compromises" reinforced by default the orthodox liberal, in the historical sequence *neoliberal*, view of capitalist society. While social development in Europe in the 1970s still proceeded largely by reference to the principle of social protection and compromise of the previous era, the actual shift in incomes was reinforcing the trend toward market solutions. From the mid-1970s on, so-called households' property income began to rise after a long decline following World War II. This is illustrated in Table 3.1.

Table 3.1
Resumption of Rentier Incomes (Rent, Dividend and Interest) in Four European Countries. (Percentage in National Income)

	1975	1980	1983
West Germany	3.8	4.5	6.0*
United Kingdom	4.3	4.7	9.2**
France	5.4	5.4	5.7
Netherlands	9.9	12.4	17.2

* Does not include rent
** Interest only

Source: OECD, *National Accounts of OECD Countries* (Paris: OECD), 1985, Vol. II (Country Tables).

The shift in actual profit distribution between industrial and bank capital (nonfinancial to financial) corporations was much more pronounced, as can be seen in Table 3.2. Financial corporations' cash flow ("total current receipts") is presented as a percentage of nonfinancial cash flow. From this table, it can be seen that the high tide of the shift to financial cash flow transpired in the 1970s, and that West Germany did not follow the other big countries (also the United States and Japan) in the shift to money capital.

The policies which from the late 1970s began to reflect the "revolt of the rentier" and the liquidation of the industrial landscape of Fordism and its Keynesian infrastructure were accordingly less pronounced in West Germany at the time. But even under corporate liberal social democrats, Germany and France eventually had to yield to privatization and deregulation, pioneered in Europe by the Thatcher government.

The deconstruction of the socially protective role of the state, which, of course, did not simply reflect a preference on the part of the ruling class but also interacted with the trend toward the globalization of capital, inaugurated a redefinition, rather than the reduction, of the state role as such. This brings us to the fourth dimension of the infrastructure of bourgeois rule, the *relationship with the state*.

Table 3.2
Cash Flow of Financial Capital as a Percentage of Cash Flow of Nonfinancial Capital

	1972	1975	1980	1985	1988
United Kingdom	46	112	146	113	112
West Germany	35	44	55	49	49*
France	73	113	150	171	145

* 1987

Source: OECD, *National Accounts of OECD Countries* (Paris: OECD), 1989, Vol. II (Country Tables).

The breakdown of the protective and modernizing state role under neoliberal governments had a particularly detrimental effect on those national bourgeoisies which had depended on such a state role to hold their own against, notably, German industrial competition, such as the French. But the ultimate attempt by the social democratic government of President Mitterrand to sustain a welfare state and step up trade protection ended in failure in 1983, one year after Chancellor Schmidt had been brought down by a desertion of the liberals from the center-left coalition. The neoliberal restructuring meanwhile had groomed the European states for a new role, backing up the new harshness of social relations.

In fact, in the field of macroeconomics an adaption to a new, neoliberal format at the member state level preceded policy convergence at Union level. To understand this EU-wide shift in policy preferences we have, again, to stress the paramount importance of the process of transnational class formation that has been part of the postwar growth of international capital accumulation, which in turn expanded enormously during the late 1970s and 1980s. The spectacular growth of foreign direct investment and the skyrocketing of short-term portfolio investment, which experienced a sixtyfold increase from SDR (special drawing rights) 2,640 billion in 1980 to SDR 156,816 billion in 1988 (cf. Junne, 1994: 88), and, in general, the spectacular rise in the volatility of transnational capital, have had a decisive impact on macroeconomic and monetary decision making.

States and social forces under these conditions were subsumed under a transnational historic bloc, reflecting the growing structural and behavioral power of internationally mobile capital. The behavioral power of transnational capital is manifested, *inter alia*, in its growing ability to play national governments off against one another with respect to international investment decisions, and in all kind of lobbying activities (Gardner, 1991: Chapter 5). An important example of the latter phenomenon is offered by the European Roundtable of Industrialists (ERT), a pressure group of the leading trans-European companies, which played a decisive role in relaunching the process of European integration in the early 1980s, as we shall see in the next section.

The *structural* power of transnational capital, on the other hand, is related to the geographically and economically extended operation of the market mechanisms:

> The movement of large amounts of capital between countries, in the form of direct foreign investment, short-term capital flows and long-term portfolio investment, in response to economic and political conditions, acts to condition, for example, the behaviour of governments, firms, trade unions and other groups. Through the market such structural power is premised upon the greater mobility of transnational capital than its "national" counterparts. . . . Thus the policies of the state toward the market, towards labour-capital relations, towards the provision of an appropriate social and economic infrastructure, are incrementally recast in an international framework. (Gill, 1990: 113-14)

In other words, national governments are constrained by the policies of other governments, and by the investment decisions of transnational capital. Here the notion of the *internationalization of the state*, understood as "the global process whereby national policies and practices have been adjusted to the exigencies of the world economy of international production" (Cox, 1987: 253; cf. Picciotto, 1991) becomes of particular importance. It is in this context that we must understand the "extended relaunch" of the process of market integration during the period 1985-92.

THE EUROPEAN ROUND TABLE AND THE RESHAPING OF EUROPE

Turning back to the synchronization of positions of the European bourgeoisies, another important change in world order structures—the emergence of the so-called New European Architecture—has to be taken into account. The collapse of the Soviet bloc has entirely altered the context in which the capitalist class in Europe finds itself. At the same time, the breakdown of barriers to capital accumulation in Eastern Europe has vastly increased the possibilities for European companies to restructure the basis for global competition. The extreme orientation toward money capital and financial forms of enrichment under neoliberalism will have to be remedied—if it is remedied at all in a capitalist context—by renewing the industrial basis of European capital.

In such a drive, of which the signs are there, the European bourgeoisie, exposed to the harsh conditions of international competition to a degree unprecedented in the twentieth century, will inevitably disintegrate into distinct fractions, differentiated in terms of their capacity to survive in world market competition. Following a distinction between import and export competition developed by Frieden (1991), we may distinguish between import-competing industrial capital in national and European markets, and export-competing industry in the world market, and capital in the global circuit of money capital relatively autonomous from European industrial capital.

These different positions in global competition have a certain correspondence with national states. Thus, the bourgeoisie in Greece and Portugal, and to a lesser extent in Spain, belong to the category of import-competing domestic producers. At the same time, German and other foreign capital producing for the European market has penetrated the economies of these countries to a considerable extent. In the case of Spain, for instance, the evolution followed by foreign direct investment shows not only a spectacular rise during the 1982-88 period but also a sharp decline of the position of the United States in exchange for a leading role of EU (then EC) countries (see Table 3.3).

Table 3.3
Authorized Investment in Spain by Country of Origin (Percent over Total)

	1960–75	1976–81	1982–88
EC	35.16	42.40	48.14
West Germany	10.54	11.33	10.09
France	5.42	10.47	7.73
United Kingdom	10.13	8.54	8.53
Netherlands	4.37	6.11	14.10
USA	40.61	25.32	9.21
total (billions current psts)	142.77	343.24	2869.60

Source: J. Molero, "German Investment in Spain: Strategies and Behaviour of German Industrial Subsidiaries," in J. van Dijck and A. Wentink (eds.), *Transnational Business in Europe* (Tilburg: Tilburg University Press), p. 163.

This foreign penetration indicates that a form of dependent accumulation has come to characterize the Spanish economy, coinciding with a virtual amalgamation of interests between national and foreign bourgeoisie. This has been accompanied by the rise to government power of a social democratic party largely shaped by the German-dominated Socialist International (Holman, 1987-88). The party's European policy in favor of monetary unification clearly shows the policy implications of this transnationalization of Spain, particularly as to the issue of sovereignty. As Spain's Prime Minister Felipe González stated in an interview with the *Financial Times*, "One cedes sovereignty in order to share it. . . . I accept that we are in a D-Mark zone. The difference between there being one day an EC institution to define monetary policy and the reality now is that we depend on the D-Mark, but according to the decisions taken in the

Bundestag and not on common decisions shared by all" (*Financial Times*, December 17, 1990).

The second "import-competing" category, industrial capital producing for a European market, is particularly strong and influential in France, notably in the case of its automobile and electronics industries. Of the direct world market exporters, Germany is the obvious stronghold, while global finance has its strongest base in the City of London. Table 3.4 illustrates these last three categories and their nationality by ranking the top fifteen companies in terms of assets, and the top fifteen in terms of employment, that is, for the greater part, industrial capital.

Table 3.4
Largest Companies in Europe, Ranked by Assets and by Employment, with Nationality (1992)

RANK	Assets		Employment	
1	Royal Dutch Shell	N/UK	Daimler Benz	Germ
2	British Telecom	UK	Siemens	Germ
3	Glaxo Holdings	UK	Fiat	Italy
4	BP	UK	Unilever	N/UK
5	Unilever	N/UK	Philips	N
6	Allianz Holding	Germ	Volkswagen	Germ
7	British Gas	UK	British Telecom	UK
8	Nestlé	Swi	BAT Industries	UK
9	Siemens	Germ	ABB Asea	Swe
10	Daimler Benz	Germ	Alcatel Alsthom	Fr
11	Hanson	UK	Nestlé	Swi
12	Deutsche Bank	Germ	Gén. des Eaux	Fr
13	Elf Aquitaine	Fr	Hoechst	Germ
14	Guinness	UK	Bayer	Germ
15	BAT Industries	UK	Peugeot	Fr

Source: *Financial Times*, January 13, 1992.

With this rough picture of internationally operating capital in Europe in mind, let us proceed to sketch the options pertaining to future strategies of European capital.

Three debates have traditionally informed the agenda of European integration (Holman, 1992: 10): (i) the debate between "Atlanticists" and "Europeanists"; (ii) the debate between proponents of, respectively, intergovern-mental cooperation and supranationalism; and (iii) the debate between those in favor of widening, and those in favor of (first) deepening integration.

From these interrelated debates, several strategies and their supporters can be deduced. First, the Atlanticist (equivalent to globalist) option, in favor of intergovernmentalism and opting for a widening rather than deepening of European integration, will be first and foremost that of globally mobile financial (and other services and commercial) capital—most of the firms located in the left column of Table 3.4. These firms constitute the corporate phalanx of the neoliberal bourgeoisie in Europe, and nine out of fifteen have their basis in Britain (two of them binational). Their vacillations on British participation in the exchange rate mechanism of the European Monetary System must be explained by fears that London might lose its dominant position as a financial center to Frankfurt (Overbeek, 1992: 146).

The contrary position, supporting some form of supranational architecture, stressing the need for deepening the process of European integration, is typically the orientation of industrial capital, especially the import-competing firms serving the European market. The firms in the lower half of the right column of Table 3.4, three of them French, may be taken as exemplary of this orientation. Philips of the Netherlands, too, must be located in this category.

Now German capital, as a whole, here occupies an intermediate position between the first, neoliberal/internationalist, and the second, conservative/regionalist strategies. For German capital, as a whole, a "catchall" strategy, therefore, seems to be the option to be favored: regionalization and globalization; deepening and widening, a mixture of intergovernmental cooperation (notably in the security and foreign policy spheres), and a suspension of national sovereignty in the monetary sphere. But this last element should be considered an expression of the sovereignty of capital over states rather than as an institutional arrangement in the federalist sense. This strategy has become the concept adopted by a key transnational grouping of the European corporate elite which in due course may become the lodestar for large sections of the European bourgeoisie in its entirety, the European Round Table of Industrialists (ERT).

The ERT was formed in 1983 as an informal group of European industry leaders, initially representing seventeen international corporations. Its principal aim was twofold: to search for common solutions for the perceived loss of competitive clout vis-à-vis U.S. and Japanese competition, and, secondly, to obtain support at the EC level for such projects as the completion of the single market, a European technology policy, and trans-European infrastructure networks. On the part of the European Commission, the ERT was seen as a useful interface to member states. "These men are very powerful and very dynamic," an aide to Jacques Delors was quoted as saying. "They seed us with ideas. And when necessary, they can ring up their own prime ministers and make their case" (quoted in Merritt, 1986: 22).

The "extended relaunch" of European integration received a critical impetus from the ERT. It acted in the process as a vanguard of the European bourgeoisie, organizing diverse business interests, governments and European institutions, as well as influencing public opinion through the media, thus shaping an emerging concept of control relevant to the immediate future of the European capitalist class. As Gardner puts it, "ERT is both the spiritual progenitor of the 1992 process and the single most powerful business group in Europe. It's not surprising, then, that when ERT talks, Eurocrats listen" (Gardner, 1991: 48).

The completion of the internal market as one of the first, main projects of the ERT received general support throughout the European Union. Its growth-generating impact (within the neoliberal framework) suited productive capital and also the import-competing firms serving the European market, such as electronics and automobiles faced with Japanese and other Asian competitors (Dekker, 1985). After the Single European Act was agreed upon in 1986, the import-competing orientation temporarily began to steer the ERT toward lobbying for protection, either from national states or in the framework of a "Fortress Europe." Several attempts were made to influence the EU decision-making process in this sense, which failed because of fierce opposition from the British and German governments. Only the French government seemed prepared to go along with these proposals for sectoral protection, notably with respect to electronics and cars. At this point, the ERT faced a significant walkout of some of its internationally oriented members such as Royal Dutch Shell and Unilever (Van Tulder and Junne, 1988: 215).

The failure to influence the Union's decisions in the field of industrial and trade policies, in combination with the collapse of the Soviet bloc after 1989, seems not only to have changed the composition of the ERT but also reshaped its strategic orientation. In September 1991 the list of ERT members, then at forty-four companies, again included Shell and Unilever and appeared to be much more heterogeneous, combining both import-competing and export-competing firms. More importantly, ERT strategy has shifted from a defensive one ("Fortress Europe") to an offensive one—meeting the challenges and "historic opportunities" offered by the new situation in Europe after the collapse of the Soviet bloc.

In its September 1991 report, *Reshaping Europe* (published right before the European Council summit in Maastricht in December), the contours of a new concept are drawn. "Perhaps more than in the past," Jérome Monod (ERT's vice-chairman, of Lyonnaise des Eaux, number 110 on the general *Financial Times* list) argues in the preface to the report, "business opinion today expresses a comprehensive world-wide vision of modern society and its problems, a vision which may in some ways go beyond the ideas of our political leaders" (Monod, Gyllenhammar, and Dekker, 1991: 2). The comprehensiveness of the ERT's proposed concept, reflecting the "catchall" strategy of the forces seeking to articulate the European industrial with the neoliberal internationalist position, resulted from "fundamental views which are widely held in the business community" (Monod, Gyllenhammar, and Dekker, 1991: 13):

The unification of Europe is the only practical way to realise its potential and harness its resources; Europe must develop through free market economics, based on open and vigorous competition and giving the maximum impulse to creativity, innovation, and long-term strategic thinking; all groups in society must have the opportunity to share in the benefits of the new Europe; deepening and widening are both needed, with the Community strengthening its policies and institutions as well as opening up to the needs of its neighbours; Europe must be open to the world and shoulder its full responsibilities in the global community; in every policy area the need is to act decisively to catch this "window of opportunity" while it is open.

This view of a "prosperous and united" Europe which is open to the outside world is further underpinned by less prominent paragraphs on social and industrial policy, a plea for monetary union (Monod, Gyllenhammar, and Dekker, 1991: 46), albeit under the precondition of economic convergence, a call for more efficient European business infrastructure, and a common security and foreign policy, for which vested economic interests are mentioned as the reference. The institutional architecture is treated in a disinterested fashion: "As businessmen, we take no ideological position for or against 'pooling' or 'merging' sovereignty" (Monod, Gyllenhammar, and Dekker, 1991: 60).

The ERT concept of reinforcing the industrial infrastructure of the expanded economic space, which European capital can control, seems well placed when one observes the trend in the United States under the incoming Clinton administration, which likewise seems committed to counterbalance the forces of global finance set free in the 1970s and 1980s by reinforcing the industrial base. In the meantime, however, the vagaries of unregulated finance as well as unequal development and the intensification of competition continue to disrupt the balance of forces on which European integration was originally based. First, the class configuration of corporate liberalism, reserving a certain countervailing power for the trade unions and making for state-monitored industrial development in addition to maintaining Keynesian controls with respect to the financial world, has been dislocated. Secondly, the Cold War context, in which the United States and the USSR effectively checked German ambitions, and which empowered France to act as an arbitrator of European integration, has given way to a configuration superficially reminiscent of the pre-World War II situation. Thirdly, the relative power position of the Arab world vis-à-vis Europe in the 1970s movement for a new international economic order, backed up by oil price hikes, has been dramatically reduced.

As a consequence of the disruption of these balances, the cohesion of both European society (especially as regards its working and landed classes) and the European periphery is correspondingly disappearing. In the resulting turmoil, which covers a broad range of mutually reinforcing phenomena ranging from warlordism and nationalism, to crime and neofascism, mass migration, and pauperization, Europe and its periphery are increasingly turned into a zone incompletely controlled by Germany. The intermittent attack on the currencies of Germany's less fortunate neighbours, as much as rampant warlordism in

Yugoslavia and the threat of war throughout Eastern Europe, is testimony to the dimensions of the disruption of social cohesion. The fact that a country like France had to throw one-half of its monetary reserves into the battle to defend the franc in the monetary unrest of October 1992, on the eve of the referendum on the Maastricht Treaty, and the disengagement of Britain from the European Monetary Union project, indicate both the destructive capacity and the narrowness of Germany's actual control of the current state of affairs and the difficult and deteriorating conditions in which a concept like the one exemplified in the ERT will have to be developed.

NOTES

1. By "world time" we mean, following Antony Giddens, "that an apparantly similar sequence of events, or formally similar social processes, may have quite dissimilar implications or consequences in different phases of world development" (Giddens, 1981: 167).

2. But as we will see, the different historical modalities of class consciousness may again complicate the picture. Some elements in the bourgeoisie in the different European countries will view the European context as the terrain in which they will have to entrench, others will not even be able to make the transition from a national frame of reference to the European one. In all cases, the fact that the bourgeoisie struggles to hold its own in between the positions of other classes, and always is a concrete bourgeoisie either up or down the hierarchy of particular capitals, determines this degree and modality of "Europeanization" (see the section below entitled "The European Round Table and the Reshaping of Europe").

3. Antonio Gramsci's notion of historic bloc refers to a particular hegemonic coalition of social and political forces, characterized by a reciprocal relationship of the political and ideological spheres of activity with the economic sphere; see Gramsci (1971) and Cox (1983). For analyses based on this and other related concepts (such as the notions of hegemony, control, and class formation) see van der Pijl (1984), Cox (1987), Gill (1990), and the different contributions in Gill (1993) and Overbeek (1993).

4. For an overview of the literature on lobbying in the EU in general and on organized business interests in particular, see the different contributions in Greenwood et al. (1992), and Mazey and Richardson (1993). Also see Gardner (1991).

REFERENCES

Bottomore, R. and R. J. Brym, eds. 1989. *The Capitalist Class: An International Study*. Hemel Hempstead, England: Harvester Wheatsheaf.

Cohen-Tanugi, L. 1987. *Le droit sans l'état: Sur la démocratie en France et en Amérique*. Paris: PUF.

Cox, R. W. 1983. "Gramsci, Hegemony and International Relations: An Essay in Method." *Millennium*, Vol. 12, No. 2.

————.1987. *Production, Power, and World Order: Social Forces in the Making of History*. New York: Columbia University Press.

Dekker, W. 1985. "Europe 1990." Speech by the president of Philips at the Centre for European Policy Studies in Brussels, January 11 mimeo.

ECE. (UN Economic Commission for Europe), 1953. *The European Steel Industry and the Wide-Strip Mill*. Geneva: United Nations.

Erhard, L. 1962. *Wohlstand für Alle*. Gütersloh: Signum.

Freyssenet, M. and F. Imbert. 1975. *La centralisation du capital dans la sidérurgie 1945-1975*. Paris: CSU.

Frieden, J. A. 1991. "Invested Interests: The Politics of National Economic Policies in a World of Global Finance." *International Organization*, Vol. 45, No. 4.

Gardner, J. N. 1991. *Effective Lobbying in the European Community*. Deventer: Kluwer.

Giddens, A. 1981. *A Contemporary Critique of Historical Materialism*. London: Macmillan.

Gill, S. 1990. *American Hegemony and the Trilateral Commission*. Cambridge: Cambridge University Press.

————, ed. 1993. *Gramsci, Historical Materialism and International Relations*. Cambridge: Cambridge University Press.

Grahl, J. and P. Teague. 1990. *The Big Market. The Future of the European Community*. London: Lawrence and Wishart.

Gramsci, A. 1971. *Selections from the "Prison Notebooks."* Edited by Q. Hoare and G. N. Smith. New York: International Publishers.

Granou, A. 1977. *La bourgeoisie financière au pouvoir et les luttes de classes en France*. Paris: Maspero.

Greenwood, J. et al., eds. *Organized Interests and the European Community*. London: Sage.

Hexner, E. 1943. *The International Steel Cartel*. Chapel Hill: University of North Carolina Press.

Holman, O. 1987-88. "Semiperipheral Fordism in Southern Europe: The National and International Context of Socialist-led Governments in Spain, Portugal, and Greece in Historical Perspective." *International Journal of Political Economy*, Vol. 17, No. 4.

————. 1992. "Transnational Class Strategy and the New Europe." *International Journal of Political Economy*, Vol. 22, No. 1.

Junne, G. 1994. "Multinational Enterprises as Actors." In W. Carlsnaes and S. Smith (eds.), *European Foreign Policy: The EC and Changing Perspectives in Europe*. London: Sage.

Landes, D. S. 1972. *The Unbound Prometheus*. Cambridge: Cambridge University Press.

Marceau, J. 1989. "France." In R. Bottomore and R. J. Brym (eds.), *The Capitalist Class: An International Study*. Hemel Hempstead, England: Harvester Wheatsheaf.

Mazey, S. and J. Richardson, eds. 1993. *Lobbying in the European Community*. Oxford: Oxford University Press.

Merritt, G. 1986. "Knights of the Roundtable: Can They Move Europe Forward Fast Enough?" *International Management*, July.

Monod, J., P. Gyllenhammar, and W. Dekker. 1991. *Reshaping Europe: A Report from the European Round Table of Industrialists*. Brussels: ERT.

Morris, J. 1982. "The Revenge of the Rentier of the Interest Rate Crisis in the United States." *Monthly Review* Vol. 33, No. 8.

Overbeek, H. W. 1980. "Finance Capital and Crisis in Britain." *Capital and Class*, Vol. 11, Summer.

———. 1990. *Global Capitalism and National Decline: The Thatcher Decade in Historical Perspective*. London: Unwin Hyman.

———. 1992. "Caught between Europe and the Atlantic: Britain's European Policy under Margaret Thatcher." In Ch. Polychroniou (ed.), *Perspectives and Issues in International Political Economy*. Westport, CT and London: Praeger.

———, ed. 1993. *Restructuring Hegemony in the Global Political Economy*. London: Routledge.

Picciotto, S. 1991. "The Internationalization of the State." *Capital and Class* Vol. 43.

van der Pijl, K. 1984. *The Making of an Atlantic Ruling Class*. London: Verso.

———. 1989. "Ruling Classes, Hegemony, and the State System: Theoretical and Historical Considerations." *International Journal of Political Economy* Vol. 19, No. 3.

Schlupp, F. 1979. "Internationalisierung und Krise—das "Modell Deutschland" im metropolitanen Kapitalismus." *Leviathan*, Vol. 7, No. 1.

Schmitter, P. C. 1991. "The European Community as an Emergent and Novel Form of Political Domination." Estudio/Working Paper 1991/26. Centro de Estudios Avanzados en Ciencias Sociales, Fundacion Juan March, Madrid, September.

SFRC: Executive Sessions of the Senate Foreign Relations Committee Historical Series [Annual volumes 1947-]. Washington: Government Printing Office [1976-].

Simon, W. 1976. *Macht und Herrschaft der Unternehmerverbände BDI, BDA und DIHT*. Cologne: Pahl-Rugenstein.

Spohn, W. and Y. M. Bodemann. 1989. "Federal Republic of Germany." In R. Bottomore and R. J. Brym (eds.), *The Capitalish Class: An International Study*. Hemel Hempstead, England: Harvester Wheatsheat.

Van Tulder, R. and G. Junne. 1988. *European Multinationals in Core Technologies*. New York: Wiley.

4

Small-Scale Industry Development Controversies and The European Union

Antigone Lyberaki and Vassilis Pesmazoglou

There appears to be a "small-scale industry renaissance" in recent academic and policy literature on industrialization and development. It is increasingly recognized that the mass production economy is in deep trouble—that large-scale industry does not "deliver" anymore, neither as the engine of growth nor as the provider of employment, in spite of substantial and consistent support in the form of financial and tax incentives as well as direct subsidies. At the same time, academic and policy attention is drawn to some prosperous and highly competitive regions, organized along principles other than those prevailing in the mass production paradigm and where small, flexible, responsive, and innovative firms play a central role.

In the face of the adversities facing mass production industries, and the successful performance of what came to be called "the flexible specialization regions," a wind of optimism concerning the role of small firms is blowing away numerous conventional arguments on backwardness and inefficiency. The body of ideas associated with the flexible specialization approach, in particular, views small firms as both offering, the magical key for overcoming the present crisis and providing the passport for long-term viable development.

Optimistic theorizations emphasizing the important role of small-scale industry are nothing new in the economic literature. There are numerous "historical precedents" with two centuries of history.[1] From Proudhon to the Russian Populists, to the search for appropriate technology, and finally to the informal sector debate, the chain of intellectual tradition is rich and multifaceted. However, the recent debate on the strengths and weaknesses of small enterprises suffers from a number of problematic aspects, mainly due to lack of clarity in definitions in two main respects. What constitutes a small firm? And, what is the meaning of flexibility?

"Small enterprise" and "small and medium-sized enterprises (SMEs)" are elusive concepts. They contain a large number of heterogeneous entities, while definitions and available typologies vary from one country to another, depending on the institutional or historical context.[2] Another area of confusion concerns the statistical definition of smallness. Different sectors and/or economies deserve different demarcation lines concerning firm size; it is therefore futile to attempt to provide uniform definitions. As has been convincingly argued, "The concern with the scale of enterprises or establishments is meaningful only in a relative or comparative context. . . . It is then sufficient to set ad hoc or convenient statistical conventions aimed at revealing as much as possible of the variation in the size composition. After all, despite the formidable problems with measurement and comparability of the data, size is still one of the most accessible indicators of productive organization across countries" (Loveman and Sengenberger, 1990: 6).

The same vagueness surrounds the notion of flexibility. Although its basic definition is rather straightforward (at its simplest, meaning adaptability and responsiveness to pressure), it is often used as a summary concept to contain a wide range of developments whose pace, causes, and nature are often assumed to be homogeneous (Standing, 1986; Blyton and Morris, 1991).

The objective of this chapter is to examine the saga of ideas and policy prescriptions associated with the persistence and proliferation of small and medium-sized enterprises, both as a response to the recession and as a means of overcoming it. An underlying assumption of our approach is that the analysis of small business cannot be carried out in isolation from the wider macro-economic trends and the dynamics of industrial restructuring under way as a response to the crisis. So, our approach is firmly situated in the context of the pervasive changes currently taking place in the terrain of industrial development internationally.

This is the reason why, although primarily concerned with small business at the European level, the focus of the following section is "the trouble with Fordism" and the challenges facing small firms in the post-Fordist era; it presents the most influential contemporary theoretical framework for small-scale development. The next section "Small-Scale Enthusiasm Revisited," examines the evidence on small and medium-sized enterprises, and deals more specifically with issues concerning employment generation, remuneration and conditions of work as well as the functioning of industrial districts. Then, the section entitled "SMEs in the European Union Context" examines more closely EU policies concerning small business development. The contemporary enthusiasm with small and medium-sized enterprises and the dismay with the performance of the large and well-established firms is further reinforced by the marked shift of employment away from the latter and in favor of the former in a number of OECD (Organization for Economic Cooperation and Development) countries

(Loveman and Sengenberger, 1990). The EU context offers some interesting insights concerning the policy issues involved in the support of smaller establishments.

CHANGES IN INDUSTRIAL ORGANIZATION PATTERNS, OR HOW THE UGLY DUCKLING OF FORDISM TURNED OUT TO BE THE CINDERELLA OF POSTMODERNISM.

Mass production has been the hegemonic paradigm of industrial organization throughout the postwar boom. Mass production or Fordism is not just about making things, but is seen as a system of technologies, markets, and institutions. It requires large investments in highly specialized equipment and narrowly trained workers, in order to realize the full potential of economies of scale. It is profitable only with markets large enough to absorb an enormous output of standardized commodities, and stable enough to keep the equipment continuously employed. Markets of this kind do not occur naturally; they have to be somehow created, notably by the operation of the "modern" corporation and the consolidation of an institutional framework ("Keynesian system") capable of matching mass production and mass consumption in the economy as a whole.

It appears, thus, that the characteristics of Fordism in its "ideal type" contrast very sharply with those of SMEs. Smaller firms do not generally realize internal economies of scale; they engage in fragmented as opposed to verticalized processes and exemplify a less clear division of labor. And although the assumption that smaller firms tend to be more labor-intensive has been called into question (Little, 1987), it appears that smaller firms tend to utilize proportionately more skilled workers than their larger counterparts. Furthermore, the skills engaged in small-scale production tend to be broader, thus allowing individual workers to perform more than one task (Schmitz, 1982). Due to low-volume production, small firms are incapable of controlling the markets or of setting prices. Last but not least, the institutional mechanism of regulation (ranging from financial assistance and incentives schemes to labor legislation and social security provisions) do not apply (or apply to a lesser extent) to smaller firms. So, against a background heavily biased in favor of economies of scale and with "best practice" common sense leaning heavily on efficiency based on high volumes of identical products, the role of small firms was seen to be marginal, ranging from "eccentricity" to "historical anachronism."[3]

The economic recession which started in the mid-1970s has triggered a process of transition, involving major changes starting from the sphere of production and increasingly affecting all spheres of social and political life. At the level of industrial organization this transition is reflected in a restructuring pattern which breaks with the principles of mass production or Fordism. The characteristics of this transition are still vague and contradictory, but they appear to involve a search for flexibility, constant innovation, and vertical disintegration with emphasis on horizontal interfirm links leading to further specialization and collective innovation. Competitiveness rests increasingly on the ability of producers to turn out batches of customized and differentiated products of high quality, high design content, and short production runs by utilizing versatile equipment and multiskilled labor.

Although these transition characteristics embrace the whole manufacturing sector irrespective of size, it is of particular interest that small firms have the potential of acquiring a competitive edge and of seriously challenging the larger and more rigid Fordist firms. Within this context, flexible specialization theorization[4] is associated with the notion that craft principles can provide a dynamic, viable, efficient, and innovative alternative mode of organization to the crisis-ridden system of mass production (Piore and Sabel, 1984). Although this new approach is primarily based on the experience of a number of developed industrial economies, it represents a challenge to peripheral economies as well, and small firms in particular.

How do small firms fit into this picture of transition? Some of the features outlined above appear, *prima facie*, best suited to the characteristics of small firms, while others can be accommodated to any firm size, provided certain requirements are met. The decentralization of production and the increase in subcontracting and outwork seem to open up more space for smaller firms in an increasing number of activities. Flatter hierarchies and skill versatility, as well as proximity and responsiveness to the market, also seem closer to the experience and *modus vivendi* of SMEs. The same applies in the case of the transactions-intensive mode of operation, closely linking a chain of independent, yet highly interdependent, small firms. Large and highly verticalized firms tend to lack such experience, and may thus find themselves at a disadvantage when dealing with the uncertainty and unpredictability of the current economic setting.

The model of flexible specialization is based on three defining characteristics: First, clusters of small firms produce a wide range of products for highly differentiated markets. The vertical disintegration of their productive system allows for constant readjustments in response to changing market requirements. Unlike the case of industrial dualism within the mass production system, small firms are not merely shock absorbers for large firms (Berger and Piore, 1980). They occupy a central role by virtue of their participation in a sophisticated network of interfirm relations. Within this network, the firms share knowledge and information and are thus capable of jointly developing new products and production methods (Piore and Sabel, 1984; Sabel and Zeitlin, 1985; Sabel, 1986).

The second defining characteristic is the use of flexible and widely applicable technologies in production: versatile and general-purpose machines and equipment, instead of large and dedicated machine systems. Product innovation is not inhibited by massive capital investment in rigid technologies; the "minimum change" strategy characteristic of mass production is replaced by a generalized drive to constant innovation. "Flexible Specialization is a strategy of permanent innovation: accommodation to ceaseless change rather than an effort to control it" (Piore and Sabel, 1984: 17). This permanent innovation strategy requires that workers possess a wide range of skills in order to produce and develop a variety of products. This upgrading of skills is incompatible with the rigid separation between conception and execution dictated by the Fordist deep technical division of labor (Piore and Sabel, 1984; Sabel, 1986; Zeitlin, 1987).

The third defining characteristic of flexible specialization is its system of microregulation aiming to balance competition and cooperation. The ideal combination of competition cum cooperation is the trigger for perpetual innovation, skills transmission, and learning-by-doing practices, ensuring that productivity does not stagnate and that competition remains "fair" (no sweating of labor). Microregulation is accomplished through learned social practices and ethical values as well as more formal rules and institutions. These sets of ideological/ethical practices and institutions tend to be regional in nature, due to the spatial agglomeration of flexible firms and their reliance on dense interfirm transactional relations.[5]

Consequently, "This model stands the principles of mass production on their heads, both with regard to the internal organization of the factory and its relation to the broader economy. Mass production is the manufacture of standard products with specialized resources (narrowly skilled workers and dedicated machines); flexible specialization is the production of specialized products with general resources (broadly skilled labor and universal, typically programmable machines)" (Sabel, 1986: 40-41). Table 4.1 summarizes the main characteristics of Fordism and flexible specialization as the ideal types of two juxtaposed systems of organizing production.

SMALL-SCALE ENTHUSIASM REVISITED: ARGUMENTS AND COUNTER ARGUMENTS

Employment Shifts and Job Generation

Statistical and empirical evidence in the OECD economies suggests that there has been a recent increase in the share of total employment in small enterprises and establishments employing less than one hundred persons, at the expense of large enterprises and establishments. Despite considerable intercountry and sectoral variations, this signifies the reversal of a historical downward trend in the employment share of small units. It appears that "the time series behavior of small unit employment shares has followed a V pattern in which declines through the late 60s and early 70s are reversed and small unit

Table 4.1
Alternative Systems for Organizing Production

	Mass Production	Flexible Specialization
Size of firm/plant	large (the corporation)	scope for small and large
Technology	specialized dedicated machinery	general purpose machinery
Labour	narrowly trained separation of conception and execution fragmented and routinized tasks narrow job classification	broadly trained integration of conception and execution multi-skilled and varied tasks broad job classification
Management	hierarchical and formal	flat hierarchy, informal
Output	high volume	large and small batch, single units
	limited range of standardized products	varied/customized products
Competitive behavior	strategy to control market	fast adaptation to change, innovation
Institutional framework	centralized national and multinational Keynesianism	decentralized local institutions which fuse competition and cooperation

Source: Schmitz, 1989: 11

employment shares increase into the 1980s. The V pattern is evident both for enterprises and establishments, and for the total economy and manufacturing" (Loveman and Sengenberger, 1990: 8).

In a pioneering study concerning the U.S. economy, Birch (1979) has claimed that small firms were responsible for creating a disproportionate share of new jobs. For the period 1969-76 Birch found that small enterprises contributed 82 percent of net job growth in the U.S. private economy, while subsequent studies found small enterprises responsible for 39 percent and 53 percent of net job creation for the periods 1978-80 and 1976-82 respectively (Armington and Odle, 1982). In his most recent and comprehensive job generation results, Birch (1987) suggests that the data for 1981-85 confirm his earlier findings: 88 percent of net job creation was in enterprises with one to nineteen employees, while small enterprises with fewer than one hundred employees accounted for essentially all net job creation (Birch, 1987; Evans,

1987). Following Birch's work, job generation studies have been undertaken in many OECD countries, reaching more or less similar results (Storey and Johnson, 1987; Hull, 1986; Fritsch, 1989).

Successful Industrial Districts

In the midst of recession and economic stagnation, a few exceptional localities exhibited a remarkable resilience and even growth. These exemplars of prosperity[6] were engaged in a variety of industries (comprising advanced and traditional sectors) and were highlighted as being localized economic constellations that "were beating the recession" (Murray, 1991; Pyke and Sengenberger, 1990). The term most often utilized to describe these localized economic constellations is "industrial district" (Goodman, 1989; Brusco, 1990; Becattini, 1990; Pyke and Sengenberger, 1992).

Industrial districts are geographically defined productive systems, characterized by a large number of firms that are involved at various stages (and in a variety of ways) in the production of a homogeneous product. These local industrial constellations combine both economic efficiency and superior standards of employment. A significant characteristic is that a very high proportion of the firms comprising the districts are small or even very small. These firms are adaptive and innovative, capable of rapidly responding to changing product demands; they rely heavily on a multiskilled and flexible labor force, and build up flexible productive networks of interfirm cooperation (Sabel, 1989; Piore, 1990; Capecchi, 1990). The most widely noted successful industrial districts are those of north-central and north-eastern Italy[7] (Goodman et. al., 1989; Pyke, Becattini and Sengenberger, 1990).

From the point of view of workers involved in flexible production, the proponents of flexible specialization suggest that multiskilling and broader skill base tend to offer workers greater control over the work process. As work becomes more skilled, wages move upward and employers are obliged to abandon authoritarian methods of control. Furthermore, job security is enhanced, as trained workers are more difficult to replace. Finally, preoccupation with quality rather than price/cost weakens the drive of employers to engage in wage-cutting practices (Piore and Sabel, 1984; Best, 1984; Zeitlin, 1987).

The Dark Side of the Moon

The above optimistic views have been challenged by a number of economists, on the grounds that formidable problems arise from the point of view of labor solidarity and collective organization. Such critiques stress the enormous unevenness of conditions of work and the disproportionate bargaining strength derived from skill: a small group of workers exploit differentiations within the labor market and pursue an active strategy of protecting and reinforcing such differences. Finally, access to skilled jobs tends to rely on existing social inequalities, regulated by gender, race/nationality, and family connections (Gough, 1986; F. Murray, 1987; Solinas, 1982; Cockburn, 1983). Thus, "The exploitation of skill as a major bargaining weapon . . . tends both to rely on and exacerbate reactionary divisions among workers" (Gough, 1986: 69). A further point of criticism to the overoptimistic generalizations focuses on the dynamics of the labor market, and more specifically on the supply of labor: in cases where there exist considerable labor reserves, employers tend to resort to sweating rather than innovation (Schmitz, 1989). Although empirical evidence supports the employment generation potential of small firms, a number of factors warn against wholesale optimism. First, the international picture suggests that the vast majority of new small firms either remain small indefinitely or fail. Therefore, their contribution to employment creation remains modest. Much of the total increase in employment among small firms is attributable to the performance of a few remarkably successful new small firms (Loveman and Sengenberger, 1990: 32). Second, some studies suggest that employment growth rates for new large firms are roughly equal to those of small firms (United States Small Business Administration, 1981; Gallagher and Stewart, 1981). And third, the notion of net job creation should be treated with caution in the case of new firms because it may simply reflect a redistribution of production from existing firms (via subcontracting), therefore hardly contributing in raising aggregate welfare (Sengenberger, Loveman and Piore, 1990).

As far as remuneration and working conditions are concerned, international data suggest that wages tend to be an increasing function of enterprise and establishment size. Despite considerable variations in wage gaps between large, medium-sized, and small establishments across countries, small firms pay lower wages than large firms in all advanced OECD countries (Loveman and Sengenberger, 1990: 33). In the case of the Italian industrial districts, however, it has been pointed out that standard compensation and working conditions data do not adequately describe worker welfare. This is so because the latter depends heavily on other, nonquantifiable elements reflecting living conditions (Becattini, 1990).

Internationally, comparable data on hours worked suggest that at least in France, Britain, and Japan small firm employees work more hours than large firm employees, although the discrepancy has narrowed in recent years (Amadieu, 1990; Koshiro, 1990; Marsden, 1990). However, labor productivity data on the same countries suggest that, due to much lower capital-labor ratios, the inferior labor productivity in small establishments is more than offsetting the lower wages (Sengenberger, 1987).

Unionization rates are positively correlated with size and reflect the differences in compensation and working conditions. Again, there is significant variation across countries. One reason accounting for the lower unionization rates of small firms may be their concentration in industries which have historically been relatively less unionized (such as the tertiary sector). Furthermore, industrial action once again appears to be positively correlated with size, although the implications of industrial disputes for the cost of production tend to be more severe in the case of smaller firms (due to lack of buffer stocks), implying thus a greater bargaining power on the part of small firms employees (Marsden, 1990; Loveman and Sengenberger, 1990).

Although it could be argued that on a statistical basis workers are less well-off in smaller enterprises and establishments, there is no "iron necessity" why this should always be the case. There is no intrinsic correlation between small size and inferior labor conditions. Indeed, the experience of the Italian industrial districts points to the substantial potential of smaller firms to contribute to the aggregate welfare, provided that there exists an adequate socioinstitutional regulating framework. Furthermore, high unionization rates among small firm employees can be found outside the Italian industrial districts, namely in Sweden, as well as in the construction, ladies' garments, and printing industries in the United States (Piore and Sabel, 1984).

Lower job stability does not necessarily contribute to greater worker insecurity, provided that there are institutions to take care of the social consequences of the instability problem. Finally, surveys on job satisfaction in various countries consistently suggest that job satisfaction levels are inversely related to establishment size. So, while on average, effective employment security is weaker in smaller firms than in large ones, some of the best employment standards and working conditions can be found in small firms (Loveman and Sengenberger, 1990).

The Limits to Flexible Specialization Paradise

The above discussion is pointing to the conclusion that there exists a viable, dynamic, competitive, and socially desirable paradigm of small and medium-sized enterprise development, following the principle of the Italian industrial districts prototype. Not all small firms comply with these principles (in fact only a minority), but at least some do, and there are good reasons to encourage the rest to move along the same lines. The question of replicability, however, is highly controversial. Can the conditions deemed to be necessary for industrial district success be dictated and repeated in different socioeconomic contexts?

In the case of the Italian successful industrial districts, a large number of necessary conditions have been held responsible for their prosperous performance. These conditions include entrepreneurial spirit and ability, the flexibility of economic activity to utilize social resources and structures, cultural and political factors preserving local consensus on commonly shared values, the provision of a local pool of skills, and, last but not least, the innovative interventionist role assumed by local government and local associations (producers, unions, and consumers) (Pyke, Becattini and Sengenberger, 1990; Capecchi, 1990; Murray, 1991).

It is the combination of these conditions that has culminated in successful economic performance, and it is doubtful whether a similar conjuncture can be dictated and encouraged out of the blue. Furthermore, it seems that the Italian experience is less homogeneous than often presented. Considerable variations in labor standards do exist, ranging from very high to instances where development has occurred on the basis of cheap labor and intolerable conditions (Amin and Robins, 1990; Brutti, 1992; Calistri, 1990).

Finally, the future prospects of successful industrial districts are seriously questioned. It might be the case that the districts took advantage of the specific conditions associated with the world recession, and that their future is uncertain as soon as economic activity and demand pick up. On the pessimistic end of the spectrum, some writers see the activities of large firms and in particular multinational corporations as a major threat (Amin and Robins, 1990; Brutti and Calistri, 1990). Others, on the more optimistic side, see no necessary incompatibility between large firms and industrial districts as two distinct, yet coexisting ways of organizing production (Zeitlin, 1987; Storper, 1990).

SMES IN THE EUROPEAN UNION CONTEXT: POLICIES AND APPROACHES

The development and future prospects of SMEs in the European Union are subject to a series of factors which can be divided methodologically along the following lines: (i) the impact of the prevailing overall socioeconomic conditions and market forces in general; (ii) the multiple indirect effects of a series of EU policy measures which, although not explicitly aiming at SMEs, affect them—often in a substantive manner—by altering their macro- or microeconomic environment; and (iii) the various Union instruments and measures which explicitly aim at assisting the SMEs. With regard to factor (ii), the protective common commercial policy measures in the field of textiles (especially clothing), contribute, to the extent that they are successful and don't simply lead to trade diversion, to the viability of a series of small Union enterprises. In this context, it has been repeatedly pointed out that the creation of a genuinely common market through the implementation of the provisions of the Single European Act clearly affect, for better or for worse, the EU's small firms (Stoker and Benson, 1990; Crossick, 1988). And to a great extent this latter concern has led to factor (iii) in the late 1980s.

Without forgetting the primacy of the basic socioeconomic forces affecting the EU's SMEs, we shall concentrate on these last policy measures taken by the EU in favor of SMEs. In particular we shall examine their basic philosophy, their mode of operation, and their impact (real or nominal) on the politico-economic processes and interests that they involve.

Basic Philosophy

EU actions/initiatives in favor of SMEs are taken in view of "1992," which sets the deadline for the completion of the Single European Market project. They reflect a growing interest in and concern for this category of firms which characterized both European policy-making centers and academic circles throughout the 1980s (Boissevain, 1981; Levicki, 1984; Burns and Dewhurst, 1986). Major points of interest, in this respect, have been the problem of defining SMEs, using the appropriate maximum number of employees threshold; the statistical studies showing an astonishing reversal of previous trends and a remarkable survival capacity of small firms, linked to substantial job creation; and SMEs' contribution to innovation and role as the seedbed of entrepreneurial effectiveness as opposed to large bureaucratic organizations. Their unfair competitive disadvantage vis-á-vis large firms is noted. And finally, the need for a policy in favor of SMEs designed with an eye toward employment and implemented on a regional or local level is addressed (Geroski and Schwalbach, 1986). This last point is indicative of the pro-decentralization mentality characterizing much of the problematic on the SMEs.

The official EU definition of SMEs (500 employees or less) is rather broad, so that on its basis SMEs comprise the quasitotality of EU enterprises. The basic philosophy behind EU actions in favor of SMEs, is to reduce their handicaps due to their small size and thus facilitate their incorporation in the large Single European Market. Such actions are also considered to benefit employment, given the importance of SMEs in job creation: in 1986, 99.9 percent of EU firms had less than 500 employees, 99.4 percent had less than one hundred, and 91.3 percent had less than ten. In the early 1980s, for which there are data available, firms with less than one hundred employees supplied fifty percent or more of total manufacturing employment in countries such as Greece, Italy, and Ireland and 40-50 percent in France, Spain, and Portugal. The participation of SMEs in employment is even more important in the services sector: firms with less than 500 (100) employees supplied 80 (72) percent of tertiary sector employment in France and 78 (60) percent in Spain (Belaud, 1990). Given the increasing importance of job creation in the services sector, it is assumed that SMEs play and will continue to play a predominant role in this dynamism.

The above data highlight the quantitative importance of SMEs in the labor market. But also in qualitative terms SME jobs are found to be characterized by part-time work, women's labor, instability, and lower wages. Such increasing flexibility constitutes a major feature of what the EU Commission calls "the secondary labor market." This creation of "different" employment is believed by Commission officials to constitute a lasting trend—especially if we include under the label SME independent, self-employed professionals supplying specialized services, which are often linked to new technologies (Belaud, 1990).

In view of the creation of the internal market, SMEs face a greater challenge than large, well-established firms which have been operating for many years on a wide European level. The SMEs' obstacles are considered to be the following: (i) Financing, especially in view of the modernization and takeoff needs entailed by the Single Market project. Both their self-financing possibilities and their access to risk capital are limited, particularly in the EU's less developed areas. (ii) The new EU-wide regimentation and harmonization process, although broadly accepted by SMEs, is often a source of difficulties, especially when it involves the implementation of stricter legislation in such areas as health standards and workplace security. (iii) SMEs also have, in comparison to large firms, a serious handicap due to lack of sufficient information as regards such issues as public procurements, EU programs and other Union policies linked to the Single Market project. (iv) Finally, again because of their limited size, SMEs often employ personnel who are inadequately trained and cannot keep up with new technologies and the EU decision-making process.

These problems are dealt with by EU member states themselves, with various government initiatives such as aiding the financing of SMEs and informing them about "1992." But especially since the late 1980s, SMEs have also constituted an explicit Union goal which is supposed to complement the national governments' efforts. Administratively, this increased interest initially led to the formation in 1986 of a specific EU Commission "SME Task Force" which was to be replaced in 1989 by a whole Directorate-General (DGXXIII) dealing with enterprises, commerce, tourism, and "social economy." This coincided with a new and more ambitious EU plan, approved in 1989, aiming at the improvement of the SMEs' environment and at the overall promotion of their activities. This plan covers the period 1989-93 and was initially granted the amount of 110 million ECUs (European currency units) as opposed to the 135 million demanded by the less developed EU regions (*Official Journal of the EC*, No. L239, August 16, 1989).

EC Policy Measures in Favor of SMEs

In practice, the EU's exact definition of SME is any firm employing less than 500 employees and having fixed assets not exceeding 75 million ECUs; furthermore, no larger company can be in control of one-third of its capital. In some cases a lower, that is, stricter definition is used (EC Commission, 1989: *Manual for SMEs*). EU actions in favor of SMEs can be classified as follows:

SME Information. Assistance to SMEs as regards their information on the Single Market has been implemented since 1986 and has led, since 1990, to the creation of the Euro-InfoCenters; these 187 centers function on a decentralized and nondiscriminatory basis and inform SMEs across the EU on legislative matters of interest to them (1992 Project), on the EU's social and regional funds' aid, on participation in research programs, and similar issues. These centers are eventually supposed to become financially independent of Union funding, by charging a certain fee for their services.

SME Cooperation.   Through the computerized Business Cooperation Network (BC-NET), founded in 1988, the EU aims to enhance to SMEs' information access. But this time the information provided relates directly to the market—to possibilities of cooperation of SMEs between themselves, either by simply selling and buying, or through joint ventures and other forms of "marriages." Since 1988 thousands of confidential "cooperation profiles" have been provided to interested SMEs by the BC-NET, which has been functioning as a *sui generis* "market substitute": it brings together small firms which, under other circumstances, would have had great difficulty in finding each other and cooperating.   Interestingly enough, since 1990 non-EU countries (EFTA countries) have started joining this network (EFTA[8] countries) (*Infobusiness*, May, 1991). A similar policy, initiated in 1988, is the "Europartenariat" program: a region (or country) of the EU selects a series of local firms able and willing to offer cooperation proposals to other firms in the EU—these proposals then circulate and trigger responses and proposals from other areas of the EU. At the third and final stage, the interested parties meet in the region in question for two days to formalize an agreement. This has taken place in Ireland (1988), Andalusia (1989), Wales (1990), Portugal (1991), and Greece (1992) (Belaud, 1990).

The EU Commission has also realized the increasing importance of subcontracting in the European economy and has taken measures facilitating this form of industrial cooperation, assisting SMEs by providing, through official EU publications, technical terminological guides in all Union languages (for the metal, plastics, textiles-clothing, and electronics sectors); providing a practical guide on legal matters; promoting joint ventures of EU SMEs with firms in third countries (organizing "business weeks," or providing through the experimental "Cheysson facility" financial support to joint ventures with Mediterranean, Asian, and Latin American countries) (COM 89: 402).

Financial support.   Assisting SMEs through various forms of financial engineering has been implemented on a EU level since 1986. In particular, the European Venture Capital Association offers risk capital to SMEs' innovatory projects transcending national boundaries (total subsidy in 1988: 0.5 million ECUs). At the same time, a pilot plan for start-up capital has been operating for the period 1989-94 with EU Commission funding of 11.6 million ECUs. A Eurotech-capital fund has financed, high-technology ventures since 1989, especially those of SMEs.   Finally, in the period 1982-89, through the successive "New Community Instruments" (NCI I, II, III, I), and with the participation of the European Investment Bank (EIB), EU SMEs have benefited from the possibility of low-interest financing. This has constituted a sort of continuation of the "global loans" policy of the EIB in the 1970s (Pinder, 1986; Belaud, 1990). Finally, the reform and reinforcement, since the late 1980s, of the EU's regional policy through the unification of the structural funds has led to a significant financing via local intermediaries of SMEs. This has been particularly striking in the case of reconversion schemes for declining industrial regions (target 2 zones), sectoral aids such as RESIDER and RENAVAL, and, of course, less developed EU regions in general (target 1 zones, Integrated Mediterranean Programs). The new EU regional development policy explicitly provides for SMEs in relation to such measures as management aid, technology transfer financing, access to capital markets and direct investment subsidies (Reg. 4254/88, *Official Journal of the EU*, No. L374, December 31, 1988). However, it is difficult to assess exact EU support to SMEs through regional policy instruments, given that it is channeled via national intermediaries. Furthermore, the extent to which the very specific SMEs' financial needs are covered successfully by the above policies remains an open question (Bissiriou, 1989). The above-mentioned policies do not exhaust the financial aspects of EU policies; on the one hand, the liberalization of the services (banking-insurance) sector within the Union will probably lead to easier and cheaper financing in general, and, *a fortiori*, for SMEs; on the other hand, other EU initiatives to this effect are envisaged, for instance, in regards to mutual guarantee systems (Zavvos, 1990, SEC (91) 1550. final).

Other forms of support. These cover a variety of measures, such as (i) training of SME management and employees, particularly in such areas as new technologies, which takes place either in the context of the European Social Fund, or in the framework of technology-oriented EU programs (COMETT, EUROTECNET); (ii) elaboration of a more appropriate and flexible legal framework for the cooperation of SMEs on a European scale (European Grouping of Economic Interests [GEIE], European company law); (iii) facilitation of SMEs' access to the increasingly liberalized public procurement procedures; (iv) adaptation and greater flexibility of EU competition legislation, especially with regard to the implementation of Articles 85 and 92 of the Treaty of Rome (which forbid agreements between companies and state subsidies respectively); (v) assistance through the CRAFT program (Cooperative Research Action For Technology), especially designed for small companies in linking up their research interests with universities and institutes (Belaud, 1990), although in the realm of mainstream EU policy in the field of research and technology (such as ESPRIT information technologies, RACE telecommunications, SPRINT technology transfer program, BRITE flexible materials technologies) SME participation is predictably rather small.

An Assessment of EU Policies toward SMEs

It is clear from the above that there is no single, easily defined EU policy vis-á-vis SMEs. This springs not only from the obvious difficulty, in the context of a free market economy, of state intervention in vast and diverse areas of economic activity, which furthermore, in the case of SMEs, can well be the underground economy; it is also a result of the many different and, to a great extent, uncoordinated EU policies, some of which incorporate as an appendix an SME dimension—this is particularly the case with regional or, even more, technology policy. But it could also be claimed that even the explicit SME policy is a by-product of the much broader and deeper European Single Market project—it stems from an increasing concern with the possible negative impact on SMEs of fuller trade liberalization within the EU. However, it is extremely difficult to predict the extent and the distribution of the overall effect of the 1992 Project on the SMEs: this will vary from region to region and from sector to sector.

The concrete EU measures toward SMEs can be methodologically divided along the following lines: they either consist in altering market conditions (Single Market legislation, common commercial policy), or they amount to a form of financial assistance (regional fund subsidies, EIB low-interest loans, training, or research funding). These two basic policy forms constitute the bulk of EU interventions in the economic sphere. The only exception in this respect is the aforementioned EU information and cooperation policies (Euro-InfoCenters, BC-NET), which effectively aim, in a very original manner, at some form of "market substitution." This "mesoeconomic policy," interesting enough, comes at a historical moment when classical tools of government economic intervention (monetarist or Keynesian) are seriously questioned. But it remains a rather marginal form of intervention, which corresponds more to the specificities of EU symbolics—the need for some policy, some Union presence in this publicly sensitive sphere. At the strictly economic level, this is limited to the whole problem of the distribution of the benefits arising from European integration in general and from the internal market project in particular.[9] At a more political level, all these measures can be seen as gestures which constitute a response to specific pressures from a specific socioeconomic group (SMEs).[10]

CONCLUSIONS: WHICH FUTURE FOR EUROPE'S SMES?

SMEs have managed to capture the attention of both academics and policy makers over the past decade. In particular, the "industrial districts model," which largely reflects the principles of the flexible specialization theorization, owes its special appeal to three important factors: the successful economic performance (exports, employment, flexibility, innovation), the capacity for endogenous regional development, and the ability to sustain high wages and labor standards despite intensified international competition.

Obviously not all SMEs fit this picture. It has been repeatedly stressed that the world of small business is highly heterogeneous, encompassing extreme cases in either direction. Some small firms are still shock absorbers for the economic cycle, but it would be misleading to suggest that small firm expansion is a mere transitory and cyclical phenomenon. The apparent variety of enterprise profiles, of restructuring responses, and of economic performance within any size category suggests that the attribution of innate economic superiority to either large or small firms contradicts present reality. In the end, "smallness" or "bigness" of a firm is not the decisive criterion for its performance. Evidence clearly reveals that the main problem for small firms is not being small but being lonely. Therefore, no single policy package can offer a panacea type of solution. There is no single policy recipe to ensure SME development, nor is there a single policy approach for "the small firms." There are different kinds of small firms and different contexts so there must be different policies adopted accordingly (Brusco and Pezzini, 1990).

The industrial districts phenomenon, itself, is far from homogeneous; there exists a wide variety of industrial districts inside and outside the Italian context, with diverse origins and internal organization. Allowing for sectoral, regional, and national variation, all the successful local constellations of SMEs meet two basic requirements. The first is the provision of common services which are beyond the capacity of individual firms to supply for themselves (training, research, market forecasting, credit, and quality control). The second is a mechanism to resolve the conflicts among local actors so that competition is not displaced from product and process innovation to sweated wages and conditions. The individual institutional solutions are bound to take the shape of the local, sectoral, and national specificities.

Deregulation and liberalization policies appear, at least *prima facie*, incompatible with the creation of a complex institutional infrastructure at the local level. The encouragement of competition and the removal of constraints on the free working of capital, labor, and product markets are likely to hinder the buildup of collective structures and relations, based not so much on antagonism, but rather on the pooling of resources. Furthermore, the dynamic stereotype of small business development requires strong and autonomous local institutions capable of formulating effective policies tailored to their needs. This does not mean that the local level of policy initiatives should always supersede the national level. What is at stake, though, is a new distribution of tasks between different levels of intervention and policy initiatives: local, regional, national, and supranational (EU). To the extent that the process of the Single European Market involves granting more "breathing space" at the local and regional levels, it could be argued that by removing the existing suffocating framework, it will open up more development options at these levels. Whether small firms are going to benefit, and which of them will "beat the recession" in the future, are open and unresolved issues, largely dependent on the strategic choices of the actors concerned.

NOTES

1. The issue originated in Proudhon's idealized and utopian craft communities (effectively criticized by Marx in *The Poverty of Philosophy*). It was taken up by the Russian populists, the Narodnilks (criticized by Lenin), as an alleged alternative to capitalism. In more recent years it was adopted by the neo-populists in development theory (appropriate technology and "small is beautiful" approaches) [Kitchincs, 1982]). In its most recent and influential guise, it informed the debate on the informal sector in the 1970s. So, it appears that the theoretical focus on small firms originated in the eighteenth century "core" economy at the dawn of the industrial revolution, then traveled to the "periphery," and now returns to its original homeland (Lyberaki, 1991).

2. Some common criteria for the definition of the small and medium-sized enterprise sector are the legal status (as in France), the ownership status (as in Hungary), the distinction between "craft" and "industrial" firms (as in Germany), and the distinction between independent and subordinate firms (as in Japan) (Loveman and Sengenberger, 1990).

3. The above should not lead to the conclusion that small-scale production was almost eradicated during the Fordist era. A number of barriers to the expansion of the fordist paradigm in a number of sectors, in combination with the strategy of certain large firms to utilize subcontractors as buffers when demand contracted, ensured the persistence of smaller establishments.

4. Other theorizations accounting for the present contradictory and transitory reality include the paradigm change literature (Freeman and Perez, 1986; Perez, 1985), the French regulation school formula on "Post-Fordism" (Lipietz, 1987; Leborgne and Lipietz, 1987; Boyer and Coriat, 1986), the concept of disorganized capitalism (Lash and Urry, 1987), Harvey's analysis on postmodernism as the cultural expression of the flexible regime of accumulation (Harvey, 1989, 1990), and last but not least, the analyses on the spatial and regional implications of flexibility and the emphasis on the politics of place (Best, 1986; Gough, 1986; Murray, 1991, 1992; Storper and Scott, 1988).

5. The idea of a cluster of small firms reaping collectively the benefits of densely populated industrial communities is neither new in economic theory, nor exclusive to the flexible specialization model. A host of issues emphasized by the latter approach can be found in the literature on the "economies of agglomeration" (Murray, 1975). They are based on the principle that "distance is the enemy of time" and they refer to economies which are external to the individual firms hut internal to the industrial community.

6. Such places of economic dynamism include Oyonnax in France, Jutland in Denmark, Baden-Württemberg in Germany, Smaland in Sweden, Barcelona in Spain, Silicon Valley in the United States, Cambridge in Britain and areas of central and northeastern Italy (Trigilia, 1992; Benton, 1992; Schmitz, 1992; Kristensen, 1992).

7. Sassuolo in Emilia-Romagna specializes in ceramic tiles, Prato in Tuscany produces textiles, Montegranaro in Marche specialists in shoe production, Cento in Emilia-Romagna is involved in mechanical engineering, Nogara in Veneto specializes in wooden furniture, while Canneto sull'Oglio in Lombardy makes toys (Sforzi, 1990; Trigilia, 1992).

8. EFTA (European Free Trade Areas) comprises Austria, Switzerland, and the Scandinavian economies.

9. On the expected overall economic benefits of the Single Market, see studies on the cost of non-Europe: for example, *European Economy*, No. 35, March 1988. On the question of the distribution of these benefits among regions and social groups, see Cutler, Haslam, Williams and Williams, (eds.) *1992: The Struggle for Europe*, (London: Berg, 1991). Also *L'Evénement Européen*, Special Issue, 1989.

10. See L'Intergroup PME du Parlement Européen, SME Intergroup, E.P. 1991., On the general issue of EC corporatism, see W. Grant, *The Political Economy of Corporatism* (London: Heineman, 1985), Chapter 9.

REFERENCES

Amadieu, J. F. 1990. "France." In W. Sengenberger, G. Loveman, and M. Piore (eds.), *The Re-Emergence of Small Enterprises: Industrial Restructuring in Industrialized Countries*. Geneva: International Institute for Labour Studies.

Amin, A. and K. Robins. 1990. "Industrial Districts and Regional Development: Limits and Possibilities" In F. Pyke, G. Becattini, and W. Sengenberger (eds.), *Industrial Districts and Inter-Firm Co-Operation in Italy*. Geneva: International Institute for Labour Studies.

Armington, C. and M. Odle. 1982. "Small Business—How Many Jobs?" *Brookings Review*, Winter.

Becattini, G. 1990. "Italy." In W. Sengenberger, G. Loveman and M. Piore (eds.), *The Re-Emergence of Small Enterprises: Industrial Restructuring in Industrialized Countries*. Geneva: International Institute for Labour Studies.

Belaud, J. F. 1990. *La nouvelle politique européenne en faveur des PME*. Club de Bruxelles.

Benton, L. 1992. "The Emergence of Industrial Districts in Spain: Industrial Restructuring and Diverging Regional Responses." In F. Pyke and W. Sengenberger (eds.), *Industrial Districts and Local Economic Regeneration*. Geneva: International Institute for Labour Studies.

Best, M. 1984. "Strategic Planning and Industrial Renewal." Greater London Enterprise Board, mimeo.

Birch, D. 1979. "The Job Generation Process." Final Report to Economic Development Administration. Cambridge: MIT Program on Neighborhood and Regional Change.

————. 1987. *Job Generation in America*. New York: Free Press.

Bissiriou, G. 1989. "La specificité des besoins financiers des PME innovatrices." *Revue Française de Gestion*, March-April-May.

Blyton, P. and J. Morris. 1991. *A Flexible Future? Prospects for Employment and Organization*. Berlin and New York: deGruyter.

Boissevain, J. 1981. *Small Entrepreneurs in Changing Europe: A Research Agenda*. Maastricht: Center for Work and Society.

Boyer, R. and B. Coriat. 1986. "Technical Flexibility and Macro-Stabilization." Paper in Venice Conference on *Innovation Diffusion*, March.

Brusco, S. 1990. "The Idea of the Industrial District: Its Genesis," In F. Pyke, G. Becattini and W. Sengenberger (eds.), *Industrial Districts and Inter-Firm Co-Operation in Italy*. Geneva: International Institute for Labour Studies.

Brusco, S. and M. Pezzini. 1990. "Small-Scale Enterprises in the Ideology of the Italian Left." In F. Pyke, G. Becattini, and W. Sengenberger (eds.), *Industrial Districts and Inter-Firm Co-Operation in Italy*. Geneva: International Institute for Labour Studies.

Brutti, P. 1992. "Industrial Districts: The Point of View of the Unions." In F. Pyke and W. Sengenberger (eds.), *Industrial Districts and Local Economic Regeneration*. Geneva: International Institute for Labour Studies.

Burns, P. and J. Dewhurst, eds. 1986. *Small Business in Europe*. Macmillans: London.

Calistri, F. 1990. "Industrial Districts and the Unions." In F. Pyke, G. Becattini, and W. Sengenberger (eds.), *Industrial Districts and Inter-Firm Co-Operation in Italy*. Geneva: International Institute for Labour Studies..

Capecchi, V. 1990. "A History of Flexible Specialization and Industrial Districts in Emilia Romagna." In F. Pyke, G. Becattini, and W. Sengenberger (eds.), *Industrial Districts and Inter-Firm Co-Operation in Italy*. Geneva: International Institute for Labour Studies.

Cockburn, C. 1983. *Brothers*. London: Pluto.

Crossick, S. 1988. "Comparative Assessment of the Impact of 1992 on SMEs and MNCs." *European Affairs*, Vol. 2, No. 3.

Cutler, T., C. Haslam, J. Williams, and K. Williams. 1991. *1992: The Struggle for Europe*. London: Berg.

EC Commission. 1989. Communication to the EC Council. COM (89) 42.

———. 1989. Business Activities in Europe. Luxembourg.

———. 1991. Communication to the Council. SC (91) 1550 final.

Evans, D. 1987. "Tests of Alternative Theories of Firm Growth." *Journal of Political Economy*, Vol. 95, No. 4, August.

Freeman, C. and C. Perez. 1986. "The Diffusion of Technical Innovation and Changes of Techno-Economic Paradigm. Sussex, mimeo.

Fritsch, M. 1989. "Einzelwirtschaftliche Analyse der Arbeitsplatzdynamik-Theoretische Ansätze und empirische Befunde." *SAMF-Arbeitspapier*, No. 4.

Gallagher, C. and H. Stewart. 1981. "Jobs and the Business Life Cycle in the UK." Research Report No. 2, University of Newcastle-Upon-Tyne, Department of Industrial Management.

Geroski, P. and J. Schwalbach. 1986. *Entrepreneurship and Small Firms*. Brussels: Center for European Policy Studies.

Goodman, E., J. Bamford, and P. Saynor. 1989. *Small Firms and Industrial Districts in Italy*. London: Routledge.

Gough, J. 1986. "Industrial Policy and Socialist Strategy." *Capital and Class*, No. 29, Summer.

Grant, W. 1985. *The Political Economy of Corporatism*. London: Heineman.

Harvey, D. 1989. *The Urban Experience*. Oxford: Blackwell.

———. 1990. The Condition of Postmodernity. Oxford: Blackwell.

Hirst, P. and J. Zeitlin, eds. 1989. *Reversing Industrial Decline?* Berg.

Hull, C. 1986. "Job Generation in the Federal Republic of Germany: Review." Discussion Paper. Berlin: Wissenschaftszentrum, Labor Market Policy Research Unit, September.

"Infobusiness." 1991. *Magazine des EIC* at BC-NET bimestriel, No. 9.

Kitchincs, G. 1982. *Development and Underdevelopment in Historical Perspective*. London and New York: Methuen.

Koshiro, K. 1990. "Japan." In W. Sengenberger, G. Loveman, and M. Piore (eds.), *The Re-Emergence of Small Enterprises: Industrial Restructuring in Industrialized Countries*. Geneva: International Institute for Labour Studies.

Kristensen, P. H. 1992. "Industrial Districts in West Jutland, Denmark." In F. Pyke, and W. Sengenberger (eds.), *Industrial Districts and Local Economic Regeneration*. Geneva: International Institute for Labour Studies.

Lash, S. and J. Urry. 1987. *The End of Organized Capitalism*. Cambridge: Polity.

Leborgne, D. and A. Lipietz. 1987. "New Technologies, New Modes of Regulation: Some Spatial Implications." Paper in conference *Changing Labour Processes and New Forms of Urbanisation*. Samos: Greece.

Levicki, C. 1984. *Small Business: Theory and Practice*. London: Croom Helm.

Lipietz, A. 1987. *Mirages and Miracles: the Crisis of Global Fordism*. London: Verso.

Little, I. 1987. "Small Manufacturing Enterprises in Developing Countries." *World Bank Economic Review*, Vol. 1, No. 2.

Loveman, G. and W. Sengenberger. 1990. "Introduction." In W. Sengenberger, G. Loveman, and M. Piore (eds.), *The Re-Emergence of Small Enterprises: Industrial Restructuring in Industrialized Countries*. Geneva: International Institute for Labour Studies.

Lyberaki, A. 1991. *Flexible Specialization? Crisis and Re-Structuring in Greek Small-Scale Industry*. Athens: Gutenberg.

Marsden, D. 1990. "United Kingdom." In W. Sengenberger, G. Loveman, and M. Piore (eds.), *The Re-Emergence of Small Enterprises: Industrial Restructuring in Industrialized Countries*. Geneva: International Institute for Labour Studies.

Murray, F. 1987. "Flexible Specialization in the Third Italy." *Capital and Class*, No. 33, winter.

Murray, R. 1975. "The Internationalisation of Capital and the Nation State." In Radice, H. (ed.) *International Firm and Modern Imperialism*. Harmondsworth: Penguin.

Murray, R. 1991. *Local Space: Europe and the New Regionalism*. CLEES and SEEDS.

———. 1992. "Flexible Specialisation in Small Island Economies: The Case of Cyprus." In F. Pyke and W. Sengenberger (eds.), *Industrial Districts and Local Economic Regeneration*. Geneva: International Institute for Labour Studies.

Perez, C. 1985. "Microelectronics, Long Waves and World Structural Change: New Perspectives for Developing Countries." In *World Development*, Vol. 13, No. 3.

Pinder, D. A. 1986. "Small Firms, Regional Development and the European Investment Bank." *Journal of Common Market Studies*, March.

Piore, M. 1990. "Work, Labour and Action: Work Experience in a System of Flexible Production." In F. Pyke, G. Becattini, and W. Sengenberger (eds.), *Industrial Districts and Inter-Firm Co-Operation in Italy*. Geneva: International Institute for Labour Studies.

Piore, M. and C. Sabel. 1984. *The Second Industrial Divide*. New York: Basic Books.

Pyke, F., G. Becattini, and W. Sengenberger, eds. 1990. *Industrial Districts and Inter-Firm Co-Operation in Italy*. Geneva: International Institute for Labour Studies.

Pyke, F. and W. Sengenberger. 1990. "Economic and Social Reorganization in the Small and Medium Enterprise Sector." In W. Sengenberger, G. Loveman, and M. Piore (eds.), *The Re-Emergence of Small Enterprises: Industrial Restructuring in Industrialized Countries*. Geneva: International Institute for Labour Studies.

———, eds. 1992. *Industrial Districts and Local Economic Regeneration*. Geneva: International Institute for Labour Studies.

Sabel, C. 1986. "Changing Models of Economic Efficiency and their Implications for Industrialization in the Third World." In A. Foxley, M. McPherson, and G. O'Donnell (eds.), *Development, Democracy and the Art of Trespassing* University of Notre Dame Press.

Sabel, C. 1989. "Flexible Specialisation and the Re-Emergence of Regional Economies." In P. Hirst and J. Zeitlin (eds.), *Reversing Industrial Decline*. London: Berg.

Sabel, C. and J. Zeitlin. 1985. "Historical Alternatives to Mass Production." In *Past and Present*, Vol. 108.

Schmitz, H. 1982. *Manufacturing in the Backyard*. London: Frances Pinter.

———. 1989. "Flexible Specialisation—A New Paradigm of Small-Scale Industrialization?" Institute of Development Studies, Discussion Paper, No. 261.

———. 1992. "Industrial Districts: Model and Reality in Baden-Württemberg, Germany." In F. Pyke and W. Sengenberger (eds.), *Industrial Districts and Local Economic Regeneration*. Geneva: International Institute for Labour Studies.

Sengenberger, W. 1987. *Struktur und Funktionsweise von Arbeits-Markten: Die Bundesrepublik Deutschland im internationalen Vergleich*, Frankfurt/Main and New York.

Sengenberger, W. and F. Pyke. 1992. "Industrial Districts and Local Economic Regeneration: Research and Policy Issues." In F. Pyke and W. Sengenberger (eds.), *Industrial Districts and Local Economic Regeneration*. Geneva: International Institute for Labour Studies.

Sengenberger, W., G. Loveman, and M. Piore, eds. 1990. *The Re-Emergence of Small Enterprises: Industrial Restructuring in Industrialized Countries*. Geneva: International Institute for Labour Studies.

Sforzi, F. 1990. "The Quantitative Importance of Marshallian Industrial Districts in the Italian Economy." In F. Pyke, G. Becattini, and W. Sengenberger (eds.), *Industrial Districts and Inter-Firm Co-Operation in Italy*. Geneva: International Institute for Labour Studies.

Solinas, G. 1982. "Labour Market Segmentation and Workers' Careers: The Case of the Italian Knitwear Industry. *Cambridge Journal of Economics*, Vol. 6.

Standing. G. 1986. *Unemployment and Labour Market Flexibility: The United Kingdom*. Geneva: International Labour Organization.

Stoker, D. and V. Benson. 1990. *The Smaller Company and "1992."* London: Gower.

Storey, D. J. and S. Johnson. 1987. "Small and Medium-Sized Enterprises and Employment Creation in the EEC Countries: Summary Report." Commission of the European Communities, Programme of Research and Actions on the Development of the Labour Market, Study No. 85/407.

Storper, M. 1990. "A Reply to Amin and Robins." In F. Pyke, G. Becattini, and W. Sengenberger (eds.), *Industrial Districts and Inter-Firm Co-Operation in Italy*. Geneva: International Institute for Labour Studies.

Trigilia, C. 1992. "Italian Industrial Districts: Neither Myth nor Interlude." In F. Pyke and W. Sengenberger (eds.), *Industrial Districts and Local Economic Regeneration.* Geneva: International Institute for Labour Studies.

Zavvos, G.   1990.   "Banking Integration and 1992: Legal Issues and Policy Implications." Harvard International Law Journal, Spring.

Zeitlin, J.   1987.   "The Third Italy: Inter-Firm Co-Operation and Technological Innovation." *South East Economic Development Strategy Conference.* Brighton: March.

———. 1992. "Industrial Districts and Local Economic Regeneration: Overview and Comment." In F. Pyke and W. Sengenberger (eds.), *Industrial Districts and Local Economic Regeneration.* Geneva: International Institute for Labour Studies.

5

The Agricultural Strata in The European Union and The Common Agricultural Policy

Napoleon Maraveyas

More than three decades after the formation of the European Economic Community and the implementation of a Common Agricultural Policy (CAP), significant differences still exist among the agricultural strata and in the structures of agriculture of all the member countries. This is the unavoidable result of the different social, political, and historical development and the natural and climatic characteristics of these countries.

As might be expected, the implementation of a Common Agricultural Policy affects the agriculture of the member countries in different ways (depending upon the level of development and the particular characteristics of each country). At the same time, it may lead to a gradual homogenization of the structure of agriculture between the countries that follow the common path of European integration. It must also not be forgotten that the creation of an institutional framework for agricultural development common to all the member countries (i.e., of the Common Agricultural Policy) means the equal handling of unequal and different subjects, that is, of different member countries. This creates serious impasses and necessitates policies of a redistributive and structural nature.

Within the confines of a chapter in this volume, we think it will be useful to attempt at the beginning an analysis of the inequalities and the differences in the agricultural structure of twelve of the member states of the European Union (formerly the European Community), in order for the variety of the interests of the agricultural strata of all these countries to be understood.

Then we will go on to a brief analysis of the mechanisms of the Common Agricultural Policy. More concretely, we will analyze the reform attempt intended to confront the impasses in the implementation of this policy, which emerged from the inequalities in the agricultural sectors and the differentiation of the interests of the agricultural strata.

This analysis of the reform of the CAP will be used as an example to clarify the contradictions in the articulation of the interests of European farmers, as those interests are expressed by the European organizations COPA/COGECA/ CEJA. (These acronyms will be explained below under "The Role of the European Agricultural Organizations.")

AGRICULTURAL STRUCTURES IN THE EUROPEAN UNION

The countries which today make up the European Union display very different historical backgrounds with regard to their economic development and their internal economic structures. As a result, agriculture in each of the countries unavoidably holds a different position and importance in the country's overall economy. This is reflected in agriculture's contribution to GDP, to employment, to foreign trade, and also to the cost of food in the total cost of living.

As Table 5.1 indicates, the differences in the key figures of agriculture are exceptionally important. It can be observed from this table that most of the member countries of the EU with the smallest GDP per capita, that is, Greece, Spain, Ireland, and Portugal, have very significant agricultural sectors. In these countries, the importance of agriculture in the economy is greater than the EU average. That is to say, agriculture is an important economic activity, both in terms of income and the employment.

Nevertheless, from the data in Table 5.1, a different grouping of countries emerges, related to the importance of agricultural exports in the total exports of each country. It can be seen that in countries such as Denmark, France, and Holland, in which the agricultural sector is not very important, agricultural exports as a percentage of total exports are higher than the EU average. Finally, there are member countries, such as Great Britain, Italy, Germany, and Belgium, in which agriculture does not constitute a significant economic sector from any perspective.

The above observations demonstrate that within the EU there are inequalities with regard to agriculture which do not correlate precisely to the inequalities of income per capita. That is to say, there are "rich" member countries in the EU which have important interests in the maintenance and the development of their agricultural sectors. As far as the poor countries are concerned, the critical problem which they confront is the productivity of their agricultural sectors and, as a result, the viability of their farms, under conditions of the complete freeing of trade and of unimpeded competition within the Union. This problem becomes even greater given the present situation with the liberalization of international trade in agricultural products within the framework of GATT (General Agreement on Tariffs and Trade), as we will see in the following sections.

Table 5.1
Basic Indicators of Agriculture in the European Union (1989)

Characteristics	EUR. 12	B	D	G	GR
1. Percentage of active farming population in total active population %	7.0	2.8	6.0	3.9	26.3
2. Percentage of farm product in GDP %	3.0	2.2	3.8	1.6	16.4
3. Percentage of farm exports in total exports %	8.7	4.7	25.0	3.9	26.0
4. Percentage of farm imports in total imports %	12.9	11.0	18.1	10.6	16.2
5. Balance of trade of farm procucts (in billion ECU)	-21.5	-2.0	1.0	-6.6	-0.2
6. Percentage of family expenses for food in total family expenses %	20.4	20.6	22.2	16.5	38.5
7. GDP Per Capita in ECU	17,106	17,508	18,224	19,286	9,303
8. Inflation %	4.9	3.4	4.5	2.5	14.2
9. Unemployment %	10.2	10.4	9.1	7.0	7.5

Table 5.1 (cont.)
Basic Indicators of Agriculture in the European Union (1989)

	E	F	IR	IT	L	N	P	U.K.
1.	13.0	6.4	15.1	9.3	3.4	4.7	18.9	2.2
2.	5.1	3.2	10.9	4.1	2.3	4.2	5.2	1.4
3.	16.2	12.7	26.4	5.6	4.7	23.9	12.9	6.5
4.	18.8	12.0	9.7	15.2	11.0	15.1	28.6	11.1
5.	-2.4	0.5	0.7	-5.9	-	-0.2	-1.2	-5.2
6.	26.1	20.0	40.6	23.5	21.9	18.7	35.1	17.9
7.	12,969	18,567	11,467	17,761	20,767	17,615	9,438	18,182
8.	6.9	3.0	5.0	6.3	3.0	1.1	12.5	6.9
9.	17.2	10.7	17.9	16.6	1.4	6.0	6.7	6.4

Source: EUROSTAT, *The Situation of Agriculture in the Community* (Brussels, 1990).

As Table 5.2 demonstrates, the inequalities in the productivity of the agricultural sector between member countries are even greater than the inequalities in the position of agriculture in the economies of the different countries, which we saw in Table 5.1. Using the data of the Network of Farm Accounting Information, we find that the differences in the size of farms' value added per annual work unit (AWU—the productivity of labor) and agricultural income are very important. Regarding the average size of farms, the relation between the smallest, which is found in Greece, and the largest, which is found in Great Britain, is approximately 1:15, while the relationship between the productivity of labor on the farms (net value added per AWU) between Holland and Portugal is approximately 1:10. The same relationship exists with respect to agricultural income. This situation does not seem to change radically, at least for the five-year period for which comparable data are available for all twelve countries shown in the table (between 1983-84 and 1988-89). It is interesting to observe that although farm size does not completely determine productivity, given that there are different methods of production and different values of produce, it remains the most important determining factor.

In the advanced capitalist countries, such as Great Britain, the importance of agriculture to the economy is minimal, while at the same time farm size is the largest of all the EU countries for which data are presented. By contrast, in Greece, a country where for historical reasons capitalist relations were not able to mature, agriculture plays a predominant role in the economy and farm size is the smallest among the EU countries represented in Table 5.2.

The combination, however, of small farms and a large percentage of agricultural population on the one hand, and a low level of development of capitalist relations on the other, is not found in all the member countries of the EU. Countries such as Ireland, Portugal, and Spain have a relatively large average size of farms and at the same time a relatively large percentage of agricultural population, without being at the height of capitalist development. Nevertheless, in all three of these countries productivity is at a low level, approaching that of Greece (Portugal is at a lower level than Greece). From the above observations, it appears that each country has followed a different path of historical evolution, something which determines the characteristics of the agricultural sector, often independently of the "general rule" of capitalist development (Mouzelis, 1978). This already complex picture of the singularity of the agricultural sectors of the various countries of the EU becomes even more complex with regard to the penetration of capitalist relations into the process of agricultural production. Table 5.3 below shows the volume of family and wage labor which is employed in the agricultural sectors of EU member countries. The percentage of wage labor in agriculture, relative to the total volume of labor, may constitute an indicator of the penetration of capitalist relations into the agricultural production process in the member countries of the EU.

Table 5.2

Efficiency of Farm Holdings in the Member Countries of the European Union (1)

	Average per holding						11000 ECU	
	Area in ha		Employment in AWU (2)		Value of production		Intermediate consumption	
	83/84	88/89	83/84	88/89	83/84	88/89	83/84	88/89
Belgium	22.0	24.8	1.60	1.66	71.0	93.6	38.4	47.4
Denmark	32.7	34.0	1.31	1.08	85.1	86.5	54.1	52.3
Germany	27.1	29.4	1.75	1.66	66.2	77.9	41.7	45.5
Greece	6.2	6.4	1.94	1.80	12.8	12.8	4.7	3.9
Spain	35.2	27.8	1.30	1.30	21.7	22.2	12.0	10.5
France	36.6	43.4	1.69	1.66	49.3	68.6	24.9	34.7
Ireland	36.0	37.2	1.35	1.28	29.2	33.0	13.9	15.7
Italy	12.0	10.5	1.83	1.49	26.0	24.9	11.0	10.2
Luxembourg	43.7	47.9	1.73	1.68	61.9	81.7	35.7	40.9
Netherlands	19.7	21.9	1.85	1.97			75.2	85.4
Portugal	24.3	11.8	2.70	1.81	19.6	8.8	8.6	4.6
U. Kingdom		93.9	2.80	2.53			77.1	75.7
EUR. 12	--	4.5	--	1.13	--	33.4	--	16.2

(1) This is a representative sample of holdings of a professional orientation. For details, see the Decision 85/377/EEC.

(2) AWU = Annual Work Unit = 275 daily wages per year.

| | Average per holding in 1000 ECU | | | | | | | |
| | Amortization | | Net value added | | Net value added per AWU (2) | | Family income per AWU (2) | |
	83/84	88/89	83/84	88/89	83/84	88/89	83/84	88/89
Belgium	4.8	7.3	29.0	40.5	18.1	24.3	16.6	23.3
Denmark	7.4	8.9	23.5	24.9	18.0	23.1	7.7	5.9
Germany	9.3	11.7	15.7	23.0	9.0	13.8	6.2	11.0
Greece	1.2	1.4	7.4	3.8	3.8	4.9	3.5	4.6
Spain	1.1	2.6	8.7	9.0	6.7	6.9	7.7	6.9
France	6.2	8.8	17.9	24.6	10.6	14.8	7.9	10.9
Ireland	2.9	2.8	13.1	16.0	9.7	12.6	8.5	11.4
Italy	2.6	2.7	12.6	12.5	6.9	8.4	6.4	7.9
Luxembourg	8.4	12.7	19.6	28.4	11.3	16.9	10.4	15.1
Netherlands	10.0	17.8	43.4	57.5	23.5	29.2	19.7	25.2
Portugal	1.3	0.9	9.5	3.7	3.5	2.1	6.7	2.1
U. Kingdom	14.5	16.3	45.5	45.8	16.3	18.1	16.9	14.7
EUR. 12	--	5.1	--	11.7	--	10.3	--	7.4

(1) This is a representative sample of holdings of a professional orientation. For details, see Decision 85/377/EEC.

(2) AWU = Annual Work Unit = 275 daily wages per year.

Source: Commission of the E.C. *The Situation of Agriculture in the Community* (Brussels, 1987-1991).

Table 5.3
Volume of Family and Wage Labor Which is Employed in Agricultural Sector and Percentage of Multiple Employment of Farm Owners among the EC Members (Year 1987)

	EUR	B	D	G	GR
1. Total volume of Labor (1)	6968	99	113	850	847
2. Family Labor	5607	94	86	763	727
3. Percentage %	80.5	95.0	76.1	89.7	85.8
4. Wage Labor	1361	5	27	87	120
5. Percentage %	19.5	5.0	23.9	10.3	14.2
6. Number of farm owners (1000)	8272	92	85	690	953
7. %	100	100	100	100	100
8. Without other employment percentage %	69.8	67.2	67.2	57.0	66.6
9. With other primary employment percentage %	23.0	29.6	10.3	38.3	26.9
10. With other secondary employment percentage %	7.1	3.0	22.5	4.7	6.5

(1) Volume of labor in 1000 AWUs (annual work units).

	E	F	IR	IT	LUX	N	P	U.K.
1.	1624	1482	254	2198	6.7	234	935	520
2.	1281	1110	223	1905	3	186	821	310
3.	78.9	74.9	87.9	86.6	4.8	79.5	87.8	59.6
4.	343	372	30	293	3.7	47	114	210
5.	11.1	15.1	12.1	13.4	55.2	20.5	12.2	40.4
6.	1601	921	210	2750	4	129	619	220
7.	100	100	100	100	100	100	100	100
8.	70.4	68.2	63.5	76.0	81.3	76.4	61.7	76.1
9.	23.2	11.8	26.0	20.5	14.4	15.5	31.8	13.9
10.	6.4	19.9	10.5	3.4	4.4	8.1	6.4	10.0

(1) Volume of labor in 1000 AWUs (annual work Units).

Source: EUROSTAT, *The Situation of Agriculture in the Community* (Brussels, 1990).

From the data in Table 5.3, the largest proportion of wage labor in agriculture is seen mainly in the more advanced capitalist countries such as Great Britain, Luxembourg, Holland, and Denmark but with the important exceptions of Belgium, Germany, and France. The volume of wage labor in agriculture is connected not only with average farm size, but also with factors such as the intensity of production, the type of cultivation, and the degree of mechanization. One further important characteristic in which these agricultural structures and, of course, the social structures of the workforce in agriculture differ from each other is the multiple sources of employment of the farmers. From the data seen in Table 5.3, important differences can be observed in the percentage of farm owners who have primary or secondary employment other than farming. As can be seen from the data on sources of employment of farmers in the different member countries, the percentage of those who have other nonagricultural activities is directly connected in certain countries with average farm size (for example, Great Britain, and Greece). It is also connected to other factors such as the type of cultivation and the possibilities of finding other forms of employment outside agriculture. It does not appear, however, to be connected with the level of development of capitalist relations in the different member countries.

A comparative analysis of the basic structural characteristics of the agricultural sectors of the EU countries must take a number of factors into account. These include the importance of agriculture in the total economy, the average farm size, the productivity of agricultural labor, the degree of penetration of capitalist relations in the production process (as a percentage of wage labor relative to family labor), and, finally, the prevalence of multiple employment among farmers. It is clear that this wide range of forms is very difficult to classify.

These differences which characterize agriculture in the European Union, become even greater when one refers to the variety of produce, the differentiation in the methods of cultivation, and the production methods. These are issues, however, which cannot be dealt with in this chapter (Maraveyas, 1989).

The issue which concerns us here is that these structural differences, and the resultant large inequalities in the efficiency of agriculture between the member countries, form at the same time differences in the economic and political stratification of the farmers in the EU. This is because it is obvious that in countries where large farms dominate there will also be large-farm owners whose interests will not necessarily be the same as those of the countries where small farms and, as a result, small farmers dominate. Furthermore, the huge differences in the efficiency of agriculture between the EU member countries, a result of different production methods, and the average size of the agricultural plots also determine the behavior of the farmers of the countries in relation to the agricultural policy of the EU which is common for all the countries.

As can be seen from EUROSTAT data, inequalities in the size of farms, both between and within member countries, are very large. In countries such as Great Britain, 83 percent of the utilized agricultural area (UAA) belongs to farms larger than 50 hectares, while only 0.15 percent of the UAA belongs to farms smaller than 5 hectares.   The percentages for Spain, France and Luxembourg are above 50 percent for farms larger than 50 hectares, and between 2 and 10 percent for farms smaller than 5 hectares.   In contrast, in countries such as Greece, Portugal, and Italy, the percentage of UAA ownership by large farms of more than 50 hectares are 10 percent, 44.5 percent, and 31.5 percent, while for small farms up to 5 hectares the figures are 32 percent, 19.6 percent, and 20.1 percent (EUROSTAT data).

It is clear that the plethora of very small farms which exists largely in Greece, Italy, and Portugal also means a plethora of small farmers with very low incomes and a large degree of multiple employment. This different reality corresponds to interests and ways of expressing those interests which are completely different from those of the large producers in Great Britain, France, and so on.

It is obvious that different sizes and levels of efficiency exist not only between the northern and southern countries of the EU, but also within those countries.   However, in the case of the national agricultural policies of the individual countries, the political and the ideological power of the large farmers was, and remains, strong enough for the smaller farmers to ally themselves more easily with the interests and the demands of the larger farmers. In this way, the national agricultural policy, which is formulated almost always for the benefit of the large farmers and the wider national interests, is legitimized and becomes accepted even by small farmers as a state intervention in favor of the total agricultural sector (Servolin, 1989).

On the contrary, in the case of the Common Agricultural Policy, which concerns all the farmers in all the member countries, the inequalities between the member countries are added to those within the countries.   There are countries in which large farms and efficient farmers dominate and other countries in which the smaller and less efficient farmers dominate. Given the multinational nature of the European Union, it is not surprising that the terms have not yet been set for the political and ideological domination of the large farmers of the northern countries over the smaller farmers of the southern countries.   The contradictions between the farmers, while they are social, become unavoidably national within the framework of the European Union and the Common Agricultural Policy.   The national delegates of the individual member countries represent the interests of the farmers of their countries (as they clash at a national level).   However, because in some member countries large farmers dominate, and in others the smaller farmers do (relative to the Union average), the confrontation takes place between large and small farmers more on a European Union level than on a national level.   As we will see in the next section, from the moment it was conceived the Common Agricultural Policy brought forth this contradiction, which of course is not unique.

As was shown above, there is another important contradiction besides the differences in size and efficiency of the farmers in the member countries. This is found in the differences which exist in the size of the agricultural sectors and their importance to the national economies of the member countries. These differences determine the position of the ministers of agriculture in the member countries and also of their governments toward the elaboration and the application of the Common Agricultural Policy. They are not, however, directly connected with the differences in size and efficiency in every country. One could argue that the differences of the first order (size and efficiency) determine the positions of the member countries with regard to the basic philosophy of the mechanism of the Common Agricultural Policy, that is, the horizontal method of price support in contrast to a more differentiated system (depending on the volume of production of each farm). The differences of the second order (the importance of agriculture in the national economy) determine the position of the member countries with regard to the level of price support, which is connected with external protection and the liberalization of the international exchange of agricultural products.

The size-efficiency combination of farms and the importance of agriculture in the national economy have determined in the final analysis the behavior of the national states in the lengthy and ongoing negotiations concerning the philosophy and the orientation of the Common Agricultural Policy from 1958 until the present day (Philipe, 1986).

THE PHILOSOPHY AND THE ORIENTATION OF THE COMMON AGRICULTURAL POLICY

The Common Agricultural Policy is an initial compromise between protection and the free market, as it emerged from the balance of interests of the founding countries of the EU. Even among the goals of the Policy, which are defined in Article 39 of the Treaty of Rome, important contradictions are apparent. These goals were and remain the following:

Increase in productivity
Assurance of an adequate standard of living for farmers
Stabilization of markets
Guaranteed regular supply of agricultural products for the population
Assurance of fair prices for consumers

If the conditions of the development of European agriculture which were agreed upon in the conference in Stresa, Italy (1958), are added, it is apparent that even at the beginning there were differences in the interests of the founding members of the Common Agricultural Policy. Indeed, at that conference, the philosophy of CAP was recorded and formulated in the following way:

For European agriculture to become competitive, but for its familial character to be maintained

For agricultural prices to be higher than international ones but not high enough to lead to overproduction

For there to be protection from international competition but not for the European Union to become self-sufficient

As can be seen from the goals and the philosophy of CAP, even at the moment of the foundation of the EU, the differences in the interests of the six founding members could not be bridged

One can detect from the formulations of Stresa that France, primarily due to the importance of its agricultural sector, and Italy, mainly due to its small and less efficient farms, asked for high prices and external protection. At the same time Holland and Germany asked for a more liberal handling of the situation (against overproduction and autarky), the first because of the high productivity of its farms and the second because of the relative unimportance of agriculture in its economy.

It is interesting to note that thirty years later virtually the same differences between the agricultural interests of these countries can be observed. Even today these interests are determined by the importance and the efficiency of their agricultural sectors (See Tables 5.1 and 5.2).

The final form of CAP was a result of the individual national interests and of the objective possibilities of the period (Kazakos, 1978). Thus CAP was made up of two parts: the common market organization and the common structural policy. It was to be expected that the common market organization would take greater priority, in order to expand the customs union and to establish common prices of agricultural products which would be set by decision of the Council of the EU (then EEC) Ministers of Agriculture. At the same time, a system of intervention and protection was adopted in order to support those common prices in the internal market at levels higher than the international ones. The system of deficiency payments was ruled out because it would have been too expensive for the EU budget, which undertook the largest part of the support of agricultural prices previously undertaken by the national states. This system, which was then in place in Great Britain, allowed the prices of agricultural products to be formed freely in the market without support against, or protection from, international competition. The farmers, however, received the difference between the price defined by the market and the "minimum price" which was defined by the state. The cost of this system was borne by the taxpayers, not the consumers, and it was applicable in situations in which the farmers constituted a relatively small percentage of the population. Of course, under this system, the importation of commodities from non-EU countries would be free and the cost of food low. On the other hand, the supply of basic commodities from non-EU countries was not always assured (e.g., in case of war), and taxation would have to be increased.

A system of interventionist measures was finally chosen, in which the price in the market was high, supported by purchasing intervention (when there was excess supply) and, of course, by tariff protection against non-EU countries, at the expense of the consumer and of industrial development (high cost of food) (Bergman and Baudin, 1989).

This system, with variations, is still in place today for more than 70 percent of agricultural production, while the system of deficiency payments is in place only for some products such as tobacco and cotton. It is obvious that under this system, the farmers of the Union take advantage of prices higher than those which would have existed without external protection. However, not only do the consumers pay higher prices, but the budget of the Union is burdened significantly by purchasing interventions in cases of excess supply, and by export subsidies which are intended to make up the difference between the high internal prices and the prices in the international market (Maraveyas, 1992).

In the first two decades in which this system was applied, the 1960s and the 1970s, serious problems did not occur, given that the European Union had not yet developed its agricultural production sufficiently to have unsold surpluses. Table 5.4 shows the development of the Union's agricultural production in relation to internal consumption.

During the last decade the rate of increase of agricultural production in the EU was 2-3 percent per year, while the rate of increase per year of internal demand did not exceed 0.5-1 percent. The result of this development is that expenditures for price support are increasing, more and more excess products are being produced, and more and more purchasing interventions are being made; the same phenomena are occurring with export subsidies. However, in spite of the increased expenditures for price support, the real incomes of the farmers are decreasing due to the continuously increasing supply, which lowers prices.

Between 1975 and 1987 (prior to the first significant attempts at reform), expenditures increased by 164 percent while farm incomes (as value added per AWU) declined by 5 percent in real terms, despite the increase of total GDP by 31.3 percent and of the value of agricultural production by 26.5 percent (Maraveyas, 1992).

Obviously, the larger and more efficient farmers and, of course, the countries which have larger farms took advantage of this increase in expenditure. The price support mechanism pays those farmers back who produce larger quantities of agricultural products and thus leads to the concentration of expenditures in the hands of a few producers. Estimates of the EC Commission show that 80 percent of the expenditures are directed toward 20 percent of farms. This strengthens the already efficient farms, so much so that today (1990) in the EU, 6 percent of the grain producers are responsible for 60 percent of grain production and 15 percent of the dairy producers for 50 percent of dairy production (Commission of the EC, 1985).

Table 5.4
Degree of Coverage % of Internal Demand by the Supply of Agricultural Products in the EU

	1968-69 (EU of 6)	1973-74 (EU of 9)	1986-87 (EU of 12)
Cereals	86	91	111
Sugar	82	100	127
Butter	92	98	105
Cheese	99	103	106
Beef	95	96	108
Fruit	80	82	85
Lamb and Goat Meat	56	66	80

Source: Commission of the European Community (1991).

Some estimates indicate that the income benefits from the support and protection mechanisms of CAP are much larger per person employed in the sector for the Dutch than for the Greek farmers, for example, given that the productivity (product per person employed) of the Dutch farmer is ten times that of his Greek counterpart. With the average Union expenditure per farmer equal to the indicator 100, the Dutch farmer receives more than 150, and the Greek farmer less than 50 (Commission of the EC, 1987). Similar inequalities are observed more generally between the most and the least efficient farmers, the former usually dominant in the northern countries and the latter in the south. The same results of CAP mechanisms also appear internally in the member countries between the regions in which the farmers are more efficient and the regions in which the farmers are less so. (For Greece, see Maraveyas, 1992 and for France, see Bonnieux, et al., 1989.)

It is clear that the philosophy of the mechanisms of CAP benefits those larger and more efficient farmers and therefore contributes to the constant increase of production by any means, even at significant ecological cost, and the lowering of the quality of the agricultural products.

We must still underline that the support and protection mechanisms of CAP do not benefit only large farmers in general, but also some groups of farmers or regions that produce products with different levels of support and protection. Table 5.5 below shows the differences in external protection which exist between the different groups of products and consequently between the farmers and regions that produce them.

Table 5.5
Percentage of Nominal Protection %
    on Import Prices

Sugar Beets	163
Olive seeds	108
Cereals	64
Beef	49
Milk and Dairy Products	47
Wine	30
Pork and Poultry	23
Fruit-Vegetables	5

Source: Bonnieux, et al., 1989.

It is to be expected that the farmers, the regions, and the countries which produce more of the products with the higher level of protection benefit more. Of course, it is not by chance that the products which have a high level of protection are produced mainly by large farmers in the northern countries of the EU, that is, those who effected favorable adjustments during the initial period of formation of the Common Agricultural Policy.

All the above mean that significant income transfers are taking place, not only from the consumers and taxpayers toward the farmers at the level of the EU, but also between the consumers of some member countries and the producers of other member countries. To put it another way, there are member countries in which the farmers benefit more, and other member countries in which the farmers do not benefit a great deal. Table 5.6 shows the relevant calculations, which were made earlier, based upon the partial equilibrium approach, and measure the welfare effects of the protective mechanisms of CAP as much for the consumers and the taxpayers, as for the farmers.

It can be seen from the table that there are member countries which have a net benefit from CAP, given that their farmers benefit more than their consumers and taxpayers lose. This is due to the fact that in some countries the farmers produce more of the types of products with a higher level of protection and therefore higher prices. These products are exported to other member countries which produce products with lower levels of protection and as a result lower prices. Thus the consumers of member countries in which farmers do not produce products with high protection levels subsidize the farmers of the other member countries which produce and export such products. In contrast, the consumers of the latter countries benefit from the importation of the products which are produced in the former countries which have lower protection levels and as a result lower prices.

Table 5.6
Welfare Effects of the CAP by Member Country
     (Million Dollars 1980)

Country	Consumers	Taxpayers	Farm producers	Net welfare effect
Germany	- 12,555	- 3,769	+ 9,045	-7.279
France	- 7,482	- 2,836	+ 7,237	-3.081
Italy	- 5,379	- 1,253	+ 3,539	-3.090
Holland	- 1,597	- 697	+ 3,081	+ .789
Belgium	- 1,440	- 544	+ 1,624	- .320
Great Britain	- 5,174	- 1,995	+ 3,461	-3.708
Ireland	- 320	- 99	+ 965	+ .546
Denmark	- 635	- 320	+ 1,736	+ .799

Source: Demekas et al. (1988).

Finally, it must not be forgotten that the southern member countries with large agricultural sectors are, generally speaking, "poorer," and the farmers smaller and less efficient. But even when they produce products with low levels of protection, CAP expenditures are very significant for the income support of these small farmers. Despite the fact that the amount, in absolute size, of CAP expenditures corresponding to each person employed in agriculture is small, it forms a necessary supplement to their incomes. In addition, the large number of farmers in these countries results in a significant total benefit from CAP expenditures, given the structural weaknesses and the difficulties of the farm population in finding alternative employment in their rural areas.

REFORM OF THE COMMON AGRICULTURAL POLICY

All the efforts at reform of CAP toward the lowering of protection and consequently of prices confront the reaction not only of the large farmers and the countries in which they dominate, but also of the smaller farmers and, of course, of the countries in which they live. Of course, it would be in the interests of the small and less efficient farmers for CAP to be reformed in the direction of an increase in expenditures for the structural policy, even at the expense of external protection and as a result of the level of prices. However, the balance of power, as much between the countries as between the farmers, at least until the end of the 1980s, did not allow the balancing of expenditures between the policy for market organization and the structural policy for the improvement of the efficiency of the smaller and less favored farmers who dominate in the less developed member countries.

The structural policy section of CAP essentially began to become active in the early 1970s when the organization of the markets of agricultural products had virtually been completed. The Mansholt Plan (Commission des C.E., 1968), that is, the suggestions of the commissioner of the European Community for agriculture, which was submitted in 1968, was the motive for the EU to become interested, not only in the organization of the markets but also in structural change in the agricultural sectors of the member countries, something which its protective policy could not achieve through common prices for all the farmers.

The aim of the Mansholt Plan was the support of the agricultural sector in the member countries (then six countries) with the funding participation of the EU in order to become more competitive relative to third countries and later for the protective measures to be reduced and for international trade to be "freed." If this policy had succeeded, it could have replaced the policy based on price support and all protective measures. However, in order to achieve such an important structural change in European agriculture, that is, for external protection not to be necessary, according to the Mansholt Plan large farms would have to be created and the agricultural population of the EU reduced. That is to say, farm amalgamations would have to take place and group forms of agricultural production would have to be pushed forward. The above would have to be accompanied by general financial incentives and also by severance payments for those smaller or older farmers who would leave agriculture.

Resistance on the part of the member countries such as France, and also Germany, was significant because it affected the structure of family agriculture and led to an uncontrolled exodus from the agricultural sector during the beginning of the 1970's, a period in which the first signs of economic crisis had begun to appear. Thus, from the Mansholt effort for a change in the orientation of CAP and from the organization of the markets and the support of prices toward the structural policy, very limited results emerged. Three guidelines were formulated in 1972 for the modernization of farms, early retirement and the cessation of farming by farmers over fifty-five years of age, and the training of farmers. Later, in 1975, a further guideline was decided upon for the severance payment of farmers in mountainous and problematic areas, aiming at the maintenance of the population and the protection of the environment (Kazakos, 1978).

As mentioned above, until the end of the 1980s, despite the problems of the high expenditures on price support and the accumulation of surplus, the market policy and the price support with external protection constituted a crushing weight upon the structural policy. Table 5.7 shows the relevant expenditures for each section of CAP. The markets section absorbs 95 to 96 percent of the total CAP expenditures. From Table 5.7 we can also see that total CAP expenditures absorb 65 to 70 percent of the total budget of the EU and represent 0.50 to 0.60 percent of the total GDP of the European Union. From the above data it becomes clear that the expenditures for the organization of the markets and the price support policy had, by the end of the 1980s, reached very high levels, while simultaneously the decline in agricultural income and the accumulation of surpluses continued. At the same time, in 1986, the Uruguay Round of GATT negotiations had begun, in which CAP found itself targeted more so than ever before. OECD calculations show that for 1984-86, total CAP support for European agriculture was higher than that of the United States, Canada, New Zealand, and Australia, that is, of the large agricultural producing countries. The Producer Subsidy Equivalent (PSE) indicator (the PSE includes the income benefits to farmers resulting from the difference between domestic and international prices and all forms of expenditures for agriculture) was 40 percent for the EU, while for the countries referred to above it was 28.2 percent, 39.2 percent, 22.8 percent, and 14.5 percent respectively. Only Japan protects its farmers to a greater degree than the EU, with a PSE of 68.9 percent (OECD, 1988). On the basis of these calculations, the United States, assisted by the CAIRNS (i.e., the countries which met in Cairns, a city of Australia) countries, after the initial discussions which had taken place during the Uruguay Round of GATT negotiations, asked for the almost complete abolition of the protective mechanisms of CAP and of the protectionist policies of the other countries. Until then, the European Union had rejected the attacks of the United States and the CAIRNS countries in the previous rounds of GATT and had not even discussed the agricultural issue. During the Uruguay Round, it agreed to negotiate the decrease of the support and protection of its agriculture.

At the same time, since 1985 the Commission of the EU had put forward proposals for the reform of CAP which were summarized in the well-known "Green Book" (Commission of the EC, 1985) at the initiative of its chairman, J. Delors. These proposals were essentially the second real attempt at reform of CAP since the Mansholt Plan. They did not, of course, have the radical character of the Mansholt Plan, given that despite the signs of recovery, the European economy still had high percentages of unemployment, while the general economic conjuncture could not be compared to the "golden" decade of the 1960s. As such, these proposals contained ideas concerning the limitation of pricing policies, the reduction of land under cultivation, quotas of production, and guaranteed quantity limits on production. At the same time, ideas were put forward for the development of rural areas, not only with agriculture as a basis, but also with other forms of activities taking place in those areas and on the farms. In addition, the protection of the environment began to seriously concern the Commission, which aimed at the limiting of intensification and of the continuous increase of productivity through the unrestricted use of industrial inputs (fertilizer, pesticides, etc.). It is extremely interesting, however, that the

Table 5.7
Expenditures of the EU on Agriculture
   (in Million ECU)

	1983	1985	1987	1991
1. EU Budget	24,807	28,085	36,168	53,823
2. Total CAP Expenditures	16,539	20,463	23,835	34,640
2:1 %	66%	72%	65%	64%
3. Market Policy	15,811	19,744	22,988	32,386
3:2 %	95%	96%	96%	93.5%
4. Structural Policy	728	676	773	2,254
4:2 %	5%	4%	4%	6.5%
5. GDP (EU 12) (*)	2,593	2,975	3,509	--
2:5 %	0.55%	0.61%	0.53%	0.63%

(*) Billion ECU

Source: Commission of the EC, *The Situation of Agriculture in the Community* (Brussels, 1987 and 1992).

family character of farming was never questioned, while particular care was given to the maintenance of the population in the agricultural sector because of the high unemployment in other sectors of the economy, though with fewer support expenditures and less protection.

The difficulty in implementing these contradictory aims is obvious, something which can be seen from the problems encountered in the introduction of measures for the application of these reform proposals. Much deliberation took place between the member countries, between the farmers of all the countries and their governments, and of course between the Commission and the European organizations COPA and COGECA. Three years later, in 1988, some of these limiting measures for agricultural products began to be applied, accompanied by counterbalances of a structural nature in favor of the less efficient farmers and the poorer countries of the EU. The entire set of reforms, which was called the "Delors Package," contained a mechanism of production "stabilizers" with limits of guaranteed quantities the exceeding of which would result in an analogous price decrease. It was intended to generalize the coresponsibility of the farmers in the increase of dairy product production (which took effect in 1984) to almost all products (for the application of quotas to milk, see Petit et al., 1987).

The possibility of differential prices analogous to the quantity produced by farmers was contained in the application of the above described measure, so long as the small farmers were excluded from the coresponsibility, that is, from the lowering of the price when a certain production limit was surpassed. As a result, this could have been the beginning of a fairer distribution of income benefits in favor of the smaller farmers with a simultaneous decrease in the total agricultural production, and the lowering of expenditures and of production surpluses. The goal which was set then could have been achieved—for the yearly increases in expenditures for agriculture not to exceed 70 percent of the yearly increase in GDP.

At the same time that the stabilizing measures were being applied, voluntary measures were being taken for the withdrawal of land from production (set aside), the extensification of production, and of course the continuation of the freezing of prices decided upon by the Council of Ministers of Agriculture of the European Union (the freezing had begun in 1984).

During the same period, important structural policy measures started to be put into effect in order to counterbalance the income problems of the farmers, mainly the smaller and less efficient ones. Since 1985, a more systematic effort had been made by the EU toward the encouragement of farmers' investments in the modernization of their farms. At the same time, incentives were legislated to set up new farmers and to reforest areas which had been withdrawn from cultivation. Within this new legislative framework, the compensation of farmers in mountainous and less favored farming areas continued and was encouraged.

More concretely, however, at the same time, with the introduction of the system of "stabilizers," structural measures were legislated which concerned early retirement, land withdrawn from cultivation (set aside), extensification, and the restructuring of agricultural production toward products with high Union and international demand (Maraveyas, 1992).

The structural policy measures described above had the obvious goal not only to encourage the less efficient farmers who dominate in the less advanced member states but also to limit the volume of production. It could therefore be maintained that, confronted with the CAP impasse (surpluses, high expenditures, pressure within GATT to lower protection), the EU was leaning toward the interests of the smaller farmers without, however, those very farmers ever having struggled for this. It appears that a political and economic conjuncture is being formed in the 1980s and the 1990s at the expense of the interests of the large and efficient farmers and the countries in which these farmers are found. Of course, the decrease in protection with the relaxing of the protective mechanism strikes primarily those farmers who derived the greatest benefit from them, that is, the efficient ones. However, one should not overlook the fact that the decrease in protection, which results in the lowering of prices and a lowering of incomes, is more painful to the smaller and less efficient farmers and to the member countries in which they dominate, that is, the less developed of those countries. This fact, in combination with the wider processes of the realization of the common internal market with the complete abolition of all barriers which was also decided upon in 1986 (with the signing of the Single European Act), led the EU to a total reshaping not only of its structural agricultural policy, but also of the entire Union practice in favor of the less developed countries Greece, Ireland, Portugal, and Spain.

This reshaping led to a doubling of the resources for structural actions of the Union and included those which concerned only the agricultural sector. This development could be considered a logical result of the Mediterranean Integrated Program (MIP) which had begun to be applied in 1985 in Greece, southern Italy, and southern France (Maraveyas and Plascovitis, 1991). The MIP, without resulting in an increase of available Union resources for development aims, gave a different orientation to the problems of regional development. The mobilization of local resources (natural and human), the taking of responsibility for development policy by those local authorities with the support of the EU and the notion of a more complete and not sectoral development made up the new quality elements together with the coordination of the funding means of the EU (i.e., of the so-called structural funds—Regional, Social, and FEOGA [European Agricultural Guidance and Guarantee Fund]).

The increase in resources of the funding sources of the EU after 1988 and the coordination of their actions, together with the new elements which had in the meantime been applied within the framework of MIP, made up the well-known structural reformation and redistribution policy of the EU known as the Delors Package.

In the context of these developments, the farmers of the less developed member countries experienced the decrease of protection and of their incomes, but they were supported directly and indirectly by the new structural policy of the EU. The resources available for investment support increased, while at the same time the regional development policy created in stages a better infrastructure for agriculture, increasing in this way the efficiency of the farmers. Moreover, with the structural policy of the EU in favor of the countries with larger developmental problems, it was hoped to create employment for those farmers who would leave agriculture or would take on a second activity to supplement their income, which was being reduced by the reformed mechanisms of CAP.

The question is, of course, how much of a decrease in prices of agricultural products goes along with an increase in productivity (without a increase in production). This increase in productivity in turn is expected to emerge from the increased investment expenditures and the improvement of the infrastructure in agriculture, thanks to the doubling of the resources of the structural policy of the EU in favor of the less developed member countries. The implementation of this new structural policy after 1988 took place with the adoption of the Common Support Framework of the developmental effort of the less developed countries. This meant that 50 percent of the public investments were funded by the EU while 45 percent of the investments of the farmers came from EU funds in the four less developed countries (Commission of the EC, 1989).

However, as was seen later, the efforts at decreases in agricultural production and expenditures which were expected following the institution of the "stabilizers" and other limiting measures (set-asides, extensification, early retirement, etc.) did not pay back tangible results in the years immediately thereafter, 1989 and 1990. At the same time, the pressure from the United States and the CAIRNS countries for a relaxing of the protective mechanisms, for a lowering of subsidies, and for a decrease in EU production continued intensifying within the framework of GATT. The European Union presented proposals for the lowering of total support to European agriculture 30 percent by 1995 in order to achieve agreement in the final round of GATT in December of 1990. The American side rejected these proposals and the negotiations were interrupted without an agreement, as was expected after four years of discussions (1986-90).

The European Union found itself in a difficult position, agreeing with larger decreases such as those which the United States and the CAIRNS countries had discussed in GATT. The proposal of the 30 percent decrease in support led to protests by farmers in various member countries, and reactions of the governments of the member countries who saw not only that their farmers were unhappy, but also that their national economies were being damaged (Maraveyas, 1992). Given that some countries benefit more than others from the continuation of the system of protection of CAP, it was to be expected that those countries would have stronger reactions. Table 5.8 shows some estimates of De Veer and Thomson (Tarditi, et. al., 1989) referring to the costs and the benefits accruing to the member countries from the decrease in protection and support of agricultural products.

In spite of the fact that these estimates cannot be considered accurate measurements, they are nevertheless indications of the direction and the size of the benefits or the losses which each member country will incur. From the above it becomes clear that the countries with a significant agricultural sector as a percentage of GDP or the countries with significant agricultural exports will have either fewer benefits or greater losses than the other countries. More specifically, Greece, Ireland, Italy, Denmark, France, and Holland will carry the weight of the decrease of protection of their agriculture to a greater extent than Great Britain and Germany. The other two countries, Spain and Portugal, have not been considered in the calculations; however, given the importance of the agricultural sector in their national economies, they should be among the countries which suffer the most damage from the relaxation of the protective mechanisms of CAP.

According to other calculations, the European Union as a whole will incur significant damage to its trade balance of agricultural products on the order of 9 billion dollars from a possible abolition of protection in all the industrial countries (Roningen and Dixit, 1989). In addition, farmers will incur decreases in income of 35 billion dollars (Tyers and Anderson, 1988). On the contrary, the countries that are asking for a decrease in protection, that is, the United

Table 5.8
Welfare Effects

Country	De Veer		Thomson
	(1)	(2)	(1)
Belgium	+ 0.37	- 0.43	+ 0.37
Denmark	- 0.18	- 0.91	- 0.79
France	+ 0.30	- 0.84	+ 0.22
W. Germany	+ 0.42	- 0.39	+ 0.65
Greece	+ 0.71	- 2.00	- 1.16
Ireland	- 1.55	- 2.68	- 3.75
Italy	+ 0.65	- 0.88	+ 0.61
Holland	- 0.05	- 0.59	- 0.42
Great Britain	+ 0.47	- 0.39	+ 0.52
EEC 10	0.38	0.62	0.35

(1) Net total benefit % of GDP

(2) Net loss to farmers % of agricultural income

Source: Tarditi et al. (1989), pp. 100 and 117.

States, Australia, and New Zealand, will benefit in their trade balance of agricultural products on the order of 3, 2.2, and 2.4 billion dollars and in their agricultural incomes 0.2, 2.3, and 1.7 billion dollars respectively.

Despite the fact that the European Union as a whole will not benefit from the decrease in the support and protection of CAP as much as the other larger producers of agricultural products (and, of course, some countries will incur net losses of welfare), the balance of power in the world system is such that it will lead the EU to compromises in the agricultural sector in order for other areas of world trade to profit. At the same time, it must not be forgotten that neoliberal ideas prevail in the question of protection of the social group of farmers as well. The problem is that this social group, which was protected traditionally not only for obvious political and social reasons but also for economic and strategic reasons (availability of food), is exceptionally heterogeneous.

As mentioned above, the largest and most efficient farmers profit more from the protective policy, which to a great extent is the outcome of the balance of political power in the different member countries and as a result in the EU. It is therefore extremely difficult to change this policy if the balance of political power does not change in all member countries. There are, of course, member countries in which the balance of power at the political level, as well as the importance of overall national interest, results in a protective stance in the EU. In other countries, conditions allow a more liberal stance. Thus, according to the positions expressed in the Council of Ministers of Agriculture of the EU, France expresses the greatest resistance to the decrease in protection, accompanied by Italy, Spain, and Greece (AGRA-EUROPE, November 1992). Great Britain is found on the other side followed by Holland, Denmark, and less so by Germany.

The heterogeneity of the social group of farmers seems to have been utilized by Commissioner McSharry in the recent attempt at the reform of CAP. In his suggestions (Commission of the EC, 1991) to the Council of Ministers of Agriculture in 1991 he proposed a differentiation in the handling of small and large farmers. The loss in income from the proposed decrease of 35-40 percent in institutional prices of wheat and other products cultivated on a large scale during a period of three years 1993-96 (so as to become aligned with international prices) is completely compensated for by hectare support only for those farmers cultivating up to twenty hectares of agricultural land. For the larger farmers, compensation is given only when they reduce their cultivated land by 15 percent. At the same time, decreases in the price of beef are suggested. Compensation is given for the loss of income only to those who have up to ninety animals. Furthermore, the proposals include decreases in guaranteed quantities (quotas) in milk and tobacco, which means either a decrease in production or a decrease in price due to coresponsibility.

Despite the initial objections of the Ministers of Agriculture of the member countries, the proposals were finally accepted with minor amendments in June 1992, that is, within a year, which means that the political, social, and economic conditions were conducive to these radical changes in CAP.

It was the larger farmers and the countries with significant agricultural sectors which were damaged the most from these changes because of the decrease in the incomes of the former, and the decrease in agricultural production of the latter. At the same time, the partial disconnection of the income of the farmers from prices in the market (of course, the protected market of the EU) creates serious problems for the improvement of the efficiency of the small farmers. Dissuaded from the intensive use of industrial inputs for the sake of the environment, farmers at the same time were discouraged from the lowering of costs with the expansion of the production scale in the less developed countries. This deepened the already serious problem of the international competitiveness of their agricultural products. The expectation of financial compensation for the decrease in incomes of the smaller farmers without productive effort led, perhaps for the first time, to the differentiation of their stance from that of the larger farmers. Thus, the member countries in which small farmers dominate did not put forward significant objections to this reform. This, in combination with the relative decline in political strength of the larger farmers in the countries in which they dominate, made the other countries agree, judging that this would contribute to the achievement of an agreement in GATT.

It is true that this reform contributed to the initial agreement between the EU and the United States in November 1992 for the lowering of protection and the limitation of exports of EU agricultural products. In this agreement, which led to a successful conclusion to the GATT negotiations in Geneva on December 15, 1993, the only country which reacted strongly is France. The other countries which have significant agricultural sectors, or smaller and less efficient agricultural sectors, that is, Greece, Italy, Spain, and Portugal, limited themselves to lower levels of reaction and primarily asked for the exception of Mediterranean products from the regulations of the imminent agreement (AGRA-EUROPE and the International Press, December 10-12, 1992, Delorme and Clerc [1994]).

It seems at the outset of the present decade that the structure of interests in almost all of the member countries of the EU defines the balance of political power at the expense of the farmers generally, and specifically at the expense of the large and productive farmers, who are considered responsible as much for the high expenditures and cost of CAP as for the ecological burden to the environment from the intensification of agricultural production.

On the other hand, the role of agriculture, as much in the development process of countries or even of rural areas, continually diminishes. In contrast, the processing and manufacturing of agricultural products is developing rapidly. From this point of view, the lowering of protection, and as a result the prices of agricultural products, fosters the competitiveness of processed food. In addition, the development of ecological attitudes in all the countries and the demand for healthier food and a cleaner environment, constitute yet another factor pressing in the direction of the lowering of protection. The wider political strategic goals for the facilitation of the integration of the former socialist countries by the EU must also be added to the above. These countries, however, for example, Hungary and Poland, have significant agricultural production potential which cannot be exported to the EU due to the protective mechanisms of CAP. At the same time, the achievement of high productivity in a significant part of European agriculture guarantees the European Union that after the lowering of protection and of prices its agricultural production will not collapse, as would have happened fifteen or twenty years ago. The biggest problem, as much for the EU as for the member countries which still have many and usually less efficient farmers, is to devise appropriate structural measures to prevent an uncontrolled agricultural exodus. Another problem which arises for these countries, the hindering of the developmental dynamics of their agriculture due to the limitation of production and the lowering of prices, does not seem to be a serious factor in the formation of EU decisions. It seems that the income compensations and counterbalances, detached from productive effort, suffice. However, this policy condemns the less efficient farmers to become even less efficient.

THE ROLE OF THE EUROPEAN AGRICULTURAL ORGANIZATIONS

As analyzed above, European agriculture displays an exceptional multiformity including farmers whose size and efficiency vary as much between member countries as within them. The differences and inequalities concern not only incomes and the productivity of labor, but also methods of production, the orientation of production, the extent of capitalist penetration, and so on. The different paths of historical development of the member countries of the European Union and the different political and cultural traditions have led to these variations.

The application of a Common Agricultural Policy in the same way to all the farmers of the member countries clearly influences the agricultural production of each country in a different way. At the same time it creates interest groups which want to exert pressure for CAP to take an orientation which will serve their particular aspirations to a greater extent. During the three decades of the application of CAP, no one could maintain that there was a substantive convergence of the structures of agriculture between the member countries. The convergence and homogenization of agricultural structures had not taken place (until the accession to the EU) even within these countries, despite the fact the their agricultural policies were applied many years in the past.

CAP does seem to have succeeded in achieving a large increase in production and productivity, as already mentioned, and in hastening the process of the centralization and the concentration of farms. This process, which emerges unavoidably from the functioning of the capitalist system, was speeded up by the philosophy of CAP, which was to "reward" to a greater extent the more productive and usually larger farmers. Obviously the equal treatment of small and large farmers works to the benefit of the large farmers while the small farmers disappear in stages from the market. Thus, within thirty years the agricultural population of the Union declined from 20 percent to 7 percent (as an average of the twelve member countries). The result of the decline in the active farming population was a decrease in the electoral importance of farmers. Of course, the process of the enlarging of farms and the decrease in the number of farmers contributed to better organization of the professional interests of the farmers for two reasons. First, the educational level rose as the farmers became bigger and richer. Secondly, the articulation and promotion of interests became more effective as the farmers acquired a higher level of professionalism (Tsinisizelis, 1985).

Thus the influence of farmers as a professional class increased, while at the same time their arithmetic importance as voters declined, and as a result their influence on political parties. Of course, the above took place primarily in the northern countries, while in the countries of the Mediterranean south—Greece, Spain, Portugal, southern Italy—these processes were exceptionally slow-moving. A large number of small farmers continue to make up the electoral clientele of the political parties and the level of their professional organization is at a low level (Mavrogordatos, 1988).

Even from the moment of the creation of the EU, the professional organizations of the six founding countries played a deciding role in the shaping of CAP (Kirchner and Schwaiger, 1981). In spite of the fact that they had been officially invited to the conference in Stresa only as observers in order to have greater influence in the new circumstances which were being shaped with the founding of the EU, these organizations decided to found a committee to remain in Brussels in September of 1957. Immediately thereafter (April 1958) COPA (Comité des Organisations Professionnelles Agricoles) emerged, which was enlarged at the same time as the EU (Delorme, 1963).

Today, COPA includes thirty organizations from the member countries, which means that some member countries have two or more organizations which are members of COPA. For a national organization to be admitted to COPA, it must be representative of its country and it must represent farmers who are farm owners. COPA is the only expression of the interests of European farmers at Union level and is in dialogue with the Commission of the EU on agricultural issues on a daily basis. It employs permanent specialized staff in Brussels, while at the same time experts on agricultural issues from the member organizations work with specialists of the Commission on the preparation of the various regulations and guidelines which are made within CAP. The Commission of the EU passes very few measures which are not first discussed with COPA, that is, with the agricultural organizations of the member countries which make it up. As with the other organizations to which we will refer below, COPA has the following internal organization. There is a general assembly at which the organizations are represented by country members, that is, a country which has more than one organization does not have a larger number of votes than a country which has only one organization. Then there is a presidium in which all the organizations take part with one representative per country. Finally, there is a presidency, which is elected every two years and includes a president and two vicepresidents.

It is well known that COPA is considered the oldest and most important lobby group in Brussels. It coordinates, moreover, the activities of all the other agricultural organizations which are found in Brussels. The leaders of COPA (presidency) frequently meet with the ministers of agriculture, in the latters' role as presidents of the Council of Ministers, with the presidents of the special committees of the European Parliament, and of course with the current commissioner responsible for agriculture. These meetings are institutionalized, and are usually the top meetings of the mixed committees between the experts of COPA and the experts of the Commission. In addition, the presidency of

COPA confers with the leaders of the agricultural organizations of such non-Union countries as the United States, Japan, and so on.

A similar role is played by the Comite General de la Cooperation Agricole (COGECA), the Conseil Européen des Jeunes Agriculteurs (CEJA) and the European Federation of Agriculture (EFA). COGECA was founded in 1959 within the framework of COPA and is recognized as advisor to the EU on issues of agricultural cooperatives. It represents the national associations of agricultural cooperatives, shares a common secretariat with COPA, and participates, as does COPA, in mixed committees of the Commission of the EU on cooperative issues. Its internal organizational structure is the same as that of COPA.

CEJA is of particular interest, given that it represents the special interests of young farmers. CEJA was founded in 1959 and includes nineteen national organizations of young farmers. Some countries have more than one organization, but do not have more votes. It has a similar internal structure to that of COPA but no one can vote or be elected if they are more than thirty-five years of age. It does not participate in mixed committees with experts of the Commission like COPA. Nevertheless, the leadership of CEJA advises those politicians responsible for shaping of the CAP. CEJA was likely based upon a French prototype, the Conseil National des Jeunes Agriculteurs (CNJA). Its goal is not only to push forward the interests of young farmers, but also to study the problems which are faced by young farmers, and to this end it organizes seminars of scientific character in various member countries of the EU.

Finally, the European Federation of Agriculture (EFA) is another organization which protects agricultural interests, from the point of view of farm workers. This organization includes twenty-two national organizations of farm workers. At the same time these organizations are members of the European Confederation of Trade Unions (CES—Confédération Européenne des Syndicats).

These twenty-two national organizations not only represent agricultural and forestry workers but also the technical cadres and employees of the agricultural organizations and businesses, altogether approximately two million workers in the European Union.

EFA has as its basic goal to improve the conditions of life and work for wage laborers in the agricultural sectors of the EU. It is directly connected with the European Confederation of Trade Unions (workers in other sectors of the economy) and at the same time it participates in working groups which are concerned in particular with the agricultural sector. In 1977 it signed a charter with COPA referring to issues of common interest such as duration of work, seasonal labor, unemployment, yearly vacations, professional agricultural training, and so on (Lefebure, 1992).

Of the four European organizations which represent agricultural interests on a Union level, the latter cannot be considered to do direct lobbying in favor of the interests of the farmers who are farm owners. The interests, however, which they represent are directly connected with the development and the prosperity of the agricultural sector in which its members work. A possible decrease in agricultural production and, more generally, the shrinking of agriculture would create direct problems of unemployment for the members of this union organization. CEJA lobbies in a more direct manner because it represents farm owners who are beginning their careers and are worried about the future of their profession. On the other hand, COGECA lobbies to protect the cooperative idea, and contributes to the strengthening of isolated producers against the private businesses of the input sector (machines, fertilizer, etc,) and against the sector which processes and manufactures agricultural products. Of course, the interests of the manufacturers of agricultural inputs coincide with the protection of agricultural production, the support of agricultural prices, and the intensification of production. In contrast, the interests of the food processors clearly lean in the direction of the lowering of the prices of agricultural products and the support and protection of European agriculture. This would enable them to buy cheaper raw materials after the liberalizing of imports from third countries (Butt, 1982: 22).

It is interesting to note the composition of agricultural interests of the individual member countries at the level of the European organizations, mainly COPA and CEJA, which more directly express the interests of the farm holders of the member countries. First of all, the representation of member countries is not equal, and neither is it proportional to the populations of the respective countries. Thus, the five large countries have six votes, the smaller three, and Luxembourg two. The national votes can be divided if there is more that one organization in each country. The presidium is mostly controlled by the large countries France, Germany, Italy, Great Britain, and Spain, usually however by France and Germany, from which the presidents of COPA, CEJA, and COGECA generally come. Italy nevertheless is, in a variety of different ways, present in the "distribution" of the most important leadership positions. Great Britain and to a larger degree Spain do not have as much influence in the leadership echelons of these organizations. The smaller countries, that is, Belgium, Holland, Denmark, Ireland, and Luxembourg, participate actively but have difficulty attaining leadership positions unless disagreements emerge between the large "players" in the distribution of leading positions. Finally, Portugal and Greece, as smaller, poorer, and newer members, play a small role, except when they are needed to form majorities between the dominant "players."

At the level of alliances between the national delegations, nearly permanent alliances can be distinguished between France, Italy, Belgium, Luxembourg, Greece, and Ireland on the one side and Great Britain, Holland, and Denmark on the other. Germany is not a stable ally, as is the case with Spain and Portugal. These countries form alliances on the basis of the particular issues which are under discussion. The foregoing grouping does not mean that many other combinations do not take place in the negotiation of farmers' problems. Nevertheless, as far as the basic philosophy of CAP is concerned, that is, the level of agricultural protection and the support of the prices of agricultural products, the above stable alliances are almost always maintained (Tsinisiselis, 1990).

In most cases, the national delegations express nearly the same positions as their respective ministers of agriculture, which means that deliberations on a national level between the national governments and the agricultural organizations have preceded discussions at the European level. The question, of course, remains to what degree the farm organizations on a national level "articulate" the interests of all the farmers, that is, do they represent the small as much as the large farmers or even the producers (e.g., those who engage in cattle breeding as much as those who produce fruit)?

It is clear that on a national level in the agricultural organizations, the large and more efficient farmers dominate, and these farmers usually produce products of large cultivation or raise cattle and produce meat and milk, depending on the countries. Thus, for example, in the French agricultural organizations, the large cereals producers, the oilseed producers, the beef producers, and so on dominate. By contrast, in the Dutch agricultural organizations the cattle breeders and in particular those who raise cows dominate. It is to be expected that within the framework of COPA the larger producers who produce products of large cultivation and cow breeders will dominate. An important role is also played by wine producers (France) and olive oil producers (Italy). It is therefore not strange that the orientation of CAP benefited the large farmers and that some products are protected more than others, as can be seen in Table 5.5.

Furthermore, the domination of national organizations of the northern countries in COPA is given, while the problems of the Mediterranean countries Greece, southern Italy, Portugal, and Spain are systematically ignored or undermined. Efforts to create a Mediterranean working group within the framework of COPA and CEJA have to date not succeeded. This, of course, is due to the fact that the main Mediterranean country, Italy, was among those that shaped the basic philosophy of CAP. It must not be forgotten that the Mediterranean countries, which recently entered the EU, do not have significant historical experience of professional agricultural unionism, and as a result, at the level of the European organizations, they cannot oppose the experienced and well-organized national organizations of the northern member countries. It is nevertheless obvious that the new direction which CAP has taken since the middle of the 1980s is in direct opposition to the dominant agricultural interests which are expressed within COPA and the other European organizations. However, it cannot be seriously assumed that the new direction of CAP, which damages primarily the large farmers of the northern countries, is due to the lobbying capability of the smaller farmers of the southernmost countries. The small farmers are hardly in a position to enforce their viewpoints in COPA, as can be seen from the positions of this organization concerning the proposals of the Commission in favor of the small farmers (*AGRA EUROPE* on the financial support per hectare for farmers who cultivate less than twenty hectares, July 10,

1991). It is also well known that CAP is moving in the direction of the strengthening of a structural policy which serves the interests of the smaller farmers of the European south. However, the breadth of this policy is not great enough to resolve the problems which emerge from the decrease in protection and the limitations on production.

Moreover, the inability of the smaller and less efficient farmers of the southern countries of the EU to intervene dynamically within COPA cannot be resolved with interventions of a more political nature, for example, by the political parties of the southern countries, given the limited role of the European Parliament in the shaping of Union policies.

As has been analyzed by some political scientists, the limited participation of the European Parliament in the shaping of Union policies has strengthened the role of the professional organizations which function at a European level. These organizations are not only lobby groups but also carry out other functions essential to the shaping and the application of Union policy. They function as belts of communication between the Commission of the EU and the farmers, ensuring exchange of information during the shaping of the policy and its legitimization during implementation (Averyt, 1975). For this reason, the Commission of the EU has supported the existence and functioning of these European organizations from the time of the Union's foundation (Peterson, 1979: 27) and it funds a large part of the functioning expenditures of COPA, COGECA, and CEJA (COPA/CEJA 1992). The question which arises and demands further analysis is the fact that since the mid 1980s, the Commission has pushed forward and finally achieved the application in stages of the reform of CAP without taking into account the views and the reactions of COPA/ COGECA/CEJA, who were and remain radically opposed to the limitation of production (stabilizers), to the introduction of financial support per hectare, and of course to all the compromises with the United States and its allies, the CAIRNS countries, within the framework of GATT.

In this chapter, only interpretive working hypotheses can be presented, and these are as follow: (i) The agricultural organizations could not adapt to the new situation in the 1980s. In addition to the decline in importance of agriculture as an economic activity and the number of farmers in the member countries of the EU, it seems that farmers as a social group have ceased to be considered by society as a group which requires protection. The belief in social protection contributed in past decades to the achievement of the goals of the agricultural organizations because they had an ideological content in addition to an economic base (H. Delorme, 1963). The change in ideological orientation from social protection toward liberalism, the decrease in state interference, the limiting of expenditures, and so on, resulted from the beginning of the 1980s in a gradual weakening in the position of farm organizations and of the other union organizations. (ii) In addition, at the European level, the development of other common policies beyond CAP allowed the Commission to increase its political and administrative role, while at the same time the importance of CAP declined.

In the previous decades such a development could not have taken place, given that the largest part of the Commission's power was based upon the application of CAP, which moreover absorbed three-fourths of the EU budget. As mentioned above, the agricultural organizations at a European level were supported in different ways by the Commission, which, in administering virtually the only common policy in cooperation with COPA/COGECA/CEJA, gained power and an important *raison d'être*. With the development of other, primarily regional policies, the focus of interest of the Commission was relocated away from CAP and in other directions (Commission of the EC, 1992). Of course, the development of a regional policy appeared in part as a counterbalancing force to the lowering of support and protection of European agriculture, with the aim of confronting the problems which the continuation of the protection policy had created (surpluses, high costs, and the distortion of international trade) without imposing the cost of structural adjustment on the less developed countries and regions of the EU (Commission of the EC, 1992).

REFERENCES

Averyt, W. F. 1975. "Eurogroups, Clientella and the European Community," *International Organization,* Vol. 29, No. 4.

Bergmann, D. and P. Baudin. 1989. "Politiques d'avenir pour l'Europe agricole," *INRA/Economica,* Paris.

Bonnieux, F. et al. 1989. "La politique européene des prix et les problèmes agricoles régionaux français," *Revue du Marche Commun,* No. 326.

Butt, Phillip A. 1982. *Pressure Groups in the European Community.* London: George Allen and Unwin.

Commission des C.E. 1968. "Mémorandum sur la reforme de l'agriculture dans la C.E.E. Brussels. (Plan Mansholt).

Commission of the EC. 1985. "Green Book," Perspectives of the C.A.P." *COM* (85) 333 final, Brussels.

———. 1987. "Third Periodic Report on the Socio-economic Situation and Evolution of the Regions of the Community." *COM* (87) 230 final, Brussels.

———. 1987 and 1991. "The Situation of the Agriculture in the Community," Brussels.

———. 1989. "Guide for the Reform of the Structural Funds," Brussels.

———. 1991. "The Evolution and the Future of the C.A.P. (Propositions of McSharry)." *COM* (91) 100 final, Brussels.

———. 1992. "From the Single Act to Maastricht and the Beyond: The Means to Match Our Ambitions." Brussels.

COPA/CEJA 1992. "Séminaire Européen CEPFAR: L'information et la formation de futurs dirigeants agricoles," Brussels, February 6-8.

Delorme, H. 1963. "Le rôle des forces paysannes dans l'élaboration de la Politique Agricole Commune." *Revue Français de Science Politique.*

Delorme, H. and D. Clerc. 1994."Un Nouveau GATT?," *Les echanges mondiaux après l' Uruguay Round.* Paris: Coplexe.

Demekas, D. et al. 1988. "The Effects of the Common Agricultural Policy of the E.C. A Survey of Literature," *Journal of Common Market Studies,* Vol. 27, No. 2.

EUROSTAT. 1988. *Agricultural Yearbook.* Brussels.

Kazakos, P. 1978. *European Economic Community* (in Greek). Athens: Papazisis.

Kirchner, E. and K. Schwaiger. 1981. *The Role of Interest Groups in the European Community.* London: Gower.

Lefebure, B. 1992. "Les organisations professionelles agricoles européennes." In COPA/CEJA 1992, Séminaire Européen du CEPFAR. Brussels.

Maraveyas, N. 1989. *The Accession of Greece to the European Community: The Effects on the Agricultural Sector* (in Greek). Athens: Foundation for Mediterranean Studies.

———. 1992. *The Process of the European Integration and the Greek Agriculture* (in Greek). Athens: Papazisis.

Maraveyas, N. and E. Plascovitis. 1991. "Integrated Mediterranean Programs" (in Greek). Paper presented at the Forum of Delphi, June 1-3, Poros, Greece.

Mavrogordatos, G. 1988. *Between Pitiokampti and Prokrousti: The Professional Organizations in Greece Today* (in Greek). Athens: Odisseas.

Mouzelis, N. 1978. *Modern Greece: Facets of Underdevelopment.* London: The Macmillan Press Ltd.

OECD. 1988. "Agricultural Politics, Markets and Trade." In *Monitoring and Outlook.* Paris.

Peterson, M. 1979. "International Interest Intermediation and Transmutation of Postwar Society." Department of History, University of Gothenburg, Bulletin No. 18.

Petit, M. et al. 1987. *Agricultural Policy Formation in the E.C.: The Birth of Milk Quotas and CAP Reform.* Amsterdam: Elsevier.

Philippe, B. 1986. *Politique agricole européenne et marches mondiales.* Paris: Economica.

Roningen, V. O. and M. P. Dixit. 1989. *Economic Implications of Agricultural Policy Reforms in Industrial Market Economies.* ERS Staff Report AGES 89-36 USDA.

Servolin C. 1989. *L' agriculture moderne.* Paris: Seuil.

Tarditi S. et al. 1989. *Agricultural Trade Liberalization and the European Community,* Oxford: Clarendon Press.

Tsinisizelis M. 1985. "The Politics of the CAP: A Study of Interest Group Politics." Ph.D. Thesis, University of Manchester.

———. 1990. "Neo-corporatism and the Common Agricultural Policy: The Case of Adjustment of the CAP." Paper presented to the European Consortium of Political Research, Bochum, Germany. April 3-7.

Tyers, R. and K. Anderson. 1988. "Liberalizing OECD Agricultural Policies in the Uruguay Round: Effects on Trade and Welfare." *Journal of Agricultural Economics,* Vol. 39 No, 2.

6

Asking for the Moon: The Political Participation of Immigrants in The European Union

Patrick R. Ireland

With the Treaty on European Union having now won passage in all fifteen member states, the European Union (EU) is trying to implement its ambitious plan to achieve economic and political unity. The treaty, drafted by the European Council at Maastricht in December 1991, reconfirms the Union's commitment to remove remaining restrictions on the free movement of goods, services, capital, and persons. As the EU heads of government and the EU Commission and the European Parliament have acknowledged, this project cannot succeed unless they develop a coordinated approach toward both regulating immigration and the influx of refugees and integrating the over eight million foreign workers and their families from outside the EU ("third-country nationals") who reside in the Union.[1]

The construction of Europe, therefore, has direct consequences for foreign-origin populations. Given the high stakes, one might expect the EU to serve as an active stimulus and focus of immigrant political mobilization. Have immigrants responded to institutional developments in the Union, fashioning European-level modes of political participation? And especially, how have the children of the foreign workers that Europe recruited after World War II reacted? Second-generation immigrants belong to Europe perhaps more than to the "homelands," and their political responses to European integration can indicate its nature, depth, and limits.

I argue here that European integration has indeed had a political "spillover" effect on immigrant communities.[2] They are generating new, European-level forms of organization and lines of solidarity. However, even more than indigenous Europeans, foreign-origin populations have run into barriers when trying to gain a say in the EU policy-making process. The distance separating immigrants from the Union and its policies, the Union's institutional structure and the trend toward intergovernmental bargaining, the diversity of national immigration policies, and the specific actions of EU authorities have all hampered immigrant participation. A legal wedge has been driven between EU and third-country nationals, and between second-generation immigrants and their parents. That they are beginning to find their European political voice in spite of such obstacles speaks to both their growing political sophistication and their fear that European unification might take place at their expense.

THE BARRIERS

Foreign-origin communities in the European Union confront a range of factors that make political mobilization at that level problematic. Civil society plays a weak role in the development of EU policy in general, and immigrants are not alone in finding it hard to penetrate the closed political world of the "Euristocrats."[3] Lacking most traditional political resources, however, foreign workers and their families have faced especially knotty problems.

The Distance from Brussels

The machinations of the EU, first of all, seem even more removed from immigrants' daily lives than from those of member-state citizens. Many noble pronouncements have emitted from Brussels and Strasbourg, but the EU has never made immigrants' needs and concerns a focus of concerted action. Immigrants "cannot attack Europe, because it is too far away and too abstract."[4] Their general awareness of the European Union and its activities has been very low. The struggle to make a living and to integrate into the host society occurs not at the European level but in the poor, working-class neighborhoods and decrepit housing projects of the continent's industrial metropolises. The young, whose socioprofessional integration has stalled in every EU member state, feel alienated in their own communities and are unlikely to seek answers from a "state of courts and technocrats."[5]

The Structure of the European Union

The institutional setup of the EU, moreover, has complicated matters for the Union's policy makers and migrants. European governments have responded to the foreign presence that their postwar labor policies created in an ad hoc manner that has exacerbated social tensions. The shortcomings of national immigration policies have heightened pressures for the Union to intervene.

It has been slow to do so. The EU has a "multitiered" structure: there is a "pooling of national sovereignties" but no truly federal system.[6] This political architecture has resulted in bitter fights between EU institutions over the locus of policy control. The European Parliament (EP), with the least power, has been the most solicitous toward immigrants. From an early date it advocated harmonized immigration and refugee policies and called for the sociopolitical integration of non-EU workers and their families. The EP has harshly criticized the EU Commission and Council of Ministers for dragging their feet and allowing antiforeigner sentiment to escalate dangerously.[7]

The European Court of Justice (ECJ) in Luxembourg, for its part, has displayed remarkable activism. EU law generally has direct effect: it becomes part of the *acquis communautaire* that domestic courts must enforce. The Court reviews the legal status of acts undertaken by Union institutions, supervises member-state compliance with the founding treaties and secondary Union legislation, and interprets EU law for domestic courts.[8] The Court has strived to rise above and mitigate the interinstitutional squabbling that has so often paralyzed the EU.[9]

In the meantime, to whom should immigrants direct their demands at the European level? The justices of the Luxembourg Court are not amenable to pressure group lobbying. The institutional turf battles and the weakness of the European Parliament have combined to reduce seriously the EU as a locus of immigrant political interest.

The Trend toward Intergovernmentalism

At the same time, the EU's multitiered institutional setting has hindered it from taking affirmative steps to manage immigration. When they shut their doors to new inflows in the mid-1970s, the host societies did not eliminate the "push" factors in Africa, Asia, and the Middle East that produced them. Family reunification added to legally resident foreign-origin populations, and much of the remaining influx simply streamed into clandestine and refugee channels.

Pressures to harmonize member state policies continued to build. Instead, only loose policy coordination has ensued, which has further discouraged immigrants from addressing their political demands to the EU. Cooperation between member state governments—outside Union institutional control—has become the preferred mechanism to reconcile national sovereignty and European interests.

In 1975 civil servants from the justice and interior ministries of the then nine member states came together for the first time as the so-called Trevi Group.[10] They set up a number of subgroups to develop joint approaches to terrorism, drugs, threats to public order, crime, and immigration. In their secret regular conferences they have acted as an intergovernmental coordinating and planning instance.

By the mid-1980s the European Union's project for a single market was exacerbating fears that the absence of true policy harmonization would allow member states to "dump" their immigration-related problems on their neighbors. In the end, though, national governments issued a declaration subsequent to the drafting of the Single European Act that affirmed: "Nothing in these provisions shall affect the right of member-states to take such measures as they consider necessary for the purpose of controlling immigration from third countries."[11]

Those member states have developed lowest-common-denominator strategies. The governments of Germany, France, and the Benelux countries, most notably, worried that Europe was too leisurely in implementing free movement. They decided to move ahead on their own and in June 1985 agreed in Schengen, Luxembourg, to remove all controls at their common frontiers by New Year's Day 1990.[12] Spurred by the example of "Schengenland" (now including Austria, Italy, Spain, Portugal, and Greece) an Ad Hoc Immigration Group emerged within the secretariat of the Council of Ministers in 1986 to work out (behind closed doors) the technicalities of removing of internal border controls.

In the years since, European Union heads of government—meeting biannually as the European Council—have taken the lead.[13] The 1988 Rhodes summit spawned the Group of Coordinators to oversee all work in EU bodies on asylum, immigration, customs, judicial, and security policies. The 1990 Dublin summit produced a convention on political asylum. The rights and the integration of third-country nationals, meanwhile, have been downgraded to a very long-term objective.

The Treaty on European Union, too, does more to strengthen national governments' veto power than to provide the EU with new institutional capacity. Articles K.1-9 of Title 6 of the accord lay out the three main areas in which common policies will be necessary and appropriate for its implementation: a common policy on visas, asylum, and the crossing of external Union borders; institutionalized judicial and police cooperation (Europol); and a Protocol on Social Policy. It drops earlier references, including those in the nonbinding 1988 Community Charter of the Fundamental Social Rights of Workers, to "living conditions" (i.e, housing, education, health, and social rights). Social integration, in a word, will no longer be on the Union docket.

In its final form the Maastricht accord says nothing about the institutional framework within which joint action is to be produced, which effectively falls to intergovernmental compromises on issues of "common interest" that relate to the principle of free mobility. Three new Steering Committees are to supersede the existing intergovernmental committees, yet the same people will sit on the new bodies: Steering Committee No. 1 (replacing the Ad Hoc Group) will treat immigration and asylum, No. 2 (replacing the Trevi groups) will deal with police and security issues, and No. 3 will oversee judicial cooperation. The Steering Committees will send their statements and proposals to a new Coordinating Committee (replacing the Rhodes Group), and COREPER

(Committee of Permanent Representatives) will be more directly involved than before.[14]   The treaty explicitly authorizes closer cooperation between two or more member states—in other words, Schengen-style arrangements.   In the immigration policy area, as in others, Maastricht embraces the "subsidiarity" principle: EU legislation is appropriate only when "legal security and uniformity provided by Community law constitutes the best instrument to achieve the desired goal."[15]

Diverse National Immigration and Other Policies

Thanks to the intergovernmental approach, immigrants in the Union still live and work within very different national policy frameworks. EU member states, the major players in the multilevel Union game, have not experienced immigration pressures to the same degree. Their foreign populations vary in size, regional concentration, and ethnic composition. In the face of such heterogeneity, governments have provided divergent policy responses.

Immigrants cannot escape domestic political and legal contexts. Non-EU nationals' rights to choose their employer, occupation, and place of residence normally expand the longer they live in a host society, yet the rate has been different in each. Residence permits have varied widely in their duration within the Union, often changing over time even in a single member state. Sometimes they have been linked to work permits (France), and sometimes not (Denmark, Greece, Ireland). National policies have likewise diverged with respect to political rights, family reunification, access to public education and state-subsidized housing, visa requirements, and measures to control illegal immigration and to combat racial and ethnic discrimination.

For second-generation immigrants the institutions of citizenship in each member state have loomed as most critical. Nation-states have held to their distinctive citizenship laws and naturalization procedures.   In attributing citizenship at birth, Germany, Denmark, Ireland, and Portugal emphasize parentage and blood ties (the principle of *jus sanguinis*) to varying degrees. Elsewhere birthplace (*jus soli*) more or less determines citizenship. Naturalization procedures, too, range from extremely liberal (in the Netherlands: five years' residence, minimal knowledge of Dutch, and no criminal offenses) to highly protectionist (in Germany: ten years' residence and strict requirements regarding language skills, employment history, and "attitude"). Britain, France, Ireland, and Italy allow dual citizenship, whereas Germany and Denmark expressly forbid it.[16]

Such differences have had a major impact on second-generation political organizing.   Some member states have witnessed the formation of bona fide social movements, whereas others have not.   In France second-generation immigrants' socioprofessional opportunities have been severely limited.   But since they can or will acquire French citizenship, what was once a mere "social category" (a group of individuals sharing recognized common traits) is becoming a "social actor" (a group having a collective identity on the basis of which it intervenes in the sociopolitical realm). By contrast, where even youngsters born and raised in a host society enjoy no special access to citizenship, their political marginalization and passivity can be nearly complete.[17]

The Actions of EU Officials

The EU's institutional structure, in sum, has restricted democratic input and has given fairly free play to national governments. Furthermore, Union authorities have themselves compounded the obstacles to European-level immigrant political mobilization. They have exacerbated discrimination between immigrants from within and outside the EU and have weakened the efforts of immigrant-origin associational movements to achieve transnational solidarity.

The Treaty of Rome, which laid the foundations for the European Economic Community (EEC) in 1958, provided for the progressive acceptance of complete labor mobility between signatory states. The Union has made significant advances toward that ideal. The five million resident migrants from within the EU command key rights when they move about the Union. They and their dependents have gained equal treatment in housing and social assistance; trade union rights; the right to remain in another member state after suffering permanent disability or involuntary unemployment; and a limited right to retire and look for employment in another member state, aggregate social security contributions, and "export" pensions. Upon demand legal EU workers receive a residence permit, valid for five years and automatically renewable. Member states can restrict freedom of movement and establishment for reasons of public safety and order, national security, and public health; then again, the European Court of Justice has defined these limitations very narrowly.[18]

Third-country nationals, in contrast, do not enjoy free movement. Member state prerogative still governs their entry into the Union and its labor market. True, the ECJ has expanded the Union's definition of "worker" and has handed down decisions that secure non-EU workers the same social, employment, and fiscal rights as EU nationals.[19] But the member states have continued to discriminate between EU and non-EU migrants. The Treaty on European Union, accordingly, advances a "Union citizenship." First discussed in 1974 and revived by the Spanish government in 1990, it would allow EU and legally resident third-country nationals to seek judicial redress in any member state, direct a petition to the European Parliament, and register complaints with the EP's Ombuds(wo)man. Another provision of this citizenship guarantees EU citizens meeting certain residency requirements the right to vote and run for office in local and European elections. In order to promote a "European consciousness," the Union thereby underscores the difference between EU and third-country nationals.[20]

The same tactic has been evident in the EU Migrants Forum. The late Greek MEP Evregenis prepared a report for the committee of inquiry examining the rise of fascism, racism, and xenophobia that was presented to the EP in 1985. It sparked the idea of assembling a forum where people of immigrant origin could find their political voice and enter into a dialogue with European institutions. Drawing on that report, as well as those drawn up by MEPs Heinz-Oskar Vetter (SPD, Germany) in 1987 and Glyn Ford (Labour, Britain) in 1991, the EP passed a resolution to set up such a body. The Commission, meanwhile, had come to believe that self-help movements had the potential to serve as critical tools by means of which "least-favored populations" like foreign workers and their families might effect at least some degree of social integration.[21] The Commission spent a year surveying and talking with immigrant associations, then assembled a constituent assembly that elected a preparatory committee, and in May 1991 the EC (EU) Migrants Forum resulted.

Southern European immigrants argue that EU citizenship has not guaranteed them equal treatment in the Union. Refusing to grant special status to EU citizens, the Commission nevertheless decided to exclude them from the Forum. The 110 immigrant organizations from throughout the Union who participate in the body represent more than fifty nationalities and most political persuasions. Yet all of them mobilize only third-country nationals. Responding to the criticism that these organizations are not representative, the director of the Migrants Forum, Stany Grudzielski, contends that it is up to public officials to set out the criteria for selecting appropriate interlocutors. And in any event, "The issue should not serve as the pretext for rejecting outright an institutionalized dialogue, which is indispensable for democracy."[22] At the Forum's general assembly in 1992, MEP Djida Tazdait, a French Green and second-generation North African, summed up its mission: "I urge the General Assembly to carve itself out a position of influence, and to lobby hard in order to carry weight in European politics. . . . [T]he main goal is to be able to represent the 8 to 9 million extra-Community residents to make sure that they do not suffer in full force from the construction of Europe."[23]

Critics have argued that the EU Migrants Forum spends too much of its 500,000 ECU annual subsidy promoting dubious pet projects. Member associations have focused on multicultural educational programs for second-generation immigrants; but they limit their concern to instruction in the language and culture of the homelands. Another top priority has been a campaign for the naming of a special European Commissioner to spearhead the fight against racism. The Union has rejected this proposal before and is unlikely to accept it any time soon: the Forum is "asking for the moon."[24]

SURMOUNTING THE OBSTACLES

The Forum does represent at least a first move toward opening EU political access for immigrants. And however difficult it might be to organize interests at a European level, there have been other attempts to overcome the barriers. Some efforts have occurred under the auspices of homeland governments, Islamic groups, trade unions, and sympathetic nongovernmental organizations (NGOs). Foreign workers and their children have also engaged in autonomous action. Though yet tentative, these initiatives demonstrate the Union's growing relevance for the immigrant communities.

Homeland-Oriented Participation and Islam

The immigrants' homeland governments, first, have constructed webs of consular services and other official organizations in EU host societies. Officials from Algeria, Mauritania, Morocco, Senegal, Tunisia, and Turkey have formed organizational networks to serve more as a means of control than representation. By comparison, southern European governments have maintained emigrants' identification with the homelands while tolerating their political and associational diversity.

As the immigration issue has acquired a European dimension, so has homeland-oriented participation. Italians resident abroad have cast ballots in elections to the European Parliament since 1979, as have Iberians and Greeks since the 1980s. Italy, Spain, Portugal, and Greece have intervened with the EU Commission and the European Court of Justice on their expatriates' behalf.

Non-EU homeland governments have adapted their approach along similar lines. The bilateral agreements that Western European governments signed with their labor-exporting counterparts after the war focused on worker recruitment. But they generally included provisos concerning the host society's responsibilities in terms of family reunification, housing, and equality of treatment of the workers and their dependents. As these agreements lapsed or fell into disuse, the EU (initially the EEC—European Economic Community) stepped into the breach. Empowered by the Treaty of Rome (Article 238) to reach treaties with third countries, the EU entered into five agreements dealing with worker mobility: the 1963 association agreement with Turkey, and cooperation agreements with the former Yugoslavia (effective in 1983, abrogated in 1991) and the Maghreb countries of Algeria, Tunisia, and Morocco (effective in 1978). Homeland governments—the Turks, Moroccans, and Algerians in particular—have protested the EU's failure to grant third-country nationals full freedom of movement and equal rights and protections.[25]

Islam's emergence as a pole of political and cultural mobilization for non-EU immigrants has upset many member states. They have dealt with the religion quite differently, ranging from a national ethnic community model in

Britain and the Netherlands to Germany's complicated federal setup that leaves religious matters up to the *Länder*. Only Belgium, meanwhile, has a bona fide Islamic policy.[26]

A number of foreign-directed religious movements have united segments of Europe's Muslims: the Saudi-based World Islamic League, the Iranian-backed Islamic Council of Europe, the pietist Sunnite *Tabligh* movement, the Turkish *Diyanet Isleri Baskanligi*, the Libyan Committee for the Islamic Vocation, and several militant terrorist organizations. Fear of Islamic fundamentalism has spurred the EU to improve relations with Islamic immigrants, their organizations, and their homelands. Authorities there have welcomed such contacts in the interests of security and political stability: "A spirit of solidarity against Islamic fundamentalist movements has created ties of complicity comparable to those found in the struggle against left-wing movements in other circumstances."[27] North African and Turkish authorities have obtained European assistance in controlling their domestic opponents, and in return they have assisted in the battle against terrorism and hostage taking in the Middle East.[28]

Trade Unions

Homeland-oriented participation has remained significant. Yet as immigration has become a durable, family affair, the immigrants' political demands have come to revolve more around the concrete problems of life in Europe. Since the first generation arrived as workers, they logically first mobilized to influence EU member state policies in the factories. There they have had their strongest legal position and most equal rights of representation. Even at that, they remain underrepresented in most of the national labor movements in the EU.

European-level collaboration between labor organizations remains embryonic. The most promising effort has been the European Trade Union Confederation (ETUC). Whereas its origins go back to the European Coal and Steel Community in the early 1950s, the ETUC emerged in its present form in 1973 to "act as a credible counterweight to the employers' European organizations and to pressure national governments to accede to the member-unions' demands."[29] The ETUC has urged the EU to do more to integrate immigrant workers from inside and outside the Union.

Unfortunately, the ETUC has not been in a position to champion their interests. For just as the member states have all had their own migratory history, so too has each had its own industrial and labor movement history. Differences in national labor markets and legislation have impeded common trade union mobilization. ETUC leaders have had their hands full fighting for the proposals on industrial democracy in the Social Charter. The Treaty on European Union codifies the Union's intention to have the ETUC and the employers' organizations work together on community legislation in the social sphere on a compulsory, consultative basis. To date, however, the European Employers' Association (UNICE) and the European Enterprise Center (CEEP) have achieved a far greater degree of effectiveness.

The ETUC's objectives, after all, are not as narrowly focused, and its constituent units not nearly as unified. The confederation grew out of a core of trade unions close to socialist and social democratic parties in the EU and EFTA countries. "Secularized" Catholic unions have been welcome, but not those with links to hard-line communist movements.   Major trade unions with large immigrant memberships such as the French CGT and the Portuguese CGTP are not ETUC members. The Spanish workers' committees (*comitados obreros*) did not win admittance until 1990.

Today, the ETUC includes forty-six member unions from twenty-two European countries. The two largest member unions, the German DGB and the British TUC, have trouble controlling their affiliate unions and little stomach for truly European syndical action; French, Italian, and Belgian confederations have pushed in just that direction. Sixteen sectorally based confederations (*comités syndicaux européens*) further complicate the organizational picture. Moreover, the ETUC prizes a consensual decision-making process; a two-thirds majority is necessary for passage on every vote. This arrangement yields vague, general proposals that have failed to improve immigrant workers' lot.

The Council of Immigrant Associations in Europe

More effective than the ETUC in enabling immigrants to articulate their political demands at the European level have been the joint initiatives of national-level immigrant associations. Cross-national linkages have strengthened in direct response to the growing importance of the EU for the Union's foreign-origin populations. The first European Conference of Immigrant Associations brought activists from six host societies to Amsterdam in 1971. Succeeding conferences produced lists of common demands addressed primarily to national governments.   In 1985, just after the introduction of the SEA, the fourth Conference of European Immigrant Associations opened in Stockholm. Delegates there called on the Union to fight racism, integrate resident foreigners, and allow EU and non-EU nationals to participate in elections to the European Parliament.[30]

At the conference an autonomous European immigration associational movement was born. Its executive body, the Council of Immigrant Associations in Europe (*Conseil des Associations Immigrées en Europe*—CAIE), includes representatives of over 2,500 immigrant associations. The CAIE has stressed inclusiveness over doctrinal purity and welcomes a wide range of class- and ethnic-based associations. Sitting on the CAIE are the largest single-nationality immigrant federations—representing hundreds of local and regional associations—in the EU fifteen, and Switzerland: the Assembly of Portuguese Associations in Europe, the Association of Young Spanish Immigrants, the Coordinating Group of Spanish Immigrant Associations in Europe, the Federation of Italian Workers and Families in France, and the European Council of Moroccan Associations (CEDAM). Alongside them are national, multiethnic coordinating bodies from France (Conseil des Associations Immigrées en France—CAIF), Britain (National Ethnic Minorities Council), the Netherlands (Landelijke Samenwerking van Organisaties van Buitenlandse Arbeiders), Luxembourg (Comité de Liaison et d'Action des Immigrés), Germany (Bundesarbeitsgemeinschaft der Immigrantenvereine), Sweden (Federation of Cooperating Immigrant Associations), and Belgium (Comité de Liaison des Organisations des Travailleurs Immigrés).[31]

Headquartered in Brussels, the CAIE monitors and reacts to developments in European integration as they affect immigrant-origin communities. The organization holds an annual European Summer University on Migration to train associational leaders and raise consciousness. The CAIE was the first immigrant association to initiate consultative discussions with EU officials. It has criticized a number of EU resolutions and directives and has filed complaints with EU officials against host-society governments whose laws or administrative procedures violate the principle of nondiscrimination.[32]

Like the national-level multiethnic networks that form a major component of its membership, the CAIE has had problems attenuating the strains caused by divergent treatment of European and non-European immigrants. Achieving equal rights for all has become a centerpiece of the CAIE program. The European Commission angered its leaders both by bypassing the CAIE when it established the Migrants Forum and by limiting participation to non-European associations.

Many CAIE member associations take part in the Forum anyway. In fact, the chief editor of the Forum's official newsletter is a leader of the French CAIF and head of the Association of Moroccans in France and the CEDAM. Such interlocking directorates have drawn criticism from some corners: "They all want a piece of the pie. It's a little Mafia gang, a business, just as at the national level. It's the same crowd."[33] Both the CAIE and the Forum remain largely elite movements, like the EU itself, and national political realities have lost little of their pertinence.

The Second Generation

Several associations of young and second-generation immigrants have worked within the CAIE and the Migrants Forum. Another segment of these young people has begun to stitch together its own transnational political network. This development started in France, where there is a long tradition of direct action and where the institutions of citizenship have been slowly but surely inserting immigrant communities into the French polity.[34]   In 1984, after a series of violent and peaceful protests had demonstrated the organizational potential of the second generation, a small band of immigrant-origin and Jewish students active in the French Socialist Party (PS) founded SOS-Racisme.   The multiethnic movement of "buddies" (potes) from France's suburban housing projects and urban slums quickly grew to include thousands of immigrants and French citizens.[35]

SOS-Racisme's Parisian headquarters provided logistical support to local clubs that sprang up in Austria, Belgium, Germany, Italy, Luxembourg, the Netherlands, Portugal, Scandinavia, Spain, and Switzerland.   In 1985 potes from across Europe took a bus tour as the "Voyagers for Equality" through the continent's northern regions.   The movement adopted a "European Charter against Racism" and in 1988 convened the "European Estates-General for Youth" at the Sorbonne in Paris.   The delegates demanded that by the "magic date 1992" all the Union's immigrants, irrespective of their national origins, gain freedom of movement, easier naturalization, and local-level voting rights.[36]

Despite its organizational and public relations successes, SOS-Racisme has not forged a very strong NGO presence in Brussels or Strasbourg.   There the second immigrant generation exerts primarily symbolic pressure.[37]   SOS-Racisme's trans-European coordination has run into complications: its component national-level movements have organized on different bases.   Thus, SOS-Racisme in France has always been close to but autonomous from the PS, and its leadership has steadfastly refused to embrace common action with French labor organizations.   In contrast, central trade union confederations have overseen the formation of SOS-Rassismus in Germany and SOS-Mitmensch in Austria, and they have proven loath to relax their tutelage.

SOS-Racisme's cozy connections to the noncommunist left have won it sympathy in EU circles but the ire of those who accuse it of having been "co-opted."[38]   The CAIE and the national federations comprising it consider SOS-Racisme a threat.   They have advanced a "unitary approach" of all immigrant generations, preaching solidarity between immigrant and minority communities and the European working classes.[39]

THE IMPERATIVE OF EUROPEAN-LEVEL ACTION

The preceding discussion shows that immigrant-origin groups have not found it easy to exert influence on an integrating Europe.   National-level movements are too weak, internally divided, and top-heavy, and the European Union has not offered many points of access.   However, with member-state governments moving in unison lately to tighten the Union's borders, and with anti-immigrant violence escalating, immigrants and their allies are under mounting pressure to overcome the barriers to European-level mobilization.

Those barriers stand as tall and imposing as ever. Institutional squabbles have not subsided and still impede Union action. The European Parliament continues to exhibit the most consistent concern about integrating immigrants and tackling the structural causes of migratory and refugee flows from the developing world.[40] Impatient with secret, intergovernmental policy making, the EP has taken the issue of free movement in the Union to the European Court of Justice.[41] Tough talk and even action notwithstanding, the Maastricht Treaty gives no real boost to the EP's influence, leaving it no more than "Europe's most powerful NGO."[42]

National policies continue to diverge. Take the institutions of citizenship as an example. Belgium changed its nationality law in June 1992, giving automatic citizenship to Belgian-born second-generation immigrants at least one of whose parents was also born in the host society and easing the process for those whose parents were born in the homeland. The Belgians eliminated the possibility of holding dual nationality, however, and naturalization has remained difficult and costly. Spain, similarly, was moving to strip Spanish nationality from most people who acquired another one. Yet the Netherlands—which has pushed more generally for liberal immigration policies in the Union—was easing its naturalization procedures and considering allowing dual nationality. In the meantime the French government of Edouard Balladur enacted a stricter nationality code, even as Germany was taking the first tentative steps away from *jus sanguinis*. Germany wants more Union involvement in immigration issues, while Britain and Denmark refuse any EU role in "internal security."[43]

As member states largely continue to go their own way on immigration, the ramifications are gradually forcing greater policy coordination. Since July 1, 1993, then, Germany has no longer recognized a constitutional right to political asylum; Britain, Portugal, and Spain have tightened up their asylum laws as well.[44] These strict new policies, enacted unilaterally, threaten simply to shift flows to other countries, such as Belgium and Denmark. Meeting outside Copenhagen as the Ad Hoc Immigration Group in June 1992, the interior ministers of the EU had to respond. They agreed to make tighter checks on immigrants, to move more quickly to expel illegal immigrants, and to "rationalize" family reunification. Hovering over the Danish capital was the "spirit of Schengen, times twelve."[45] In fact, the EU's immigration policy is starting to converge with the emerging Schengen system. The EU/non-EU dichotomy has grown starker, as European governments emphasize policies on visas, admissions, and political asylum. Their intergovernmental negotiations emit resolutions that are not subject to review by the European Court of Justice.

Across the Union attacks against foreigners and electoral gains for right-wing nationalists have shaken the political establishment. The racist epidemic and the EU's tough new policies of closure have provoked a more intense reaction than before from organizations close to the foreign-origin population. Backed by the Commission to the tune of 500,000 ECUs, the European Trade Union Confederation (ETUC) has drawn up an action program, "For the

Integration of Migrant Workers, against Racism and Xenophobia," and hosted a conference in Brussels last December. Member unions and confederations are to open their decision-making structures more completely. The ETUC is trying to surmount the "differing national approaches and policies, coupled with the paucity of information," that make it difficult to develop common proposals.[46]

Similarly, Christian churches have begun to organize a European-level mission. They have been among the immigrants' most faithful defenders against hatred and discrimination. Catholic churches have long looked to Rome, not Brussels, for guidance. And Protestant churches, true to their tradition, have proved nationalistic, if not localistic. Even so, the outbreaks of anti-immigrant violence across Europe, together with what have been perceived as EU attacks against the "holy family" (i.e., restrictions on family reunification),[47] have been compelling churches to get involved. They have organized cross-national rallies to decry racism and conferences to discuss the effects of European integration on immigrants. The Churches' Committee for Migrants in Europe (CCME)[48] has joined the British Commission for Racial Equality, the Dutch National Bureau against Racism, and the Berlin Senate's Commissioner for Foreigners' Affairs in writing up a proposal for a draft council directive, the "Starting Line," on the elimination of racial discrimination. It would impose a deadline for member states to produce legislation and would lay down minimum standards to provide a guarantee of legal recourse to victims of bias. Whereas the sponsoring organizations would prefer Union legislation, they will accept national legislation achieving a similar outcome.[49] The European Parliament has incorporated the Starting Line into its new four-year action program to combat racism and xenophobia.[50]

The second generation and young immigrants have also been incited to action. The Standing Conference on Racial Equality (SCORE), created in London in 1990, is concerned that European immigration policy ignores minority communities in Britain, where skin color counts more than citizenship status. It urges the EU to adopt British-style legislation on racial equality and "positive discrimination."[51]

More symbolic actions have emerged over recent months as well. In April 1993 an antiracist rally from Rabat to Bonn kicked off in the Moroccan capital. Moroccan celebrities devised the event to heighten popular concern about racism in Europe. Some two hundred young athletes from both sides of the Mediterranean ran and cycled through Spain, France, Belgium, the Netherlands, and Germany, arriving in Bonn on May 1 for a rock concert. There activists read aloud a declaration against racism in six languages.[52]

Out of necessity, then, trans-European networks of voluntary associations and immigrant groups have been forming.[53] This development might appear a case of too little, too late. Elections to the European Parliament in June, 1994 increased the number of MEPs belonging to the extreme right. Referring to the upsurge in extremist political movements and anti-immigrant violence, Antonio Cruz of the Migration News Sheet is skeptical: "All of this had to happen for a few thousand people believing in justice, equality, and peace—what ridiculous numbers!—to begin to organize a few anti-racist demonstrations." Though there is truth in that assessment, it would be wrong to underestimate the growing sophistication of immigrant associations and their supporters.

One cannot yet speak of a true "European immigration lobby." Yet the beginnings of a truly European antiracist social movement are visible, one that is linking together immigrants and "native" social activists, foreign workers and the second generation, in coordinated actions that respect the identity and organizational autonomy of each component group. In February 1993 organizers of this embryonic Anti-Racist Network for Equality in Europe met in Berlin. Leading the movement are the Anti-Racist Alliance (Britain), the Forum Buntes Deutschland (Germany), the Mouvement contre le Racisme, l'Anti-Sémitisme et la Xénophobie (MRAX/Belgium), Nederlant Bekent Kleur (the Netherlands), Nero e Non Solo (Italy), SCORE (Britain), SOS-Racisme (France), SOS-Racismo (Spain), and SOS-Rassismus/Berlin (Germany). Several dozen antiracist groups from every EU member state and Switzerland—some headed by immigrants and others by indigenous activists—have expressed support for the initiative.

By choosing to hold their first meeting at the old Reichstag building, organizers underlined their upset over attacks against refugees and immigrants in Germany and across Europe. Those associations in attendance agreed on a number of demands: an EU directive against racism, antidiscrimination and *jus soli* citizenship laws in all member states, joint action against skinhead rock bands and racist literature, cooperation with antiracist organizations in Eastern Europe, the right to vote and to be elected for all immigrants, a European right to asylum in accordance with the Geneva Convention of 1951, and greater acceptance of war refugees from ex-Yugoslavia throughout Europe.[54]

Leaders of this broad-based, loosely structured movement are busy buttonholing EU officials. Also planned are symbolic events designed to attract European media attention and raise public consciousness. Network activists are learning, however, that they cannot afford to be doctrinaire. Once one Dutch group opposed to the Schengen accords realized that the agreements were not to be stopped, therefore, it formulated proposals that officials in the Netherlands (whose government then held the rotating Union presidency) found difficult to refuse: that every decision of the Council of Ministers and European Council first be submitted to the national parliaments (so as to facilitate the exchange of information) and, once accepted, be subject to review by the ECJ. The Dutch parliament has accepted these proposals. Italy has also voiced support, and Germany has agreed to consider them.[55] Though it has been weakened lately by internecine squabbling, the EU Migrants Forum, meanwhile, has met with Belgian, French, and German authorities in an attempt to influence domestic policy and to lobby for common European action.[56] Immigrants and their allies argue that the intergovernmental approach opens up twelve opportunities for NGOs, national legislatures, and the European Parliament to "raise hell." Would it not be better to have a Union approach?[57]

Charta 91, a coalition of Belgian nonprofit associations, tried that line on the Belgian government when it took over the EU presidency in July 1993. Charta wants Belgium to intercede to ensure that NGOs gain a real voice in Union policy making: "To many questions raised by civil society, the political world does nothing but reply that 'that should be regulated at the European level.' The dysfunctions at the national level thus risk being repeated at the level of European policy."[58]

Fighting this trend will not be easy. Many observers doubt that immigrants, bereft of most political rights, and their motley collection of allies in the trade unions, churches, and antiracist movements can navigate and influence the complex, multitiered game that the European Union is playing. Perhaps they are, in fact, asking for the moon. Yet they must at least try to exert pressure on the member states and EU institutions: "Since the European governments are taking decisions that affect us, we are obliged to try to 'comprehend' (*concevoir*) Europe. It is a reaction to the danger, no, the reality of seeing the member states construct a Europe without the immigrants."[59]

NOTES

I am grateful for the financial assistance from the German Marshall Fund of the United States (grant #8-90714-3) and the University of Denver that made the research for this chapter possible.

1. On February 23, 1994, the Commission adopted its Second Communication to the Council and the European Parliament on Immigration and Asylum Policies. Failure to tackle "on a cooperative basis" the "challenges that immigration pressures and the integration of legal immigrants pose for the Union as a whole," warned the Commission, "would be to the detriment of attempts to promote cohesion and solidarity within the Union and could, indeed, endanger the future stability of the Union itself." See *Migration News Sheet*, No. 132, March 1994, p. 1.

2. See Patrick Ireland, "Facing the True 'Fortress Europe': Immigrant and Politics in the EC," *Journal of Common Market Studies*, Vol. 29, No. 5, September 1991, pp. 466-67.

3. Dieter Grimm, "Der Mangel an europäischer Demokratie," *Der Spiegel*, Vol. 43, 1992, pp. 57-59.

4. Personal interview with Jan Niessen, General Secretary, Churches' Committee for Migrants in Europe (CCME), Brussels.

5. Stephan Leibfried, "Towards a European Welfare State?" In Szusza Ferge and John Eivind Kolberg (eds.), *Social Policy in a Changing Europe* (Frankfurt/Boulder: Campus Verlag/Westview Press, 1992), p. 227.

6. Stephan Leibfried and Paul Pierson, "Prospects for Social Europe," *Politics and Society*, Vol. 20, No. 3, September 1992, pp. 333-66. See also Patrick R. Ireland, "Immigration: The E.C. and Social Policy Coordination," paper prepared for delivery

at the Annual Meeting of the American Political Science Association, Washington, D.C., September 2-5, 1993.

7. "Entschließung zur Bekämpfung von Rassismus und Fremdenfeindlichkeit," *Information zur Ausländerdienst*, Vol. 1, 1991, p. 4.

8. G. Federico Mancini, "The Making of a Constitution for Europe," *Common Market Law Review*, Vol. 26, 1989, p. 599.

9. Kai Haibronner, "Perspektiven einer europäischen Asylrechtsharmonisierung nach der Maastrichter Gipfelkonferenz," *Zeitschrift für Ausländerrecht und Ausländerpolitik*, Vol. 2, 1992, pp. 51-59.

10. For details see Antonio Cruz, "Schengen, Ad Hoc Immigration Group and Other European Intergovernmental Bodies," Briefing Paper No. 12 (Brussels: CCME, May 1993), pp. 18-19.

11. Quoted in Giuseppe Callovi, "Regulation of Immigration in 1993: Pieces of the European Community Jig-Saw Puzzle," *International Migration Review*, Vol. 26, No. 2, Summer 1992, p. 354.

12. The Schenger convention has finally been applied, as of March 26, 1995, in the five original signatory states, Spain and Portugal. Austria, Italy, and Greece are to follow "soon," but they have yet to announce a date. See *Migration News Sheet*, No. 145, April 1995, p. 1.

13. Though the Single European Act finally mentioned the European Council, it is not really a Union institution.

14. Under the treaty of Maastricht, immigration and asylum come under the third and final "pillar"—justice and home affairs—on which the European Union is to be built. See Ann Dummett and Jan Niessen, "Immigration and Citizenship in the European Union," Briefing Paper No. 14 (Brussels: CCME, November 1993), pp. 15-20.

15. Callovi, op. cit. (note 11), p. 360.

16. Martin Baldwin-Edwards, "The Socio-Political Rights of Migrants in the European Community," in Graham Room (ed.), *Towards a European Welfare State?* (Bristol: School for Advanced Urban Studies, 1991), pp. 213-215. "What Is a European?" *The Economist*, August 17, 1991, pp. 42-43.

17. See Patrick R. Ireland, *The Policy Challenge of Ethnic Diversity: Immigrants and Politics in France and Switzerland* (Cambridge, MA: Harvard University Press, 1994), Conclusion.

18. Danièle Lochak, "La liberté de circulation et ses limites," *Plein Droit*, special issue (Paris: GISTI, 1989-90), pp. 61-65. Member states have also set aside categories of "privileged" foreigners, those from former colonies or otherwise favored countries who face fewer restrictions.

19. See Elspeth Guild, *Protecting Migrants' Rights*, Briefing Paper No. 10 (Brussels: CCME, November 1992).

20. Patrick Weil, "Immigrés: Les risques d'une dérive," *Le Monde*, September 9, 1992, p. 2. In December 1993 the "General Affairs" Council adopted the directive on the right to vote and stand for EP elections, and the process of transposing it into the national laws of the member states has already begun. See *Migration News Sheet*, No. 130, January 1994, p. 11.

21. European Centre for Work and Society (ECWS), "Rencontre sur les mouvements d'auto-organisation des moins-favorisés en Europe: Le cas des populations immigrées" (Maastricht: ECWS and the EC Commission, November-December 1989).

22. Stany Grudzielski, "Pour un lobby européen des immigrés," *Forum*, No. 2 (Brussels: Forum des Migrants des Communautés Européennes, 1992), p. 23.

23. Quoted in "A Successful General Assembly," *Forum*, No. 3 (Brussels: Migrants Forum of the EC, 1993), p. 2.

24. Personal interview with Jan Niessen, CCME.

25. Bichara Khader, "Immigration maghrébine face à l'Europe 1992," *Migrations-Société*, Vol. 3, No. 15, May-June 1991, pp. 17-48.

26. See Hecham Abdessamad, "Islam in Europe," *Forum*, No. 3 (Brussels: Migrants Forum of the European Communities, 1993), pp. 17-19.

27. Rémy Leveau, "Inquiétudes du Sud," *Esprit*, Vol. 7, No. 132, July 1992, p. 136.

28. See Edgar Auth, "Kurdisches Dilemma," *Frankfurter Rundschau*, June 29, 1993, p. 3.

29. Pierre Blaise, *Les syndicats en Europe*, Dossiers du Centre de Recherche et d'Information Socio-Politiques (CRISP), Vol. 37 (Brussels: CRISP, December 1992), p. 18.

30. Personal interview with Abderrazak Bouazizi, Conseil des Associations Immigrées en France (CAIF), Paris. See "Résolutions de la IVe Conférence des Associations des Immigrés en Europe," reprinted in *Presse et immigrés en France*, No. 128 (March 1985), pp. 9-13.

31. Ireland, op. cit. (note 2), pp. 470-71.

32. ECWS 1989. *Informations-Communautés-Immigrés* (Brussels: CAIE, October 1988), p. 1.

33. Telephone interview with Antonio Cruz, editor in chief, *Migration News Sheet*, Brussels.

34. See W. Rogers Brubaker, *Citizenship and Nationhood* (Cambridge, MA: Harvard University Press, 1992).

35. Serge Malik, *L'histoire secrète de SOS-Racisme* (Paris: Albin Michel, 1990).

36. *Libération*, December 20, 1988, p. 3.

37. Personal interview with Jan Niessen, CCME.

38. Personal interview with CAIF officials, Paris. Under new leadership, SOS-Racisme has officially broken with the PS and has announced its intention to "expand our action at the European level." See *Migration News Sheet*, No. 115, October 1992, p. 9.

39. Antonio Perotti, "Le mouvement associatif immigré face à l'Europe sans frontières," *Presses et immigrés en France*, No. 164 July-August 1988.

40. See "EP/Human Rights," *Europe*, No. 5939, March 13, 1993, pp. 3-4; *Official Journal of the EC*, English edition, Vol. 36, No. C81, March 22, 1993, p. 19.

41. *Migration News Sheet*, No. 122, May 1993, p. 1; and No. 131, February 1994, p. 1.

42. Personal interview with Jan Niessen, CCME.

43. "On the Borderline," *The Economist*, November 23, 1991, p. 58. Yvan Mayeur, "Code de la nationalité," *MRAX Information*, No. 70 (Brussels: Mouvement Contre le Racisme, l'Anti-Sémitisme et la Xénophobie, May 1993, p. 37). Hermann Bleich, "Ausländer in den Niederlanden," *Frankfurter Rundschau*, June 24, 1993, p. 2.

44. Jean-Christoph Cambadélis, "L'Europe entre chien et loup," *Le Monde*, November 12, 1992, p. 9. Martin Baldwin-Edwards, "Recent Changes in European Immigration Policies," *Journal of European Social Policy*, Vol. 2, No. 1, 1992, pp. 53-56.

45. "L'Europe tente d'endiguer l'afflux des réfugiés," *Le Soir* (Brussels), June 3, 1993, p. 1.

46. Personal interview with officials of the ETUC, Brussels. See ETUC Working Group on Migration and Racism, "Summary Record, Luxembourg, October 1 and 2, 1992" (Brussels: ETUC, 1992).

47. Personal interview with Jan Niessen, CCME.

48. The CCME, founded in 1964, is a Brussels-based organization of Europe's Protestant, Anglican, and Orthodox churches, part of the ecumenical network of the World Council of Churches.

49. CCME et al., "The Starting Line" (Brussels: CCME, April 1993), p. 2.

50. *Migration News Sheet*, No. 130, January 1994, p. 9.

51. Personal interview with Jan Niessen, CCME.

52. *Migration News Sheet*, No. 120, March 1993, p. 9; and No. 122, May 1993, p. 1.

53. See Elizabeth Meehan, "Citizenship and the European Community," *Political Quarterly*, Vol. 64, No. 2, 1993, pp. 172-186.

54. Forum Buntes Deutschland e.V., "Results of the Meeting of the Anti-Racist Network for Equality in Europe," tract (Bonn, February 1993).

55. Personal interview with Jan Niessen, CCME.

56. Representatives of fourteen Turkish associations walked out of the Forum's general assembly in December 1993, angry at a proposal to limit the voting weight of any ethnic group to 10 percent; Turks constitute fully a one-third of the EU's immigrants. See *Migration News Sheet*, No. 133, April 1994 p 7

57. Personal interview with Jan Niessen, CCME.

58. Charta 91, "Proposition d'initiative européenne," *MRAX Information*, No. 70 (Brussels, May 1993), p. 17.

59. Personal interview with MRAX activists, Brussels.

7

Attitudes Toward European Integration: Ethnic and Cultural Dimensions

Andreas G. Kourvetaris and
George A. Kourvetaris

On September 5, 1929, the French Prime Minister Briand, speaking before the assembly of the League of Nations, proposed a European federation. While his nascent idea of a united states of Europe was received favorably by more than two dozen European nation-states, both the worldwide economic crisis of the 1930s and the onset of World War II postponed the notion of European integration. The idea was again revived with the signing of the Treaty of Rome in 1957 and subsequent treaties for the creation of the European Economic Community. Previously, in 1950, Jean Monnet and Robert Schuman had already proposed the formation of the European Coal and Steel Community. This became the predecessor of the European Economic Community (EEC), which later became known as the Common Market. The actual formation of the EEC in 1958, however, represented a radical departure from the more limited concept of the European Coal and Steel Community. The architects of the Treaties of Paris and Rome believed that it was desirable to replace nationalism and national competition in Europe with an integrated industrial and commercial European entity which, in the long run and in theory, would strengthen European economic competitiveness vis-à-vis other world economies. The ultimate goal of integration for the "new" architects of the EEC was, as Prime Minister Briand had proposed twenty-nine years before, to transform the nation-states of Europe into a politically united Europe, akin to the United States of America.

Even a cursory examination of recent studies on European integration reveals that emphasis has been primarily on economic issues and secondarily on political issues. Furthermore, while many surveys of EU (the EEC has since evolved into the European Union—EU) member nation-states depict attitudes toward economic and political integration as positive and desirable, this does not seem to be the case with respect to the more "nationalistic" and intangible cultural and ethnic issues.   The revival of ethnic nationalism in the former Yugoslavia and the former Soviet republics, for example, and the rise of xenophobia and racism against foreign workers in many Western European countries show that ethnic nationalism is not peculiar to former socialist societies but also pervasive in many EU member states.

The presence of foreign residents in Western Europe (most of whom live in the more affluent EU countries such as Germany) has become a major divisive issue in those host countries, especially during periods of high unemployment.   While public support for unification and a single market economy remains high among the member states, it seems apparent that what is meant by "unification" does not necessarily encompass the cultural and ethnic dimensions of true European integration.   Though far from an exhaustive list, cultural and ethnic dimensions include the following: cultural pluralism versus assimilation, European identity versus national identity, ethnic nationalism versus European union, multi- versus monolingualism, unity within diversity versus unity within conformity.

In general, cultural pluralism is characteristic of ethnically, religiously, and racially diverse societies and cultures, whereas assimilation is prevalent in largely homogeneous, monolingual societies.   It can be argued that the former model emphasizes unity within diversity while the latter promotes unity within conformity to a dominant perspective of intergroup ethnic relations.

Liberalism and democracy can be considered more compatible with cultural pluralism and diversity.   Nationalism, on the other hand, can be understood as more supportive of the conformity or assimilative model.   Theoretically, then, the greater the diversity of a country, the more culturally plural it should be. In the United States, however, this is not the case.   For example, a great deal more assimilation, or fusion of cultures, is taking place in the United States, especially among European immigrants and their descendants, than cultural pluralism.   Thus, the cultural pluralism model has been more of a minority model of intergroup race relations in the United States than the more dominant assimilative one.   Despite the fact that the U.S. Immigration and Naturalization Service identifies four major racial groupings in the United States, namely whites, Hispanics, blacks, and Asians, the dominant social paradigm is the assimilative model.   By this example, can there feasibly be a United States of Europe similar to the United States of America?   After all, each European country, unlike the United States, has its own distinct language, customs, and traditions.   Can there be a "melting pot" or assimilation of European nationalities into one conglomerate European identity comparable to that of the American experience?   Such sociocultural and ethnic terms are not adequately addressed in studies of European integration.   Instead, as mentioned previously, European integration is understood primarily in economic and political structural terms.

In this chapter, we will argue that while economic and political integration of European communities has been advanced and, in many respects, achieved, cultural and ethnic integration of European nation-states will be less achievable, if at all, in the foreseeable future. Once again, it must be stressed that ethnic nationalism remains a strong divisive force not only in the former Soviet republics but also in other parts of Europe, Eastern and Western. Here, the scope of ethnic nationalism includes the establishment of a sovereign and independent nation-state, defined not in terms of a common citizenship and a public political philosophy but rather in terms of a common ethnic ancestry.

In general, the criteria of ethnicity include race or physical characteristics, nationality, and, to some extent, a common religion. More specifically, European ethnicity refers primarily to that specific European nationality. For example, Yugoslavia, after Tito and prior to its breakup, was a multiethnic and multireligious state. It is now being transformed from a unitary, integrated nation-state to a fractured group of nation-states seeking self-determination and independence (e.g., Croatia, Slovenia, Bosnia-Herzegovina). Whether or not this transformation and subsequent reemergence of ethnic nationalism will lead to democratization is debatable and uncertain. Issues and examples such as these will be discussed in this chapter. In addition, the conceptual framework of cultural and ethnic European and American divergences and convergences will be briefly discussed; the research procedures and data collection will be presented; an analysis and discussion of findings supplemented by other published material will be offered; and finally, a number of conclusions for further exploration of the cultural and ethnic issues will be suggested.

CULTURAL AND ETHNIC CONVERGENCES AND DIVERGENCES: UNITED STATES AND EUROPE

The process of state/nation formation in Europe evolved over centuries and was coincidental with the development of European cultures, which are predominantly rooted in the ancient worlds of Greece and Rome. In contrast, no such slow historical evolution occurred in the formation of the United States, where peoples of different backgrounds and origins ventured to the shores of the "new world" primarily for economic reasons.

Historically, the creation of nation-states was the outcome of artificial boundaries etched out by the victors in wars and through treaties. Because of this arbitrariness, the map of Europe has been altered repeatedly throughout history. To give one specific example, Belgium was created by the great powers (especially Britain) after the Belgium revolt against Dutch rule in 1830. Other artificial entities abounded in Europe, especially as recently as after the breakup of the Austro-Hungarian Empire in the early twentieth century. Similarly, in the "new world," a number of territories conquered previously by Spain were eventually annexed by the United States after Spain's expulsion from Mexico. As a result, southwestern states such as Arizona, Texas, and New Mexico arose.

As should be evident already, one way to conceptualize the cultural and ethnic diversity of the European Union is, as will be done throughout this analysis, to contrast and compare Europe with the United States. To understand Europe as well as the United States, one must first understand that they are, as a whole, multicultural and ethnically diverse continents. Of course the United States is not a continent per se. North America includes Canada as well. But for the sake of argument and with respect to sheer size, for all practical purposes the United States can be considered a "continent" comparable to the European continent. However, while the United States is a conglomerate "nation of nations," which includes diverse nationalities, subcultures, races, and religions, Europe is a continent of distinct and diverse national, cultural, and independent sovereign nation-states. Each country has its own borders and its own history, traditions, language, and culture. Though the United States is often considered a multicultural, multiethnic, multireligious, and multiracial society, it is only one country. But since the forefathers of the United States were European by descent (or more specifically, pariahs from British rule who established the thirteen colonies as an extension of British colonization and hegemony), the United States even today, and for the immediate future, remains Eurocentric in its politics and general social outlook. While distinctly European, the heterogeneous European cultural heritages are nourished by competing ideas, values, and historical antagonisms which have resulted in many conflicts and wars throughout Europe's turbulent history. In contrast, with the exception of the Civil War (1861-65) and occasional racial conflict, serious, massive, and prolonged ethnic and cultural conflicts have not been the case in the United States. Furthermore, unlike the United States, Europe does not have one central governing body. Instead, Europe is a polycentric system of nation-states divided into rival metropoles, each with its own specific cultural physiognomy and uniqueness. In addition, contrary to the United States overall, each European country taken singly is more or less ethnically homogeneous.

Another fundamental difference between the United States and Europe is the fact that by law in the United States attributes such as ethnicity, race, religion, or national origin are not criteria for American citizenship. The American nation was founded on a constitution and a public philosophy which grants American citizenship to all those who meet certain legal and naturalized citizen requirements. This is not the case in most European countries, however. In Germany, for example, one cannot become a citizen unless one has German ancestry.

Another important factor of divergence between Europe and the United States is religion. While both Europe and the United States are predominantly Christian (Roman Catholic and Protestant and, to a lesser extent, Eastern Orthodox), there is no officially recognized religion in the United States. Furthermore, unlike most European countries, there is a constitutional freedom of religious affiliation in the United States. In addition, the United States separates the church from the state. And, as a result, religion is not taught in public schools. This is not the case in most European countries, where religious affiliation directly corresponds to nationality or a nation-state. For example, Italy, Spain, Portugal, Poland, France, Ireland, and Croatia are predominantly Roman Catholic countries. England, Sweden, Norway, (Germany is half Roman Catholic and half Protestant) are predominantly Protestant. Greece, Serbia, Bulgaria, Romania, and Russia are predominantly Eastern Orthodox. It must also be pointed out that while the United States claims to have no state religion, it is fundamentally and dominantly a Protestant state.

In terms of racial composition, according to the U.S. Immigration and Naturalization Service, it is estimated that by the year 2030 the United States will be half nonWhite, Hispanics being the largest group after whites. This is not the case with the European communities despite the fact that many nonWhite immigrant families reside in Western European nations as guest workers. Europe is still predominantly white and Christian by religion. Thus it can be argued that in contrast to Europe, racial, ethnic, and cultural diversity in the United States can take different forms. One such form is known as the Anglo-Saxon model. Implicit in this model is the understanding that any incoming immigrant group must conform to or adopt the dominant--in this case, Anglo-Saxon--cultural and political values. As a result of this assimilation and acculturation, over the course of two to three generations, the majority of descendants of European immigrants in the United States have surrendered most of their unique ethnic identities, withdrawn from their ethnic subcultures, and adopted the Anglo-Saxon core values. The few ethnic ties that they have maintained are those that pertain particularly to what we call the "Dionysian" or symbolic aspects of their ethnic subcultures.[1]

The primary reasons for such acculturation were that the majority of these European ethnics strove for equality with the dominant Anglo-Saxon groups. As a result and mentioned above, they conformed to the dominant values of old stock Euro-Americans. Known also as the Anglo-conformity assimilation model, it has been the dominant, one-sided view in the United States, according to which ethnic intergroup conflict is minimized so long as any incoming immigrant groups adopt the dominant Anglo-Saxon values over time, or in terms of immigration, over generations. In general, the Anglo-Saxon dominant model includes the old stock European-Americans whose ancestors came primarily from countries of Western Europe, which includes such nationalities as English, Scottish, Irish, German, Dutch, Swedish, and Norwegian. The predominant religion of these nationalities, with the exception of the Irish, is Protestant. In fact, the 1990 United States Census revealed that the predominant ethnic components of the U.S. population are, in descending order, German, Irish, English, and Italian. As stated earlier, the United States is predominantly a Christian country, whose power structure is predominantly Protestant. Roman Catholics, however, are the largest single Christian group, followed by Baptists (*Yearbook of American Churches*, 1990). Eastern Orthodoxy is the third largest

Christian faith in the United States. Somewhat similar patterns are found in Europe.

In addition to the Anglo-conformity assimilation model, another model of intergroup relations exists in the United States along pluralist lines. Known as the cultural pluralist model, it suggests an ideal paradigm in which all ethnic groups are treated equally within a multicultural and multiethnic inclusive culture. In actuality, however, assimilation occurs even in this "ideal and equal" type of adaptation. As mentioned previously, one can argue that while most ethnic groups retain certain cultural and primary group distinctions along religious, marital, and kinship lines, assimilation occurs along the Anglo-Saxon core culture even in the pluralist model. Thus, an ethnic identity for many has become a symbolic identity. So while the descendants of ethnic and ethnorelig-ious groups in the United States, who originated primarily from Southern, Eastern, and Central Europe, achieve political and economic equality and, in some instances, surpass the dominant Anglo-Saxon groups in terms of economic status, they remain symbolically Greek, Italian, Irish, Russian, Serbian, and so on (Gans, 1979).

Many political pundits believed that European union would precipitate the end of the traditional nation-states, which would be replaced by a supranational state beyond the national interests of each nation. This conclusion, however, was premature. Evidence suggests that economic and political integration of Europe does not translate into the end of the nation-state. Moreover, it appears that European union does not mean centralization but rather decentralization and diversification. Indeed, there are two opposing views of European union: a superstate in which each member state relinquishes some of its sovereign power to a centralized federal state, versus a weaker system of centralized government, with authority dispersed among nation-states, something resembling a confederation. Contrary to those opposing views, others posit a middle ground, embodied in the concept of subsidiarity.

According to the concept of subsidiarity, the European Union undertakes responsibilities of governance as a collectivity only if the solution to a problem by the Union is thought to produce more effectual results than if the individual country tackled the issue alone (Scott, Peterson, and Millar, 1994: 47-67). While the principle of subsidiarity is more easily applied to political and economic issues, it is far more problematic when broadened to include cultural (nontechnical or nonmaterial) and ethnic issues. In short, Europe's cultural diversity is a mixed blessing. It is a strength in that it enriches the European community and thus is compatible with liberal values and democracy. However, it is a weakness as well in that within diversity are often conflicting cultural and ethnic particularities. It must be understood that these peculiarities are the very essence of ethnic nationalism. And ethnic nationalism often results in problems or lack of coordination, cohesiveness, and unity of purpose. Extreme ethnic nationalism can result in hegemonic chauvinism and ultimately war. The challenge to the EU thus becomes one of fostering unity within diversity, without sacrificing unity for diversity, and vice versa. Some of these cultural and ethnic particularities were addressed in a survey undertaken in the spring of 1991. More specific variables examined were the European values concerning language, religion, history, tradition, literature, nationalism, ethnic identity, intermarriage, education, and the like.

RESEARCH PROCEDURES AND DATA COLLECTION

The following data were gathered in the spring of 1991 from interviews and research conducted in Brussels, Belgium (the location of the EU headquarters), Greece, and the United States. During this period interviews were conducted with representatives and delegates from seven EU countries, including Belgium, Germany, Spain, Italy, Luxembourg, Denmark, and Greece. Most of the interviews took place in the interviewees' offices around Schuman Square near the EU headquarters in early May 1991. Prior to the interviews in Brussels, a questionnaire was mailed to all twelve representatives of the EU as a form of pilot study. Six of the twelve responded and provided useful suggestions for improvement of the final interview schedule.

One interviewee was a German graduate student who was working with the German delegation in Brussels at the time. He answered all of the questions in the interview schedule as part of his Ph.D. research on the EU. In addition, both the interviewee from Greece and one from the United States were professors whose extensive research and academic interests were on issues of the EU.

The interview schedule encompassed general structural, social-psychological, and cultural/ethnic questions. The structural component consisted of political and economic questions; the social-psychological dimension included questions on European and national identity, nationalism, and Europeanism; and the cultural/ethnic component included questions about issues such as cultural pluralism, assimilation, consensus, conflict, ethnicity, cultural values, language, history, literature, and traditions. Due to the complexity of the ethnic and cultural issues being discussed, no effort was made to quantify or operationalize some of these qualitative concepts. The interview questions were open-ended, and the analysis and discussion of the findings will be entirely qualitative and supplemented by other published material. It must be stressed that what follows below is more of a general sampling of the opinions and attitudes of a small number of official representatives from seven European Union members rather than a comprehensive study.

PRESENTATION OF FINDINGS: DISCUSSION AND ANALYSIS

Supplemented by similar studies, the presentation of findings will be organized around two broad frameworks. The ethnic dimension of our research included issues of (i) European versus national identity and (ii) nation-state versus federal state. Despite the above frameworks' interrelatedness, here European versus national identity can be considered the extent to which individuals of European Union nation-states perceive themselves as Europeans and/or whether they perceive themselves as nationals. The question was asked, "Given the fact that the European Union is proceeding on schedule and becomes a reality in the near future, do you think a European identity in the long run will replace a national identity?" Only one of the respondents felt that perhaps in three or four generations a European identity could be possible but was not at the present time. Most respondents stressed such factors as history, traditions, geographical distribution, distinct regions, past conflicts, diverse nationalities, different languages, and cultures as factors operating against Europeanization. While most respondents made no distinction between cultural and ethnic issues, they stressed overwhelmingly the idea of European citizenship as a common denominator of European identity. National identity was seen as synonymous with cultural and ethnic diversity, which, according to the respondents, gives Europe its strength and vitality.

Although there is a dearth of research on ethnic and cultural issues, a number of studies dealing with the issue of European versus national identity can be discerned (see Mann, 1993; Riffault, 1991; McGowan, 1992; Lepsius, 1992; Habermas, 1992; Orstrum, 1993). Basically, these studies argue that Europe cannot replicate the United States. Their evidence stems from the fact that in the United States national/ethnic identity is secondary or part of a hyphenated identity (e.g., Greek-American, Italian-American, Jewish-American). This ethnic identity, however, is basically lost after the second or third generation. In addition, the United States no longer maintains statistical records of European ancestry, with the exception of those who voluntarily mention the name(s) of their European ancestors or religion. This is exactly opposite the case in European societies, where ethnicity is the primary characteristic of identity and a European (or more universalistic) identity is secondary. As one researcher stated, "The effort to turn Europe into a unified superstate is now at a standstill as Europeans confront their fears of losing their individual national policies and identities" (McGowan, 1992). Stated more bluntly, another researcher said that "the type of centralization required by a federal model would be unacceptable to extant nation-states and would engender an array of intractable nationality problems that would dwarf the ethnic hostilities currently on display in the Balkans." He added that "Europeanization of national parliaments promises greater democratization of regional politics than a 'denationalization' of the European parliament" (Lepsius, 1992).

National State Versus Federal State

While the concept of a nation is a broader sociological idea denoting a group of people who share a sense of peoplehood and ethnic consciousness, the notion of the state is a newer and narrower political and territorial concept. Throughout history and up to modern times, we can identify more nations but fewer states. Nations can also exist without being states. For example, the Kurds and the Palestinians are nations who have struggled for years to establish their own states. With the end of the Cold War and the reemergence of ethnic nationalism and subnationalism, more nations will demand and struggle for statehood (Kourvetaris, 1993).[2]

In order to determine how our respondents felt about supporting the creation of an EU superstate (federal state), we presented a number of statements on our questionnaire to elicit their opinions of national versus European issues. On a scale from one (disagree), to two (unsure), to three (agree), their answers revealed ambivalent feelings. First, regarding the statement that European interests in general should take precedence over national interests, four respondents opposed this assertion, three supported it, and two were unsure. Second, concerning the issue of national interests versus European interests in all international negotiations, six were against the notion that all national interests should come first in all international relations, two were in favor, and one was in favor of both. Third, on the notion of European citizenship versus national citizenship, five of the respondents were in favor of both a European citizenship and preserving national citizenship, three opposed the idea of European citizenship at the expense of national citizenship, and one was in favor of European over national citizenship. Finally, concerning the idea of a world federalism as opposed to a national state, five respondents disagreed with the idea of world federalism and one was in favor of both.

From the results, it is evident that a European identity is not going to replace a national identity very soon. However, it is possible that both identities could coexist. At the summit of the twelve members of the European Union in Maastricht, Holland, the principle of multiple identity (Articles A-F, Part 2) was emphasized; it was decided that, in the first stage, a European identity will be introduced coexistentially with national identity (Stavropoulos, 1992: 6). While national identity has had a long and tumultuous history, European identity is a relatively new idea. The difficulty surrounding this idea is the existence of distinct nationalities and nation-states in Europe, each with its own national culture and history, which, as a result, makes a European collective identity more difficult. It can be argued, however, that a European identity may be enhanced by the concept of European citizenship and political union. A political union, however, does not automatically lead to the attenuation of national identities. While a European identity may have certain advantages in world affairs and decision-making processes, it may not be desirable for all the nation-states of Europe. European identity is especially problematic for smaller nations, because of their fear of being absorbed by bigger nations. This concern can be partly explained by the cultural and ethnic imperialism and domination of bigger nations over smaller ones, which has been the earmark of the European experience throughout the centuries of its turbulent and violent history.

Our respondents referred repeatedly, as discussed previously, to the notion of subsidiarity. Speaking in more economic terms, if the Union as a whole is more competent in solving some European problems so as to minimize cost and maximize efficiency, the respondents argued that Union action should take precedence over national pride. The principle of *subsidiarity* (Article 36, Paragraph 2) was one of the major decisions at the Maastricht conference. The application of this principle has a dual function: (i) It relieves the member states of competencies or expertise which they are not capable of putting into practice (the principle of sufficiency); and (ii) it releases the centralizing activities of the center in favor of the periphery. In this way it is possible to operate on the regional or local level, utilizing mechanisms of regional development and reconstruction which are more effective (the principle of effectiveness). The principle of subsidiarity combines the mandates of democratic government with those of effective government, and it is considered one of the most important federal principles of the EU (Stavropoulos, 1992: 6; Scott, Peterson, and Millar, 1994; Genscher, 1993). In his article "Nationalism Has No Home in Europe" Genscher, the former foreign minister of United Germany, linked the notion of European Union with the principle of subsidiarity. He felt that without unification, Europe will be doomed to "economic stagnation and nationalist conflict" (Genscher, 1993). In his words, "[T]he subsidiarity principle, which states that the central institutions of the European Community should deal only with those matters that cannot be handled by individual member states, must be reaffirmed to reassure those who worry about loss of national sovereignty" (Genscher, 1993).

To reiterate, the resurgence of ethnic nationalism in the Balkans and the former Soviet republics is not something unique to the former socialist societies. Indeed, European nationalism emerged in its most destructive aspect in Western Europe during World Wars I and II and was exported to many other regions of Europe and the world. The scope of this present analysis, however, does not allow us to expand on this point. The rise of neofascism and the waves of antiforeign movements in Western Europe against foreign workers are blatant indications of the continuing survival of fanatical nationalism in European countries. Such nationalism ironically parallels Western Europe's increasing political and economic integration. The continuing conflict between Protestants and Roman Catholics in Northern Ireland, as well as strife in Spain, Scotland, Wales, Belgium, and many Central and Eastern European societies, is indicative of continuing survival of and animosity between nationalisms. Contrary to modernization and development theories, the idea of the nation-state is not declining but rather diversifying and still developing. Indeed, the end of the

Cold War and the demise of state socialism have contributed to the increase rather than the decrease of ethnic nationalism and subnationalism.

The Cultural Dimension

Closely related to ethnic aspects of European integration is what we have termed the cultural component of integration. We define culture as a way of life, including values, norms, traditions, histories, and ideologies, that is embodied, shared, and transmitted among the people and their social and cultural institutions, such as religion, education, marriage, and the family. Language is the most important medium of culture and, as such, can be considered the very foundation of one's cultural and ethnic identity; it gives each nation its national, cultural identity and uniqueness. The respondents' attitudes toward this cultural dimension were examined by a number of questions pertaining to issues of education, history, religion, language, intermarriage, and mass media.

Most respondents were opposed to any attempt by the Union to centralize or establish a uniform system of education. One respondent summarily stated the following:

Education should be left to the member states or its federal subentities. Education is the area in which the different national traditions are most evident. All nations of the member states are most sensitive about it. History has shown that education can be abused for indoctrination. People remember these experiences very well. Respect for these sensitivities requires abstention from any sort of a compulsory uniform system of education. Apart from these considerations there is no conceivable need for a uniform education system on community level.

While most respondents were against the idea of a uniform educational system, many expressed views of devising educational programs which incorporated the principle of subsidiarity, especially with respect to technical and more scientific areas of higher education.

Asked whether they believed that the EU should stress within an educational system more common or core values rather than differences among its EU member states, seven of the nine respondents stressed common European values but with respect to economic and political issues only, such as European citizenship, common law, common economic interests, democracy, and free market. They opposed common cultural and ethnic issues. Two of the respondents expressed the view that the EU educational system should include not only what is common or a core of European cultural values, traditions, and histories but what is different or what distinguishes one country from another. In addition, with one exception, all respondents felt that each country should have full control of what is taught in its schools about history and politics and in no way be determined by the EU. One respondent summarized his views as follows:

The Community will develop its own values. Yet these values will be its own. They cannot be taken artificially as the lowest common denominator of the different national traditions. They will evolve in the ongoing process of integration. There is no need to stress them particularly. On the contrary, nothing would harm more the idea of integration, than a sort of artificial eurochauvinism. On the other hand stressing differences between the Member States does not necessarily mean stressing dissensus. Differences are a fact. They are due to the history of Europe. They cannot be denied and they should not be neglected. A respect for different traditions and cultures does not mean encouraging dissensus, but accepting the given frame, in which European integration works.

One index of assimilation and convergence is ethnic intermarriage, including interfaith marriages. While most respondents believed that there should be a basic freedom of religion in Europe (Article 9 of the EU constitution)—even though in practice Europe is predominantly Christian—none of the respondents opposed the idea of interethnic marriage. The right to marry whomever one wishes is laid down in Article 12 of the European convention on human rights. Most marriages, however, tend to be intraethnic or intrafaith rather than interethnic or interfaith. Contrary to Europe, in the United States most marriages tend to be interethnic and interfaith, especially once we move beyond the first two generations of European immigrants.

In the United States, as ethnicity declines as a form of identity, religious identification seems to takes its place. This is what Herberg (1955) called the "triple melting pot theory." Herberg argued that most marriages are intradenominational. For example, Roman Catholics marry other Catholics, Protestants marry other Protestants, and so on. In Europe, with the exception of the Jewish religion, it can be argued that most marriages are also intrafaith marriages due to the fact that nationality and religion overlap. Thus, Italians, who are primarily Roman Catholics, usually marry other Italian Catholics; British, who are Anglican or Episcopalian Protestant, usually marry within their own religion and nationality. The same pattern is evident for Scandinavians, who are predominantly Lutheran, and Greeks, Serbians, and Russians, who are predominantly Eastern Orthodox. Despite the predominance of intraethnic and intrafaith marriages, it is projected that eventually, as Europe becomes more unified, interethnic and interfaith marriages will increase substantially among the European Union members.

One of the most fundamental and important issues facing the EU is language. As mentioned previously, it alone underscores all of culture. In fact, it can be argued that culture would not be possible without the system of symbols and meanings conveyed by language. Some argue as well that only through language, including both the spoken and written word, are we able to maintain our cultural identity, social heritage, and ethnic consciousness. Only through a particular language can we express the nuances of meaning, feeling, and ways of thought. Thus the argument for a common EU language seems to ignore the subtleties of a mother or native tongue.

Seven of the nine respondents opposed the idea of a common EU language. One of the respondents who favored a common language believed that since English was already an international medium of communication, it should be the common language of the EU. The other respondent believed that the EU should be bilingual. Those that favored a common language argued that the simultaneous translations of EU documents into nine languages has become not only a bureaucratic nightmare but also an expensive one for the Union. The other seven respondents' advocacy for the maintenance of national languages supports the view of distinct ethnic identities rather than a European one. Furthermore, they argued that only multilingualism could preserve the more intangible aspects of culture, such as literature, values, history, traditions, and the like. But those who stressed the need for a common language argued that using a common language would contribute to more effective communication among the EU member communities. One such respondent said the following about language and, in general, about the cultural and ethnic dimensions of European integration:

One of the main resources of the community is the richness of its different national cultures and traditions. These have to be preserved. A European identity is gradually evolving. It will be enhanced further by the concept of European citizenship as it is projected for the political union. Yet it does not follow necessarily that all citizens of the EEC automatically think of themselves as Europeans first. They will certainly not swear allegiance to the European flag every morning in school or anywhere else. It will rather depend on the specific context, whether an individual will primarily feel as a European citizen or as a national one. It seems possible that a person might feel as a national citizen at home and as a European citizen while living in a third country, not being a member state of the EC. The different national identities must not be suppressed. Therefore the idea of a common language is out of the question.

In a related study on "European national identities and cultural values," based on secondary analysis data from the Eurobarometer surveys, Riffault (1991) summarized her findings as follows: "While ethnic groups all over the world are striving for greater autonomy and recognition, the peoples of Europe are moving toward an integrated society composed of multiple ethnicities. . . . Results reveal that, despite obvious differences among countries, Europeans generally share values relating to family, work, politics, and religion. Most Europeans are in favor of unification and recognize its economic and political benefits. Although very few think of themselves as 'Europeans' most do not feel that unification will put their ethnic identity at risk. Rather, they see unity as the only way to ensure that their common interests are represented at a global level."

SUMMARY AND CONCLUSION

In this chapter an effort was made to look at a number of cultural and ethnic dimensions of European integration. While Europeans have made significant strides toward economic and political integration, they continue to lag behind with respect to cultural and ethnic matters. Although most Europeans support the goals of European economic and, to some extent, political union, they are reluctant to relinquish their national cultural heritages in favor of a common supranational Union or superstate. Nationalism, history, traditions, values, beliefs, and language remain sensitive and oftentimes volatile issues. No European nation-state researched in this analysis is willing to abdicate its sovereignty and national right for a superstate. Thus for now, they reject the assimilation model, which is more prevalent in the Anglo-Saxon countries such as United States, Canada, Australia, and New Zealand, and advocate the cultural pluralism model.

Of course further research is necessary in order to understand more fully the role of ethnic and cultural dimensions in European integration. A future agenda for further research on the issues of European integration could include such questions as: Is there an emerging European culture? What is the relationship between European citizenship and national citizenship? The majority of the respondents stressed the notion and maintenance of cultural diversity, which was seen by them as a strength rather than a weakness for a united Europe. Of course, Europe has always been culturally diverse with respect to its diverse traditions, languages, geography, nationalities, cultural heritage, and population distribution. One respondent argued that the notion of European citizenship and the rights of European citizens should not detract from the belief in cultural diversity. Overall, however, the respondents believed that distinct nationalities and nation-states will make the realization of a true European union and collective identity more problematic. As a result, it can be argued that the existence of distinct nationalities and nation-states hinders a common European identity. Other factors mentioned as contributing to a lack of a European collective identity were issues such as cultural diversity, distinct regions, separate countries, distinct nationalities, different languages, historical roots, and national traditions.

Europeans more than Americans think of themselves primarily as nationals or members of distinct nationalities (e.g., Germans, French, Italians, Greeks) and only secondarily as Europeans. While this attitude is changing somewhat in the EU countries, the opposite is true in the United States, particularly after the second generation, or the children of European immigrants. In the United States, the ethnic identity of most European immigrants, especially the second and subsequent generations, has been replaced by an American common identity. In short, while in Europe distinct ethnic identities are primary, in the United States these ethnic identities become secondary.

The geographic boundaries of each European nation-state gives each nationality its uniqueness. The same phenomenon existed in the former Soviet Union and former Yugoslavia. However, the reemergence of ethnic nationalism in these former republics reveals how fragile and artificial the notion of federalism was. Needless to say, communism in these former socialist societies was imposed by force, following the Bolshevik Revolution of 1917. But nationalism proved to be a more powerful force of self-definition than socialist ideology did.

The concepts of ethnicity, assimilation, identity, and culture have different implications and meanings in Europe than in the United States. While in both Europe and the United States there is an emphasis on cultural and ethnic diversity, there is a fundamental difference between theory and practice. From its inception, the United States was an Anglo-Saxon core culture to which subsequent generations of immigrants had no choice but to adopt. This adaptation became known as the assimilation-acculturation model. On the contrary, in Europe, there was no singe dominant cultural/ethnic model. Instead, different national cultures identified themselves as French, British, German, Italian, Greek, and so on.

In the United States, ethnicity beyond the second generation eventually becomes more and more what Herbert Gans (1979) referred to as "symbolic ethnicity." In other words, life in the United States does not promote the preservation of distinct ethnicities among its citizens whose ancestors immigrated to the United States from abroad. Members of third, fourth, and subsequent generations of "new" immigration resort to ethnic symbols. As a result, visible symbols or Dionysian aspects of ethnicity rather than genuine or Apollonian ethnic identification become the last remaining remnants of ethnic identity (Kourvetaris, 1994). Perhaps European Union members are fearful of becoming symbolically ethnic.

In Europe, while we can identify certain core values shared by most Europeans, Europeans identify themselves first as members of distinct nationalities and second as Europeans. The opposite is characteristic in the United States. It appears that the movement toward economic and political integration may bring Europeans closer to ethnic and cultural integration. Only time will reveal the extent to which such ethnic and cultural integration will take place. However, the rise of ethnic nationalism in the former Yugoslavia and the former Soviet republics, and the persistent intensification of conflict in Northern Ireland and in other parts of Europe are not encouraging "beginnings" for a unified and integrated Europe.

NOTES

We would like to express our thanks to Professors Pierre Gravel and Gustaaf Van Cromphout of Northern Illinois University for their invaluable comments and insights, which helped us to improve the analysis. However, it must be stressed that the usual caveat that the authors alone accept the responsibility for the interpretation is especially relevant here.

1. Dionysian aspects of ethnic subculture in the American context include emphasis on the material or external aspects of an ethnic subculture such as food, music, dance, or artifacts rather than the Apollonian or esoteric aspects of ethnic subculture such as literature, philosophy, history, language. Americans know very little about the Apollonian aspects of various ethnic and racial groups. When we think of Chinese, Thais, Mexicans, or any other ethnic group there is the tendency to think of them in stereotypical and Dionysian terms, especially in terms of food. We are exposed to the culinary aspects of the ethnic subculture first and only secondarily learn anything about the culture as a whole. Our knowledge and perception about various ethnic subcultures are limited. We only know what is visible or exotic, including colorful parades, exotic dances, special dishes, and so on. The terms "Dionysian" and "Apollonian" were taken from Greek mythology and used by the German philosopher Nietzsche (1844-1900) and later applied to culture by the American anthropologist Ruth Benedict (1887-1948). (See Kourvetaris, 1994.)

2. Ethnic nationalism has challenged the existence of many nations. Within a multiethnic nation-state an ethnic group can mobilize its power and establish a separate nation-state. The emergence of ethnic nationalism in former Yugoslavia is a case in point. Subnationalism refers to the ethnic, religious, or racial movements within a multiethnic state for self-determination or independence, for example, the insurgency among the Kurds in Turkey. The end of the Cold War has strengthened rather than weakened the forces of ethnic nationalism and subnationalism (Kourvetaris, 1995).

REFERENCES

Denton, G. R., ed. 1969. *Economic Integration in Europe*. London: Weidenfeld and Nicolson.

Gans, Herbert J. 1979. "Symbolic Ethnicity: The Future of Ethnic Groups and Cultures in America." In Herbert Gans (ed.), *On the Making of Americans*. Philadelphia, PA: University of Pennsylvania Press.

Genscher, Hans Dietrich. 1993. "Nationalism Has No Home in Europe." *New Perspectives Quarterly*, Vol. 10, Winter.

Glazer, Nathan and Daniel P. Moynihan. 1963. *Beyond the Melting Pot*. Cambridge, MA: MIT Press.

Gordon, Milton. 1964. *Assimilation in American Life: The Role of Race, Religion and National Origins*. New York: Oxford University Press.

Greeley, Andrew. 1974. *Ethnicity in the United States*. New York: John Wiley and Sons.

Habermas, Jurgen. 1992. "Citizenship and National Identity: Some Reflections on the Future of Europe." *Praxis-International*, Vol. 12, No. 1, April, pp. 1-19

Herberg, William. 1955. *Protestant, Catholic, Jew*. New York: Doubleday and Co.

Kourvetaris, George. 1993. "Greek Attitudes toward Political and Economic Integration into the EEC." *East European Quarterly*, Vol. 27, No. 3, September, pp. 375-415.

————. 1995. "Ethnonationalism and Subnationalism: The Case of Former Yugoslavia." Paper presented at the Second International Hellenic-American Conference on "Nationalism and Sexuality: Crises of Identity." Thessaloniki, Macedonia, Greece, May 17-22.

————. 1994. "The Apollonian and Dionysian Dimensions of Ethnicity." Paper presented at the Illinois Sociological Association at Springfield, IL, April.

Lepsius, M. Rainer. 1992. "Beyond the Nation-State: The Multinational State as the Model for the European Community." *Telos*, Spring, pp. 57-76.

Mann, Michael. 1993. "Nation-States in Europe and Other Continents: Diversifying, Developing, Not Dying." *Daedalus*, Vol. 122, No. 4, Summer, pp. 115-40.

McGowan, William. 1992. "European Disunity." *Scholastic Update*, Vol. 125, No. 20, November, p. 10.

Mendès, M. A. J. *Economic Integration and Growth in Europe.* London: Croonhelm.

Messas, Kostas. 1994. *Return to Decadent Europe: Debating Europe's Security.* Westport, CT: Greenwood.

Orstrum, Muller. 1993. "Europe: The Coming of the 'Nonmaterial' Society." *The Futurist*, Vol. 27, November/December, pp. 23-27.

Overturf, Stephen F. 1986. *The Economic Principles of European Integration.* New York: Praeger.

Paterson, William E. 1973. "Nationalism and European Integration: The Nationalist Movements in Scotland, Wales, Ireland and Belgium." *Europa–Archiv*, Vol. 28, No. 18, pp. 651-56.

Riffault, Helene. 1991. "Comparative Research on National Identities." *Innovation*, Vol. 4, No. 1, pp. 31-40.

Scott, Andrew, John Peterson, and David Millar. 1994. "Subsidiarity: A 'Europe of the Regions' the British Constitution?" *Journal of Common Market Studies*, Vol. 32, No. 1, March, pp. 47-67.

Stavropoulos, C. J. 1992. "Maastricht: Some Conclusions." *Athena Magazine*, Vol. 53, pp. 6-7.

Tsoukalis, Loukas. 1981. *The European Community and Its Mediterranean Enlargement.* London: George Allen and Unwin.

————. 1983. *The European Community: Past, Present, and Future.* Oxford: Basil Blackwell.

8

Organized Interests in
The European Union

Wolfgang Streeck and Philippe C. Schmitter

Whatever the differences between the various versions of the theory, or "pre-theory,"[1] of European regional integration, organized interest groups were always assigned a prominent place in it. Especially in the "neofunctionalist" image of "Europe's would-be polity"[2] and of the path to that polity, supranational interest group formation was expected to serve, in an important and indispensable sense, as a substitute for popular identification with the emerging new political community above and beyond the nation-state.[3] Most observers and in fact most participants in the integration process fully expected that the citizens of Europe would for a long time continue to adhere to traditional national passions and identities. They knew that if the united Europe had to wait until its citizens began to feel as "Europeans" rather than as the French, Germans, Italians, and so forth, it would not come about in any foreseeable future, and Europe as a political entity would in their lifetime never be more than a small bureaucracy in Brussels with very fragile support in national politics.

One reason why there nevertheless appeared to be hope was that things were believed to be different with the professional leaders of organized interest groups. Unlike the voters, they were seen as likely to orient themselves rationally and calculatedly to where the action was—that is, under the presumed logic of the neofunctionalist spillover process,[4] to "Brussels." Indeed in attitude and outlook, interest group officials and European civil servants could

---

*Wolfgang Streeck and Philippe C. Schmitter, "From National Corporatism to Transnational Pluralism: Organized Interests in the Single European Market." *Politics and Society* 19 (1991), No. 2, 133-64. Reprinted by permission of Sage Publications Inc. Slightly revised version in: V. Eichener and H. Voelzkow, eds., 1994: *Europäische Integration und verbandliche Interessenvermittlung*, Marburg: Metropolis Verlag, 181-215. Reprinted in: Colin Hay and Bob Jessop, eds., 1995: *Beyond the State? New Directions in State Theory*, London: Macmillan.

easily appear as birds of a feather: both appointed rather than elected, both experts and technocrats, both susceptible to a cosmopolitan orientation and lifestyle, and both professionally interested in the smooth management of complex interdependencies and likely to be distinctly disinterested in the traditional rituals and symbolism of nationhood. Just as civil servants like Jean Monnet had been persuading, cajoling, and manipulating the elected politicians and the administrative machineries of national states into emergent supranationalism, so the *Geschäftsführer* of business associations and trade unions were expected to inform their elected leaders that their interests had migrated to a new place and that the offices and decisions of their representatives had to follow suit.

In fact, the relationship between European bureaucrats and the full-time managers of collective interests that was envisaged by integration theory was even more intimate. As has been pointed out, interest groups were believed to have a much better, sharper, more intense perception of the effects of spillover on the situs and locus of decisions than did the average voter and as a result were expected to make their appearance at the supranational level earlier than their less insightful fellow citizens. But more importantly perhaps, the move of organized interests onto the European scene was expected to be further accelerated by European bureaucrats, who, in their search for a constituency, would be more than willing to promote interest organization on a scale coterminous with their supranational jurisdiction. Indeed in the perception of early integration theory, especially its neofunctionalist version, there was hardly anything in which "Brussels" could be more interested than in cultivating an environment, around the Commission in particular, of powerful interest organizations negotiating with Union officials and each other—as an *Ersatz* for the elusive pan-European citizen humming a pan-European supranational anthem when facing the Berlaymont office building.

Attracting a growing number of supranational lobbyists into the Union's decision-making process was seen as offering important payoffs, especially for the Commission. Cooperation with organized interests would not only provide civil servants with an indispensable input of detailed factual information in complex decisions. It also and above all was to bring about the socialization of powerful forces in European civil society into a worldview compatible with that of European bureaucrats and with the requirements of continued spillover. Having been drawn into the ambit of the Commission, a multitude of political players would learn from experience that management from the top, from the center, and from Brussels was more efficient and effective than national policy making. When they returned to their national capitals,—it was hoped and in fact predicted—would again become a lobby; this time not of their interest group vis-à-vis Brussels, but of Brussels vis-à-vis their national leaders, including their governments. By fostering a transnational system of organized interest representation, the Union and its Commission in particular would thus contribute to its own growth as a policy arena and executive body and lift itself out of the parochial entanglements of national politics and intergovernmental nondecision making into a safely anchored new world of supranational political management.

In many ways, the status provided for organized interests in the future European polity bore strong resemblance to a model of interest politics that some time later came to be known to students of politics as "neocorporatism." As in the latter, the integrated European polity was to be one that was primarily concerned with governing a "mixed economy" according to rules of technical and professional expertise whose prudent application was to help avoid social conflict and disruption. There also was to be a shift away from the territorial-electoral-parliamentary realm of politics toward powerful mechanisms of functional representation of producer groups, and there was an emphasis on close linkage between state and society through privileged participation of organized interests in policy and through mutually supportive organizational arrangements between the machineries of government on the one hand and of large, centralized interest organizations on the other. Above all, there was the idea of the future European political economy being kept together by a combination of technocratic professionalism shared among all major players regardless of divergent, specific interests and a web of dense and durable, bi-, tri-, and multilateral bargaining relationships involving both public and private bodies. This bargaining system would contribute to order less through shared values and interests of the bargainers than through common strategic imperatives of self restraint and compromise reflecting and respecting the complexity of a modern society and economy.

But while motivated speculation about the politics of a unified Europe prepared the ground for the (re)discovery of (neo)corporatism as a concept,[5] at the European level the reality of corporatism was not found. When in the early 1970s students of European integration, in despair over their subject, searching for new themes,[6] turned their energies to comparative politics, they recognized at the level of European nation-states something that looked conspicuously like what integration theory had long had in mind for Europe as whole. At the time, European nation-states were almost universally turning to centralized bargaining between firmly institutionalized class and sectoral interest groups. Facilitated, moderated, and supplemented by the government, this bargaining emerged as a reaction to the turmoil of 1968 and 1969 and as a recourse against the dislocations of the economic crises after 1973 and especially of the threat of inflation in societies with a strong labor movement whose governments were afraid of reneging on the postwar Keynesian welfare state commitment to politically guaranteed full employment. In turning to "neocorporatist concertation," as it came to be called, national governments appeared to be doing precisely what integration theorists had been counseling the European Union and its Commission. In order to integrate their political systems, they were relying more and more on deals with interest groups as distinct from electoral and parliamentary participation; they were sometimes bypassing and generally downgrading their parliaments as places of political decision making;

they attempted to govern through compromises with and between organized interests; and they were generating obligations of special interests to the collective good not through legislation passed by parliamentary majority but through collective bargaining in all possible forms and manners.[7]

THE FAILURE OF EURO-CORPORATISM

Not that there was nothing like that at all at the European level. But compared to the paradigmatic national political systems of the time, interest representation around and within the Union was always much more "pluralist" than it was corporatist: more organizationally fragmented, less hierarchically integrated, more internally competitive, and with a lot less control vested in peak associations over its affiliates or in associations over its members. Union and business association officials that were transferred to Brussels in the 1970s more often than not perceived this as a falling from grace at home and as a usually well-paid elimination from the excitement of domestic power games and succession struggles rather than as accession to the new center of political power. Belying the predictions of integration theory, by the mid-1970s at the latest it had become clear that the Brussels system of functional representation had failed to develop into a corporatist engine of supranationalism.

The history of organized supranational interests in Europe is short. Prior to the formation of the European Economic Community in 1958, European class, sectoral, and professional interest groups had only vague memories of collective action across national lines, and very little of it had been successful. Around the turn of the century, industry cartels among business firms, "proletarian internationalism" between trade unions, and some cooperative ventures involving professional groups emerged, but World War I seems to have put an end to most of this activity. After 1945, the insistence of the United States under the Marshall Plan that European countries act in concert on matters of postwar reconstruction laid a new foundation. But there is little evidence until the stimulus of the Treaty of Rome that national interest associations were prepared to establish permanent European-level organizations.[8]

Immediately after 1958, European peak associations began to form, especially for the representation of broadly encompassing industrial, commercial, and agricultural business interests: UNICE (European Confederation of National Employers' Federations) for industry (1958), COPA (Comité des Organisations Professionelles Agricoles) for agriculture (1958), a permanent conference for chambers of commerce (1958), UNACEE for craft industries (1958), COGECA (Comité Général de la Coopération Agricole) for agricultural cooperatives (1959), BFEC for banking (1960), and GCECEE for savings banks (1963). Workers and consumers look much longer to build their peak associations: both the European Trade Union Confederation (ETUC) and BEUC were established only in 1973. SEPLIS, representing the liberal, intellectual, and social professions, was created in 1975. By then, roughly the time of the first enlargement to include Great Britain, Ireland, and Denmark, all of the major functional groups were present. Affiliated to their broadly encompassing European peak organizations were exclusively national associations, most of which continued to command far greater resources than their nominally superior *Spitzenverbände* and all of which reserved the right to act on their own on matters of particular importance to them. For example, demonstrating their continued autonomy, the national associations of industrialists for each member state opened their own offices in Brussels. None of the European peak associations of this first wave had individuals or firms as direct members.[9]

Meanwhile, a myriad of more specialized, sectoral associations were also being formed. Some of these did have direct membership, but then they were rarely affiliated (and never subordinated) to the European peak associations. By 1985, the number of interest associations registered in Brussels had reached 654, according to a census carried out by the Commission.[10] Associations of business interests vastly outnumbered those of labor, with 20 unions and 79 professional associations facing 332 associations from industry, 139 from commerce, 6 representing craft and artisanal interests, and 5 associations of small and medium-sized enterprises. This mirrors a similar situation at the national level, where business interests also prefer to work through a greater number and variety of specialized intermediaries than do workers.[11]

The Commission seems to have deliberately encouraged the formation of these associations[12] and very quickly established a procedure for recognizing their special European status. This implied privileged access to its deliberations[13] even if recognition was typically not limited to only one organization per category. Each of the Commission's Directorates-General soon surrounded itself with a vast number of standing, advisory, and management committees, most of which were based on functional rather than territorial principles of representation.[14] Apparently in the early stages, the Commission attempted to confine lobbying to certified European associations, but this was subsequently relaxed to permit an increasing volume of direct contacts with national interest representatives.[15]

Advisory committees and expert groups mushroomed in subsequent years. The Commission itself has never employed very many officials[16] and has depended heavily on consultation with interest representatives, national government employees, and experts for drafting its directives and monitoring compliance with them. By the time the Single European Act was signed in 1986, the number of consultative bodies had grown to about 700, and it has almost doubled since then to 1,336 in 1988.[17] Interest representatives are well remunerated for attending meetings in Brussels, and indeed these payments might be interpreted as a subsidy for the development of an "appropriately structured" system of interest intermediation related and obligated to the European Union.

The corporatist capstone of the emerging system of Europe-wide functional representation might have been the Economic and Social Committee (ESC). This body was inserted in the Treaty of Rome and persists to the present day. Its 189 members (as of 1985) represent three "grand categories" of interest: employers, workers, and "others"—that is, agricultural and transportation interests, shopkeepers, artisans, consumers, environmental groups, and so forth. ESC members do not, however, represent European interest associations; rather, they are nominated as individuals by member governments and appointed by the Council of Ministers (*not* the supranational Commission) to four year-terms. While the ESC likes to think of itself as the "other European Assembly"—a sort of functional shadow to the territorially based European Parliament—there is general agreement that it has, in fact, accomplished very little.[18] In particular, it was never able to serve as a privileged access point for organized interests to European-level decision making and therefore failed completely in providing focus and structure to the growing pluralist system of European interest associations. It also proved entirely unsuitable to accommodate labor's ritual demands for a "social Europe" and prevent the "common market" from remaining exactly that—a customs union committed to liberalism and free trade.[19]

For a few years after 1968, this seemed to be about to change. With the accession to power of social democratic parties in major member countries and with national political elites still suffering from the shocks of their respective *autunni caldi*, the first Paris summit of the heads of state and government inaugurated an ambitious program to extend the domain of the European Union to a wide range of social policies. Subsequently for a short, intensive period between 1970 and roughly 1974, it seemed that labor was about to capture the same or similar substantive concessions and institutional privileges at the European level as it was picking up simultaneously in individual countries. If at all, it was then that labor leaders, in the way predicted by early integration theorists like Ernst Haas, began to take "Europe" seriously as a political arena in which to launch strategic initiatives.[20] Characteristically at that point, the ESC was set aside as too cumbersome and insufficiently *paritaire* to bear the burden of leading the Union into the era of "social partnership." Instead, the ministers of social affairs and, later, of economic and financial affairs decided to convoke a series of "tripartite conferences" bringing together the European peak associations and national representa-tives of capital and labor with officials of national governments and the Commission. These met six times until 1978—often in highly publicized settings—to discuss a wide range of macroeco-nomic and social policies. Their agenda paralleled that of the national concert efforts of the same period: full employment, inflation, wage restraint, fiscal policy, worker training, and productivity measures. A standing committee on employment with tripartite representation was established, and there was even a plan for creating a set of sectoral councils wherein capital, labor, and state officials were expected to come up with proposals for governing the steel, shipbuilding, textiles, aerospace, and telecommunications industries.

All this effort came to naught in 1978 when the strongest proponent of Euro-corporatism, the ETUC, withdrew its support under complaints about lack of progress and also confronted with rising dissent within its ranks. Especially after the defeat in the councils of Europe of the draft European company statute that was to expand codetermination from Germany to companies incorporated in Union law and with the demise in the 1970s of the draft directive on consultation and information in multinational enterprises (the so-called Vredelinck Directive), there was not much left that would have justified the enormous effort labor had invested in the building of a corporatist Social Dimension for the Union. By the end of the 1970s, all that remained of Euro-corporatism was the standing committee on employment and a few specialized working groups that continued to recycle the by now tattered idea of concert.

Why was it that a centralized pattern of interest politics did not emerge at the European level when it was so common in national polities? Rather than in neofunctionalist terms, the answer to the puzzle of the stagnant record of European interest politics has to be given in a language that recognizes the significance of conflict and power and does not submerge politics in the technicalities of managing sectoral spillovers. In particular, our argument emphasizes the importance for the growth of a centralized, publicly institutional ized interest politics of highly developed organizational and political capacities of *labor* during a polity's formative period—adding to whatever incentives *capital* may have on its own to get organized as well as contributing to the emergence of an active, interventionist, nonliberal *state* which may then in turn institutionalize labor as well as capital as principal participants in a centralized structure of political bargaining. That latter relation, we believe, is in itself crucial for the (further) growth of labor's political capacity as is the availability of partners for mutually centralizing cross-class alliances on the side of capital. In a nutshell, our point is that in uniting supranational Europe, it was not only the case that labor was, and continues to be, *underorganized* but there also was never a real possibility of a mutually organizing *interaction effect*, a *Wechselwirkung*, between labor and the two other major players in the political economy, capital and the state.

As to labor itself, there is no doubt that as a European actor labor is afflicted by *specific disabilities* that are not usually present at the national level and that do not in the same way affect business. Business, for example, finds it easier than does labor to overcome the problems posed by different national languages (at least nine in the Europe of the Twelve). It also is much less hampered by ideological divisions between different political orientations like that most prominently on the labor side between communists and social democrats. More importantly, however, the low organizational capacities of labor at the European Union level also reflect the wide regional disparities in Europe and the resulting divisions of interest between national labor movements.[21] The vast divergence in union concerns and strategies to which this gives rise are reflected, among other things, in the traditionally low significance for their affiliates of European sectoral and intersectoral union confederations. While for unions from advanced economies a joint European strategy is unlikely to offer improvements over what they have already gained on their own, to unions from weaker countries common demands tend to appear unrealistically ambitious and remote from their everyday practical concerns. Moreover, to unions in rich countries, common labor standards, even if they are intended to do no more than set a floor, may appear to threaten their own, higher standards. Still and at the same time, they may *exceed* the marginal productivity of the workforces of less wealthy countries, thereby undermining their ability to take advantage of increased capital mobility and attract foreign investment.[22] While it is *also* true that common standards may help unions in weaker economies to make more progress than they otherwise would and while they may make it easier for more affluent working classes to defend their employment against capital migration, bringing the different interests together and finding a compromise acceptable for both sides is far from simple. Indeed, uniting national union movements behind European programs and policies always required great political effort and skill. Even where these were successfully applied, the joint platforms that were in the end adopted often had to be left deliberately vague and rarely were more than symbolic in character.[23]

As a consequence of fundamental national differences, European union officials always had to face tendencies among their constituents either to seek national solutions for their problems and ignore the supranational level altogether or to pursue their "European" interests through intergovernmental channels, using their access to home governments to work either through the national embassy in Brussels lobbying the Commission or, more likely, through the Council of Ministers.[24] Frequently such initiatives were coordinated with the respective national peak associations of employers, resulting in trilateral national coalitions pursuing joint objectives in competition with other countries and thereby effectively cutting out or starving off the European system of functional representation.

On the other hand, labor fragmentation had originally been a condition in many countries whose labor movements later proved able to propel themselves into a trajectory of growing unification and centralization. Indeed we believe that the specific disabilities of European labor are often overrated in comparison to two other factors that would have frustrated progress toward comprehensive organization of labor and toward corporatist modes of interest intermediation and concertation even in the best of circumstances.

The first of these factors is the complete absence of significant *business* factions with an active interest in centralized negotiations with labor. While European capital is strongly represented in Brussels by both lobbyists for individual firms and sectoral and subsectoral trade associations, the interests that these defend are primarily those of enterprises and industries demanding protection and/or (de)regulation of their *product markets*. Although sometimes the same channels are also used to address social policy and labor market concerns—for example, in the 1970s to defeat the European Union directives on workforce participation and consultation—this is not their principal purpose. In fact, the *producer interests* pursued by firms and trade associations in Brussels are by and large and more or less tacitly shared by their workforces, with business interests often functioning in effect as vertical associations representing important firm-specific or sectoral interests of labor as well as of capital.[25]

By comparison, the interests of firms *as employers* are typically not directed at extracting favorable policies from Union bodies. European business has from the beginning refused to contribute to a transfer of social policy matters from the national arenas to (tripartite political bargaining in) Brussels. While firms and their associations are always available to European officials for formal and informal consultations, binding decisions are opposed usually with reference to the widely different conditions in member states and the economic need for "flexibility." It is important to note in this context that getting its will and keeping supranationalism and tripartism from growing did not require major organizational efforts from business. To protect the Brussels body politic from contagion by the neocorporatist disease that befell European nation-states in the 1970s, all business had to do was refuse its European peak associations the competence to enter into binding obligations on behalf of their national constituents. A trilateral polity can exist and grow only if all three sides are sufficiently centralized to take part in it. By not delegating authority upward to the European level, employers were, and still are, able to confine institutions like the Social Dialogue to a strictly nonbinding, consultative status. The growing frustration of European unions in the late 1970s with the minuscule results of long and complicated discussions in Brussels and increasingly with the European Union as such, was in large part due to the political strength business was able to draw from its organizational weakness.

Nowhere else is the neofunctionalist image of interest groups centralizing their organizations and activities at European level and thereby pushing regional integration forward as far from reality as it is in the case of European business associations. The implicit assumption in much of neofunctionalist writing is that in a set of interdependent economies a centralized pursuit of group interests is always and unproblematically the superior alternative to traditional, national, or subnational strategies. The evidence shows, however, that there may indeed be policy arenas such as social policy and industrial relations where different levels of regulation favor different social interests and where groups that are favored by decentralized regulation or by the unfettered operation of "market forces" find it easy to prevent centralization of regulatory capacity simply by refusing to build the organizations necessary for them to be able to make binding commitments at the central level. The result is growing interdependence between national economies due to progressing market integration without proportionate growth of regulatory institutions—with the consequence of integration and deregulation becoming one and the same.

The second factor that frustrated progress is the presence inside the European Union's quasi-state, or *nonstate*, of a strong *centrifugal center*, in the form of the Council of Ministers, which halted any attempt by supranational bodies, especially the Commission and the Parliament, to cultivate a strong constituency of organized interests that would in turn have enhanced the status of supranational Union institutions as an incipient sovereign government. No comparable barrier to central state formation and state growth has ever been present in a traditional nation-state. It should be noted that "intergovernmentalism," as it came to be called, had the same discouraging impact on the organization of business as it had on labor with opposite consequences for the realization of the respective interests. This is because under the unanimity principle of decision making, which is the hallmark of intergovernmentalism, a European interest group that wants to *prevent* a specific decision needs just one national government willing to veto that decision in the Council, frustrating even the most sophisticated lobbying efforts vis-à-vis the Commission. Where such a veto is not cast on ideological or interest-political grounds, a class like business, whose interest was and is essentially not in *shaping* but rather in *preventing* a centralized European social policy, could always hope to find allies in national governments concerned about their sovereignty. Intergovernmentalism thus made both encompassing organization and centralized negotiations with labor largely dispensable for European business, whose social policy interests, under the specific configuration of markets, national states, and supranational institutions that is the European Union, tend to be realized as it were by default.

Much of the corporatist debate of the 1970s was on the question of whether a strong state is a precondition for strong associations or whether strong associations can develop without, and may even substitute for, a strong state. Based on national observations and cross-national comparison, what seemed to emerge as a tentative consensus assigned a prominent place to the indispensable contribution of public power even in cases of "societal corporatism."[26] The European Union has never been permitted to develop the organizational design capacities necessary to reshape powerful interest organizations rooted in civil society. Whatever capacity it may have in this respect is vastly inferior to that of the Union's nation states, from which it is derived in the first place. Moreover the policy-making process in the Union is too fragmented and dispersed to place a high premium on interest organizational centralization at the European level. In the history of the Union up to the present, intergovernmentalism and the veto powers of individual nations were always strong enough to preempt or modify centrally made decisions. Organized interests thus had no other choice, even if they were otherwise inclined, than to maintain a strong national base and to cultivate established national channels of influence. This, as has been pointed out, holds in particular for groups and in policy arenas *where the interest is more in nondecisions than it is in decisions*. As long as the

Union—that is, its nonintergovernmental institutions such as the Parliament and the Commission—cannot autonomously determine the range of policy issues that come under its jurisdiction, its ability to influence the structure of organized group interests will remain low indeed.

CORPORATISM, THE NATION-STATE, AND THE DEREGULATION OF EUROPEAN ECONOMIES

There are, however, more and equally important and vexing relationships between corporatism, nationalism, supranationalism, and the distribution of power in the political economy. The heyday of corporatism in the 1970s was a period of distinctly *national* responses to the catastrophic deinstitutionalization of the capitalist world economy that started in the late 1960s and to the domestic and international disorder that ensued. Apart from the United States, where the absence of a European-style resurgence of labor militancy in 1968[27] had set the stage for a strategy of economic recovery through deunionization and deregulation, governments almost everywhere experimented with centrally negotiated "social contracts" of all sorts. These agreements served as a homemade replacement or functional equivalent for the now defunct set of international institutions that had in the past provided at least some form of stability for and among competing capitalist nations by, for example, imposing and enforcing external "balance of payments constraints" that helped national governments keep domestic "discipline." To an important degree, corporatist concert in the 1970s must be understood as a sometimes desperate turn to domestic political and institutional resources in a search for solutions to what really were international problems—a turn that reflected the almost complete absence on the eve of the crisis, in spite of three decades of international institution building, of technically viable and politically legitimate mechanisms of international cooperation.[28]

Member states of the European Union in particular had recourse to corporatism or attempted corporatism in the early 1970s. Indeed if the Union was mentioned in Europe at all during that period, it was to point out how useless it had proven as an instrument for tasks like the restoration of a stable monetary environment, for working out a common energy policy with the United States and perhaps OPEC (Organization of Petroleum Exporting Countries), or for fighting inflation and unemployment. The "dark age" of the European Union was above all a time when European national elites seemed to believe as a matter of course that the supranational European institutions they had set up in the 1950s and 1960s, embedded in a relatively stable world order, could not serve as a suitable tool for the restoration of that order and that therefore everybody had to find their own national solutions.[29]

National corporatism, we have maintained, was adopted as an alterative to an international response including a European one. At the same time, the use of domestic concert on a large scale was bound to make international concert even more difficult and thus contributed further to bringing the process of European integration, including the building of a European-level system of interest politics, to a halt. This was not only because emerging national corporatisms diverted the attention of policy makers and association officials away from "Brussels" and back to national capitals or because attempts at international cooperation would have added further complexity to the domestic bargaining process, thus reducing the elites' degrees of freedom and making compromise more difficult. It was also, and more importantly, because different countries turned out to be differently equipped institutionally for corporatist concert. While corporatism worked in some places, it failed dismally in others, and in yet others it worked for a while but created accumulated problems that later came home to roost. The economic performance of different capitalist economies thus became more divergent than ever in the 1970s, and as the history of European integration testifies, divergent performance is not at all conducive to countries giving up a share of their sovereignty—the weak ones being afraid of becoming subservient to the strong ones and the strong ones seeing no need to dilute, and even being afraid of diluting, their national success.

Second, it almost follows from the above that the resurgence of European integration, as signified by the Single European Act and the internal market project, was more than just incidentally related to the demise of national corporatism in the early 1980s. If anything, it had been the rapid decline of their "effective sovereignties"[30] that had undermined the capacity of national states in the developed capitalist world to sustain the kind of social contracts that they had entered into in response to the crisis. The neocorporatist exercises of the 1970s had in large part been attempts to shore up the systems of economic and social policy-making that had been put in place under the postwar settlement[31] and to prolong their lives beyond that of the international environment in which they had originally been embedded. Ultimately it turned out that this was not possible. The changes in the international position of the United States that had exhausted its capacity to act as a benevolent hegemon had gradually given rise in the 1970s to a domestic move away from the New Deal compromise, to a political economy that sought competitiveness through deregulation and deunionization and abandoned the social democratic principle that wages and social conditions were to be taken out of competition. After the final defeat of the Labor Law Reform Act in 1978, the Federal Reserve could feel free to respond to the second oil crisis with a dramatic increase in interest rates, ending inflation at the price of deindustrialization and causing a further, probably irreversible, decline in union organization. In the early 1980s, with effectively deregulated worldwide integrated capital markets, the destruction of American trade unions paid off handsomely in that it gave the United States the "flexible" markets and the "confidence" of financial investors required to underwrite an expansionist fiscal policy that has been ironically characterized as "Keynesianism in one country."

From the perspective of other capitalist countries, that term would appear to have carried a particularly ominous connotation. As the French socialist government after 1981 was soon to find out under the watchful eyes of other political elites, the dynamics of the international political economy after the second oil shock were governed by the old Roman imperial maxim, *quod licet Jovi non licet bovi*. Keynesianism had ceased to be universally available; it had become limited not just to one but to *only* one country. Being so much larger than everybody else and as a consequence so much less internationalized, having broken its unions, being still in control of the *de facto* world currency while no longer accepting the responsibilities of world banker, and for all these and other reasons being able to attract and maintain the confidence of what is euphemistically called "the financial markets" in spite of gigantic and growing deficits in its budget and foreign trade—the United States could effectively and successfully apply fiscal stimulus whereas the others could do so only at the expense of their capital running away and holders of financial assets dropping their currencies at their doorsteps.

The important point here is that some sort of effective Keynesian-expansionist capacity seems indispensable for the kind of corporatist concert and social contract bargaining that was to stabilize non-American capitalism in the 1970s. As much as these systems may otherwise have differed, under the rules of corporatist bargaining a state that cannot with any reasonable prospect of success promise to apply its fiscal and monetary policy tools to alleviate unemployment cannot possibly hope to gain concessions from unions or to influence settlements between unions and employers by, for example, offering to improve the terms of the bargain through a corresponding economic policy.[32] To put the use of its sovereignty up for negotiation, a state needs to have sovereignty in the first place. As the effective sovereignty and subsequently the Keynesian capacity of European nation-states faded, so did corporatism and with it the social-democratic project of politically guaranteed full employment.

Of course, not all of the causes for the demise of sovereignty and, therefore, national corporatism originated in the deinstitutionalization of the international economy or in the internal politics of the United States and the deflationary bias it introduced in the world capitalist system. A more general explanation lies in the growing interpenetration of capitalist economies that has now increased the external contribution to a typical western European country's national accounts to a level where it can no longer be treated as a mere addition to a primarily domestic economy. As the French have learned and as everybody else has learned from the French, interdependence does not make it impossible to create jobs by Keynesian stimulus, but unless a country has the size, the currency, and the social system of the United States, chances are that many of those jobs will emerge outside the territory whose government has increased the national debt to create them. Given the absence of international institutions to manage such interdependence, governments in the early 1980s felt hard-pressed, or saw a golden opportunity, depending on their political complexion, to withdraw the political full employment promise of the postwar period and yield control over the restoration of prosperity and employment in their international-ized national economies to "the market," including a deregulated labor market, thereby in effect accepting the increasingly demanding conditions placed by capital holders on industrial investment and conceding what Burnham once called "domestic sovereignty" to what is referred to in the jargon of international capitalism as "market forces." It is true that the decay of national corporatism in the late 1970s and in the 1980s was also rooted in domestic developments like qualitative changes in social structures, in the economy, and in domestic political systems that had imperceptibly at first eaten away at corporatism's structural and perhaps cultural foundations. While this is not the place to review these trends in any detail, three of them will be briefly discussed, adding to the reasons why a restoration of neocorporatism at either national or supranational level has become unlikely now and in the future.[33]

Increasing Differentiation of Social Structures and Collective Interests in Advanced Capitalist Societies

Neocorporatism assumed an underlying social structure that could be plausibly conceived of as polarized in to two large producer classes, "capital" and "labor." With hindsight, that assumption appears to have been already highly counterfactual when Western European countries in the late 1960s were increasingly moving toward neocorporatist forms of governance. While the corporatist working hypothesis of a bipolar organization of societal cleavages and identities was never more than a *heroic simplification* of a much more complex reality, it could be kept alive with the help of the powerful institutional reinforcement that both business and labor as organized actors had received from their beleaguered governments. Underneath the organizational and institutional structures, however, social change continued and perhaps even accelerated. In addition to strengthening the institutional position of labor movements, 1968 was also the birthdate of a new, highly educated, and politically outspoken *middle class* that increasingly found its specific concerns insufficiently represented in the post-1968, class-political institutional setup. Subsequently during the 1970s and 1980s, the substantive content of interest conflicts and the focus of policy attention shifted away from class-based lines of cleavage toward a panoply of discrete issues focusing on consumer protection, quality of life, gender, environmental, ethical, and other problems, each with its respective movements. As is well known, in most countries this weakened the capacity of social democratic parties to govern or alternatively strained the alliance between social democracy and the union movement. Neither was conducive to corporatist governance.

Market Instability and Volatility and Pressures on Firms to Increase the Flexibility" of Their Product Ranges, Technologies, and Social Organization

New production technologies based on microelectronics and cutting across traditional job classifications and professional categories have created possibilities for flexible production in relatively small units. In one sense, these processes increased the need for active assent on the part of workers and therefore the need for employers to bargain with them over the quality as well as the quantity of their contribution. But in another sense, they are occurring in highly differentiated settings that are not easy to cover by a standard contract and difficult for intermediaries to control. Indeed both unions and employer associations are today finding themselves increasingly shut out of an expanding range of workplace-specific deliberations and bargaining between their respective local constituents.

Changing Roles and Structures of Interest Associations

In the new social and market environment, negotiations aimed at establishing standard national solutions for the regulation of the employment relationship appear of decreasing relevance and at times may even be counterproductive when what is demanded are policies tailored to improving the productivity and international competitiveness of specific sectors and individual enterprises. As a result, the role of intermediary institutions, especially trade unions and employer associations, changed from the point of view of members and interlocutors, both of whom are searching for more differentiated mechanisms of representation. While decentralization may have taken very different courses in different countries, what it inevitably had in common was a weakening of the center, and it is there that corporatist bargains are traditionally struck.

Moreover the shift of employment from traditional manufacturing to the services and in some cases to public employment in a number of countries changed the character of unions in that unions from the public and private service sector became the largest units in national confederations. This seems to have weakened the organizational discipline that was traditionally maintained by unionized manual workers, especially from the metalworking sector.[34] These unions, whose industries were exposed to world market competition, have in the past typically been willing to observe wage restraint in exchange for political concessions. Their sectors have often been hard hit by deindustrialization, and such workers as remained after successful restructuring—if they joined

unions at all—were employed in more scattered sites with much more individu-
ated tasks. The very categories upon which macrocorporatist compromises were
built have thus become disaggregated and dispersed, and as a result centralized
negotiations on wages, benefits, and working conditions came under severe
pressure. In some cases (for example, that of Sweden), the system only
survived by shifting to a sectoral level.

Deregulation thus spread from the United States to Britain, the country with
the most open capital markets, and from there to the European continent,
meeting with declining resistance in changing domestic political economies.
What it involved was a more or less forceful, and more or less successful, attack
on the accumulated "rigidities" that more than three decades of "mixed
economy" had installed. In many cases, this included the dismantling or at least
the disregard of structures of collective bargaining and domestic compromise
that already under the late Keynesian regime had more and more been perceived
as obstructing industrial adjustment. Where dismantling got stuck, the proven
inability of governments to deliver on employment, and their growing
unwillingness to try, together with the insistence of unions on concessions and
institutional monopolies that capital and governments felt they no longer needed
to provide, created the atmosphere of "Europessimism" and "Euromalaise," not
to mention "Eurosclerosis," that was so pervasive in Europe during the first half
of the 1980s. The internal market project emerged at this time and in this
context.

THE RELAUNCHING OF THE EUROPEAN UNION: CUTTING THE CURRENCY OF NATIONAL POWER RESOURCES

If one wants a shorthand explanation for the renewed momentum of
European integration in the mid-1980s,[35] one would probably account for it
as the result of an alignment between two broad interests—that of large
European firms struggling to overcome perceived competitive disadvantages in
relation to Japanese and U.S. capital and that of state elites seeking to restore
at least part of the political sovereignty they had gradually lost at the national
level as a result of growing international interdependence. Unlike in the crisis
years of the 1970s, European large firms seem to have resolved at some point
in the early 1980s that the increased size of production runs and investments
required for world market competitiveness made it counterproductive to use their
clout in national political arenas to get protection from foreign competition
through subsidies, technical standards serving as nontariff trade barriers, or
privileged access to public procurement contracts. Instead of trying to benefit
from the economic nationalism that made European integration grind to a halt
in the 1970s, business throughout Europe seems to have become willing in the
1980s to join forces with political elites which, under the impact of their
economies' poor performances and with worldwide policy coordination with the

United States and Japan out of reach, found themselves under pressure to seek a *supranational pooling of eroded national sovereignties over economic policy*, to recapture collective autonomy in relation to the United States, and to begin to organize a competitive response to the Japanese challenge.

The main concession governments seem to have made in return for business giving up previous claims for national protection was that the future European political economy was to be significantly less subject to institutional regulation—*national or supranational*—than it would have been in the harmonization-minded *and* social democratic 1970s, when employers found themselves forced to struggle against a Union directive that would have made German-style codetermination obligatory for all large European firms. In the 1992 compromise, the project of European integration became finally and formally bound up with a deregulation project. While 1992 is all about sovereignty, it is about sovereignty vis-à-vis Europe's external environment, *not* its domestic economy. Indeed part and parcel of the pooling of sovereignties[36] under the Single European Act and of the political deals that made it possible is a redefinition of the relationship between the Union's "domestic" institutions and "the market" under which the latter stands to gain unprecedented freedom from intervention by the former. The mechanism to accomplish this, and a powerful reassurance for business that supranational sovereignty will indeed be used exclusively for the *external reassertion of*, as opposed to *internal intervention in*, the European economy, is "negative integration" through preemption of national regulatory regimes without a simultaneous supranational restoration of regulatory capacity. The adoption of "mutual recognition" as a novel method of defining and governing the internal market—a method that for all practical purposes amounts to a subtle form of deregulation[37]—can only be fully explained in this light.

Seen from a national perspective, 1992 amounts to a formal devaluation of vast political resources that have come to be organized in and around the nation-state. Declining effective sovereignty had long been chopping away at the value of investments in national political power that had been accumulated and cultivated for more than a century; this, after all, was why corporatism was eventually becoming untenable. The 1992 principle of mutual recognition may well be understood in analogy to the cut of a collapsed currency—an inevitable but nevertheless painful adjustment to reality with significant distributional side effects in that currency holders are more severely affected than are owners of real estate or productive capital. In present-day European nation-states with the successive layers of political, industrial, and social rights that have been built into them in the domestic struggles of the nineteenth and twentieth centuries, it is clearly labor that is in the former and capital that is in the latter position. While mutual recognition and the resulting interregime competition devalue nationally institutionalized power resources, they leave property rights untouched or even increase their value. As neocorporatism has always been conditional on a measure of political strength of organized labor, the prospects for its restoration in the post-1992 European nation-states are therefore dim.

This is not to say that everything that, in the analyses of the 1970s and 1980s, has come to be associated with corporatist modes of governance will disappear in Europe. Pragmatic sectoral partnerships between state agencies and groups of business firms, oscillating as it were between agency capture and *Selbstverwaltung*, are likely to continue to the extent that they are comfortably embedded in national policy styles and as long as they do not run afoul of European Union competition law, which well may happen. Especially if they have been labor-exclusive "private interest governments" from the beginning, as we have called them elsewhere,[38] they may remain viable for some time due to the savings on transaction costs they entail and regardless of the weakening of their sponsors in national state and legal systems. Multiemployer collective bargaining arrangements between trade unions and employers associations, where they already exist, may not disappear either—at least, again, for the time being. But corporatism as a national-level accord between encompassingly organized socioeconomic classes and the state by which an entire national economy is comprehensively governed would seem to be a matter of the past.

TOWARD A NEW EUROPEAN INTEREST POLITICS

The character of the emerging European polity has puzzled the literature on European integration from its beginnings. As it became clear that "regional integration" was an exclusively European phenomenon—the number of cases being no higher than one—the question became irrepressible of what the "dependent variable" was that integration theory expected to explain,[39] toward what "final state" (if at all) the integration process was moving, and what "the nature of the beast" was that students of European integration—like in the parable of the blind men and the elephant—were trying to grasp.[40]

Unlike in the early, "motivated" theorizing (until de Gaulle rehabilitated realism, both with and without a capital "R"), today hardly anybody[41] expects that the supranational European polity of the future will be a replication of the European nation-state of the past. Wherever else students of European politics may disagree, and they like to disagree a lot, as a minimum it now seems to be accepted that the political system of the post-1992 European Union will be fundamentally and by a quantum leap *more complex* than anything that has preceded it. For example, while Europe as whole will undoubtedly exist as a unified political entity of some as yet undetermined sort, the nation-states that now constitute the European Union will not disappear in that entity but will coexist with it.[42] Nor will Europe be simply an institutionalized system of international or intergovernmental relations; yet at the same time such relations will continue to play an important part in Europe alongside, and in interaction with, others.[43]   And similarly Europe will have supranational institutions contributing to the governance of what will be a domestic Western European polity, but these will have to share authority with national as well as with a dense web of international and transnational institutions which, too, will be constitutive elements of the emerging political system of Western Europe.[44]

Europe's future polity, that is to say, will be composed of traditional domestic relations *within countries*, traditional international relations *between countries*, less traditional transnational relations between both individuals and organizations across national boundaries, and entirely nontraditional supranational relations *between European-level public institutions* on the one hand and, on the other, a *European civil society* consisting of domestic, international, and transnational forces and relations and including both nation-states and, in manifold national and cross-national combinations, their constituents.   The possible dynamics of this unique and uniquely complex system of governance are as yet only poorly understood, and there is very little theory, if any at all, to guide such understanding.   This applies not the least to the literature on state formation and the role of class conflict in it.   While there always were more and other actors involved in the shaping of state structures than in the shaping of socioeconomic classes—for example, regional, ethnic, and cultural communities and interest groups—in the case of European integration classes, as well as other forces in civil society, have to compete for control over the newly emerging central level of governance with a qualitatively different set of players: a number of already existing, sovereign (or better and increasingly "semisovereign") nation-states.   One reason why the latter's continued presence inside the European polity makes a difference is that the international boundaries between them constitute powerful, additional lines of cross-cutting cleavage inside classes and interest groups that stand in the way of their fast and effective polity-wide organization.   Moreover, unlike in the nineteenth century, when the system of European nation-states was formed, social structures today appear too differentiated and political problems too variegated to be easily organizable along bipolar class lines—a condition that, while it is gradually yet fundamentally transforming the political makeup of established nation-states, can be expected to exert a much more powerful formative influence on the only now emerging polity of the integrated European Union.

There is, furthermore, a growing suspicion that conventional models of the growth of the modern European welfare state may not be applicable to the European Union.   For some time to come, whatever will occupy the place of the supranational aingle European state governing the Single European Market will likely resemble a pre-New Deal liberal state, with the following characteristics, in Marshall's terms:[45]

(i) A high level of *civil rights* enabling citizens to engage freely in contractual relationships inside and across national borders, accompanied by well-protected *human rights* to equal treatment before the law, freedom of movement, and so forth. Here the

European Court of Justice is of crucial importance and also the Council of Europe although the latter is not, of course, a European Union institution.

(ii) A low level of *political rights*, with the European Parliament continuing to play only a minor role in the system of European institutions. This holds in spite of the fact that the Parliament's direct election and its new powers under the Single European Act have vastly improved its status over what it was in the mid-1970s.

(iii) An even lower level of *social rights*, these being essentially limited to a set of European-wide health and safety standards. Historically, intervention on health and safety matters represents the earliest stage in the history of the modern welfare state. Present efforts to attach a "social dimension" to the internal market by starting with a set of generally binding health and safety standards are aimed at replicating the familiar national trajectory of welfare state development. But in the face of the retarded advancement of European-level political rights, there is little reason to expect such efforts to be particularly successful.

(iv) The almost complete absence of a European system of *industrial citizenship* that would give workers and unions rights to representation in industry as a functional domain at the European level, separate from the territorial domain of electoral politics. The closest the European Union will come to being a source of industrial citizenship—that is, to creating and safeguarding European-wide institutions of industrial relations and collective bargaining—is in providing for some form of labor participation under the European company statute. But, whatever this will in the end entail, it is likely to pale into insignificance when compared to some of the national systems of union rights that were part of the post-World War II national settlements.

The emerging shape of the European supranational nonstate—or even "post-Hobbesian" state[46]—does not bode well for a reappearance of neocorporatism above the disorganizing nation-state. We will now try to trace some of the implications of what we think we know about the future contours of the European polity for the structure and function of organized interests at the two newly emerging, additional levels of policy making and interest articulation in Europe: the subnational, or regional, and the supranational levels. Together with the member states, regional and supranational political entities share in the diffuse and fragmented sovereignty of the Union, blending into a highly interdependent but incompletely unified, loosely coupled, and diverse institutional complex—the new type of state that is the European Union—that confronts an at least equally diverse civil society acting in what after 1992 will be an integrated market.

INTEREST POLITICS AT THE SUBNATIONAL LEVEL

At the core of the 1992 process is the abolition of national boundaries between the markets of the 12 member states of the European Union.[47] As a result, the twelve formerly national economies will turn into regional subunits of a larger economic entity—a *region* being defined as a territorial society without sovereignty over its borders. Also, the existing regional subunits of

European nations, being no longer fenced in by common, national economic boundaries, will themselves become subunits in their own right of the larger, integrated European economy. This transformation of national into regional economies and of subnational regions into subunits of a supranational economy amounts to a regionalization of Europe as well as at the same time a Europeanization of its regions.

The potential importance of the regional level for the developing politics of Europe is underlined by the rich literature on industrial districts.[48] Its common theme is that of a strong, positive contribution of a dense, social-institutional infrastructure to the vitality of regional economies, like Baden-Württemberg in West Germany or parts of the "Third Italy," which engage in "high valued-added," "flexibly specialized,"[49] or "diversified quality"[50] modes of production. In many of these prosperous and world market-competitive areas, interest associations and apparently often unions seem to play an indispensable part in the negotiation of distributional compromises, the building of growth and productivity coalitions, the formation of public-private interfaces, the provision of a protective institutional exoskeleton for small, innovative firms, the generation of collective factor inputs, and the creation of institutions that allow for nonzero-sum cooperation among firms as well as between capital and labor at the workplace and beyond.

Recent developments seem to indicate that the former regional subunits of European national economies may be about to become independent actors on the European Union stage.[51] A number of European regions, most prominent among them Catalonia, Lombardy, and Baden-Württemberg, have set up permanent offices in Brussels that bear conspicuous resemblance to embassies. Moreover, their heads of government have met several times to discuss strategy and form coalitions concerning their interests vis-à-vis the European Union. If this trend were to continue, regions would join nations, classes, sectors, and firms as participants in European-interest politics, adding another category of players and further complexities to a scene that is already highly complex and pluralistic.

Europeanization of regional interests, and especially interregional political competition for Union resources, is far from being universally welcomed.[52] For one thing, while it would improve the position of the Commission, it would also and *ipso facto* tend to weaken further what is left of sovereignty at the national level, which is why national governments have been found to resent actively the formation of direct connections between Brussels and "their" subnational territories. Also, if regions are admitted to European politics, regional subunits of *federal* states, having independent powers of legislation, taxation, budgeting, and so on, will likely have an advantage over regions in more centralized countries; note the absence from the above list of, say, the Midlands in England.

An important question with respect to the possible emergence of a regional level of European-interest politics concerns the sources and conditions of labor inclusiveness of regional regimes—especially whether regional power resources of labor can be generated endogenously inside the region or need to be mobilized exogenously using national power resources under the protection of a sovereign border. Regions, as has been pointed out, are societies that lack control over their borders. As European nation-states turn into regions of an integrated market economy, nationally legislated labor market regimes are likely to lose much of their force, and the same holds for protective barriers against cross-border competition; this, after all, is what the expected deregulatory effect of 1992 is all about. The survival and growth of regional labor-inclusive institutions inside the integrated internal market and with it, perhaps, that of regionally based non-price-competitive production, would then have to depend on nonnational, regionally indigenous forces or would require that functional equivalents for national-level supports be found at the supranational level to balance the decline in national political capacities that is associated with 1992.

Much of the literature on regional political economies seems to take the position that the composition and survival of their regimes is indeed, and always was, largely independent from national institutions. Typically the institutional infrastructure of economically successful European regions is described as based in *local* cultures, traditions, and politics that, by implication, would be unlikely to be destabilized by an attenuation of national sovereignty. Apart from the fact that culture and tradition may rapidly lose vitality in the modernizing, internationalizing post-1992 European economy, however, a case could be made that, certainly as far as the presence of unions and of a tripartite power balance in regional economies is concerned, this severely underestimates the role played in the past by *national* power resources,[53] like labor law creating or supporting various overt or covert mechanisms of union security or protective monetary and trade policies.

Regions, not being states, are by definition unable to insert coercive power in the voluntary contractual and communitarian relations between their citizens. Their social organization is that of a civil society largely undistorted, as it were, by public intervention. In particular, regions would seem to lack the capacity to provide the kind of public support that has generally been found to be required to transform unstable, voluntaristic, pluralistic unions into institutionally "mature" ones that are capable of looking in corporatist fashion beyond the individual enterprise or occupational group to the sector, the country, or for that matter the region as a whole. Regionally based unionism in the European Union would have to do without external sources of associational monopoly, without authoritative stabilization of bargaining arenas, and without recourse to a public sphere balancing the manifold advantages employers enjoy in the marketplace. It is not easy to see how the disabling effects on union movements of the erosion of institutional supports at the national level should be counterbalanced by unions turning to the regional level where such supports have never existed.

In any case, even if it were somehow possible to create stable tripartite systems of regional governance, referring to this as "regional corporatism" may be highly misleading. Corporatism requires encompassing organizations that internalize a significant part of the externalities of a group's collective action and interests, and allow for hierarchical coordination between different levels of interest aggregation and group activity. Neither condition would be met in a Europe of regional tripartisms. If national-level corporatism has been undermined by growing international interdependence beyond the control of the parties at the bargaining table, regional arrangements are even more affected by the shrinking effective size of modern polities. The tyranny of external effects, as it has been called, may be and clearly is on the advance at the national level; but it certainly is incomparably more severe in the much smaller action space of a subnational region, especially after the demise of national regulations that in the past have taken a core set of social and constitutional conditions out of interregional competition.

Moreover, in moving their organizational center of gravity toward the region, as most of the industrial district literature more or less explicitly advises them to do, unions would write off any aspiration they may have had for playing a role in the political management of interregional externalities. Regionalized unions would inevitably be partners, junior or not, of regional capital trying to survive in interregional free market competition. Such unions would have to cease trying to act as agents of interregional redistribution. While the *mezzogiorno* policy of Italian unions in the 1970s, which relied on the movement's centralized, national power to demand regional development programs for the impoverished south of the country, may not have been particularly successful, a regionally decentralized union movement would have been unable to agree on any such policy in the first place. Today regionalized unionism would for the same reasons be incapable of a political, as opposed to a market-driven, response to the deep interdependence of regional economies with the larger European and global economic context—a condition that has become more profound than ever and that incidentally fundamentally distinguishes today's regional economies from those of the past.

It is conceivable that political control over economic interdependence is presently beyond recapture and that union organizational domains may for a long time or forever be bound to be significantly narrower than whatever the relevant "market" may be. But decentralization of unions and industrial relations toward regional arenas will clearly not remedy this condition, and to the extent that it ratifies the possibly inevitable fragmentation of organized interests, it actually amounts to the very opposite of corporatism. The emergence of regional arenas of interest politics seems to advance, not the organization of labor or for that matter of capital, but rather its *disorganization*. In the 1992 environment in particular, new opportunities for interest articulation at the regional level would appear to increase actors' range of choice between political channels widely beyond what would be compatible with the orderly world of corporatism. In addition to the enterprise, the sector, the nation, and perhaps Europe as a whole, struggling factions inside interest associations, including unions, would have yet another option for pursuing sectional interests separately and on their own in coalition with other categories of equally fragmented interests or with ambitious local governments. By undermining associational monopoly and interassociational hierarchy, the fragmentation of interests and the pluralist proliferation of political opportunities that is entailed in the "regionalization of Europe" adds to the decomposition of national-level corporatisms as well as to the obstacles to its supranational resurrection.

INTEREST POLITICS AT SUPRANATIONAL LEVEL

Tripartism never really worked in Brussels,[54] and where it was tried, it was always too encapsulated and marginal to come in any way close to a neocorporatist model of governance. There is no reason to believe that this will change. The negative integration mode of the 1992 process—the move away from harmonization to mutual recognition—ensures that the eroded domestic sovereignty of nation-states will only partly, if at all, be re-created at the Community level. Unlike older, more naive images of regional integration, allowance has to be made today for the possibility that national political arenas, themes, and regulatory instruments that are rendered obsolete by integration are not always and necessarily reconstructed at the level of the emerging supranational polity. Rather than being moved upward, they are as likely to dissipate in a larger, less orderly, or less mature institutional complex and may thereby more or less intentionally be turned over to, or replaced by, the voluntarism of market and civil society. Where this happens, it deprives what might aspire to become a European federal government of a range of subject matter and decisional discretion that it otherwise could use and indeed would need to build the mutual give-and-take in and between interest groups and public bodies that is the indispensable basis for stable neocorporatist exchange.

A case of limited state capacity at the European level reducing the incentives for comprehensive organization of economic interests is the absence of a European central bank.[55] Historically, tripartite corporatist bargaining has typically involved the government's use not only of fiscal but also of monetary policy instruments. The need to be represented in bargaining over monetary policy was an important reason for socioeconomic interests, in particular for employers, to get organized. The European system of central banks, however, provided it will some day come into being, will be carefully shielded from political pressures, not least by its diffuse and decentralized internal structure. Moreover, a European central bank is likely for a long time to continue to be subject to strongly institutionalized deflationary, "monetarist" preferences[56]—if only because the European Union as an imperfectly unified actor in the world economy will need time to get used to the reflationary possibilities offered by a large economy with a currency that could in principle compete for the role of world money.

Another important ingredient of 1970s-style neocorporatism—centralized collective bargaining between capital and labor—is entirely missing at the European level, and nothing is in sight that would indicate its impending appearance.   In national industrial relations systems, centralized collective bargaining was often advanced by encompassing employers' associations forcing unions to unify their policies and organizational structures.[57] No such support will be forthcoming at the European level in the foreseeable future, not least because the interregional mobility of capital will perhaps indefinitely now exceed that of labor and because centralization would deprive capital of the strategic advantages of competition-driven industrial relations at regional or enterprise level.   The same applies to the other historical source of external facilitation, government intervention.   Europe-wide institutions are unlikely to develop a capacity to serve as carryover mechanisms from the unionized to the nonunionized sector so as to protect employers in the former from competition by employers in the latter.

The emergence of European-level collective bargaining is further impeded by mutual incompatibility of existing national industrial relations systems. While in some countries collective agreements are negotiated at the enterprise level, in others they are concluded for all firms that belong to a specific sector or a given national or subnational territory.   The latter, in addition to requiring the presence of strong employers' associations and preferably state-sponsored extension mechanisms making agreements binding on nonaffiliated firms, depends crucially on the large and more prosperous firms being included in the territorially defined bargaining units; otherwise industrial unions would be deprived of the opportunity to increase their bargaining power in small firms by enlisting as their ally the willingness to settle and the ability to pay of large firms.   In the absence of supranational employer associations and facilitating state intervention, however, all unions can hope to accomplish in building what the Commission has euphemistically called a "European industrial relations system"[58] are consultations and perhaps negotiations with the headquarters of large multinational firms.[59] But while this would be compatible with national industrial relations systems based on enterprise bargaining, European enterprise agreements would over time inevitably tend to exempt the national subsidiaries of the respective enterprises from the domain of sectoral-territorial bargaining. The result would be a weakening of existing national multiemployer bargaining regimes.   Since sectoral-territorial bargaining is used by unions to reduce regional and interfirm wage differentials, unions would have not just organizational but also political reasons for objecting to European enterprise-level bargaining even if this is likely to be the only form of supranational collective bargaining on offer.

Also, there is no reason to believe that an increase in political opportunities for labor at the European level, assuming that it will ever come to pass, will make consensus building in European labor organizations less difficult. In fact, if outcomes matter more, interest differences assume more weight. Organizational, political, and ideological divergence may be even less crippling in this respect than would different national labor market structures, training systems, or living standards.[60]   Trade unions from rich countries traditionally offer their poorer counterparts assistance in the pursuit of aggressive demands for wages, holidays, social security benefits, and so forth. But what to them may appear to be internationalist concern for their fellow workers' rights and well-being, the latter may eventually perceive as designed to protect their richer brothers and sisters from capital outflow and subsequent job loss.[61]   As long as calls for Union-wide labor standards have no practical consequences, they are likely not to be opposed by unions in weaker economies. When confederal policies may have a real impact, their formulation could become more contested.[62]

European-level relations between capital and labor, instead of constituting the core of the European political economy, will for the foreseeable future remain compartmentalized in the private sphere of large multinational enterprises and will thus be essentially nonpolitical and voluntaristic in character. Where labor-capital relations enter the political arena, they will mainly take the form of a set of discrete "labor" and "social policy" issues. As such, they will lend themselves to being dealt with by bureaucrats, experts, and intergovernmental committees in the same way as are, for example, labeling rules regarding the cholesterol content of palm oil or regulations for the recycling of mineral water containers. Rather than driving the constitutional bargain underlying the political system, the traditional class issues of industrial society will have to compete on an equal plane with "postindustrial" themes like environmental protection, consumer rights, equality between men and women, and so forth—issues that by their nature defy integration into an encompassing framework of "class" politics.[63]

The evolutionary alternative to neoliberalism as a model for the European political economy is clearly not (German or Scandinavian) neocorporatism. More likely appears an American-style pattern of "disjointed pluralism" or "competitive federalism," organized over no less than three levels—regions, nation-states, and "Brussels." As in the United States and perhaps more so, this system would be characterized by a profound absence of hierarchy and monopoly among a wide variety of players of different but uncertain status. Interest associations, and quite a few of them, will certainly be among those players. But they will have to compete for attention with national states, subnational regions, large firms, and specialized lobbyists, leaving their constituents with a wide range of choices among different paths of access to the Union's political center and enabling them to use threats of exit to coerce their representatives into pluralist responsiveness. Just as fundamental constitutional questions of sovereignty and hierarchy inside the Union's quasi-state concerning, for example, the relative status of regions, nations, and supranational bodies—will remain unsettled and uncertain, so will the hierarchical relations between firms, sectoral associations, and peak associations in its system of functional representation.

Given the constitutional bargain that underlies the relaunching of the European Union in the 1980s, no mechanism is in sight that could rationalize its political system, help crystallize its *mélange* of actors and processes, and establish corporatist monopolies of representation, interassociational hierarchies, or for that matter a predominant position for the Commission's bureaucracy and technocracy. Whatever turn the European Union may take after 1992, it will not reverse the tide and reorganize European capitalism in the neocorporatist cast.

NOTES

1. Ernst B. Haas, "The Study of Regional Integration: Reflections on the Joy and Anguish of Pretheorizing," in Leon N. Lindberg and Stuart Scheingold, (eds.), *Regional Integration: Theory and Research* (Cambridge, MA: Harvard University Press, 1971), pp. 3-42.

2. Leon N. Lindberg and Stuart A. Scheingold, *Europe's Would-Be Polity: Patterns of Change in the European Community* (Englewood Cliffs, NJ: Prentice Hall, 1970).

3. On the following, see in particular Ernst B. Haas, *The Uniting of Europe: Political, Social and Economic Forces 1950-1957* (London: Stevens and Son, 1958).

4. Which was, of course, the core concept of Haas's seminal, "neofunctionalist" theory of European and regional integration. Haas, op. cit. (note 9).

5. See especially Philippe C. Schmitter, "Still the Century of Corporatism?" in Philippe C. Schmitter and Gerhard Lehmbruch (eds.), *Trends towards Corporatist Intermediation* (London: Sage, 1979), pp. 7-52; "Corporatism (Corporativism)," forthcoming in *The Encyclopedia of the Social Sciences*; Philippe C. Schmitter, "A Sketch of an Eventual Article on the European Community as an Extreme Example of a Newly Emergent Form of Political Domination," unpublished manuscript, 1989.

6. Ernst B. Haas, "Turbulent Fields and the Theory of Regional Integration," *International Organization*, Vol. 30, No. 2, Spring 1976, pp. 173-212.

7. Gerhard Lehmbruch, "Liberal Corporatism and Party Government," in Philippe C. Schmitter and Gerhard Lehmbruch (eds.), *Trends towards Corporatist Intermediation* (London: Sage, 1979).

8. The exceptions seem to be CIC (professional association of executive workers, founded in 1951), FIPMEC (small business associations for artisanal and craft trades, 1951), CEA (business association for the insurance industry, 1953), CIF (association for public service employees, 1955), COCCEE (trade and commerce, 1957), and EUROCOOP (association of consumer cooperatives, 1957).

9. It should be noted that many of these associations affiliated national associations from countries that are not, or were not at the time, members of the European Union. For example, UNICE had twenty-seven affiliates in 1980, of which fourteen were from (then) non-European Union countries. The ETUC has, in addition to most union confederations from the twelve member nations, representatives from all EFTA countries and from Malta, Cyprus, and Turkey. For by now more or less outdated descriptive surveys of European-level interest organizations, see Alan Butt Philip, "Pressure Groups

in the European Community," *UACES Occasional Essay 2* (London: University Association for Contemporary European Studies, 1985); Economic and Social Committee of the European Communities, *European Interest Groups and Their Relations to the Economic and Social Committee* (Farnborough, England: Saxon House, 1980); Emil J. Kirchner and K. Schwaiger, *The Role of Interest Groups in the European Community* (Farnborough, England: Gower, 1981); J. Meynaud and D. Sidjanski, *Les groupes de pression dans la Communauté Européenne* (Brussels: Institut de Sociologie, 1971).

10. Commission of the European Communities, *Répertoire des organisations professionelles crées dans le cadre des Communautés Européennes* (Brussels: Edition Delta, several editions).

11. Wolfgang Streeck, "Interest Heterogeneity and Organizing Capacity: Two Class Logic of Collective Action?" in Roland Czada and Adrienne Windhoff-Heretier (eds.), *Rational Actors in Institutional Settings* (Boulder, CO: Westview Press, 1990).

12. For example, Sicco Mansholt seems to have played a major role in the founding of COPA; See Lindberg and Scheingold, op. cit. (note 2), p. 173. In the extreme case of EUROFER, the Union sponsored the creation of a Europe-wide cartel; see op. cit. (note 9), Butt Philip, p. 45.

13. Lindberg and Scheingold, op. cit. (note 2), p. 173; Jane Sargent, "Corporatism and the European Community," in Wyn Grant (ed.), *The Political Economy of Corporatism* (London: Macmillan, 1985), pp. 229-53.

14. Not all access to these committees was, however, restricted to functional representatives. Many involve "experts," which admittedly may often be difficult to distinguish from lobbyists. For a description of forty-six of these consultative bodies, see Economic and Social Committee of the European Communities, op. cit. (note 9), pp. 23-52.

15. J. A. Caporaso, *The Structure and Function of European Integration* (Pacific Palisades, CA: Goodyear, 1974), pp. 23-52.

16. As of 1989, there were 3,277 officials assisted by 9,202 staff personnel in the employ of the Commission.

17. Jurgen Grote, "Guidance and Control in Transnational Committee Networks: The Associational Basis of Policy Cycles at the EC Level," unpublished manuscript, 1989.

18. N. Nugent, *The Government and Politics of the European Community* (Durham, NC: Duke University Press, 1989); J. Lodge and V. Herman, "The Economic and Social Committee in EEC Decision-Making," *International Organization*, Vol. 34, No. 2, Spring 1980, pp. 265-84. Even the Committee's own propaganda literature admits that "it was regarded as the most unobtrusive of Community institutions" (Economic and Social Committee of the European Communities, *The Other European Assembly* [Brussels: ESC Press, Information and Publications Division, 1986], pp. 13-14).

19. Where, in addition, the principal lines of cleavage were not between capital and labor but rather between "Gaullists" and "Atlanticists" and between the proponents of supranationalism and national sovereignty. As these conflicts began to dominate and eventually block the Union's agenda in the 1960s, introducing social questions in addition was a hopeless endeavor from the outset.

20. Not that Haas would have predicted or approved the substance of those initiatives, which to a large extent was clearly outside the spectrum of the "pluralist industrialism" of the 1950s, and in the eyes of many observers signaled a return to "class conflict" and "ideology." See Haas, op. cit. (note 6).

21. D. C. Campbell, "Multinational Labor Relations in the European Community," *ILR Report*, Vol. 27, No. 1, Fall 1989, pp. 7-14; J. Alexander, "Divergent European Community Unionism: A Threat to Single Market Unification?" unpublished manuscript, 1989; Jelle Visser, "Trade Union Diversity in Western Europe: Dimensions, Origins, and Consequences," paper presented at the IRRU Conference on Industrial Relations and the European Community, University of Warwick, Coventry, England, 1989.

22. Tommaso Padoa-Schioppa, "Questions about Creating a European Capital Market," in R. Bieber, R. Dehousse, J. Pinder, J. H. H. Weiler (eds.), *1992: One European Market?* (Baden-Baden, Germany: Nomos Verlagsgesellschaft, 1988), pp. 283-292.

23. P. Cressey, "Trade Unions and the Social Dialogue," paper presented at the IRRU Conference on Industrial Relations and the European Community, University of Warwick, Coventry, England, 1989. In that sense, the encompassingness of labor's organizational structure at the European level, as indicated by the low number of unions compared to business associations, is illusory. If the internal policy-making capacities of European union confederations are taken into account, the picture changes dramatically.

24. For a case study, see Paul Teague, "Trade Unions and Extra-National Industrial Policies: A Case Study of the Response of the British NUM and ISTC to Membership in the European Coal and Steel Community," *Economic and Industrial Democracy*, Vol. 10, No. 2, May 1989, pp. 211-37.

25. On the difference between class and producer interests and its reflection in the organizational structures and strategies of business, see Streeck, op. cit. (note 11).

26. Alan Cawson (ed.), *Organized Interests and the State: Studies in Meso-Corporatism* (London: Sage, 1985); Wyn Grant (ed.), *The Political Economy of Corporatism* (London: Macmillan, 1985).

27. See the book by Colin Crouch and Alessandro Pizzorno (eds.), *The Resurgence of Class Conflict in Western Europe since 1968*, 2 vols. (London: Macmillan, 1978).

28. Paul McCracken et al., *Towards Full Employment and Price Stability: A Report to the OECD by a Group of Independent Experts* (Paris: Organisation for Economic Co-operation and Development, 1977).

29. Of course, as has been pointed out, the period in question was also notable for attempts by unions and social democratic governments to move the European Union to the left. With hindsight, this may be seen as another manifestation of the general confusion and indecision of the time when the left was still benefiting from the momentum of 1968 while the right was beginning to launch its counterattack with the support of, as it were, 1973. Moves toward a "social Europe" may in this situation have been an important reason for business and its political allies to hold back on European integration. Having not been able to escape national corporatism after 1968, it made little sense for them to accept supranational corporatism in addition at a time when the tide was already beginning to turn in their favor.

30. Stanley Hoffmann, "The European Community and 1992," *Foreign Affairs*, No. 4, Fall 1989.

31. Peter Gourevitch, *Politics in Hard Times* (Ithaca, NY: Cornell University Press, 1986).

32. Marino Regini, "Political Bargaining in Western Europe during the Economic Crisis of the 1980s," in O. Jacobi et al. (eds.), *Economic Crisis, Trade Unions and the State* (London: Croom Helm, 1986) pp. 61-76.

33. On the following, see Philippe C. Schmitter, "'Corporatism Is Dead! Long Live Corporatism!' Reflections on Andrew Shonfield's 'Modern Capitalism'," *Government and Opposition*, Vol. 24, No. 1, Winter 1989, pp. 54-73.

34. Colin Crouch, "Trade Unions in the Exposed Sector: Their Influence on Neo-Corporatist Behavior," unpublished manuscript, 1988.

35. For more detail, see J. Sandholtz and J. Zysman, "1992: Recasting the European Bargain," *World Politics*, No. 1, October 1989; Wolfgang Streeck, *The Social Dimension of the European Economy: A Discussion Paper Prepared for the 1989 Meeting of the Andrew Shonfield Association* (London: Andrew Shonfield Association, 1989).

36. Robert O. Keohane and Stanley Hoffmann, "European Integration and Neo-Functional Theory: Community Politics and Institutional Change," unpublished manuscript, 1989.

37. Hoffmann, op. cit. (note 30); Streeck, op. cit. (note 35).

38. Wolfgang Streeck and Philippe C. Schmitter, "Community, Market, State—and Associations? The Prospective Contribution of Interest Governance to Social Order," *European Sociological Review*, Vol. 1, No. 2, September 1985, pp. 119-38.

39. Ernst B. Haas, *The Obsolescence of Regional Integration Theory* (Berkeley: Institute of International Studies, University of California at Berkeley, 1975).

40. Don Puchala, "Of Blind Men, Elephants and International Integration," *Journal of Common Market Studies*, No. 3, March 1972, pp. 267-84.

41. The exception being the "federalist" tradition of thinking about the European Union with its strongholds in Italy (the tradition of Spinelli) and remarkably in the United Kingdom (compare Michael Burgess, "Federalism and European Union: Past, Present and Future in the European Community," unpublished manuscript, 1989).

42. Puchala, op. cit. (note 40).

43. Keohane and Hoffmann, op. cit. (note 36).

44. Schmitter, op. cit. (note 5).

45. Th. H. Marshall, *Class, Citizenship and Social Development* (Garden City, N.Y.: Doubleday, 1964).

46. Schmitter, op. cit. (note 5).

47. R. Bieber, R. Dehousse, J. Pinder, J. H. H. Weiler, "Introduction. Back to the Future: Policy, Strategy and Tactics of the White Paper on the Creation of a Single European Market," in Bieber et al. (eds.), *1992: One European Market?* pp. 13-31; Michael Calingaert, *The 1992 Challenge from Europe: Development of the European Community's Internal Market* (Washington, DC: National Planning Association, 1988).

48. Sebastiano Brusco, "The Emilian Model: Production Decentralization and Social Integration," *Cambridge Journal of Economics*, Vol. 6, No. 2, June 1982, pp. 167-84; Charles F. Sabel, "Flexible Specialization and the Re-emergence of Regional Economies," in Paul Hirst and Jonathan Zeitlin (eds.), *Reversing Industrial Decline? Industrial Structure and Policy in Britain and Her Competitors* (New York: St. Martin's, 1989), pp. 17-70.

49. Michael J. Piore and Charles F. Sabel, *The Second Industrial Divide: Possibilities for Prosperity* (New York: Basic Books, 1984).

50. Arndt Sorge and Wolfgang Streeck, "Industrial Relations and Technical Change: The Case for an Extended Perspective," in Richard Hyman and Wolfgang Streeck (eds.), *New Technology and Industrial Relations* (Oxford, England: Basil Blackwell, 1988).

51. For a strong statement to this effect, see G. Majone, "Preservation of Cultural Diversity in a Federal System: The Role of the Regions," unpublished manuscript, 1989.

53. Walter Korpi, *The Working Class under Welfare Capitalism: Work, Unions and Politics in Sweden* (London: Routledge and Kegan Paul, 1978).

54. Sargent, op. cit. (note 13).

55. E. Holm, "The Politics of Europe's Money," in B. Crawford and P. Schulze (eds.), *European Self-Assertion: A New Role for Europe in International Affairs* (forthcoming).

56. Committee for the Study of Economic and Monetary Union, "1989: Report on Economic and Monetary Union in the European Community."

57. Peter Swenson, *Fair Shares: Unions, Pay and Politics in Sweden and West Germany* (Ithaca, NY: Cornell University Press, 1989).

58. Commission of the European Communities, *The Social Dimension of the Internal Market: Interim Report of the Intergovernmental Working Party*, Special Edition of *Social Europe* (1988).

59. Campbell, op. cit. (note 21).

60. While this condition has existed for a long time, it was exacerbated in the mid-1980s by the accession to membership of three Mediterranean countries: Spain, Portugal, and Greece. Today regional disparities in Europe are much wider than they are in the United States. According to *Eurostat Review 1977-1986*, hourly labor costs in Portugal for manual and nonmanual workers in 1984, expressed in ECUs, amounted to 16 percent of German labor costs. The respective figure for Greece was 28 percent (U.K., 63 percent, France, 86 percent). Later data or more exact measures are not at present available.

61. Wolfgang Streeck, "More Uncertainties: West German Unions Facing 1992," *Industrial Relations* (forthcoming, 1991).

62. We owe this point to a recent, as yet unpublished, paper by Peter Lange (1990).

63. To this extent, they would be subject to a "policy style" that is specifically "European"—that is, Union-European. In brief, the Brussels policy process seems to depend on successful decontextualization and depoliticization of the issues at stake— "pragmatically" isolating them from "ideological" meanings and as much as possible avoiding their incorporation in any coherent political symbolism. Didactically helpful for this kind of exercise is the recurrent discovery in European Union bodies that apparently identical political arrangements and outcomes can sometimes be of completely contrary significance in different national, political and ideological environments—for example, legally based codetermination rights at the workplace in Britain and Germany. After policy "issues" have been divested of their emotional and ideological aura and fragmented and individualized, their treatment can be assigned to "experts"—specialists, that is, in comparative inventories of decontextualized and depoliticized problems, positions, and compromises and in the extraction of the smallest common denominator from such inventories.

9

The Nature of Political Parties in The European Union

Karl Magnus Johansson

Hrbek comments as follows on the emergence of transnational links between European political parties:

> If one sees the EC as a multi-level system . . . and if one understands integration as a process during which mutual links between these levels grow, then the existence and activities of transnational party organisations are important for the integration progress. They help to establish and maintain links between different levels; they are a component of the sociopolitical infrastructure of the EC system which can be regarded as an emerging political system (Hrbek, 1988: 457; see also Henig, 1979: 5).

In their seminal work the Pridhams (1981: 5) concluded that transnational party cooperation had been "something of a 'forgotten' aspect of Community studies." The few studies that had been conducted until then had focused on the political groups in the Common Assembly and the European Parliament (see Fitzmaurice, 1975; Haas, 1958; Oudenhove, 1965). However, the founding of transnational party federations in the mid-1970s, as a response to the decision in 1974 that the Members of the European Parliament would be directly elected, acted as a stimulus for further research (see Gresch, 1978; Lodge and Herman, 1982; Niedermayer, 1983; Pridham and Pridham, 1981; Rutschke, 1986). Today, further stimulus is provided by the call for European parties, the obvious interest on the part of various political parties in establishing transnational party networks, and the enhanced powers of the European Parliament.

The overall aims of this chapter are to shed some light on the nature of transnational party cooperation within the European Union and on the nexus

---

*Submitted for publication in February, 1994.

between political parties, national and transnational, and the integration process. The chapter begins with a conceptual and party-theoretical framework, which, as a starting assumption, contributes to an understanding of the transnational party organizations and the political groups in the European Parliament. These two types of political organization will be discussed below, even though neither of them is "strictly analogous to national parties" (Lodge, 1986: 23). Is this ad hoc analogy between national political parties and transnational party organizations fruitful or misleading? What are the obstacles to the formation of genuine and integrated European parties? What are the roles of political parties and transnational party organizations in the integration process and to what extent do they fulfill these roles?

UNITS AND SYSTEMS: APPROACHES TO THE STUDY OF POLITICAL PARTIES

The Party within the National Political System

The study of political parties has traditionally been two-faceted. One involves the study of party units in their own right (Panebianco, 1988), the other the study of parties in party systems (Sartori, 1976). However, this is an artificial distinction since "one cannot really deal adequately with either without reference to the other. Interactions among parties are so affected by the nature of the interacting units, while the interactions in turn have repercussions on the units themselves" (Eckstein, 1968: 436). Insofar as parties form a system they do not exist in a vacuum (Sartori, 1976: ix). They are involved in iterative games and their leaders have to be observant of the moves of opposing units, that is to say, of "the different positions of parties on the political chessboard" (Duverger, 1951/78: 337). What is the number of units? Is the party system polarized? Is it fragmented? Is there a dominant party? How remote are the units from each other? The ideological space for maneuver, and strategic and tactical reasons for cooperative or conflictual relations, are all essential.

Let us ponder two definitions of a political party, definitions to which we will return later in the chapter:

Party is defined simply as an organization that appoints candidates at general elections to the system's representative assembly and also to other political positions. (Sjöblom, 1968: 21; see also Sartori, 1976: 63)

[W]e may define "political party" generally as *the articulate organization of society's active political agents, those who are concerned with the control of governmental power and who compete for popular support with another group or groups holding divergent views*. As such, it is *the great intermediary which links social forces and ideologies to official governmental institutions and relates them to political action within the larger political community.* (Neumann, 1956: 396; italics in original)

Neumann's (1956:405) conception of the "party of democratic integration" generally refers to the centralization, structure, and degree of cohesion within political parties. However, the concept could also be useful in analyzing the role of political parties in processes of nation building and community formation. Historically, parties have been of great importance to the outcome of such processes:

[P]arties have served as essential agencies of mobilization and as such have helped to integrate local communities into the nation or the broader federation. . . . In competitive party systems this process of integration can be analyzed at two levels: on the one hand, each party establishes a network of cross-local communication channels and in that way helps to strengthen national identities; on the other hand, its very competitiveness helps to set the national system of government *above* any particular set of officeholders (Lipset and Rokkan, 1967: 4; see also Rokkan, 1966; Rokkan and Urwin, 1982).

A party organization could be described as a network in which the central body has a coordinating function. Ideally, top-down and bottom-up communication occur and provide links within the entire organization. A political party is to be conceived of as a coalition of subunits. Duverger (1951/78: 17) has referred to these component subunits of a party organization as "basic elements" which are integrated vertically. Likewise, Sartori (1976: 62) has focused on the party as system, that is, the important relationship between the party unit itself and its subunits. It follows that party theorists should move beyond the limiting notion of party as a unitary actor, except for analytical simplification. Like Rose (1964: 35) the present author distinguishes between parties as electoral and policy institutions in order to give recognition "both to the differences *between* electoral parties and to the differences *within* electoral parties." When analyzing conflicting pressures on party behavior—"nested games"—a party's internal arena as well as the electoral and parliamentary arenas must be taken into account (see Sjöblom, 1968; Tsebelis, 1990).

It is important to stress that the experiences of the American and European party systems are different in that Europe's parties generally are more cohesive and integrated. The differences between federal and unitary political systems must, of course, be taken into account here (see Key, 1942/64). In a federal party system tendencies of separatism and autonomy are, if not manifest, always latent (Truman, 1955: 117-18). The U.S. parties have primarily functioned as electoral machines and not as integrative mass parties to the same extent as the parties in Europe. Moreover, the parties in Europe are generally more programmatic and more nervous about their ideological orientation. However, like most political parties they share one and the same *raison d'être*, which is to be found in the four functions they are expected to carry out within *mature* political systems (von Beyme, 1985: 13; cf. Lipset and Rokkan, 1967: 5): (i) identification of goals (ideology and programe); (ii) articulation and aggregation of social interests; (iii) mobilization and socialization of the general public within the system, particularly at elections; and (iv) elite recruitment and government function.

These functions contain an underlying normative element in that it is expected that a political party *should* mobilize opinion and be integrative. These used to be the functions of the mass party in national political systems and it could be misleading to argue that transnational party organizations, inherently looser and federal in structure, should be able to carry out the same missions, or even embrace the same goals, as far as the functions are concerned. Transnational party federations and party organizations in federal political systems have several characteristics in common. To take the Swiss example, parties at the federal level are no more than coalitions of regional parties. Similarly, a transnational party federation, working within a transnational political system, is nothing less than a coalition of national parties.

To what extent the traditional functions are carried out by the transnational party organizations within the framework of the EU international regional subsystem and its emerging political system will be analyzed further in the chapter. Prior to this another approach will be discussed in regard to the study of political parties—one which regards parties as transnational actors in the international system.

THE PARTY WITHIN THE INTERNATIONAL SYSTEM

Sigmund Neumann (1956: 416) pointed out as early as the mid-1950s that "in our times—when the frontiers between domestic and international affairs are blurred . . .— political parties have become international forces that must be studied" (see also Goldman, 1983; Jerneck, 1990; Kuper, 1991; Seidelmann, 1993; Sjöblom, 1989). However, he seems to be the exception to the rule; most party theorists and theoreticians working within the subfield of comparative politics have tended to neglect the fact that parties are transnational actors and in this capacity could influence domestic politics. On the basis of the last section we can confirm the description of a political party as "a channel of expression both upward and downward" (Hague and Harrop, 1987: 149), but have to add that there is an international arena and an outward and an inward dimension as well.

To the extent that there is an increasing domesticization of foreign policy and an increasing internationalization of domestic politics (Goldmann, 1989), it becomes even more relevant to study transnational party organizations as well as "party diplomacy" (Jerneck, 1990). Nonstate actors like these have also been neglected within the subfield of international politics, particularly by "realists," with a few notable exceptions. Wolfers (1962/68) found fault with the realist "states-as-the-sole-actor approach," and Aron (1962/84: 113-19) coined the expression "transnational society" to draw attention to the fact that international nongovernmental organizations (INGOs) exist side by side with states on the international arena.

Rosenau (1969,1990) offers the most fruitful attempt to move beyond the realist paradigm and the "state-is-still-predominant" tendency to the study of international relations. He draws attention to the myriad of actors in our multicentric world and suggests the distinction between "sovereignty-free" actors, among which he identifies political parties, and "sovereignty-bound" actors (Rosenau, 1990: 36). This terminology is, however, not without problems in that political parties might be supportive of a regime and committed to the preservation of national values and state sovereignty. In the literature we are often reminded that political parties first and foremost are national actors and reluctant to subordinate themselves to a supranational decision-making structure (see Ware, 1986). Thus, it is often suggested that political parties struggle for their autonomy and that they are less likely than other groupings "to have strong, institutionalized transnational links" (Willets, 1982: 8). It is important to emphasize that there is a fundamental difference between government and opposition parties as well as between antisystem parties and established parties in this respect. Consequently, the term "sovereignty-restrained actors" is a more appropriate label for political parties when they are crossing borders.

Establishing networks and linkages constitutes one type of transnational party strategy (Oldlund, 1992). In a "penetrative process" (Rosenau, 1969:46) a transnational organization could influence not only the conduct or norms of its subunits but those of states as well:

Foreign social actors or transnational coalitions can influence a state in two ways. They can work directly by lobbying officials, organizing letter-writing campaigns or *helping sympathetic political parties win elections*. Such efforts can affect policy by changing the balance of influence among contending policy networks within the target government. More often, they work indirectly, by reinforcing the efforts of like-minded groups within a country in the expectation that they will be able to influence their own government. (Peterson, 1992: 384; my emphasis)

The transnational party organizations studied in this chapter will be referred to as PINGOs—party international nongovernmental organizations—despite the fact that we are dealing with nonstate actors. The same reservation goes for the acronyms INGO (international nongovernmental organization) and BINGO (business international nongovernmental organization). PINGOs have been rationalized as counterforces to increasingly transnationalized capital and one could argue that, to the extent transnational companies, or BINGOs, penetrate national political systems the more important PINGOs become as a counterbalance and as promotors of democratic ideals (cf. Kaiser, 1971a, 1971b).

Multilateral cooperation between like-minded political parties within the framework of "internationals" has a long history. Liberal, conservative, Christian democratic, and socialist/social democratic parties all have their own internationals, of which the Socialist International is the oldest, originating from 1864. That there are inherent tensions involved in this kind of cooperation is best illustrated with the breakdown of the *Second International* in 1914 when national priorities proved to be more important than international solidarity among the working-class parties (Joll, 1955; May, 1977).

The internationals, like all transnational party organizations, provide channels through which personal contacts can be established and ideas can flow. Thus, they contribute to transnational socialization and to diffusion of democratic ideals, however defined. Thanks to national party foundations, such as those associated with the German political parties, internationals were successful in their mission to support social movements working for democracy in the transition processes in Portugal, Spain, and Greece in the 1970s (Pridham, 1991). The countries in Eastern and Central Europe are in the midst of such democratization processes, and new or reborn parties have linked up to various PINGOs, which offer "liberal-democratic know-how;" for example, how to organize elections and parliamentary work (interview no. 5).

The German party foundations are active all over Europe. One of them (Konrad-Adenauer-Stiftung) has set up a branch of offices in European capitals; these offices function as "embassies" to the mother party CDU (Christian Democratic Union). Interestingly enough, the networking and "private diplomacy" conducted by these nongovernmental organizations, often by informal means, act as an alternative to rigid traditional intergovernmental diplomacy.

THE PARTY WITHIN THE INTERNATIONAL REGIONAL SUBSYSTEM OF THE EUROPEAN UNION

The German political scientist Karl Kaiser (1968: 92) has distinguished three "ideal types" of international regional subsystems: first, the transnational society subsystem of the regional type; second, the intergovernmental regional subsystem; and third, the comprehensive regional subsystem. The EU resembles the third type, in which both governmental and nongovernmental elites are important actors. In that system, Haas (1958: 5) argued, attention should be paid to the role of interest groups and political parties, which he "singled out as the significant carriers of values and ideologies whose opposition, identity or convergence determines the success or failure of a transnational ideology" (see also Claude, 1956/64: 105). The process of "political spillover" implied that élites would undergo a learning process and shift loyalties and activities to the new center beyond the nation-state (Haas, 1964a). However, as far as "political spillover" is concerned, neofunctionalist integration theory proved to be too optimistic in that the importance of domestic politics was more or less ignored (George, 1991: 26). However, attention is again being paid to neofunctionalist theory (Taylor, 1989; Tranholm-Mikkelsen, 1991), and the early integration theorists have, to a certain extent, been rehabilitated. Perhaps they were right when they pointed out that transnational actors such as parties *could* help bringing legitimacy to a process in which people are not involved to the same extent as in nation-states (cf. Lindberg, 1963: 9)?

In this context a democratic and normative problem touched upon earlier concerns what role political parties can play for the sake of democracy in a wider framework than the nation-state, that is to say, in "a 'democratic' transnational political community," and whether parties could, as in national political systems, traditionally constitute "the link between the delegates and the demos" (Dahl, 1989: 320). The idea of European parties as instruments for integration and democracy is given legitimacy in Article 138a of the Maastricht Treaty:

Political parties at the European level are important as a factor for integration within the Union. They contribute to forming a European awareness and to expressing the political will of the citizens of the Union. (Treaty on European Union)

Such a Europe of the parties—*Europe des partis*—has been contrasted to a Gaullist intergovernmental *Europe des patries* (Marquand, 1978: 445). To federalists, the formation of European parties is a litmus test of the integration process in that it is hard to believe that politicians incapable of integrating political parties would ever be able to agree on deeper integration between nation-states. Interestingly enough, formation of genuine parties at the European level has been prescribed by Professor Duverger (1992) as the most important means to come to grips with the so-called democratic deficit.

It seems, however, as if some functions carried out by political parties at the national level are not applicable to their acting in the regional subsystem of the EU. So far they have not, at the European level, been successful as "the great intermediary." From the very beginning the process has, on the whole, been exclusively an elite-level phenomenon. In this respect, the transnational integration process is different from the process of nation building outlined earlier. The relation between the elite and the mass is more distant and the communication process between the *demos* and elected politicians less successful. While political parties have been decisive instruments for integration and legitimacy within nation-states they have to date been less successful in this role at the European level. This is indeed a challenge for the parties and their transnational party organizations because within the EU framework they can serve "to transmit political concerns from the base to the center, and, at a more critical level, to establish the future ideological patterns" (Ward, 1980: 556; see also Colchester and Buchan, 1990: 184-90).

THE PARTY FAMILIES OF WESTERN EUROPE AND THE ARENAS
ON WHICH THEY PERFORM

Traditionally, the party families of Western Europe are the conservative, or secular conservative, the Christian democratic, the liberal, the socialist/social semocratic, the communist, and the ecologist party families. A party family is a wider conception than an ideological *famille spirituelle*. Each of the party families includes more than one more or less distinct ideological tendency, and it goes without saying that considerable diversities could exist within the same party family.

Christian democrats, for ideological and domestic reasons, are often anxious to separate themselves from conservatives, but due to closer cooperation at the European level it has become increasingly appropriate to include them in one and the same party family. However, one can identify at least three broad ideological tendencies within this family: first, the liberal-conservative; second, the conservative; and, third, the Christian democratic (Girvin, 1988: 9-10; see also Layton-Henry, 1982; Morgan and Silvestri, 1982). These tendencies could be divided even further since the Christian democratic parties differ in their programes, in particular with regard to degree of confessionalism (see Irving, 1979; von Beyme, 1985: 94). In this respect a German Christian democrat is different from an Italian, a Belgian, or a Dutch, not to mention a Nordic, Christian democrat. Similarly, there are several strands among secular conservative parties (Gallagher et al., 1992: 74). One such strand is concerned with the preservation of national values, values traditionally of high priority to conservative parties such as the Fianna Fáil of Ireland and the Gaullists of France. Another concerns the preoccupation with libertarian ideas. In fact, secular conservative parties, like the British and Swedish, are flirting with neoliberalism and communitarianism at the same time. A theme taken up with some degree of enthusiasm by conservative parties concerns the social market economy, an idea developed by the German Christian Democrats.

The Liberal party family is ideologically incoherent. As Gordon Smith (1988: 16) has pointed out, "there is a streak of ambiguity running through European liberalism which is seen in the varied character of liberal parties: some are regarded as belonging to the left, some are more home on the right, while others hover uneasily between the two." This diversity can be explained with reference to two historic roots of liberalism, that is, the Anglo-Saxon version and the continental (primarily French) version (Kirchner, 1988: 3). The former has its origin in an empiricist political culture and the latter in a rationalistic one.[1] In countries where there is a large Christian democratic party, as in the Benelux countries, the Federal Republic of Germany, and Austria liberal parties are more to the right of the left-right spectrum than in countries where there is large secular conservative party, as in the United Kingdom and the Nordic countries (Gallagher et al, 1992: 75-77). Historically, it is the church-state cleavage which to a large extent explains the relations between center-right parties. Where this cleavage has been salient a conflictual relationship between a Christian democratic and a liberal party could be identified, and where the religious dimension has been less important a secular conservative party has generally been predominant on the right.

The socialist/social democratic party family includes reformist parties, whose leaders have rejected the revolutionary, Leninist rhetoric and instead played the parliamentary game (Padgett and Paterson, 1991; Paterson and Campbell, 1974; Paterson and Thomas, 1977, 1986; Pelinka, 1983). The distinction between socialist and social democratic is of little relevance, as witnessed by the practiced policies of socialist governments, such as the French and Spanish socialist governments from the early and mid-1980s. Nonetheless, it has a certain symbolic meaning in that socialism generally connotes a more radical approach to the ownership of means of production.

The communist party family of Western Europe has been heavily influenced by the collapse of the communist model in the former Soviet Union and Central and Eastern Europe. Traditionally, it has been divided between pro-Moscow and more autonomous parties, but this has become an obsolete distinction. However, the family must still be considered as incoherent, and some communist parties are more orthodox than others. These parties are undergoing critical self-examination, and if they are developing into pragmatic leftist parties one could imagine one single leftist socialist/social democratic party family in the future.

The ecologist or green party family is a broad church indeed. As a relatively young family it contains individuals and tendencies of different shades; some of them more red than green (similar to a water melon: green outside, red inside). Discord within the family has been a salient feature, not least over attitudes to European integration (Buck, 1989; Parkin, 1989; Spretnak and Capra, 1986).

These party families are the most important in Western Europe of today. However, a few others must be mentioned. Even though the agrarian party family is of minor importance in Western Europe as a whole, agrarian parties have a long tradition in the Nordic and Central and Eastern European countries and will thus gain ground if and when the EU widens. Finally, there are the regional and ethnic parties, which have done well in elections in Belgium, Italy, and Spain, and the far right parties (see Gallagher et al., 1992: 80-83; von Beyme, 1985).

The rest of this chapter will adopt the party-theoretical conception of arenas (see Sjöblom, 1968). In this context the internal arena refers to the transnational party organizations, the electoral arena to the Euro-elections, and, finally, the parliamentary arena refers to the political groups in the European Parliament.

THE INTERNAL ARENA

As mentioned earlier a party could be conceived of as a system, or network, with vertical linkages and, ideally, an ongoing internal communication process. Likewise, the transnational party organizations dealt with in this section consist of subunits, national member parties, and resemble parties in federal political systems in structure in that they are coalitions or amalgams of such subunits. Besides having bilateral horizontal contacts the relations between the transnational unit and the national subunits take place vertically. This relationship could be characterized as a two-level game in which interests, concerns, party profiles, and strategies at the national level determine party behavior at the European level (Bogdanor, 1986, 1989; Niedermayer, 1984: 236; Smith, 1989: 301; Taylor, 1983: 47-48; interviews no. 1, 4, 5, and 7).[2] True, the main battlefield for political parties is at the national level, where they have their roots. It follows that the PINGOs suffer domestic constraints, which impinge upon their degree of cohesion. Once such political restrictions are taken into account the conclusion that the PINGOs have not been able to reach genuine party integration is hardly surprising. It is also important to emphasize that party elites, as witnessed by the battle over the Maastricht Treaty, have proved to be far ahead of public opinion with regard to views on the speed and final destination of European integration.

When party doctrines and programs are to be coordinated in a transnational context, a relevant question concerns whether the final outcome is the result of compromises on the level of "the lowest common denominator," in which the least cooperative unit, as in intergovernmental negotiations based on the unanimity rule, could slow down or hinder the entire process. Is the internal arena to consider a supranational system, which features a bargaining process best described as "upgrading common interests," or is it more "intergovernmental" in character (cf. Haas, 1964b: 65)?

As stated, government parties generally act differently in this respect in that they are more reluctant to commit themselves than opposition parties, which have a freer hand (interview no. 6). This distinction is helpful in explaining the different behavior and attitudes of the British political parties in the run-up to the 1994 European elections. While the Labour Party and the Liberal Democrats were fully signed up to common manifestoes with like-minded parties, the governing Conservatives decided to fight the European elections wholly and exclusively on a domestic manifesto—a "distinctively British" platform in the words of the prime minister and leader of the Conservative Party, Mr. John Major (quoted in *Financial Times*, February 11, 1994). The commitments made by the Labour Party and the Liberal Democrats, their signing a federalist Eurosocialist and a federalist Euroliberal manifesto respectively, were exploited by the Conservatives (see *The Guardian*, February 15, 1994; *Sunday Times*, November 7, 1993). However, the Liberal Democrats had got a hold on the Conservatives—the latter's alliance in the European Parliament with outspoken federalist Christian democrats (*The Times*, February 8, 1994). Because of this alliance it was hard for the Conservative Party to attack the other parties for being federalists advocating a centralized superstate. This episode—to be elaborated upon in the author's doctoral thesis—offers empirical evidence for the central argument made in this chapter about the interrelationship between the national and the European levels. Due to transnational alliances each of the parties found itself on the defensive after attack from political enemies, and this very political warfare within the national political system illustrates the inherent domestic constraints circumscribing a party's search for friends and allies across borders. Even though the Labour Party and the Liberal Democrats had agreed on common platforms with sister parties they nevertheless drafted manifestoes with a distinctively national flavor. And it is important to emphasize that had they decided not to sign up to the common platforms in the first place, instead referring to a conscience clause and opting out of particular policy proposals, there would not have been any legal consequences of such behavior. However, they would have had to justify such a lack of solidarity to their transnational allies.

The EU-PINGOs to which the British political parties, directly or indirectly, are linked up are the three existing ones: The European Liberal, Democrat and Reform Party (ELDR); the European People's Party—Federation of Christian Democrat Parties of the European Community (EPP); and the Party of European Socialists (PES). The PES was born at the Socialist parties' Congress in November 1992 (*Agence Europe*, November 16/17, 1992). From 1974 until then the name had been Confederation of the Socialist Parties of the European Community (CSP). Membership in the Socialist International (SI) is a requirement for membership in the PES. That the word "confederation" was replaced by the word "party" should not be interpreted as merely symbolic, since procedures for decision making have changed. Until the formation of the PES decisions were taken on the basis of unanimity, but from then on majority decision making has been applied in those issue areas where the Council of Ministers applies this procedure. At the 1992 Congress the socialist/social democratic parties of the states which have applied for membership in the EU were adopted as new members. The PES would undoubtedly profit from a widening of the EU, since social democratic parties are of considerable size and importance in Austria, Sweden, Norway, and Finland.

Conservative parties, and some Christian democratic parties, are members of the European Democrat Union (EDU), established in 1978. Some Christian democratic parties are also members of the European Union of Christian Democrats (EUCD), founded in 1965 as a successor to the Nouvelles Equipes Internationales. The more "purist" of the Christian democratic parties, those of Belgium, Italy and the Netherlands, have stayed at arm's length from the EDU, which they regarded during the days of the Cold War as a suspect right-wing organization with the sole purpose of combatting communism. The EDU was set up as a forum where the German and Austrian Christian democratic parties could meet with conservative parties of the United Kingdom, France, and Scandinavia. The secretary-generals of the EDU and EUCD are currently discussing the future of these organizations against the background of a considerable overlap in membership. The EDU and the EUCD are to be considered as pan-European organizations, linked to non-EU parties and to the respective internationals—the Christian Democratic International and, in the case of the EDU, the conservative International Democrat Union. A few years ago the intention was to dissolve the EUCD, but the events in Eastern and Central Europe have led to its revival (interview no. 5). That the EUCD should be in harmony with the European People's Party (EPP), formed in 1976 as a true party federation of only EU members, is best illustrated with the fact that they have one and the same secretary-general. At the Ninth Congress of the EPP, held in Athens in November 1992, it was decided that the conservative parties of the states which had applied for membership in the EU would be accepted as "permanent observers" of the EPP. The Swedish Christian Democratic Party (KdS) is an associated member of the EPP and opposes conservative membership to the utmost (Johansson, 1993). At congresses the British Conservatives, who sit as allied members of the EPP group of the European Parliament, have the right to propose changes of the EPP programe but not to vote. The two pillars of the EPP are the Christian vision of man and the common will to found a federal United States of Europe (Burgess, 1989: 5; Johansson, 1993).[3] The EPP does not compromise its federalist vocation; in 1993 the Portuguese member party CDS was expelled because of a critical attitude toward the Maastricht Treaty.

The European Liberal, Democrat and Reform Party (ELDR) was transformed into a "party" at a Congress held in December 1993, following the models of the EPP and the PES (*Agence Europe*, December 11, 1993). However, in this case the new name seems to be more symbolic than substantial in that decisions were taken by two-thirds majority also within the various organs of its forerunner, the ELDR Federation. The Federation was launched in 1976 and had its origin in the Mouvement Libéral pour l'Europe Unie, founded in 1952. Like the other PINGOs of Western Europe the ELDR is linked to an international, the Liberal International, and like the EPP and the PES it is committed to federal ideals.

The transnational party organization of the ecologist party family, the former European Greens, took the name European Federation of Green Parties in 1993. It is a pan-European organization, including parties from non-EU countries. It will apply the majority decision-making principle, while the member parties "will maintain their name, identity and autonomy acting within the scope of their national and regional responsibilities" (*Statutes of the European Federation of Green Parties*, 1993). It stresses dialogue with the states of the former Soviet Union and Central and Eastern Europe. Its First Congress, held in early 1994, failed to resolve differences over environmental policies as well as the European Union, and a common manifesto for the 1994 European elections could not be agreed upon (*The Guardian*, February 1, 1994).

Whether or not these PINGOs will develop into true European parties in the future can only be speculated upon. Earlier students of transnational party cooperation have shared a skeptical view in this respect and have tended to conclude that such an outcome is more likely in the cases of the EPP and the ELDR, since "the majority of the CSP (PES) member parties shares the concept of a transnational cooperation of absolutely autonomous national parties" (Niedermayer, 1984: 241; cf. Pridham and Pridham, 1979b). Even though member parties of the then CSP, as well as those of the European Greens, have until recently not been able to agree on the need for a supranational decision-making structure, they seem willing to work in this direction. Moreover, it is an outspoken ambition generally, not only among PES representatives (interviews no. 2, 5, and 6). In fact, there is an increasing awareness of the fact that nation-states have become more interdependent and that transnational issues must be tackled in a transnational context.

Most tellingly, the article in the Maastricht Treaty which calls for the establishment of European parties was the result of a common effort by the presidents, all of whom were Belgians, of the then CSP, ELDR, and EPP (interviews no. 4 and 5). The initiative was taken by Dr. Martens, the president of the EPP, and he gained support not only from fellow party federation presidents but also from the then president of the European Parliament, Mr. Baron Crespo (*Agence Europe*, November 16/17, 1992).

While member parties of the CSP until recently have had a veto right, the EPP and ELDR members have accepted the majority principle. In practice, however, consensus and compromises at the level of the lowest common denominator are generally strived for at congresses as well as bureau and council meetings, and one could argue that none of the party federations are genuine European parties. It is the national member parties which have the final say concerning programes and goals of the party federations. Likewise, their secretariats are very small compared with those of the member parties, which are the most important paymasters along with the political groups of the European Parliament (see Bardi, 1992). The federations' financial dependence upon the European Parliament is being discussed at the present, and as a consequence of the call for European parties in the Maastricht Treaty these might eventually receive direct support (interview no. 3). However, not all political parties in the European Parliament are affiliated to a transnational party federation.

Party leader meetings have become an increasingly important part of transnational party cooperation. Such meetings take place a couple of times yearly, normally the week preceding European Council summits. One dimension of these meetings concerns the ambition to influence discussions and agreements in the European Council. Another concerns the convergence of national party positions. The Maastricht Treaty is to a large extent influenced by party leader meetings; among its signatories no less than six out of twelve heads of government were Christian democrats and members of the EPP. Prior to the Maastricht summit party leader meetings were held, also by the liberals and socialists, in connection with the Intergovernmental Conferences on Monetary and Political Union (Hix, 1993; Jacobs et al., 1992: 86). Party leaders as well as national and European parliamentarians, through various channels and regular meetings, were able to shape the debate and put pressure on governments (Corbett, 1992, 1993). Such informal integration processes must be highlighted whenever hidden agendas are being traced. Moreover, they have been important for some parties' attitudes to the EU generally as well as for their stances in different issue areas. Consequently, they are of importance to domestic politics and contribute to party-to-party as well as party system convergence (cf. Katz and Mair, 1993). More often than not such massive transnationalization processes are neglected in the various textbooks on the EU, most of which are written by theorists in the "intergovernmentalist" camp.

Hrbek (1988: 456-57) has put forward five reasons for the formation of the transnational party organizations (EPP, ELDR, CSP) in the 1970s (cf. Nugent, 1991: 145-46): contributing to reduce the democratic "deficit" of the EU, following other socioeconomic associations which had established Euro-organizations; adapting to the further and "positive" integration of the EU, supplying the political groups in the European Parliament with an extraparliamentary basis and thereby strengthening their political weight and impact on EU decision making, and, finally, responding to the challenge of direct elections to the European Parliament.

Of these reasons, the last-mentioned must be considered the most important. As in various national political systems undergoing electoral reform, there was a need for party organizations outside the parliament (Stammen, 1980: 199). Through participation in Euro-elections they could give these "a 'European' character by presenting to the electorate a common programme agreed upon by all member parties, by campaigning in a transnational framework, and perhaps by co-operating in the selection of candidates" (Hrbek, 1988: 456). To what extent have the transnational party organizations been successful in these missions? To answer this question we must turn to the electoral arena.

THE ELECTORAL ARENA

The institution of direct elections to the European Parliament is unique in several respects and of great academic interest. It is, just like transnational party cooperation in general, to be considered as a two-level game and each and one of the elections as a two-level election. Even though the elections are supposed to form a "European" event in a transnational context, party politics at the national level have tended to determine the character of debates and issues as well as outcomes (Lodge, 1986,1990; Sweeney, 1984a: 154). Lodge has

pointed out that this hybrid character of the Euro-elections must be described as
"the supreme irony" (1990: 1).

Reif has, together with colleagues at the University of Mannheim, developed
a sophisticated model and a conceptual framework for the analysis of Euro-
elections (Reif and Schmitt, 1980; Reif, 1984, 1985). He distinguishes between
first- and second-order elections. National parliamentary elections are the most
crucial first-order elections, while the direct elections to the European
Parliament are to be considered as second-order elections, since less is at stake.
Second-order election campaigns are "characterized by a mix of specific second-
order arena issues and general, mostly first-order arena issues" (Reif, 1984:
247). Consequently, the voter's behavior is different in the two kind of
elections. In second-order elections the voter can afford to send a warning
signal to the government and vote for the parties of the opposition. This is
exactly what happened in France in 1984 (Frears, 1991: 190-91), and in the
United Kingdom and Germany in 1989 (Lodge, 1990), corroborating Reif's
hypothesis as well as the argument that the Euro-elections are not transnational
elections but instead national contests and "plebiscites on the performance of
each member state's government" (Bogdanor, 1986: 167; see also Bogdanor,
1989: 214; Lodge, 1986: 258; Reif, 1984).

All in all, the general conclusion drawn from the first and second Euro-
elections in 1979 and 1984 is that they were low stimulus elections" (Blumler
and Fox, 1980: 379, Schmitt and Mannheimer, 1991: 47), and "second-order
elections," which brought losses for governmental parties, brighter prospects for
small and new parties and lower turnout (Reif, 1985: 9). The French National
Front is a party which had its breakthrough in a Euro-election (Frears, 1991:
191). Denmark is a case where the salience of the European cleavage has given
birth to new parties, to the extent that they can be described as political parties,
which only take part in European elections: the People's Movement Against EU
and the June Movement (cf. Worre, 1987).

The conclusion to be drawn from the 1989 elections is slightly different
from earlier elections in that small parties in general, apart from the Green
parties and the National Front, did not do particularly well. Even though an
antigovernmental swing was present, it is "by no means inevitable at a European
election held in midterm" (Curtice, 1989: 225). Nevertheless, the average
turnout from the first and second direct elections actually declined from 62.5 and
59.0 percent respectively to a disappointingly low 57.2 percent in 1989.[4]

The voter's incentive for participating is negligible and it may be argued
that abstention is a rational act when the voter perceives that so little is at stake
(Reif and Schmitt, 1980: 34). However, the European Parliament has increased
its powers, and if this message is successfully communicated the Euro-electorate
might go to the polls in larger numbers than previously (cf. *The Economist*,
January 22, 1994). Nevertheless, it is evident that transnational issues are
remote to the average voter, to whom also the European Parliament is a distant
entity. In this respect the media have been accused of being parochial and of

being ineffective as "socializing agents vis-à-vis the electorate" (Lodge and Herman, 1980: 60; cf. Pridham and Pridham, 1981: 258-59).

As stated, the standard definition of a political party prescribes that it is "an organization that appoints candidates at general elections." This is a function which is still carried out by national political parties, despite the existence of transnational party organizations at the EU level. These publish common manifestoes, but obviously play a subordinate role when it comes to the nomination of candidates to the Euro-elections (cf. Holland, 1986). Another function of political parties is involvement in the formation of government. This function is not applicable, since there is no clear alternative between government and opposition and since the Commission's responsibility to the European Parliament is limited and the commissioners, including the president, have not been selected by Parliament (Bogdanor, 1986; Nord and Taylor, 1979: 413; Steed, 1984: 228). However, in accordance with Article 158 of the Maastricht Treaty the European Parliament will be more influential in this respect in the future. The European Parliament shall be consulted prior to the nomination of the president of the Commission, and the president and the other members of the Commission shall be subject as a body to a vote of approval by the European Parliament ("Treaty on European Union").

The fact that there is no uniform electoral system contributes to the deficiencies and to the variations in turnout (see Appendix).[5] It has been argued that a "single system would pave the way to much closer cooperation among Europe's political parties. It is not inconceivable that national political parties might consult each other as to the order of names on the party lists" (Williams, 1991: 173). So far just a few candidates, of whom Sir David Steel and Professor Maurice Duverger (the party theorist quoted earlier) are the most prominent examples, have participated as representatives of parties, Italian ones, from other states than their own. Another transnational element has concerned the fact that politicians have crossed borders and participated in campaigns of sister parties (see Lodge and Herman, 1982; Lodge, 1986, 1990). A citizen of the EU will be able "to vote and to stand as a candidate in elections to the European Parliament in the Member State in which he resides, under the same conditions as nationals of that State" ("Treaty on European Union," Article 8b).

The overall conclusion from the direct elections is that the transnational party organizations have failed to live up to the expectations concerning their role of bringing a transnational dimension to the Euro-elections (Fenner, 1981; Lodge and Herman, 1980; Lodge, 1986: 253; 1990: 214-15; Niedermayer, 1984; Sweeney, 1984a). Nevertheless, common manifestoes have been adopted and one could argue that this is an impressive achievement and that the degree of integration within these organizations has increased gradually due to the challenges of European elections. In this respect, the Christian democrats and liberals have been more successful than the socialist party family, whose member parties until the 1994 European elections have failed to forge common manifestoes (cf. Niedermayer, 1983: 205; Pridham and Pridham, 1981: 187, 248; Steed, 1984: 232).

As extraparliamentary organizations the party federations are linked to the political groups in the European Parliament. It is to them and the parliamentary arena the last section of this chapter is devoted.

THE PARLIAMENTARY ARENA

Just as party cohesion is important for parties within national political systems, it is also a concept which demands close attention in the transnational context. A low degree of cohesion has implications for parliamentary efficacy as well as for a party's credibility (Sjöblom, 1968: 191; cf. Epstein, 1967: 316). In the framework of the European Parliamentary arena electoral results and the variation in electoral systems have implications for group cohesion and for the power balance between as well as within different groups. The fact that the United Kingdom (except Northern Ireland) has retained the majority, or first-past-the-post system, implying that "the winner takes it all," contributed to overrepresentation for the Conservatives in the former European Democratic Group after the 1979 and 1984 direct elections and for the Labour Party in the Socialist Group following the 1989 elections. Due to this electoral system the Liberal/Social Democratic alliance failed to obtain representation in 1984 despite obtaining 18.5 percent of the vote, and so did the Green Party, with 14.9 percent, in 1989 (Bardi, 1992: 933).

Most Members of the European Parliament (MEPs) take part in a transnational grouping and are no longer mere national delegates. Until the introduction of direct elections in 1979 all MEPs were nominated by national parliaments, which reinforced the importance of national considerations.[6] According to one school of thought, the so-called national mandate theory, "the delegate owes his distinctive status to the fact that he has been appointed by the State he represents" (Oudenhove, 1965: 11; cf. Kirchner, 1984: 141). This ambiguity of roles, stemming from the dual mandate, implied that delegates played boundary roles (Fitzmaurice, 1975: 47). Some still hold a dual mandate, and conflicts of loyalty did not simply disappear once direct elections were introduced. The conflict of interests is enhanced by the fact that MEPs have to pay attention not only to sectoral, regional, party, and national interests but to European concerns as well (see Hagger and Wing, 1979). To some the federal vocation is important, to others the nation or the region are instead the most important points of reference. Nationality and political cultures matter here and so does the issue area at stake. Whenever the Common Agricultural Policy and the structural funds are debated national and regional concerns tend to predominate. The fact that an MEP works on a day-by-day basis with like-minded colleagues implies, however, that he or she forms part of a transnational socialization process where there are cross-pressures arising from national preoccupations and party group discipline and ideological concerns (cf. Kerr, 1973).

It follows that there is a permanent potential for conflict between the national and the European levels in the parliamentary arena too (cf. Herman and Van Schendelen, 1979). This tension could also be illustrated with reference to the sensitive issue of extending the powers of the European Parliament, which is one of the most supranational, and probably the most integrative, of the European institutions. Whenever MEPs put this issue on the agenda national parties and parliaments are provoked into "creating stronger controls over the European groups" (Taylor, 1983: 48). Ironically, one could argue that a more powerful European Parliament, in accordance with Article 189b of the Maastricht Treaty, would "encourage the more hesitant governments to whip members of their party in the European Parliament into towing the party line, and would tend to weaken the development of European parties" (Taylor, 1992: 24).

The establishing of links between national parliaments and the European Parliament is encouraged in an annex of the Maastricht Treaty and should be further developed as a means to democratize the EU (interviews no. 1, 5, 7, and 8; Williams, 1991). The parliamentary "assizes" convened occasionally have met with success; on these occasions MEPs and national parliamentarians are brought together for discussions on topical issues (Corbett, 1992: 274-75). Professor Duverger (1992) has drawn attention to the historical conference in Rome in November 1990:

Spontanément, les deux catégories de parlementaires se sont groupées suivant leurs affinités politiques et non suivant leurs pays---De cette initiative date la conception, sinon la naissance, des partis européens.

Informal meetings are also held now and then among presidents of parliaments, including the European Parliament. In most parliaments specialist committees dealing with EU affairs have been set up and in some cases common meetings with committee members and MEPs are organized (Jacobs et al., 1992: 259-62). Despite such constructive innovations the degree of coordination and communication is insufficient, resulting in communication failures and sometimes a deep mistrust between politicians and officials at the two levels. An illustrative example is the British MEP who told the present writer that "we [MEPs] understand Europe better than MPs back home. Some at home are very parochial."

Overall the most important role of the group chairmen is that of consensus seeking—to balance the subgroups, or national delegations, within the groups at the same time as ideological concerns are taken into consideration (Kieffer and Millar, 1979: 35). However, whipping is of less importance than in national parliaments, which is why it is hard to impose discipline when national delegations decide to obstruct (Jacobs et al., 1992: 83). At the same time there are group norms and moral pressures on members to arrive at compromises. At the end of the day even the most outspoken opponent can fall into line, or as one interviewee put it: "You think twice before you defect!"

As in national parliaments there are elements of pragmatic intragroup as well as intergroup bargaining and compromise in the transnational European Parliament. Indeed, since the groups are in no way unitary actors and do not exist in a vacuum they must, just as parties in national political systems, be cooperative besides being conflictual and competitive. All bargaining units have to choose between a "conflictual" and an "integrative" strategy (Pruitt, 1991: 79). An integrative strategy is encouraged by the fact that none of the groups has a majority on its own and therefore has to seek support from other groups. The institutional imperatives, following upon the cooperation procedure as stated in the Single European Act, encourage technical cooperation between the groups.

Ideological affinities have been important from the outset, that is to say, from the days of the European Coal and Steel Community Common Assembly, which held its first meeting in 1952. This was the first transnational Assembly where members sat according to their ideological affiliation. Until 1965, there were only three political groups: the liberals, the Christian democrats, and the socialists. As of spring 1994 there were eight political groups, and each one of them will, at the risk of oversimplification, be briefly presented here (in declining order of size).

The Group of the Party of European Socialists, the former Socialist Group, became the largest group in 1975 when the British Labour Party joined after having boycotted transnational party activities within the European Parliament for two years. It is linked to the Socialist International and, more tightly, to the Party of European Socialists. The group is, together with the Group of the European People's Party, the most transnational of all the groups in that it comprises parties from all EU member countries. It used to be regarded as the most cohesive of all the groups (Fitzmaurice, 1975: 105, 164-71; Haas, 1958: 392-93; Oudenhove, 1965: 27; Pridham and Pridham, 1979a: 250; 1981: 54, 261). However, the adoption of the British Labour Party, the Danish Social Democratic Party and the Greek Panhellenic Socialist Movement (PASOK) contributed to a drop in cohesion (see Featherstone, 1988; Haahr, 1992). A quantitative analysis of group cohesion, published in 1990, led to the general conclusion that there is a drop in cohesion when MEPs are asked to express themselves on questions and acts directly relevant to the Union decision-making process and that the Socialist Group "reveal this drop in cohesion more than other Groups" (Attinà, 1990: 568). However, the secretary-general of the group, Julian Priestley, argues that the group's cohesion has increased recently and that this is due to the fact that the member parties have converged in their approaches to European integration; particularly the British Labour Party and the Danish Social Democratic Party have become more positive (interview no. 6; cf. Haahr, 1992). The former Italian Communist Party (PCI), which in 1991 changed its name to the Democratic Party of the Left, left the Group of the

United European Left in September 1992 and joined the Socialist Group, which thereby could become more heterogeneous. Mr. Priestley, however, did not foresee any serious cooperation problems (interview no. 6). But despite the fact that the former PCI was a relatively pragmatic Eurocommunist party it has previously not been ideologically acceptable to some member parties of the Socialist International (Sweeney, 1984b: 183).

The Group of the European People's Party, until 1979 called the Christian Democratic Group, is linked to the party federation European People's Party (EPP). On the basis of his analysis Attinà (1990: 575) suggests that the Christian democrats show a higher degree of cohesion in their voting behavior than the socialists. Nevertheless, there are reasons to expect less unity in the long run following the widening of the group that took place in the spring of 1992. At that time an alliance was formed between the group and the conservative MEPs of the European Democratic Group, which included thirty-two British Tory MEPs and two Danes. Some kind of linkup has been under way for a long time, but has stumbled upon opposition due to ideological differences between the conservative and Christian democratic parties (Johansson, 1993; Kohler and Myrzik, 1982; Lodge and Herman, 1982: Chapter 8; Pridham, 1982). The Belgian, Dutch and Italian Christian democrats have been most reluctant to accept the British Conservatives as group members. The alliance, which was the outcome of a series of meetings within the Bureau and Conference of the party federation EPP and a top-level agreement between Helmut Kohl and John Major,[7] raises several interesting questions, such as how the cooperation between Christian-inspired and secular conservative parties will develop, not to mention how British Conservatives will be able to embrace the idea of federalism, so wholeheartedly supported by Christian democratic parties. However, contrary to their national counterparts, a majority of the Tory MEPs share the federalist vision and have therefore been attacked by Euroskeptics back home. The major factor behind the alliance is the lure of political power in that smaller groups are increasingly marginalized due to the institutional imperatives. Moreover, the Christian democrats are fully aware of the fact that they stand to lose seats to the socialists once the EU widens, since the Nordic Christian democratic parties are quite small. The argument made is therefore that the Christian democrats must open up to conservative parties, but some parties fear that the very Christian democratic identity is at stake. As a matter of fact, the group has shown a willingness to open up to non-Christian democrats; it expanded in 1989 when the Spanish Partido Popular left the European Democratic Group immediately after the Euro-elections. Also the Greek party Nea Demokratia is a member of the group. The former president of France, Valéry Giscard d'Estaing, joined the group in December 1991 with a few compatriots but was not allowed, according to French rules, to remain as an MEP because of his seat in the French parliament.

Not even the third largest political group, the Liberal, Democratic, and Reformist Group, seemed to provide a sufficient power base to Giscard d'Estaing; this was the group of which he was chairman until he suddenly joined the EPP Group. The Liberal, Democratic and Reformist Group is linked to the ELDR Party. Compared with the PES Group and the EPP Group this group has been less cohesive from the outset, reflecting the various strands within the liberal party family (cf. Fitzmaurice, 1975: 167). In general, it is more free market-orientated than the two largest groupings.

The Green Group in the European Parliament was founded in 1989. Green parties were represented in the Rainbow Group in the 1984-89 Parliament. The group suffers from the British electoral system, since the Green Party of the United Kingdom would achieve a higher level of votes under a system of proportional representation. At the same time, however, the group has profited from the character of second-order elections in that each of the Euro-elections "was perceived by the public as less important than national elections and thus it was easier for the voters to take risks with new ideas" (Spretnak and Capra, 1986: 165). Its member parties reflect the ideological diversity within the ecologist party family, and a split has been forecast because of these ideological differences among Green parties, some of which position themselves on the left while others maintain their neutral position on the left-right spectrum (Jacobs et al., 1992: 71).

The Group of the European Democratic Alliance has its origin in the European Democratic Union, which was formed in 1965, and is dominated by the French Gaullists and the Irish Fianna Fáil. It must be regarded as an incoherent group. There have been moves on the part of the Gaullists to join the EPP Group and it seems likely that they will do so following the 1994 European elections. A Gaullist has already joined the EPP Group on an individual basis. On the other hand, it is unlikely that the Gaullist party RPR, which has been ambivalent in its approach toward the EU, not to mention toward the Maastricht Treaty, would be accepted as a member of the federalist EPP Party in the foreseeable future.

The Rainbow Group in the European Parliament, mentioned earlier, has its origin in the Technical Coordination Group, formed in 1979. The member parties reflect divergent views, but most of them have ethnic and regional concerns in common. This is a group with which the agrarian parties of the Nordic countries eventually may affiliate.

The Technical Group of the European Right was launched in 1984. It is right-wing and nationalistic, containing such parties as the Belgian Vlaams Blok, the French National Front, and the German Republican Party. It is, together with the group presented next, the least transnational of all the groups. There was a split in 1989 when the Italian neofascist MSI left the group.

The Left Unity Group is the smallest and, in terms of the number of national delegations, the least transnational group. It was founded in 1989 following a split within the former Communist and Allies Group. The other left-wing group that was founded then, the Group of the United European Left, dissolved after its largest delegation, the Italian Democratic Party of the Left, joined the Group of the Party of European Socialists. Unlike the Group of the United European Left this group has been wary of, if not hostile to, further integration. The French Communist Party is the largest member party.

Finally, attention must be paid to the small number of nonattached, or independent, MEPs. They have preferred to stay out of the political groups mainly for ideological reasons, despite the fact that it is more advantageous to belong to a group as far as financing and intrainstitutional powers are concerned.

In the European Parliament the left-right dimension is not always the predominant one, and a consensus between the socialists and Christian democrats is often mustered prior to votings (cf. Corbett and Jacobs, 1989: 175). This "consensus-politics approach," to some extent reflecting "consociational" political systems like Belgium and the Netherlands, can be contrasted to the polarized political system of the Westminster model. In the European Parliament you must compromise if you are to win support for policy proposals. After all, half a loaf is better than none.

The party system at the European level is becoming less fragmented and more bipolarized (cf. Abélès, 1992: 171; Quermonne, 1993: 87-88). Because of the institutional imperatives in the European Parliament there are incentives to form large groupings and the smaller groups have become marginalized (see *European Parliament-EP News*, 1992). In the run-up to the 1994 European elections the two largest groups, the Group of the Party of European Socialists and the Group of the European People's Party, comprise no less than 361 out of 518 seats (70 percent). There is a clear trend, however imperfect, toward the formation of a two-and-a-half-party system in the European Parliament.[8] Except for the socialist and conservative/Christian democratic poles, the liberal grouping is the third largest and forms one of the three most influential blocs. It goes without saying that ideological clashes abound in such broad, catchall groups and that it meets with difficulties in imposing group discipline.

CONCLUDING REMARKS

The subject studied in this chapter constitutes a turbulent field of EU studies. The party federations in general and the political groups in particular are undergoing constant alignments and mergers. However, a functioning party system is a fundamental attribute of any political system, federal or not. If, as one can predict, a leftist and a center-right bloc will be the outcome of the present maneuverings, then it is hard to see how the national party systems will not be affected. There are pressures to party and party system convergence, pressures that should be further analyzed.

The analogy between party organizations of federal political systems and transnational party federations is helpful indeed. The transnational party organizations, as well as the political groups of the European Parliament, could be conceived of as coalitions of parties, and the theoretical approach to the study of political parties as systems seems to have relevance in a transnational context as well. It is important to emphasize, however, that transnational party organizations should be judged on their own merits and not by the same strict criteria as are usually applied to Europe's national political parties. The emerging European parties are not mass parties and they have not been successful as mobilizers of public opinion. They resemble American parties in that they above all are active in regard to elections and work as channels for competing elites.

Whether or not genuinely supranational European parties will take form is difficult to predict. Earlier scholars have been skeptical in this respect, and if we were to base our forecast on experiences it is hard not to agree with these assessments. Even though the ambition to work in this direction is strong, the final result will depend on the outcome of the integration process overall. Given the present anticommunautaire mood of public opinion, politicians are cautious in embarking upon new routes to deeper integration. However, if European parties cannot be formed will it ever be possible to found a United States of Europe?

The national and the European levels are interrelated and communication between them is of fundamental importance. Today, there is a mutual distrust due to a lack of communication, and ameliorating this situation requires that the number of links and degree of communication between party representatives, parliamentarians, and officials at the two levels increase. There is a need for increased contact and exchange, bilaterally as well as multilaterally, vertically as well as horizontally.

The importance of domestic politics has been emphasized throughout this chapter. The inside-out dimension is the most important one, despite existing outside-in pressures on party and party system convergence. It is at the national level that we find the most important determinants, such as the character of party systems, party politics, and ideological space of maneuver, of the obstacles to and the prospects for transnational party cooperation and the formation of parties at the European level.

LIST OF INTERVIEWS

1. *Biesmans, John*, Deputy Secretary-General, Group of the European People's Party, Brussels, June 25, 1992.
2. *Fitzmaurice, John*, Administrator, Commission of the European Union, Brussels, June 25, 1992.
3. *Gresch, Norbert*, Political Advisor, President's Office, European Parliament, Strasbourg, June 23-24, 1993.
4. *Hanisch, Axel*, Secretary-General, Party of European Socialists, Brussels, June 26, 1992.
5. *Jansen, Thomas*, Secretary-General, European People's Party, and European Union of Christian Democrats, Brussels, June 26, 1992.

6. *Priestley, Julian*, Secretary-General, Group of the Party of European Socialists, Brussels, June 26, 1992.
7. *Rφmer, Harald*, Special Advisor, Group of the European People's Party, former Secretary-General of the European Democratic Group, Brussels, June 23, 1992.
8. *Tindemans, Leo*, Chairman of the Group of the European People's Party, Prime Minister of Belgium, 1974-78, Brussels, June 24, 1992.

In addition to Tindemans, some thirty Members of the European Parliament have been interviewed.

APPENDIX

Arrangements for the European Elections

State	Number of MEPs/From	Electoral System	Turnout	
	1994	1994	1984	1989
Belgium[1]	24/25	PR with PV[2]	92.2	90.7
Denmark	16/16	PR with PV	52.4	46.2
Federal Republic of Germany	81/99	PR with PV[3]	56.8	62.3
France	81/87	PR without PV	56.7	48.7
Greece[1]	24/25	PR without PV	77.2	79.9[7]
Ireland	15/15	PR with STV[4]	47.6	68.3[7]
Italy	81/87	PR with PV	83.4	81.0
Luxembourg[1]	6/6	PR with vote splitting	88.8	87.4[7]
The Netherlands	25/31	PR with PV	50.6	47.2
Portugal	24/25	PR without PV	72.4[5]	51.2
Spain	60/64	PR without PV	68.9[6]	54.6
United Kingdom	81/87	Majority Vote System (Northern Ireland: PR with STV)	32.6	36.2

Total number of MEPs 518/567[8]

[1] Voting compulsory.
[2] Proportional representation with preferential vote.
[3] Proportional representation without preferential vote.
[4] Proportional representation with single transferable vote.
[5] Elections of July 1987.

APPENDIX, (cont.)

[6] Elections of June 1987.
[7] General election held on the same day.
[8] At the European Council summit in Edinburgh, December 1992, compromises on new national quotas were arrived at and the total number of Eurocandidates to be elected in the 1994 European elections, June 9-12, will be 567.

Sources: Nugent (1991); adapted with permission from the author. See also European Parliament, Research and Documentation Papers, *Electoral Laws for European Elections* (1989). For turnout, see Jacobs et al., (1992) and Niedermayer (1991).

NOTES

1. For a discussion of the political theoretical concepts of rationalism and empiricism, see Giovanni Sartori's essay "Politics, Ideology, and Belief Systems," *American Political Science Review*, Vol. 63, No. 2, 1969.

2. The present writer leans heavily upon the so-called domestic-politics approach to studies of European integration (see Bulmer, 1983), and to studies of international politics and foreign policy overall (see Putnam, 1988).

3. The principle of subsidiarity runs like a continuous thread throughout the basic programes and documents of the EPP. This principle, reflecting Catholic social teachings, has a long history in Christian democratic thinking.

4. Voting is compulsory in Belgium, Greece, and Luxembourg (European Parliament, Research and Documentation Papers, *Electoral Laws for European Elections*, 1989). Otherwise, average voter turnout would probably have been even lower.

5. With regard to a uniform electoral system, Article 138 of the EEC Treaty included the following provision: "The Assembly shall draw up proposals for elections by direct universal suffrage in accordance with a uniform procedure in all Member States" (quoted in Nugent, 1991: 142). This article is again to be found in the Maastricht Treaty; the word "Assembly" is, however, replaced by "the European Parliament." According to an act of September 1976, "the European Parliament shall draw up a proposal for a uniform electoral procedure to serve as a basis for deliberations by the Council with a view to the adoption of this proposal by the Member States" (source: see note 4)

6. The act referred to in note 5 states that membership in the European Parliament is compatible with membership in a national parliament. However, the electoral laws of Belgium, Greece, and Spain prohibit such dual mandates (source: see note 4).

7. The then secretary-general of CDU, Volker Rühe, and the party chairman of the British Conservative Party, Chris Patten, were instrumental in this process, as were the chairman of the former European Democratic Group, Sir Christopher Prout, and the group's secretary-general, Harald Rømer, not to mention Drs. Thomas Jansen and Wilfried Martens, the Secretary-General and President, respectively, of the EPP and EUCD (interviews no. 1, 5, and 7). With regard to these interpersonal relations one can identify a network of party elites, who are familiar with each other and share basic values. I would argue that the EU is based upon this kind of networking and personal contacts established through transnational party networks, often in the context of youth associations.

8. In an illuminating article Hix (1993) argues that the emerging party system at the European level, as far as the number of significant parties and the issue cleavages are concerned, is strikingly similar to the German one (cf. Pappi, 1984).

REFERENCES

Abélès, M. 1992. *La vie quotidienne au parlement européen*. Paris: Hachette.

Agence Europe, 1992. "The 'European Socialist Party' Is Born." November 16/17.

———. 1993. "EU/Liberals: Federation Congress in Torquay." December 11.

Aron, R. 1962/84. *Paix et guerre entre les nations*. Eighth edition. Paris: Calmann-Lévy.

Attinà, F. 1990. "The Voting Behaviour of the European Parliament Members and the Problem of the Europarties." *European Journal of Political Research*, Vol. 18, No. 5.

Bardi, L. 1992. "Transnational Party Federations in the European Community." In R. S. Katz, and P. Mair (eds.), *Party Organizations: A Data Handbook on Party Organizations in Western Democracies, 1960-90*. London: Sage Publications.

Blumler, J. G. and A. D. Fox. 1980. "The Involvement of Voters in the European Elections of 1979: Its Extent and Sources," *European Journal of Political Research*, Vol. 8, No. 4.

Bogdanor, V. 1986. "The Future of the European Community: Two Models of Democracy." *Government and Opposition*, Vol. 21, No. 2.

———. 1989. "Direct Elections, Representative Democracy and European Integration." *Electoral Studies*, Vol. 8, No. 3.

Buck, K. H. 1989. "Europe: The 'Greens' and the 'Rainbow Group' in the European Parliament." In F. Müller-Rommel (ed.), *New Politics in Western Europe: The Rise and Success of Green Parties and Alternative Lists*. Boulder (CO), San Francisco, and London: Westview Press.

Bulmer, S. 1983. "Domestic Politics and European Community Policy-Making." *Journal of Common Market Studies*, Vol. 21 No. 4.

Burgess, M. 1989. *Federalism and European Union: Political Ideas, Influences and Strategies in the European Community, 1972-1987*. London and New York: Routledge.

Claude, I. L., Jr. 1956/64. *Swords into Plowshares: The Problems and Progress of International Organization*. Third revised edition. New York: Random House.

Colchester, N. and D. Buchan. 1990. *Europe Relaunched: Truths and Illusions on the Way to 1992*. London: Hutchinson/The Economist Books.

Corbett, R. 1992. "The Intergovernmental Conference on Political Union." *Journal of Common Market Studies*, Vol. 30, No. 3.

———. 1993. *The Treaty of Maastricht. From Conception to Ratification: A Comprehensive Reference Guide*. Marlow: Longman.

Corbett, R. and F. Jacobs. 1989. "Aktivitäten und Arbeitsstrukturen des Europäischen Parlaments." In O. Schmuck and W. Wessels (eds.), *Das Europäische Parlament im dynamischen Integrationsprozeß: Auf der Suche nach einem zeitgemäßen Leitbild*. Bonn: Europa Union Verlag.

Curtice, J. 1989. "The 1989 European Election: Protest or Green Tide?" *Electoral Studies*, Vol. 8, No. 3.

Dahl, R. A. 1989. *Democracy and Its Critics*. New Haven and London: Yale University Press.

Duverger, M. 1951/78. *Political Parties: Their Organization and Activity in the Modern State*. Third edition. London: Methuen and Co.

———. 1992. "Vers des partis européens," *Le Monde*, January 25, 1992.

Eckstein, H. 1968. "Party Systems." In Sills, D. L. (ed.), *International Encyclopedia of the Social Sciences*. Vol. 11. London: The Macmillan Company and New York: The Free Press.

Economist, The. 1994. "Europe's Feeble Parliament." January 22.

Epstein, L. D. 1967. *Political Parties in Western Democracies*. London: Pall Mall Press.

European Parliament-EP News. 1992. "Larger Groups Grow Stronger." January 13-17.

European Parliament, Research and Documention Papers. 1989. *Electoral laws for European elections*. Second revised edition.

Featherstone, K. 1988. *Socialist Parties and European Integration: A Comparative History*. Manchester: Manchester University Press.

Fenner, C. 1981. "Grenzen einer Europäisierung der Parteien: Europa kann man nicht wählen." *Politische Vierteljahresschrift*. Vol. 22, No. 1.

Financial Times. 1994. "Major Deepens Tory Divisions on Europe." February 11.

Fitzmaurice, J. 1975. *The Party Groups in the European Parliament* Westmead: Saxon House.

Frears, J. 1991. *Parties and Voters in France*. London: Hurst and Company.

Gallagher, M. et al. 1992. *Representative Government in Western Europe*. New York: McGraw-Hill.

George, S. 1991. *Politics and Policy in the European Community*. Second edition. Oxford: Oxford University Press.

Gidlund, G. 1992. *Partiernas Europa*. Stockholm: Natur and Kultur.

Girvin, B., ed. 1988. *The Transformation of Contemporary Conservatism*. London: Sage.

Goldman, R. M., ed. 1983. *Transnational Parties: Organizing the World's Precincts*. Lanham (MD) and London: University Press of America.

Goldmann, K. 1989. "The Line in Water: International and Domestic Politics." *Cooperation and Conflict*, Vol. 24, No 314.

Gresch, N. 1978. *Transnationale Parteienzusammenarbeit in der EG*. Baden-Baden: Nomos Verlagsgesellschaft.

Guardian, The. 1994. "New Green Alliance Fails to Find Common Ground on Union Poll." February 1.

———. 1994. "Hurd Attacks Lib-Lab EU Pact." February 15.

Haahr, J. H. 1992. "European Integration and the Left in Britain and Denmark." *Journal of Common Market Studies*, Vol. 30, No. 1.

Haas, E. B. 1958. *The Uniting of Europe: Political, Social and Economical Forces 1950-1957*. London: Stevens and Sons.

———. 1964a. *Beyond the Nation-State: Functionalism and International Organization*. Stanford, CA: Stanford University Press.

———. 1964b. "Technocracy, Pluralism and the New Europe." In S. R. Graubard (ed.), *A New Europe?* Boston: Houghton Mifflin Company.

Hagger, M. and M. Wing. 1979. "Legislative Roles and Clientele Orientations in the European Parliament." *Legislative Studies Quarterly*, Vol. 4, No. 2.

Hague, R. and M. Harrop. 1982/87. *Comparative Government and Politics*. Second edition. London: Macmillan.

Henig, S., ed. 1979. *Political Parties in the European Community*. London: George Allen and Unwin.

Herman, V. and R. Van Schendelen, eds. 1979. *The European Parliament and the National Parliaments*. Westmead: Saxon House.

Hix, S. 1993. "The Emerging EC Party System? The European Party Federations in the Intergovernmental Conferences." *Politics*, Vol. 13, No. 2.

Holland, M. 1986. *Candidates for Europe*. Aldershot: Gower House.

Hrbek, R. 1988. "Transnational Links: The ELD and Liberal Party Group in the European Parliament." In E. J. Kirchner (ed.), *Liberal Parties in Western Europe*. Cambridge: Cambridge University Press.

Irving, R. E. M. 1979. *The Christian Democratic Parties of Western Europe*. London: The Royal Institute of International Affairs/George Allen and Unwin.

Jacobs, F. et al. 1992. *The European Parliament*. Second edition. Harlow: Longman.

Jerneck, M. 1990. "Internationalisering och svensk partidiplomati." In G. Hansson, and L.-G. Stenelo (eds.), *Makt och internationalisering*. Stockholm: Carlssons.

Johansson, K. M. 1993. "Transnational Party Co-operation: The Case of the European People's Party." Paper for ECPR Workshop "Inter-Party Relationships in National and European Parliamentary Arenas." University of Leiden, Netherlands, April 2-8.

Joll, J. 1955. *The Second International 1889-1914*. London: Weidenfeld and Nicolson.

Kaiser, K. 1968. "The Interaction of Regional Subsystems: Some Preliminary Notes on Recurrent Patterns and the Role of Superpowers." *World Politics*, Vol. 21, No. 1.

———. 1971a. "Transnational Relations as a Threat to the Democratic Process." *International Organization*, Vol. 25, No. 3.

———. 1971b. "Transnational Politics: Toward a Theory of Multinational Politics." *International Organization*, Vol. 25, No. 4.

Katz, R. S. and P. Mair. 1993. "Varieties of Convergence and Patterns of Incorporation in West European Party Systems." Paper for ECPR Workshop "Inter-Party Relationships in National and European Parliamentary Arenas." University of Leiden, Netherlands, April 2-8.

Keohane, R. O. and S. Hoffmann, eds. 1991. *The New European Community: Decisionmaking and Institutional Change*. Boulder, CO: Westview Press.

Kerr, H. H., Jr. 1973. "Changing Attitudes through International Participation: European Parliamentarians and Integration." *International Organization*, Vol. 27, No. 1.

Key, V. O., Jr. 1942/64. *Politics, Parties, and Pressure Groups*. Fifth edition. New York: Thomas Y. Crowell Company.

Kieffer, G. and D. Millar. 1979. "Relations between the European Parliament and the National Parliaments." In V. Herman and R. van Schendelen (eds.), *The European Parliament and the National Parliaments*. Westmead: Saxon House.

Kirchner, E. J. 1984. *The European Parliament: Performance and Prospects*. Aldershot: Gower House.

————, ed. 1988. *Liberal Parties in Western Europe*. Cambridge: Cambridge University Press.

Kohler, B. and B. Myrzik. 1982. "Transnational Party Links." In R. Morgan and S. Silvestri (eds.), *Moderates and Conservatives in Western Europe: Political Parties, the European Community and the Atlantic Alliance*. London: Heinemann.

Kuper, E. 1991. "Transnational Party Federations in Action." Paper prepared for the ISA convention in Vancouver, Canada, March 19-23.

Layton-Henry, Z., ed. 1982. *Conservative Politics in Western Europe*. London: Macmillan.

Lindberg, L. N. 1963. *The Political Dynamics of European Economic Integration*. Stanford, CA: Stanford University Press and London: Oxford University Press.

Lipset, S. M. and S. Rokkan, eds. 1967. *Party Systems and Voter Alignments: Cross-National Perspectives*. New York: The Free Press.

Lodge, J. and V. Herman. 1980. "Direct Elections to the European Parliament: A Supranational Perspective." *European Journal of Political Research*, Vol. 8, No. 1.

————. 1982. *Direct Elections to the European Parliament: A Community Perspective*. London: Macmillan.

Lodge, J., ed. 1986. *Direct Elections to the European Parliament 1984*. London: Macmillan.

————, ed. 1990. *The 1989 Election of the European Parliament*. London: Macmillan.

Marquand, D. 1978. "Towards a Europe of the Parties. *Political Quarterly*, Vol. 49, No. 4.

May, J. 1977. "Co-operation between Socialist Parties." In W. E. Paterson, and A. H. Thomas (eds.), *Social Democratic Parties in Western Europe*. London: Croom Helm.

Morgan, R. and S. Silvestri, eds. 1982. *Moderates and Conservatives in Western Europe: Political Parties, the European Community and the Atlantic Alliance*, London: Heinemann.

Neumann, S. 1956. *Modern Political Parties: Approaches to Comparative Politics*. Chicago: The University of Chicago Press.

Niedermayer, O. 1983. *Europäische Parteien? Zur grenzüberschreitenden Interaktion politischer Parteien im Rahmen der Europäischen Gemeinschaft*. Frankfurt and New York: Campus Verlag.

————. 1984. "The Transnational Dimension of the Election." *Electoral Studies*, Vol. 3, No. 3,

————. 1991. "European Elections 1989." *European Journal of Political Research*, Vol. 19, No. 1.

Nord, H. and J. Taylor. 1979. "The European Parliament before and after Direct Elections." *Government and Opposition*, Vol. 14, No. 4.

Nugent, N. 1991. *The Government and Politics of the European Community*. Second edition. London: Macmillan.

Oudenhove, G. van. 1965. *The Political Parties in the European Parliament: The First Ten Years (September 1952-September 1962)*. Leiden: A. W. Sijthoff.

Padgett, S. and W. E. Paterson. 1991. *A History of Social Democracy in Postwar Europe*. London and New York: Longman.

Panebianco, A. 1988. *Political Parties: Organization and Power*. Cambridge: Cambridge University Press.

Pappi, F.-U. 1984. "The West German Party System." *West European Politics*, Vol. 7, No. 4.

Parkin, S. 1989. *Green Parties: An International Guide*, London: Heretic Books.

Paterson, W. E. and I. Campbell. 1974. *Social Democracy in Post-War Europe*. New York: St. Martin's Press.

Paterson, W. E. and A. H. Thomas, eds. 1977. *Social Democratic Parties in Western Europe*. London: Croom Helm.

———, eds. 1986. *The Future of Social Democracy: Problems and Prospects of Social Democratic Parties in Western Europe*. Oxford: Clarendon Press.

Pelinka, A. 1983. *Social Democratic Parties in Europe*. New York: Praeger.

Peterson, M. J. 1992. "Transnational Activity, International Society and World Politics." *Millennium: Journal of International Studies*, Vol. 21, No. 3.

Pridham, G. and P. Pridham. 1979a. "Transnational Parties in the European Community I: The Party Groups in the European Parliament." In S. Henig (ed.), *Political Parties in the European Community*. London: George Allen and Unwin.

———. 1979b. "Transnational Parties in the European Community II: The Development of European Party Federations." In S. Henig (ed.), *Political Parties in the European Community*. London: George Allen and Unwin.

———. 1981. *Transnational Party Co-operation and European Integration: The Process towards Direct Elections*. London: George Allen and Unwin.

Pridham, G. 1982. "Christian Democrats, Conservatives and Transnational Party Cooperation in the European Community: Centre-Forward or Centre-Right?" In Z. Layton-Henry (ed.), *Conservative Politics in Western Europe*. London: Macmillan.

———, ed. 1991. *Encouraging Democracy: The International Context of Regime Transition in Southern Europe*. Leicester and London: Leicester University Press.

Pruitt, D. G. 1991. "Strategy in Negotiation." In V. A. Kremenyuk (ed.), *International Negotiation: Analysis, Approaches, Issues*. Oxford and San Francisco: Jossey-Bass Publishers.

Putnam, R. D. 1988. "Diplomacy and Domestic Politics: The Logic of Two-Level Games." *International Organization*, Vol. 42, No. 3.

Quermonne, J.-L. 1993. *Le système politique européen*. Paris: Montchrestien.

Reif, K. 1984. "National Electoral Cycles and European Elections 1979 and 1984." *Electoral Studies*, Vol. 3, No. 3.

———. 1985. *Ten European Elections: Campaigns and Results of the 1979/81 First Direct Elections to the European Parliament*. Aldershot: Gower House.

Reif, K. and H. Schmitt. 1980. "Nine Second Order National Elections: A Conceptual Framework for the Analysis of European Election Results." *European Journal of Political Research*, Vol. 8, No. 1.

Rokkan, S. 1966. "Electoral Mobilization, Party Competition, and National Integration." In J. LaPalombara and M. Weiner (eds.), *Political Parties and Political Development*. Princeton, NJ: Princeton University Press.

Rokkan, S. and D. W. Urwin, eds. 1982. *The Politics of Territorial Identity: Studies in European Regionalism*. London: Sage.

Rose, R. 1964. "Parties, Factions and Tendencies in Britain." *Political Studies*, Vol. 12, No. 1.

Rosenau, J. N. 1969. *Linkage Politics: Essays on the Convergence of National and International Systems*. New York: The Free Press and London: Collier-Macmillan.

————. 1990. *Turbulence in World Politics: A Theory of Change and Continuity.* New York: Harvester Wheatsheaf.

Rutschke, G. 1986. *Die Mitwirkung der Fraktionen bei der parlamentarischen Willensbildung im Europäischen Parlament im Vergleich zu den Parlamenten der Mitgliedstaaten.* Frankfurt am Main: Peter Lang.

Sartori, G. 1969. "Politics, Ideology, and Belief Systems." *American Political Science Review*, Vol. 63, No. 2.

————. 1976. *Parties and Party Systems: A Framework for Analysis.* Cambridge: Cambridge University Press.

Schmitt, H. and R. Mannheimer. 1991. "About Voting and Non-Voting in the European Elections of June 1989." *European Journal of Political Research*, Vol. 19, No. 1.

Seidelmann, R. 1993. "Parteien und Internationale Politik." In W. Woyke (ed.), *Handwörterbuch Internationale Politik.* Fifth edition. Opladen: Leske+Budrich.

Sjöblom, G. 1968. *Party Strategies in a Multiparty System.* Lund: Studentlitteratur.

————. 1989. "Notater om politiska partier och internationalisering." In *Danmark og det internationale system: Festskrift till Ole Karup Pedersen.* Köpenhamn: Politiske studier.

Smith, G. 1988. "Between Left and Right: The Ambivalence of European Liberalism." In E. J. Kirchner (ed.), *Liberal Parties in Western Europe.* Cambridge: Cambridge University Press.

————. 1989. *Politics in Western Europe: A Comparative Analysis.* Fifth edition. Aldershot: Gower House.

Spretnak, C. and F. Capra. 1986. *Green Politics.* London: Paladin.

Stammen, T. 1980. *Political Parties in Europe.* London: John Martin Publishing Ltd.

Statutes of the European Federation of Green Parties. 1993. Masala, June.

Steed, M. 1983. "The European Parliament." In V. Bogdanor, and D. Butler (eds.), *Democracy and Elections: Electoral Systems and Their Political Consequences.* Cambridge: Cambridge University Press.

————. 1984. "Failure or Long-haul? European Elections and European Integration." *Electoral Studies*, Vol. 3, No. 3.

Sunday Times, The. "Smith in Row over Socialist Euro Charter." 1993. November 7.

Sweeney, J. P. 1984a. *The First European Elections: Neo-Functionalism and the European Parliament.* Boulder, CO: Westview Press.

————. 1984b. "The Left in Europe's Parliament: The Problematic Effects of Integration Theory." *Comparative Politics*, Vol. 16, No. 2.

Taylor, P. 1983. *The Limits of European Integration.* London and Canberra: Croom Helm.

————. 1989. "The New Dynamics of EC Integration in the 1980s." In J. Lodge (ed.), *The European Community and the Challenge of the Future.* London: Pinter Publishers.

————. 1992. "Consociation and Symbiosis in the European Community." Version of a paper which was published in *Review of International Studies*, January 1991.

Times, The. "Lib Dems Play Down European Message." February 8, 1994.

Tranholm-Mikkelsen, J. 1991. "Neo-functionalism: Obstinate or Obsolete? A Reappraisal in the Light of the New Dynamism of the EC." *Millennium: Journal of International Studies*, Vol. 20, No. 1.

"Treaty on European Union."

Truman, D. B. 1955. "Federalism and the Party System." In A. W. Macmahon (ed.), *Federalism: Mature and Emergent*. New York: Doubleday.

Tsebelis, G. 1990. *Nested Games: Rational Choice in Comparative Politics*. Berkeley: University of California Press.

von Beyme, K. 1985. *Political Parties in Western Democracies*. Aldershot: Gower House.

Ward, Z. A. 1980. "Pan-European Parties: Proselytes of the European Community." In P. II. Merkl (ed.), *Western European Party Systems*. New York: The Free Press and London: Collier Macmillan.

Ware, A. 1986. "Political Parties." In D. Held and C. Pollitt (eds.), *New Forms of Democracy*. London: Sage.

Willets, P., ed. 1982. *Pressure Groups in the Global System: The Transnational Relations of Issue-Orientated Non-Governmental Organizations*. London: Frances Pinter.

Williams, S. 1991. "Sovereignty and Accountability in the European Community." In R. O. Keohane and S. Hoffmann (eds.), *The New European Community. Decisionmaking and Institutional Change*. Boulder, CO: Westview Press.

Wolfers, A. 1962/68. *Discord and Collaboration: Essays on International Politics*. Baltimore: The Johns Hopkins University Press.

Worre, T. 1987. "The Danish Euro-Party System." *Scandinavian Political Studies*, Vol. 10, No. 1.

10

The European Parliament

Juliet Lodge

The European Parliament is arguably one of the most vital EU institutions. It is one that assumes a system-transformative role in the EU; one that sets the political agenda and tries to define the emergent European Union's *raison d'être*; yet is one that, until relatively recently, had few entrenched powers. The absence of legislative authority meant that for much of its history, it was derided as impotent and unfavorably compared to national parliaments. Its mere existence, however, aroused acute anxiety among national parliamentarians and governments who feared that it would snatch away their sovereignty. The degree of fear and presentiments of rivalry require explanation, for though powerless, the European Parliament was never irrelevant to the development of European integration and the realization of European Union.

ORIGINS

The European Parliament originated as the Common Assembly of the European Coal and Steel Community, set up in 1950. By the 1960s, it served the merged communities. Its members were initially appointed from among the ranks of national parliamentarians. While mainly elected MPs, their number included appointments from second, sometimes nonelected, chambers such as the House of Lords (following Britain's accession in 1973). The national nominees were said to hold a "dual mandate" and this dual mandate was often seen as the chief obstacle to Members of the European Parliament (MEPs) acquiring real power.

The Common Assembly referred to itself as the European Parliament but this name was not adopted officially until the reforms introduced through the Single European Act made even the most reluctant government (in this case, the British under Mrs. Thatcher) use this nomenclature. The name was not just symbolically and psychologically important. Nor was it mere rhetoric. It was part of the EP's gambit to inject vision into the emergent EU polity and to transform it, and itself, into something that was a recognizable feature of a liberal democratic, representative form of government.

From the outset, the EP performed important socializing functions alongside the exercise of its "advisory and supervisory" roles ascribed to it in the EU treaties. The Common Assembly fairly quickly abandoned the practice of national delegations sitting together in favor of alphabetical ordering in line with broad party allegiance. This provided an ideal forum for European conditioning and socialization. Though this arrangement was much maligned as a "talking shop," the value of establishing such a forum among nationals who had been but shortly before vicious enemies was soon proven. What is remarkable is that the seemingly simple device of alphabetical seating swiftly moved to one of seating according to party preference and that this developed into a rudimentary party system and formed the basis of an enduring political consensus geared toward transformation of the then EC into a European Union.

The roles and functions of the EP, and with them those of its political party groups, have changed dramatically since the end of the 1970s, when the first Euro-elections were held. The symbiotic relationship between the parties and the EP has become increasingly significant and will be one of the main features of institutional development during the 1990s. The tensions underlying this relationship have existed since the inception of the EUs. They derive from the rivalry between national parliaments and the EP; the jealousy with which member governments have safeguarded their omnipotence, via the Council of Ministers and the European Council, in the EC legislative process; the continuing debate about the democratic deficit; the continuing misapprehension over the implications of a federal Union for national sovereignty and for the transformation of the EU into a liberal, democratic polity; and the contested roles and functions of the EP in the incipient and continuously evolving, flexible European Union. Yet the EP, via the political parties, has played one of the most significant, if undervalued, system-transformative roles in the EU of all the Union institutions. It is a role that it developed with a vengeance during the early 1980s and one to which it has returned on the eve of the realization of the Single Market.

Before examining the EP's powers and functions in more detail, it is important to understand how the EP is organized and how and why the question of it's powers cannot be separated from the issue of it's *raison d'être*. It must be remembered that the EP's role in the EU has always been a contested one. Governments have always been deeply skeptical about the need for a European Parliament and sorely worried lest such a body acquire the kind of legislative prerogatives and powers that would curtail their own primacy in determining the pace of integration and which would render the Council of Ministers less than supreme as the EU's legislative arm. However, a complicating factor arises from the very organization of the EP and from the question as to what its purpose should be in the EU. Given its parliamentary pretensions and the linkage of parliaments with liberal democratic practice, the EP has been bedeviled by a struggle to assert itself as a legitimate EU institution imbued with real legislative power. Overcoming government resistance to its aspirations has proved difficult and complex. However, successive generations of MEPs have developed a number of innovative strategies for achieving its objectives. These have hinged on, first, the quest for direct election, and secondly, democratic legitimacy. Every time that the EP has managed to expand its powers, often by skillfully interpreting the narrow roles prescribed for it in the Rome Treaty, and latterly the Single European Act, an important change in the nature of the EU's emerging polity has occurred. Therefore, changes in the EP's powers always parallel change in the development of the EU and, in the deepening of political integration.

A contested but symbiotic role: parties, national parliaments and the EP. From the outset, the political parties' roles have been rudimentary and viewed with a good deal of suspicion by their national parliamentary counterparts. The latter saw MEPs as their agents and to a degree still see them as such. This position is essentially untenable since MEPs have an independent mandate and cannot be bound by national parties. This is undoubtedly a source of friction between the two groups of parliamentarians and partly accounts for the relatively weak party cohesion among some of the EP's party groups. However, this must not be overstressed since the contested role of the EP and the evolution of its powers continues to condition the evolution of the parties. Moreover, the symbiotic relationship between the two has yet to be fully exploited to mutual benefit: something that will happen following the implementation of the Maastricht agreements (in whole or in part) before the next wave of EU enlargement.

Initially, the political parties (still known mostly as party groups) in the European Parliament only reflected the political allegiances of those members appointed from national parliaments. This had two consequences. First, for the most part, the caliber of MEPs was impoverished and MEPs' career advancement was tied to the priority most afforded their national parliamentary obligations. Secondly, it meant that for many years, there were no communist members from either France or Italy. So long as the communists adhered to the view that the EU was a bastion of imperial American capitalism against the USSR, they refused to participate in one of its agencies. The Italians relented by 1968 and the French thereafter.

The implications of this for the evolution of the EP's powers and the development of its treaty-given functions were negative: without sufficient time and commitment to the EP, the national delegates (many of whom were undoubted Euro-enthusiasts) were unable to focus adequately on distilling from the EP's limited functions a genuinely influential role for the EP in the conduct of the EU's legislative business. This is not to say that they were uninterested in the promotion of European union but to suggest that because their own and the EP's stature were low, because the EP's work remained largely invisible, unintelligible, and irrelevant to national electorates, national parliaments, and national governments, it was difficult for them to have a real impact on the progress of European integration.

Moreover, so long as the EP failed to adopt a flexible and innovative approach to capitalizing on its existing, limited powers, it was unable to insert itself effectively into the decision-making process. Since its opinions were often ignored by the Council of Ministers, and even by the Commission, there was little incentive for either to heed its views. This also meant that the party groups (whose membership could alter with every intervening national election) had little reason for developing greater cohesion and policy-making capabilities within their ranks.

Not until after the first Euro-elections, when the famous Isoglucose case confirmed the innovative exploitation of the EP's rules of procedure and called the Council of Ministers to account, did things change.[1] By then, the context was propititious and the cross-party commitment to European Union was unassailable. This also coincided with the period in the EU's development when anxiety about the EU's declining competitiveness in the international political economy induced member governments to heed Commission and EP reports on the costs of non-Europe and to commit themselves to a timetable of reform culminating in the Single Market and the realization of European Union.

There is still only a rudimentary party system in the EU. This exists at several levels and the most important is clearly the party organization within the European Parliament. The EP's power and that of its political parties remain mutually dependent, but this political and strategic interdependence is more vital now than at any other stage in the EU's history. This owes much to the reforms introduced through the Single Act and especially to those signaled by the Maastricht Treaty. However, it is important to recall that such a development had been foreseen, indeed feared, by successive member governments and treaty framers who, in relegating the Common Assembly initially to a minor role, were anxious to demote it to the status of a perpetual "talking shop" devoid of power (as the name implies)[2] and to prevent the development of a relationship between the Commission and the EP that would mirror the weakness of the French Fourth Republic by giving political parties real influence over the executive. That the progress and future of European union would demand a politicization of both the Commission and the EP was not properly appreciated. That this would have significant implications for the relationship between the EP and national parliaments was only grasped during the run-up to the signature of the Maastricht Treaty.

THE DEMOCRATIC DEFICIT

The democratic deficit is a concept which is used to refer to an implied gap between democratic practice in theory and democratic practice in reality. It refers principally to weaknesses and deficiencies in the relationship between the

European Parliament and the other key institutions. In particular, the notion of a democratic deficit has often been explained by reference to the European Parliament's relationship with the EU Commission and the Council of Ministers. Consequently, the democratic deficit is seen as the product of flaws in that relationship. These are conceived of in two ways: first, the actual legislative and control powers possessed and exercised by the European Parliament; and secondly, the impact of Euro-elections on the composition of the decision-making institutions.

The EP's intrinsically weak legislative and control powers—notably vis-à-vis the Council of Ministers—are seen as a major cause of the democratic deficit. This deficiency is bolstered by the fact that there is no correspondence between elections to the EP and the composition of an "EU government." This is because there is no EU government. However, the lack of correspondence is often seen as a means of explaining relatively low turnout at Euro-elections, which itself is seen as eroding the European Parliament's democratic legitimacy and hence its claim to greater legislative power. However, strict analogies between national polities and the incipient EU polity are often unhelpful, misleading, and implausible.

PARTIES, ELECTIONS AND DEMOCRATIC LEGITIMACY

Nevertheless, parties are responsible, at times of elections, for mobilizing the electorate and ensuring that it turns out to vote. The fear among the ranks of national parties and national parliaments that the EP (and its parties) were rivals for the loyalty of voters meant that national parties did not sufficiently engage themselves in the electoral campaigns to mobilize a high turnout. This chapter is not the place to go into this, but it must be remembered that the disjunction between the transnational, supranational, and national party levels in the EU has had important repercussions both for turnout, for public confidence in the EP, and ultimately for the EP's quest for greater power.[3]

Getting a high turnout (which is still on average above the average turnout in U.S. presidential elections) is important to the EP party groups and to the EP's quest for real legislative authority. This is because the EP has traditionally argued that a democratic deficit exists in the EU and that it can be partly rectified by the holding of Euro-elections, which would then justify the granting of a directly elected body in the EU real legislative power.

The problems of mobilizing turnout are legion. The EP's weak legislative authority makes it difficult for it to campaign on a record of achievement at Euro-election time. It is even more difficult for the different EP party groups to put forward distinctive claims in terms of their political records during the EP's preceding term. Again, this owes much to the actual role of the EP in the legislative process. It is also a product of the fact that the EP still lacks a formal right of initiative and therefore does not set the legislative agenda of the

EU. Too much should not be made of this, since in national parliaments the members normally initiate less than 8 percent of all legislation, the rest being driven by the agenda set by the government.

ELECTIONS

Party representation was distorted until the first Euro-elections, held in 1979 after being postponed from 1978. The member states had resisted adhering to the letter of the Rome Treaty prescribing Euro-elections, as they were concerned that the elections would so transform the EU's and especially the European Parliament's legitimacy that their sovereignty would be compromised. This argument derived largely from the view that national parliaments, because directly elected, were the repositories of popular sovereignty and that sovereignty was indivisible. The notion that people voting for representatives in a European Parliament would through that act become citizens of the EU as well as of its component states (much as in federal states) disquietened them, to say the least. Their fears were also compounded by the continuing pressure, even among appointed MEPs, for an accretion in the European Parliament's powers. Insofar as the quest for greater power was rooted in the presumed enhanced legitimacy deriving from election, low turnout could be used as an excuse by national governments to reject the EP's claims for greater powers.

DEMOCRATIC LEGITIMACY

The realization of democratic legitimacy has rested on the attainment of two objectives: first expanding the European Parliament's decision-making powers to enable it to approximate the role traditionally associated with legislatures in Western European democracies; and secondly, to ensure that the way in which its members are chosen and exercise their powers conforms to accepted democratic practices. Exploitating the rules of procedure, the European Parliament developed a dual-pronged strategy for augmenting its influence over the content and direction of EU legislation during the 1980s. This strategy divided into two complementary tactics: the minimalist tactic rested on MEPs fully utilizing both their own rules of procedure and the EP's treaty-given powers, and the maximalist tactic rested on exploiting its right to set its own agenda by initiating a debate on the future of European union and so playing a grand forum and constitution-framing role for the EU.[4]

The EP possesses a unique right: the right to set its own agenda. It is this right that it has fully made use of with a view to expand the domain of its own debates, investigations, and own-initiative reports. While it is true that since the adoption of the cooperation procedure under the Single Act and the interinstitutional agreement on a legislative programe, the EP's agenda is partly determined by the exigencies of the legislative timetable, the EP still has the right to look into any matter it chooses. This enables it to influence the context within which debate unfurls on all manner of issues. Moreover, it is often the case that the EP initiates debate in areas which the other institutions, notably the Commission, have to avoid lest they be seen as overstepping their treaty-given competences. In using this power, the EP does indeed expand the scope of European integration and herald the direction in which the EU is moving. A good example of this lies with the debates both on intensifying European union and, more poignantly, on the evolution of some responsibility in the taboo area of foreign and security affairs.[5]

EP POWERS AND FUNCTIONS AFTER MAASTRICHT

The EP decided that it should take the lead in developing a constructive forum for a permanent, institutionalized dialogue with national parliaments. In this it was partly inspired by the need to augment its own democratic legitimacy and to convince national parliaments that the democratic deficit afflicted them too in terms of their actual power vis-à-vis national ministers in the Council of Ministers. The EP was also partly encouraged by the strategic and tactical desirability of promoting effective communication with putative rival, and often skeptical, national parliaments. It had learned the lesson of Spinelli: during the run-up to the Single Act and during the deliberations over the EP's draft treaty establishing the European Union, MEPs had been careful to engage in a dialogue with national MPs. This had two functions. On the one hand, it created an additional legitimate parliamentary base and informed voice favorable to European union in the national arena which could partially offset opposition and skepticism, notably among government ranks. On the other hand, it created the basis for a symbiotic relationship between the national and supranational arms of a functioning parliamentary system. It was designed both to promote communication and set the foundations for long-term intercourse: the two sets of parliamentarians not only were mutually dependent but could be mutually beneficial to each other if only they cooperated constructively in an effort to scrutinize, control, influence, and hold accountable national government ministers[6].

THE ASSIZES

Only a year before the signature of the Single European Act, the EP had argued during the 1984 election campaign that it should be invested with the task of devising a draft constitution for the EU. While this was not enthusiastically received by governments (who were in a position to deny it such a role), only a year after the implementation of the Single European Act, steps were taken to rectify the democratic deficit by concerted parliamentary cooperation. Through a series of reports in 1987-89, the EP put treaty revision back on the political agenda[7]. It was to lobby hard for real reform following the decision to hold an IGC (Intergovernmental Conference) on EMU (European Monetary Union).

The EP called on national parliaments in June 1988 to work with it to overcome the democratic deficit. The Italian parliament took the initiative and called for the establishment of a European Etats Généraux. The EP put forward its own strategy for the attainment of European union which owed a good deal to the EUT (draft Treaty establishing the European Union) and to the Spinelli strategy: that is, it used its experience of its newly won legislative powers under the cooperation procedure combined with a strategy justifying a deepening of European integration, in part through further institutional reforms. Like Spinelli, the EP continued to see the realization of European union in terms of augmenting the EC institutions' capacity to act effectively, efficiently, accountably, responsively, transparently and democratically.[8] It timed its interventions on these issues carefully to coincide with a change in the EC Commission, successive EC presidencies, the 1989 Euro-election, and the launch at the 1989 Madrid European Council of the Intergovernmental Conference on EMU, in which, it argued, it should participate.

While the EP was not successful in gaining a role either in respect of the IGC on EMU on the later conceded IGC on political union, for which it had lobbied hard, its experience of the cooperation procedure was instrumental in bringing about further changes to the legislative process agreed by the Maastricht Treaty negotiators. The cooperation procedure had not only made decision making more transparent but significantly expedited the passage of legislation (cuffing it to under two years from start to finish) and begun to ensure that the Council of Ministers was publicly held accountable by the EP for its decisions or indecision.[9] This experience could be used to justify its claims for further institutional and legislative change to its advantage but, as in the earlier negotiations leading to the adoption of the Single Act, it was not enough to guarantee it a direct voice in the deliberations leading to the Maastricht Treaty.

The EP had been able to use a document which had been transformed into treaty format—its EUT—to press for change during the SEA (Single European Act) negotiations: the EUT lay on the table alongside the documents of the permanent representatives and there are striking parallels between the two. There was not an exact equivalent during the Maastricht process. The Martin report emanated from the Institutional Affairs Committee in three phases. Martin I (March 14, 1990)[10] defined the subjects which the EP wanted to see as part of the process of treaty revision. This report was especially important in terms of the strategy subsequently developed. The report had advocated an inter-institutional conference to prepare an IGC on political union at a time when the governments merely envisaged one on EMU. More importantly, it had called for a meeting with all national parliaments—the assizes. Four preconferences were eventually held[11] and the assizes convened in November 1990 with

250 parliamentarians (two-thirds national MPs to one-third MEPs) for one week to deliberate on issues due to come up in the IGCs. Martin II set out detailed proposals[12] in all areas, which were translated into legal language, complete with the EP's Opinion, just before the IGCs convened in November.

The EP had argued in favor of including the following in the treaty revision process: the integration of EPC into the supranational framework (which conformed to the notion of [a single structure] as opposed to the three-pillar approach eventually adopted); greater EU competence in social, R & D, and environmental sectors; fundamental rights and citizenship; majority voting in the Council of Ministers; stronger executive powers for the Commission; reform of the own resources system; and, of course, greater powers for the EP. These broke down into a right of codecision, a role in the appointment of the Commission, a right of inquiry, right of initiative, and expansion of the assent procedure to international agreements and treaty revision[13] (a particularly sensitive issue in view of the EP's exclusion from deliberating on and granting assent to the special treaties concluded with Central Europe following German unification and the opening to the East).

The Martin reports certainly conditioned the climate of debate and helped to expand the EU's overall competence and scope of policy activity but they lacked the legitimizing impact and hence potential of the EUT. On the one hand this was because there was less extensive and continuous consultation with national parliamentarians, political elites, opinion makers and those in a position to transmit information to others compared to the Spinelli process. On the other hand, it was because a treaty format did not emerge swiftly enough and the EP had to work hard to reestablish dialogue with members of national parliaments in which, by dint of intervening national elections, the pro-European union constituencies had altered—sometimes radically so. However, it would be wrong to underestimate the amount of strategic planning that went into the initiative to establish an Etats Généraux.

The Italian initiative had called for the conventions of the Etats Généraux to ensure that political union proceeded following the expression of the popular will in the member states' parliaments. The EP's Institutional Affairs Committee responded and prepared a report which concluded that the convening of the "assizes" (as they were to be known) would (i) redress the democratic deficit by retransferring national parliaments' transfer of authority to the Council of Ministers through the Rome Treaty back to the EP; (ii) promote *ex ante* cooperation and consensus building between the two parliamentary levels on European union; and (iii) determine the guidelines for the attainment of European union to be incorporated into a draft constitution.[14] Following the assizes in Rome in November 1990, the European and national parliaments agreed on the need to transform relations between the member states and the EU on the basis of a proposal for a constitution drawing inspiration from and refining the EUT.[15] The assizes ended with the adoption of declaration which endorsed nearly all the EP's main proposals by a vote of 150 to 13. Whether the alliance will endure remains to be seen. Given that it did have some impact on expectations that were generated then in wider political and government circles, it is open to conjecture whether that kind of momentum could be institutionalized and turned to good effect during the daily cut and thrust of domestic politics. Certainly, national parliaments (notably Italy's and Belgium's) that had been sympathetic to the EP during the ratification phase of the SEA (when, unlike in 1991 the results of the SEA were put to the EP) were to align themselves similarly with EP views this time and were to argue that they would not ratify pending the EP's approval. Again, however, EP approval was not necessary, but an alliance between the EP and the national parliaments of this nature exerted a kind of moral suasion which was not without effect. Like the EP, they were to stress the desirability of deeper integration and expanded powers for the EP as a condition of ratification.

In the future, there must be far more cooperation between the two levels of parliaments on a daily basis to ensure effective communication and mutually beneficial information exchange designed to enhance the capacity of both sets of parliaments to influence legislative outcomes. This will inevitably affect the nature of party interaction and the way in which Euro-elections come to be conducted. The problem will lie in ensuring that the national parties do not try to interfere with MEPs' treaty-guaranteed individual autonomy. This would be detrimental to the overall independence of the EP and would undermine the nascent EP party system. Constructive cooperation will have to be developed in an empathetic way, and, at least in part as a result of the wrangling over the ratification of the Maastricht Treaty, some genuine attempt will have to be made to define the locus of political authority in the European Union.[16]

POWERS OF THE EP AFTER MAASTRICHT: FROM COOPERATION TO CODECISION

The Single European Act expanded the EP's legislative authority and also gave it some additional powers which can be used to further it's influence. Compared to the EUT, the SEA's provisions for the EP were modest. But skillful exploitation of their possibilities by the EP has shown how modest increments can be turned to good effect.

A basic premise behind the EP's strategy was to ensure that if EU policy competences were expanded, a legislative system should be put in place that allowed maximum input from the EP. In brief, the EP wished to ensure that no new policies could be adopted without its consent. However, while the cooperation procedure had shown itself to be useful, it still fell short of the bicameral legislative arrangement wanted by the EP. Moreover, there was no chance of the cooperation procedure's being extended from the ten treaty articles it covered to the whole of the EU's work. Short of this, the EP had to argue for an effective right of codecision over EU policy making. This it did with some success but at the cost of rendering decision making if anything more complex than before. Now, different legislative rules cover different treaty articles with the result that any one of up to around eight procedures can be prescribed, and squabbles between the Council and the EP over the appropriateness of one over the other are not inconceivable. Indeed, the cooperation procedure proved that such wrangling can be fertile ground for legislative delay and institutional confrontation.

MAASTRICHT AND THE EUROPEAN PARLIAMENT

The Maastricht Treaty sections dealing with political union are perhaps more important in terms of the intentions they reflect than the actual goals achieved. Above all, they signal the intention to realize a liberal democratic polity at supranational level complete with bicameral legislature. This shows through most clearly in the adoption of a codecision procedure, discussed below. A further strengthening of the role and position of the European Parliament is heralded by other seemingly minor revisions which are highly significant. Among these is the fact that the term of office of the Commission is to be brought in line, or synchronized, with that of the European Parliament to coincide with the five-year cycle of Euro-elections. The next are scheduled for summer 1994 and the new Commission would be expected to take office on January 7, 1995. A drafting oversight, however, has failed to deal with the immediate gap occasioned by the extension of the Delors Commission term of office for a two-year period from January 7, 1993. The "old" Commission will still be in office and in a position to initiate legislation and run the legislative programme when the new EP takes office.

The European Parliament has acquired the right to approve the composition of the Commission. While the final decision on its appointment remains with the member governments, it is unlikely that they will seek to appoint someone lacking the EP's confidence. This new power for the EP is one that it developed itself through its practice of giving a vote of investiture to the Commission following the president's speech on the annual programme to the EP. The formalization of the vote of confidence provides the essential counterpart power to the EP's right to censure the Commission *en bloc* if dissatisfied with its performance—a right which has rarely been invoked and which has never been successfully applied (largely because the Council rather than the Commission bears responsibility for the content of legislation adopted of which the EP disapproves). While the EP did not seek and has not obtained a power to appoint or censure individual commissioners, there can be little doubt that a politicization of the relationship between the Commission and the EP will result.

The New Powers of the European Parliament may: (i) request the Commission to submit a proposal (Article 138b); (ii) set up a temporary Committee of Inquiry to investigate alleged maladministration of contraventions

(Article 138c); (iii) shall appoint an Ombudsman (Article 138e); (iv) shall approve the Commission President and Commission (Article 158); (v) shall exercise a limited right of co-decision (Article 189b); and (vi) shall be petitioned by citizens (Article 138d).

The Commission as a whole can only take up office after a vote of confidence. This will occur after a very political and public process following the "consultation" of the EP by the European Council on the election of the Commission president. The EP will interpret this to imply a public vote on an individual. It is inconceivable that a Commission president-elect would wish to stand or to continue if rejected in such circumstances.[17]

Given the EP's role also in endorsing the Commission's legislative programe, and the need for interinstitutional cooperation to facilitate the adoption of the legislation to give effect to this programe, the need for closer links between the Commission and the European Parliament will be not only paramount but essential if the legislative programe outlined by the Commission is to be implemented on time. This is because the European Parliament, unlike most national parliaments, determines its own agenda and is therefore in a position to politicize and prioritize its agenda and the ranking of legislative proposals due for discussion. Given the constraints of the cooperation procedure and the new codecision procedure, legislative items necessarily have priority on Parliament's agenda. However, both the Council and the Commission try and influence it by requesting that the item be given urgent treatment (this is often turned down unless the EP's responsible committee agrees, something that happens mainly on technical or minor issues).[18]

Closer links between the three institutions are essential to the working of the legislative process. Closer links between the European Parliament and the Commission are bound to reinforce politicization in both institutions. Article 138b gives MEPs yet another potential source of influence vis-à-vis the Commission in that it introduces another element to the Commission's right of initiative. This has been effectively a unique right and a Commission preroga-tive deemed essential to ensuring that legislative proposals were drafted in terms of the "common good" and, as far as possible, based on the principle of "upgrading the common interest." Under Article 138b, the Commission can be asked to submit an appropriate proposal by the European Parliament if MEPs feel that EU legislation is needed to implement the Treaty. If a majority is of this opinion, the Commission must respond. The Council of Ministers has had a similar right under Article 152 of the EEC (European Economic Community) treaty since the EEC's inception, but it is not tantamount to the Council having either an explicit right of initiative or power to demand that the Commission act. The European Parliament's position differs, however, because MEPs are in a position to sack the Commission. The practice has long been for the Commis-sion to sound out MEPs on legislative proposals, and a sinister erosion of Commission autonomy should not be inferred from Article 138b. Used judiciously, both the EP and the Commission could benefit if they bolster each other when necessary (for example, in the face of Council prevarication or intransigence). Moreover, since the Commission has also been endowed with the task of reporting and supervising specific areas of policy—from R & D, to social policy, economic and social cohesion, and economic and monetary policy—and with publishing the results, it could use its findings tactically and in the name of decision making openness indicate which states are preventing the EU from attaining its stated goals. Indeed, the IGC appended a Declaration on the Implementation of Community Law to the Final Act. This states:

The Conference calls on the Commission to ensure, in exercising its powers under Article 155 of this Treaty, that member States fulfil their obligations. It asks the Commission to publish periodically a full report for the Member States and the European Parliament.[19]

MEPs could no doubt infer much from the reports and use them in a politically more visible manner to secure action or to prompt the Council's members to toe the line. In brief, small incremental changes to the Commission's role have potentially large implications for the exercise of influence and authority by the EU's increasingly bicameral legislature: the Council and the European Parliament.

The ideological composition of parliamentary majorities may well take on a new importance, as may the ideological content of legislation. This view must be qualified, however, by recognizing that a coherent ideological orientation over several legislative items may be seriously diluted if party discipline and voting discipline are weak or desultory. However, the officials from both institutions are likely to be more closely involved in each other's deliberations at all stages of the predecisional and legislative processes. The EP had hoped to strengthen this even more by dint of the Commission president being given the right to choose, in agreement with the member states, individual commissioners from a preselected list drawn up by the member governments. However, the Commission president will merely be consulted. Even so, it is possible to envisage politicization of this process and an alliance between the EP and the Commission on the next Commission designate. The new procedure will run after the 1994 Euro-elections with the new Commission taking up office in January 1995. The Commission that comes in 1993 will serve two years only. It is also likely that after 1994 the number of commissioners will be cut (possibly to one per member state) and that an overt hierarchy will develop inside the Commission, especially following enlargement.

THE CODECISION PROCEDURE

Given the positive experience of the cooperation procedure over the continuing difficulties and protracted arguments using the traditional single-reading procedure (which covered all treaty items except the ten isolated for the cooperation procedure under the Single Act), there was support within the EP and the Commission for abolishing the traditional system in favor of generalized majority voting based on the cooperation procedure. This came to be known as the quest for generalized codecision. Following practice under the Single Act, it was argued that codecision should also apply to all new or expanded areas of Union competence. Many were already subject to existing Article 235 or 100a procedures. However, these were cumbersome and protracted, not least because revisions had to secure the unanimous approval of the member governments.

The codecision procedure replaces the cooperation procedure in some instances (such as the free movement of labor (Article 49), services (Article 66), right of establishment (Articles 54-56[i], mutual recognition of diplomas, etc. 57[i], and[ii]), and completion of the Internal Market (Article 100a and 100b). It is to be applied to new areas where the European Union has acquired competence—such as education (Article 126), public health (Article 129), trans-European networks (Article 129d), culture (Article 128), R & D framework programs (Article 130), and aspects of research and environmental policy, and pluriannual framework programes. On other new policy areas—such as culture—the codecision is to apply, but unanimity is required in the Council of Ministers.

Codecision institutes a system of up to three readings. This departs from what the EP had asked for during the IGC negotiations, when it had advocated the extension of qualified majority voting (QMV) in the Council to all matters, and an equal right of decision for itself with the Council.

First Reading

Under codecision, the Commission submits a proposal to the EP and to the Council. The Council, acting by qualified majority after obtaining the EP's opinion, adopts a common position (as under the cooperation procedure). It transmits its common position to the EP together with information explaining its position. The Commission is likewise bound to inform the EP fully of its view. The EP may then adopt it the common position within three months of receiving it. If it does so, the Council definitively adopts the act in question in line with the common position. If the EP fails to act, the Council position stands. The EP has other possibilities at this stage. It may amend the proposal by an absolute majority of its component members. The amended text is then forwarded to the Council and the Commission. Both have to deliver an opinion on those amendments. Alternatively, the EP can opt for outright rejection of the proposal with the approval of an absolute majority of MEPs. It has then to inform the Council immediately of this intent.

Second Reading

The Council must respond within three months. Acting by qualified majority, it may approve the EP's amendments and accordingly amend its common position and adopt the act in question. The Council cannot do this, however, in instances where the Commission disapproves of EP amendments: if the Commission issues a negative opinion, it must act unanimously. If the Council does not approve the act in question, the Council president has to enter into dialogue with the EP. With the EP president's agreement, the Council presidency then convenes a meeting of the conciliation committee. (The conciliation committee procedure was first introduced in the 1970s to deal with disagreements between the Council and the EP over the draft budget. It did not prove to be an unmitigated success, but extending the concept of conciliation through exploiting the EP's rules of procedure was seen as a way of increasing the EP's influence. This is another instance where past practice has been adapted to confront contemporary needs.)

The conciliation committee is composed of Council members or their representatives and an equal number of EP representatives. Their job is to reach agreement on a joint text by a qualified majority of the Council representatives and by a simple majority of EP representatives. The Commission participates in the conciliation committee's proceedings and has the right to take necessary initiatives in order to reconcile divergencies between the Council and the EP.

Third Reading

If, after six weeks, the conciliation committee approves a joint text, it is referred back to the EP (which may adopt it acting by an absolute majority of the votes cast) and to the Council (acting by qualified majority). The text has to be adopted within six weeks of receipt. If either fails to approve the proposed act within this time, it falls.

If the conciliation committee does not approve a joint text, the proposed act falls unless the Council, acting by a qualified majority within six weeks of expiry of the period granted to the conciliation committee, confirms the common position to which it agreed before the conciliation procedure was initiated. This common position may incorporate amendments proposed by the EP. In this case, the act is finally adopted unless the EP, within six weeks of the date of confirmation by the Council, rejects the text by an absolute majority of its component members. In such a case, the text falls. This provision is extremely important since it gave rise to much debate about the new role of the EP. MEPs argued that this newly conferred right amounted to a negative veto and that the EP would much rather be in a position to work constructively for compromise.

The deadlines built into the codecision procedure are important and serve to keep the process under way. They may be extended by common accord of the EP and the Council. A two month extension is automatic in the case where the EP, at first reading, indicates that it will reject the common position.

That the codecision procedure is seen as potentially the legislative process to be widely applied in future is made clear by the provision for its application to be expanded on the basis of a report to be submitted to the Council by the Commission by 1996 at the latest.

FUTURE POWERS OF THE EP

The development of the EP's powers and functions continues to hinge upon MEPs' ability to exploit fully the EP's own rules of procedure to capitalize on the new treaty provisions which have given the EP additional means of playing a genuine legislative role. It is true that its powers still fall short of those of some national legislatures. It is equally true that it is gaining powers at a time when those of national parliaments have been in steady decline: though an alliance between the two parliamentary levels sensitizes MPs to the need for vigilance vis-à-vis the expanding powers of the executive.

In short, in exercising the original supervisory and advisory powers bestowed on it by the Rome Treaty, the EP will have to continue to be innovative, adaptable, flexible, and persuasive. It will have to develop communication with the other institutions and to ensure that it is effective. It will have to honor the task of being the EU's grand forum by continuing to use its right to set its own agenda imaginatively, even though the demands of the codecision procedure are bound to encroach on the time set aside for this. It will also have to ensure that dialogue with the new committee of regions as well as with national parliaments is genuine and effective. As guardian of the quest for democratics, effective, efficient, transparent, and accountable government, the EP will have to continue to press for institutional reform. In addition, the imminent enlargement of the EU beyond EFTA will give it additional responsibilities in terms of integrating new parties and nascent democrats into EP practice.

The new legislative procedure has additional implications for the EP's future responsibilities. The question of future financing inevitably impinges on the EP's existing budgetary rights and financial obligations in respect of expenditure. However, it sees the possibilities of new policy areas in a constructive way and will have its own priorities to argue for in the distribution of available funds. This will become an increasingly politicized process, given its powers to influence outcomes through the codecision procedure. In addition, it will use its power of assent to assert its voice in international affairs, much as it has done in the past. An added *frisson* is present, short-term, however, in that it can veto the admission of new applicants—and has threatened to do so—pending accommodation of some of its demand in respect of its role in the European Union.

Moreover, its assent (by majority of voting MEPs except under Articles 237 and 138) is now needed for citizenship issues, for structural funds (Article 130), cohesion funds (Article 130d[ii]), Euro-election procedure (Article 138), international agreements (Article 228) including association and cooperation agreements outside Article 238, agreements with important financial implications, and those involving modifications to decisions taken under codecision. Additionally, the assent procedure applies to special tasks of the Central European Bank (Article 105[vi] and Article 106[v]). The foreign and security arena, as well as judicial and home affairs, offers further arenas where the EP is likely to become more active, not only because of individuals' right of petition, the concept of EU citizenship, and the existence of a Euro-ombudsman, but because the EP itself will become increasingly visible and comprehensible to citizens. National MPs will also perhaps begin to lobby it more and to direct constituency matters to MEPs where appropriate. The implications of subsidiarity[20] will also affect the evolution of the EP's role, as will the interpretation of the new policy responsibilities and competence bestowed on the EU by the Maastricht Treaty.

The external relations role of the EP is also like to grow. The number of interparliamentary committees has grown in number and in importance. In addition, the EP continues to be seen by foreign statesmen as an institution that should be addressed. It is the target of an ever increasing number of lobbyists. It has engaged in fact-finding missions abroad, and its high profile in international affairs (regardless of its very limited competences in this field) will continue. Indeed, as the common foreign and security provisions of the Maastricht Treaty begin to be realized, the number of debates and reports on the areas covered will rise, as will the interaction with the Commission and Council. Again, this will happen without the EP's powers being appreciably augmented.

CONCLUSION

The EP has come of age and its stature is steadily increasing. It faces innumerable tasks in terms of reorganizing and refining its working methods in order to ensure that it is able to fulfill the new demands confronting it. In addition, links with the Commission (always seen as one of its protagonists) and the Council (typically portrayed as its adversary) will be strengthened, if only because of the demands of the codecision and legislative procedures. This has to be done carefully and systematically. Automatic sympathy on the part of the Commission for the EP cannot be taken for granted, nor should the opposite for the Council be inferred. The EP's potential influence vis-à-vis the Commission has grown in a constructive way. Its ability to exercise a control and scrutiny function over the formerly completely unaccountable Council of Ministers has also undergone significant improvement since the mid-1980s. Even so, in the legislative relationship, the Council still occupies a superior rather than a coequal position. Areas of policy still escape effective parliamentary supervision, scrutiny, and control as well as judicial control.

The Commission, Council, and EP now have an institutionalized symbiotic relationship which will be given expression during the coming years, when further, possibly even radically, institutional reforms will follow. The European Parliament will continue to expand the agenda of such deliberations and to make an important contribution to the debate and content of a constitution for the European Union. It will play its part in generating support for and discussion about the transformation of the European Union into a recognizably federal, liberal democratic polity complete with a representative, democratic, transparent, effective, accountable, and efficient legislature.

NOTES

1. J. Lodge, "The European Parliament: Talking Shop or Putative Legislature," *Journal of European Integration*, Vol. 12, 1982.

2. V. Herman and J. Lodge, *The European Parliament and the European Community* (London and New York: Macmillan, 1978).

3. J. Lodge (ed.), *The 1989 Election to the European Parliament* (London: Macmillan, 1990).

4. R. Cardoso and R. Corbett, "The Crocodile Initiative," in J. Lodge (ed.), *European Union: the European Community in Search of a Future* (London: Macmillan, 1986).

5. M. Telo (ed.), *Vers une nouvelle Europe?* (Brussels: ULB, 1992).

6. See the Martin reports and the Peottering report of June 10, 1990 entitled "The Outlook for European Security," EP *Document A3-0107/91*.

7. See the Toussaint report on the democratic deficit, the Graziani report on the application of the SEA, and the Herrnan report on European union.

8. D.Martin, *Europe: An Ever Closer Union* (London: Elf, 1991).

9. J. Lodge, "The Single European Act: Towards a new Euro-Dynamism?" *Journal of Common Market Studies*, Vol. 24, 1986, pp. 47-69; and her "The European Parliament: From Assembly to Co-legislature—Changing the Institutional Dynamics," in Lodge (ed.), *The EC and the Challenge of the Future* (London: Pinter, 1989).

10. *Official Journal* C96 March 14, 1990, p. 114.

11. R. Corbett, "The Intergovernmental Conference on Political Union," *Journal of Common Market Studies*, Vol. 30, 1992, pp. 271-98.

12. *Official Journal* C231 July 11, 1990, p. 97.

13. See W. Paterson (ed.), *Beyond the IGCs: European Union in the 1990s* (Edinburgh: Europa Institute, 1990).

14. Known as the Duverger report. See EP document A3-162/90 (June 22, 1990).

15. See final *Declaration of the Conference of the Parliaments of the European Community,* November 27-30. 1990.

16. J. Lodge, *The EC and the Crisis of Political Authority* (London: Elgar, forthcoming).

17. R. Corbett, "The Intergovernmental Conference on Political Union," *Journal of Common Market Studies*, Vol. 30, 1992, p. 294.

18. F. Jacobs and R. Corbett, *The European Parliament* (London: Longman, 1990), p. 131.

19. Declaration Part 2, "Treaty on European Union," Maastricht, February 7, 1992.

20. For details see EP Document A3-163/90 (June 22, 1990) and Part B (July 4, 1990) on subsidiarity, known after the *rapporteur* as the Giscard D'Estaing reports.

11

European Union and Local Government: The Challenges of Integration and Internationalization

Andreas Moschonas

The European Union (EU) has been experiencing two contradictory tendencies: (i) the tendency toward economic integration, albeit in an uneven manner, under the force of the logic of capital and the resultant internationalization of the process of production and of exchange, and (ii) the tendency toward the restructuring of the national state so as to meet the needs of economic integration, at the supranational level, and the demands for political legitimization and democratization, at the local-national and supranational level.

In the context of the provisions of the Maastricht Treaty, and the principle of subsidiarity associated with it, this chapter intends to examine the content and the form of the triangular institutional relationship between local government, the national state, and EU institutions. The focus of the analysis will be on the European regions within the EU economy and the issue of work (forms of work organization) and employment (local labor markets).

The discussion begins with the presentation of an analytical framework concerning the process of internationalization, integration, and institutional transformation. Then, in the main section of the chapter the analysis concentrates on the three issues raised and discussed here: the regulation of the labor markets, the restructuring of the labor process and the organization of work, and the activation of the regional and local authorities in the EU political structure. On these issues I shall try to argue for the following points: (i) the restructuring of the production process reinforces the segmentation of the labor market, and reinforces the alteration of the labor policies from the traditional defensive labor policies designed to provide unemployment protection to more active labor policies designed to regulate the labor market so as to meet the demands of capital accumulation. This entails, in accordance with the neoliberal logic adopted by the EU countries, market-oriented employment solutions and, therefore, decentralized (local state or employer-led) practices to training and job creation. (ii) the current discussions in the EU about the content and the prospects of the so-called anthropocentric production systems are ideologically biased. (iii) the principle of subsidiarity, which gives institutional form to the process of socioeconomic restructuring described above, implies political decentralization with the aim not so much to strengthen democracy at the local-regional level, but mainly to decentralize and thus privatize the social costs of innovation and structural competitiveness. Finally, in the last section of the chapter some concluding remarks are offered.

THE ANALYTICAL FRAMEWORK

The expanded economic and social reproduction of capitalism has been associated with a specific regime of accumulation and a specific mode of social regulation. This means that the state has historically played and continues to play a strategic role in relation to the reproduction of both capital and labor power. The development, however, of the new technologies in the era of the so-called electronics revolution has actually reinforced the restructuring of both (i) the regime of accumulation and (ii) the mode of social regulation, thereby changing (iii) the role of the state itself.

The restructuring of the regime of accumulation entails the transformation from Fordist to post-Fordist patterns of organization of the production process: Fordist capitalism has been characterized by mass production in large factories based on assembly-line principles, a high degree of state intervention based on Keynesian principles, and welfare policies based on institutionalized trade union practices. Post–Fordist capitalism, on the other hand, is said to be characterized by high–quality production based on general–purpose machines (micro-electronics) and flexible working practices, reduced state intervention based on Shumpeterian principles, and workfare policies based on a new individualism and a much reduced role for trade union practices (Bonefeld and Holloway, 1993; Jessop, 1993).

The reasons behind this transformation are both economic and social. First of all, the Fordist pattern of organization entered in the late 1960s into a process of crisis which had two characteristics: it was a market crisis because mass consumption seemed to have reached its limits under a growing need for high-quality new products, and it was also a production crisis because the improvement of the organic composition of capital seemed to have put in operation the declining tendency of the rate of profit (Moschonas, 1990; Hirsch, 1993). This latter factor makes the transformation of Fordism the result not only of the objective tendencies of capitalist development, but also of a process of constant class struggle. Because, as Holloway (1993) points out, "The 'laws of capitalist development' are nothing other than the movement of class struggle" (p. 98), which means that "it is the presence of the working class as an antagonistic force inside capital which is the key to understanding the development and the instability of capitalism" (p. 100).

The development of the new technologies based on microelectronics has contributed to the management of the crisis of Fordist capitalism through its transformation into a post-Fordist pattern of organization. First of all, the new technologies have managed to overcome the obstacles posed by mass consumption and thus enlarge the market through the improvement of the quality of the products produced.   More than this, however, the new technologies have restraining effects on capital's tendency toward a declining rate of profit. This happens because, contrary to the previous techniques, the new technologies are able to produce simultaneous increases in the productivity of labor and in the technical composition of capital. In fact, the new technologies sustain general-purpose machines able to offer not just a specialized operation but a variety of complex functions. This characteristic makes possible the technical division of the production process, that is, it enables the introduction of flexible changes in the production process.   In this sense production can now be carried out by a number of relatively independent groups of direct producers organized either inside the traditional manufacturing units in the context of the process of centralization and concentration of capital, or in autonomous small and medium-sized units in the context of a decentralized production process. The objective of this transformation is obvious: to produce more varied and customized products; to reduce the cost of production, and to avoid trade union pressures through the restructuring of the mode of social regulation (Moschonas, 1990; Sabel, 1982; Brusco, 1982).

The restructuring of the mode of social regulation entails the transformation from Taylorist to neo-Taylorist or post-Taylorist patterns of work organization in the production process. The Taylorist organization of the labor process has been characterized by the intensification of exploitation based on far-reaching diskilling processes, the destruction of traditional craft forms of workers' power, and the use of efficient techniques of managerial control and supervision. Neo-or post-Taylorist forms of work organization, on the other hand, have been associated with the "microelectronic revolution" and signify the reorganization of the labor process based on more flexible combinations of workers and machines, the creation of new hierarchies among the wage earners, and a systematic individualization of work relations (Braverman, 1974; Hirsch, 1993).

More specifically, the Taylorist organization of the labor process implies the concentration of workers under the direction of a single capitalist and the development of the technical division of labor, that is, the division of labor within the factory. This division of labor contains despotism and fragmentation as functions of capital and as preconditions for the reproduction of the capital-labor relationship. In this context, the rationalization of the labor process in fact implies the division of the various activities into three interrelated levels: first, the level of the initial planning, the organization of methods, and engineering, all of which become autonomous; second, the level of skilled manufacturing, which requires a fairly skilled labor force; and finally, the level of unskilled assembly and execution, which in theory requires no skills (Lipietz, 1987: 71). Thus, from a sociological perspective, the rationalization of the labor process implies the creation and reproduction of a social stratification: manual work is separated from mental work, which means not only the separation of the process of conception from that of execution but also the separation of skilled from unskilled work (Sabel, 1982; Braverman, 1974; Moschonas, 1990).

Post-Taylorist forms of work organization, necessitated by the crisis of Fordism and Taylorism, are supposed to overcome the separation of mental and manual labor, and of skilled and unskilled work. This is because the specific and specialized work of Taylorism is supposed to be substituted by a general work composed of the functions of management and supervision. As Hirsch (1993) points out, the new labor policy, under the "information processing, planning and regulating technologies," aims at "the formation of a small, privileged core of highly qualified employees entrusted with complex tasks of supervision and direction," while "unskilled, monotonous jobs directed by others will still be retained" (p. 26). More than this, the microelectronic reorganization of Taylorism brings a qualitively new element into the labor process: "Beside the skilled and relatively autonomous core workers there arises on the basis of the new technologies a new type of mass worker," that is, a worker who is "not spatially concentrated, unified and subject to homogeneous working conditions," but "individualized to a high degree, flexibilized and segmented." However, the "Taylorized and deskilled mass worker will by no means disappear—especially when there is a structural over-supply of cheap labor power." On the contrary, "peripheral and insecure jobs, part-time, home and temporary work will not only remain but will even expand," although "there is a reduction in employment in the core sectors of material production, in administration and in services as a whole, and an increase in mass unemployment" (p. 26). It is exactly in this context that the role of the state tends to undergo changes.

The restructuring of the state has been conceptualized as the "hollowing out" of the national state. This implies a triple displacement of state powers: "upward" displacement where state powers are transferred to supranational bodies, "downward" displacement where state powers are transferred to regional-local bodies inside the national state, and "outward" displacement where state powers are assumed by emerging horizontal networks—regional or local— which bypass central states. In other words, the national state's gradual loss of autonomy creates the need for supranational coordination and the space for subnational resurgence.

In a theoretically penetrating article, Jessop advances the thesis that the transition in Western economies from Fordism to post–Fordism has reinforced the reorientation of the state's principal economic and social functions (Jessop,

1993). Specifically, it is well documented that the Keynesian welfare state regimes, developed during the periods of the Fordist forms of organization, had the objective, regarding economic and social reproduction, of promoting full employment and generalizing norms of collective consumption. The crisis of Fordism, however, has given rise to a new mode of social regulation called the Schumpeterian workfare state: while Keynes was the theorist cited to justify the state's role in securing full employment, Schumpeter is the theorist rediscovered to justify the state's new role in promoting innovation. As Jessop puts it, the distinctive features of the Schumpeterian workfare state are "a concern to promote innovation and structural competitiveness in the field of economic policy, and a concern to promote flexibility and competitiveness in the field of social policy" (p. 18). This latter feature implies that while the welfare state "tried to extend the social rights of its citizens," the workfare state "is concerned to provide welfare services that benefit business with the result that individual needs take second place" (pp. 18-19). Thus, there is according to Jessop a major reorientation of social policy "away from redistributive concerns based on expanding welfare rights in a nation-state toward more productivist and cost-saving concerns in an open economy" (pp. 17-18).

The openness of the economy subjects the national state to a complex series of changes similar to those the national corporations themselves have undergone in the process of becoming "hollow corporations," that is, "transnationals headquartered in one country whose operations are mostly pursued elsewhere" (Jessop, 1993: 22). By the same token, the term "hollow state" is used to indicate two trends: (i) that the national state "retains many of its headquarters functions—including the trappings of central executive authority and national sovereignty as well as the discourses that sustain them," and (ii) that "its capacities to translate this authority and sovereignty into effective control are becoming limited by a complex displacement of powers" (p. 22).

Specifically, there is the displacement of powers that occurs through the expansion of supranational institutions, established to coordinate policies and thus to safeguard the functioning of the internationalized economies. There is also the displacement of powers occurring through the strengthening of the role of the local state, as a reflection of both the growing internationalization and the economic retreat of the nation-state. And, finally, there is the displacement of powers occurring through the growing development of links among local states, as nations become more open to transsovereign contacts at the local and the regional level as well (Jessop, 1993: 22-25).

THE EU EXPERIENCE

European integration, as both socioeconomic organization and institutional construction, exemplifies these historical tendencies of restructuring of the regime of accumulation, the mode of social regulation, and the form of state organization. In this connection, this section concentrates on three interrelated topics: (i) the organization of local labor markets, (ii) the new tendencies of work organization in the labor process, and (iii) the role of local states and regional institutions in the context of the principle of subsidiarity adopted with the Treaty of the European Union.

The process of European integration creates conditions conducive to the integration of the European labor markets. This entails a gradual shift from the traditional labor markets, where a distinction has been made between national labor markets and local labor markets, to the post-Fordist labor markets. Here, a distinction can be made between the internal labor market (i.e., the labor market which operates within the multinational corporations themselves) and the external labor market (i.e., the labor market regulated by the forces of supply and demand). In both cases there is a tendency to differentiate between EU labor market, national labor market, and local-regional labor market. In the latter category there are advanced and less developed regions, and this distinction tends to differentiate the characteristics of the local labor market itself.

The problem of unemployment has been for many years at the center of the discussions in Europe and elsewhere. In the European Union, the rate of unemployment has moved, for instance, from 2.1 percent in 1965 to 4.1 percent in 1975, 10.8 percent in 1985, 8.4 percent in 1990, and 10.5 percent in 1993, which amounts to 16 million people for 1993 (EC, 1991: 41; EC, 1993). Moreover, the ratio of total employment over the total amount of the labor force (persons of age between fifteen and sixty-four) has been since 1990 as low as 60 percent, compared to an average of 73 percent in the United States and Japan, and this percentage is below the levels of 1970 (EC, 1991: 21; EC, 1993).

At the same time there has been a shortage in the EU labor market of certain skills and professions, and this too has been recognized as a major problem. The reason is that while the quality of the skills which one can find in the EU depends on the efficiency of the system of training and education of the member states, the technology embodied in the capital goods and the production process of the Union is mainly produced internationally. This means that the rhythm of the development of the new technologies is faster than the acquisition of the skills required. For this reason the quality of the labor offered in the EU is not always what the technology employed requires. In simple terms, in the EU there is an imbalance between the needs of the labor market on the one hand, and the systems developed for training and education on the other—a fact which contributes to the problem of unemployment (EC, 1991; EC, 1993).

The problem of unemployment, reinforced in a period of restructuring of the production process, has made necessary the formulation of a more active employment policy: while in the past the main objective of the employment policy was to provide unemployment and social security benefits, the current policies of employment have as their prime objective (i) the improvement of the quality of the labor force and (ii) the regulation of the labor market (Gravaris, 1991).

As stated above, the rapid technological development in the so-called information societies not only produces technological unemployment but also requires a well-qualified labor force. Thus the various training and education structures are integral parts of the policies of employment: education and vocational training, explains the EU's White Paper, are aimed at contributing not only to the enrichment of the knowledge of the individual person but also to the improvement of the economic performance. The promotion of the vocational qualifications, through training and retraining, makes possible the adjustment of the individual skills to the needs of the labor market, thereby contributing to the fight against unemployment, and also becomes a factor conducive to the assimilation of new technology and thus to the enhancement of competitiveness (EC, 1993, Chapter 7; Blanke et al., 1992).

The competitiveness of the economy is closely related to the regulation of the labor market. This implies the development of flexible labor markets. Here, the notion of flexibility has a double meaning: first, it means internal labor market flexibility to the extent that the individual employer has the right to make substantial adjustments to the working conditions; and, second, it means external labor market flexibility to the extent that the labor market becomes sensitive to the forces of supply and demand of labor. This flexibility concentrates on the duration of the working time and actually implies reductions in working time by means of various schemes such as flexible work hours, part-time employment, job sharing and so on, not for the enhancement of the individual welfare but rather to improve the productivity of the economy. In the context of neoliberalism, as Jessop states, this is reflected "in government promotion of hire-and-fire, flex-time, and flex-wage labor markets" (Jessop, 1993: 29; EC, 1993, Chapter 7; OECD, 1986, 1989; Hinrichs et al., 1988; Toutziarakis, 1990).

The measures, indicated above, for the improvement of the quality of the labor force and the regulation of the labor market are introduced not only by the EU institutions and the national states but also by the local authorities. The EU's White Paper of 1993, for instance, argues that, because the market economy operates according to the principles of decentralization, the role of the local institutions becomes of great importance. This means that the efficient operation of the labor market requires a significant degree of decentralization at the level of the actually existing "pools of employment." And this argument has been reinforced by the experience of many countries, which has shown the significance of the participation of the social partners in the decentralized management of the sources of employment. Similarly, the White Paper states, the adjustment of the working time can better contribute to both the improvement of the productivity of labor and the maintenance or creation of positions of employment if that measure is taken in the context of a decentralized approach at the level of the individual firms (EC, 1993, Part A; Tonge, 1993). Here, the regulation of the labor market becomes an issue closely related to the organization of the labor process itself.

The restructuring of the production regime, with the introduction of flexible manufacturing systems, affects the organization of work and the composition of the working class. In the fields where new technologies are introduced the tendency is toward the formation of a new nucleus of the working class composed of highly skilled workers, namely; engineers and systems analysts, programmers and operators, and technical staff of lower skills. The traditional professions, on the other hand, tend to undergo changes in the following directions: the reskilling of work, the degradation of work, the adoption of flexible forms of work, and the loss of work. Thus, the social stratification in the production process tends to be shaped around the following three categories: the traditional workers, whose main characteristic is the standard duration of employment; the modern workers, who tend to work on flexible schemes of employment; and the postindustrial proletarians, who are either unemployed or occasionally employed usually in positions outside the production itself.

These trends in the social stratification of the labor force tend to reinforce not only the social functions of the state, even at the local-regional level, as indicated below, but also the transformation of the regime of work organization from the traditional Taylorist to post-Taylorist forms of organization. Several studies on the EU experience are indicative of these trends. Before, however, entering into this question it is important to state that the relationship between technological development and the organization of the labor process is a complex one, in the sense that in a given kind of technology one can possibly find more than one system of work organization. Thus, it is conceivable to visualize a field of possibilities whose limits are, on the one hand, the traditional Taylorist system of work organization characterized by the primacy of the administrative prerogative of the entrepreneur, and, on the other, the system of work organization wherein the administrative prerogative of the entrepreneur tends to be refuted. From the various factors which condition the form of a system of work organization, the following three seem to be of great importance: (i) the degree of development of the so-called industrial democracy, (ii) the level and the extent of the skills of the labor force, and (iii) the intensity of the social antagonisms and their effect on the social cohesion of society and on the operation of the production process itself (Moschonas, 1993).

In the traditional Taylorist system of work organization there is, as indicated above, a high division of labor and high functional specialization in the labor process, while the decision making is taken away from the workers and centralized in a factory planning office. Following, however, the introduction of the new technologies, based on microelectronic systems, the traditional Taylorist system tends to undergo changes toward a new system called the neo-Taylorist system of work organization. What is "new" here is that a part of the conception-supervision function is now transferred from the engineers and the technicians, who actually work in the planning office outside the production area itself, to highly skilled workers working in the shop floor, that is, the area of production (Kidd, 1990: 3-4; Lehner, 1991: 69, 72).

These changes, however, were not able to eliminate the rigidities of the traditional system of work organization, which themselves tended to become, with the introduction of the new technologies, an obstacle to the improvement of the productivity of labor. Thus, the traditional system of work organization began to undergo changes toward a more cooperative production system, that is, a system which combines individual and group responsibility, at the lowest possible operational level, and stimulates motivation. The key idea here is to avoid the traditional fragmentation of work into a variety of jobs, functions, and departments by integrating tasks into multidimensional jobs and into teams, thereby making departments collaborate. In this system, called the lean production system in the Japanese experience, conception and technical planning continue to be functions under the responsibility of the engineers and the highly skilled technicians, but most of these highly skilled personnel have now been transferred from the factory planning office to the shop floor (Lerner, 1991: 69, 73; Wobbe, 1991: 45-50; cf. Lipietz, 1992: 320-22).

A third system of work organization, which has even been adopted in various EU publications, is the so-called anthropocentric production system. The aim of this system is to combine the new technologies with the appropriate human skills in a holistic and cooperative work structure, thereby limiting both the division of labor and the hierarchical structures. Thus the anthropocentric production systems are defined as the "computer-aided production systems which are strongly based on skilled work and human decision-making." That is, they are production systems combining the following elements: (i) "flexible automation supporting human work and decision-making," (ii) "a decentralized organization of work with flat hierarchies and a far reaching delegation of power and responsibilities especially to the shop-floor level," (iii) "a minimized division of labor based on some form of integrated work system design;" (iv) "a continuous, product–oriented upskilling of workers at work," and (v) "a product-oriented integration of the whole productions process including R & D, manufacturing, marketing and servicing" (Lehner, 1991: 29 30). What really characterizes this system, compared with the other two mentioned above, is that the functions of execution, design, and supervision are now assigned to the workers as a whole, both skilled and unskilled, while the conception and the strategic planning continue to represent a prerogative of the entrepreneur and responsibility of the engineers and the highly skilled technicians (Lehner, 1991: 69-73; Wobbe, 1991; Kidd, 1990).

This implies that the anthropocentric production systems are intended not so much to strengthen the position of the workers in the labor process but rather to minimize the negative social effects produced by the introduction of the new technologies and the restructuring of the production process. Even so, the use of anthropocentric production systems proposed by the EU presupposes the existence of the necessary objective and subjective conditions. In fact, according to EU reports, the use of anthropocentric production systems in the EU member states is very limited or even non-existent.

Specifically, (i) in Greece and Portugal the use of new technologies is very limited, and wherever this happens it is usually combined with traditional Taylorist or neo-Taylorist systems of work organization (Lehner, 1991; Wobbe, 1991; Papadimitriou, 1991). (ii) In Belgium, Spain, Ireland, and Italy the use of new technologies has been combined with only an experimental employment of elements of the anthropocentric systems. In Belgium there are experiments in the car industry, the chemical industry, and the metal industry. In Spain and Ireland there are only a few experiments, mainly due to the low degree of industrialization and the predominance of small and medium–sized enterprises. In the large enterprises the use of the new technologies is usually combined with traditional Taylorist systems of work organization. In Italy the various experiments on anthropocentric production systems take place in the large corporations of the north and in the decentralized production systems of central Italy (Lehner, 1991; Wobbe, 1991; Anquetl, 1990; Ruggiero, 1987; Hancke, 1991). (iii) In the Netherlands and the United Kingdom the use of the new technologies has been associated with the introduction of anthropocentric production systems only in a limited number of firms or industries. In the United Kingdom, for instance, such experiments are found in high–technology firms, both domestic and foreign (Lerner, 1991; Wobbe, 1991; Charles et al., 1990). (iv) In Denmark and France the employment of the new technologies is associated with broader experiments in the introduction of major elements of the anthropocentric systems in several firms or industries. In Denmark, anthropocentric systems have been introduced especially in the metal industry, wherein there is a tradition of Taylorist systems of work organization. In the textile and clothing industry, however, where no such tradition exists, the new technologies are associated with Taylorist systems of work organization. In France, anthropocentric systems have been introduced in the steel industry, while in the industry of metallurgical construction the use of the new technologies is combined with traditional systems of Taylorism (Lehner, 1991; Wobbe, 1991; Lojkine, 1986; Wilson, 1991; Howell, 1992). (v) Finally (the former West) Germany represents the country where the anthropocentric production systems have found the greatest application. Among the various factors conducive to this development, one must single out the German tradition of advanced industrial organization based on highly skilled and cooperative production work (Lehner, 1991; Wobbe, 1991; Kern and Sabel, 1991).

In conclusion, the high level of vocational education and training, that is, the existence of a highly skilled labor force, combined with the development of a system of cooperative work and codetermination, is the factor which contributes to the application of the anthropocentric production systems (cf. Windolf, 1993).

In the social field, the use of the anthropocentric production systems tends to give rise to social conflicts to the extent that it undermines the administrative prerogative of the entrepreneur, the degree of which varies from country to country. In Germany, for instance, about 72 percent of the personnel of an enterprise are production and maintenance workers, without essential differences between the two, while the remaining 28 percent are administrative personnel, that is, technical-clerical and supervisory staff. By contrast, in two other major countries, the U.K. and France, the administrative personnel amount to about 37 and 42 percent of the total, respectively. This means that, compared with Germany, the U.K. and France cannot but experience strong resistance in the development of decentralized systems of work organization—systems which entail the delegation of authority to the highly skilled production workers (Lehner, 1991: 76-78; Kern and Sabel, 1991; Wilson, 1991).

The point which needs to be underlined here is that both the regulation of the labor market and the restructuring of the production systems of work organization, discussed above, are in themselves politically sensitive social processes. This means that they are processes which require political intervention. What we are going to discuss now is that this intervention is not confined to the national state alone but in the process of European integration involves, besides the institutions of the European Union, the local-regional authorities as well.

The rationale for the activation of the local-regional authorities in the era of economic crisis and restructuring lies in the need to foster the development of the endogenous forces of the regions. The post-World War II redistribution policies seemed to have reached their limits by the end of the 1970s. Thus a new strategy was formed in the 1980s to promote local development in an effort to restructure production and to create employment. The regionalization of Europe, institutionalized with the Maastricht Treaty, is a direct response to these socioeconomic and political imperatives.

Let us be more specific. The Treaty on European Union of 1992 establishes for the first time in EU history a "Commission of the Regions," which consists of representatives of the local-regional authorities of the Union member states. The Commission is an advisory body, similar to the Economic and Social Commission, and expresses opinions on matters which affect the local communities and the regions of the European Union (Article 198 A, B, C). Thus, parallel to the traditional structure of authority established between local governments, national states and supranational institutions, the Treaty on European Union institutionalizes the idea of the urban network and gives new content to the notion of the region (cf. Van den Berg and Van Klink, 1992).

It is an institutional arrangement which reflects the forces unleashed by the abolition of the national boundaries between the markets and the establishment of a Single European Market. As Streeck and Schmitter point out, the result will be that "the 12 formerly national economies will turn into *regional subunits* of a larger economic entity—a region being defined as a *territorial society without sovereignty over its borders."* Moreover, "The existing regional subunits of European nations, being no longer fenced in by common, national economic boundaries, will themselves become subunits in their own right of the larger, integrated European economy." This transformation, the authors argue, of "national into regional economies and of subnational regions into subunits of a supranational economy amounts to a *regionalization of Europe* as well as at the same time a *Europeanization of its regions"* (Streeck and Schmitter, 1991: 153, emphasis in the original).

This regionalization expresses the contradictory tendencies of internationalization, regional integration, and productive decentralization. In a penetrating article, Brusco has argued that the principal sources of the movement towards decentralization of the productive structure have been, first, the rise of trade union power since the 1960s and the consequent need imposed upon the large employers to offset the effect of unionism by shifting production toward the small firm sector, and, secondly, the emergence of a significant demand for more varied and customized goods, produced in short series by using flexible technology, alongside that of standardized goods (Brusco, 1982: 171-73).

The result of this productive decentralization is the tendency for local governments to become more actively involved in the local economy and society. According to Brusco, two areas of intervention stand out in this respect: first, the area of the local social services, following the financial restrictions imposed upon the welfare services of the central state administra tions, and second, the area of urban planning and development, in an effort to control speculative building development and foster the growth of the endogenous forces of the region (Brusco, 1982: 181-82; cf. Kratke and Schmoll, 1991).

The new role of the local government, however, reflects not only the requirements of productive decentralization but also the growing needs of the local societies in periods of economic crisis. In this sense, the policy for local development actually amounts to a contribution of the regions to the development and restructuring of the national economy, and this mainly through the development of the productive potential of the regions and the enhancement of technological innovation. It is a policy aiming at the restructuring of the economy and the creation of positions of employment, mainly through local initiatives and entrepreneurial activities of small and medium scope. What the European Union actually supports here is the development of integrated programes, which take into account economic, social, and cultural problems and rely on the cooperation between local governments and development agencies (Tonge, 1993; Kratke and Schmoll, 1991; Potamianos, 1991).

These are policies reinforced by the historical process of internationalization and integration. As Kresl put it, European integration tends to undermine the role of the national states, thereby making local governments important actors: it is at the level of the city that (i) "workable partnerships between the public and private sectors are established," (ii) "effective linking of company, university and institute research laboratories is created," (iii) "adequate investment in infrastructure is made," and (iv) "local energies and institutions are mobilized on behalf of a well designed strategic response to the challenges and opportunities inherent in internationalization" (Kresl, 1992: 152). In other words, local states and regional authorities, faced with the challenges of integration and internationalization, are in many ways engaged in the two processes discussed above, that is, the regulation of the local labor markets and the restructuring of the economy, which involves the reorganization of the labor process itself.

The increasing internationalization and specialization of the economy and the completion of the internal market of the EU, however, are processes which tend to reinforce not only the competition between the various cities for a better position in the EU urban system, but also the cooperation between cities at the European level. Cooperation networks, being horizontally oriented and decentralized urban systems, range from "activities of simple exchange of experiences to projects where cities commit themselves to work together over a long period of time to achieve specific objectivies," and "aim to create economies of scale, technology transfers and increased efficiency through joint ventures" (Camphis and Fox, 1993: 100; Van den Berg and Van Klink, 1992: 139-50; cf. Article 129B of the Treaty on European Union).

These economically and historically conditioned transformations have also been expressed at the political level as a specific form of power structure conceptualized in the EU around the notion of subsidiarity. According to the meaning given in EU documents (Article 130 P of the Single European Act, Article 3B of the Treaty on European Union), the EU acts in accordance with the principle of subsidiarity in the areas which do not fall under its absolute jurisdiction only if Union action in these areas will yield better results than action by the individual member states.

The principle of subsidiarity takes two forms: the vertical form, wherein a distinction is made between the powers of the Union and the powers of the member states, and the horizontal form, which draws a distinction between the area of jurisdiction of the public authorities (both national and supranational) and the area of jurisdiction given to civil society, that is, to the individual citizens. In this sense one can identify two interrelated dimensions in the principle of subsidiarity: the political dimension, wherein subsidiarity actually defines democracy in a more or less federalist institutional construction, and the social dimension, wherein subsidiarity tends to define the degree of regulation of society and thus the degree of privatization of social and economic action (cf. Wilke and Wallace, 1990).

The point is that these two dimensions found in the principle of subsidiarity are to a certain extent contradictory. The reason for this is that though in political terms subsidiarity entails decentralization of authority, thereby strengthening democracy, in actual practice subsidiarity is a principle which tends to legitimize the restriction of the EU's positive action on socioeconomic and political questions, thereby perpetuating existing social inequalities. The rule seems to be, as some analysts point out, that "the principle of subsidiarity means that national and urban governments in the member states will play a major, and the Commission a more limited, role in responding to urban problems" (Parkinson, 1993: 150). This actually reflects the adoption by the EU of a market-driven notion of subsidiarity wherein state action tends to be subordinated to the requirements of the Single Market strategy and the neoliberal approach to social organization and economic competitiveness (cf. Jessop, 1993: 32; Wise and Gibb, 1993).

CONCLUSIONS

In conclusion, the preceding analysis has brought to the fore several points which are now presented in a summary form. First of all, we have argued that the deepening of European economic integration, in the context of the completion of the internal market, has been associated by a clear tendency toward the formation of a European labor market. The regulation of this labor market, however, is not confined to the supranational institutions nor to the national states but also involves the local and regional authorities of the EU area, thereby producing several local labor markets.

Similarly, the internationalization of the mode of production and of exchange and the subsequent deepening of European economic integration, in the context of the completion of the internal market, has been accompanied by a tendency toward the decentralization of production and the restructuring of the European economies. The regulation, however, of this economic restructuring, which affects the labor market and the work organization itself, is a very complex process involving not only supranational and national institutions but also local and regional authorities of the entire EU area.

These tendencies entail the activation of the role of the regional and local bodies of the EU institutionalized by the Commission of the Regions and the principle of subsidiarity. The application of this principle of institutional engineering and power sharing, however, has been interpreted from three differing perspectives: (i) as a driving principle toward the formation of a truly federal political system in the European Union (the position advanced by the Commission, the Benelux countries, the Mediterranean countries, Ireland, and to some extent Germany); (ii) as a political framework aiming at the establishment of a loose confederal political system or even an intergovernmental decision-making structure (the position shared by the U.K. and Denmark); and (iii) as a policy mainly directed toward the political legitimization of the neoliberal strategy aiming at the privatization of the social costs (the position supported by the neoliberal governments of the U.K. and to some extent of Germany) (cf. Ioakeimidis, 1993: 467-68, 491-93).

This being the case, one can only say that positions of power and reasons of expediency will in the end shape the form and influence the content of this contradictory social and political process.

REFERENCES

Anquetl, D. 1990. "Automation and Work Organization in the Car Industry." *Theses*, Vol. 32, pp. 107–24.

Blanke, B. et al. 1992. "Explaining Different Approaches to Local Labor Market Policy in the F.R.G." *Policy and Politics*, Vol. 20, pp. 15–29.

Bonefeld, W. and J. Holloway, eds. 1993. *Post-Fordism and Social Form*. London: Macmillan.

Braverman, H. 1974. *Labor and Monopoly Capital: The Degradation of Work in the Twentieth Century*. New York: Monthly Review.

Brusco, S. 1982. "The Emilian Model: Production Decentralization and Social Integration." *Cambridge Journal of Economics* Vol. 6, pp. 167-84.

Burawoy, M. 1985. *The Politics of Production*. London: New Left Books.

Camphis, M. and S. Fox. 1993. "Urban Networking in the Development of the European Community's Territory." In P. Getimis and G. Kafkalas (eds.), *Urban and Regional Development in the New Europe*. ed. Athens: URDP, TOPOS.

Charles, T. et al. 1990. *Prospects for Anthropocentric Production Systems in Britain*, Brussels: Com. of the EC Res. Rpt. FAST.

Commission of the EC. 1993. *White Paper*. Brussels.

Dunford, M. and G. Kafkalas, eds. *Cities and Regions in the New Europe*. London: Bellhaven.

EC. 1991, 1993. *Employment in Europe*. Brussels: Commission of the EC.

Getimis, P. and G. Kafkalas, eds. 1993. *Urban and Regional Development in the New Europe*. Athens: URDP, TOPOS.

Gravaris, D. 1991. "Employment Policies and the Role of the State in the Labor Market." *TOPOS, Review of Urban and Regional Studies*, Vol. 3, pp. 3-36.

Hancke, B. 1991. "The Crisis of National Unions: Belgian Labor in Decline." *Politics and Society*, Vol. 19 pp. 463-87.

Hinrichs, K. et al. 1988. "Time, Money, and Welfare-Capitalism." In J. Keane (ed.), *Civil Society and the State*. London: New Left Editions.

Hirsch, J. 1993. "Fordism and Post-Fordism: The Present Social Crisis and Its Consequences." In W. Bonefeld and J. Holloway, (eds.), *Post-Fordism and Social Form*. London: Macmillan.

Holloway, J. 1993. "The Great Bear: Post-Fordism and Class Struggle." In W. Bonefeld and J. Holloway (eds.), *Post-Fordism and Social Form*. London: Macmillan.

Howell, C. 1992. "The Dilemmas of Post-Fordism: Socialists, Flexibility, and Labor Market Deregulation in France." *Politics and Society*, Vol. 20, pp. 71-79.

Ioakeimidis, P. 1993. *European Political Union*. Athens: Themelion.

Jessop, B. 1993. "Toward a Schumpeterian Workfare State." *Studies in Political Economy*, Vol. 40, pp. 7-39.

Kern, H. and C. F. Sabel. 1991. "Trade Unions and Decentralized Production: A Sketch of Strategic Problems in the West German Labor Movement." *Politics and Society*, Vol. 19, pp. 373–402.

Kidd, P. 1990. *Organization, People and Technology in European Manufacturing*. Brussels: Com. of the EC Res. Rpt. FAST.

Kratke, S. and F. Schmoll. 1991. "The Local State and Social Restructuring." *International Journal of Urban and Regional Research*, Vol. 15, pp. 542–52.

Kresl, P. K. 1992. "The Response of European Cities to EC 1992." *Journal of European Integration*, Vol. 25, pp. 151–72.

Lehner, F. 1991. *Anthropocentric Production Systems: The European Response to Advanced Manufacturing and Globalization*. Brussels: Com. of the EC Res. Rpt. FAST.

Lipietz, A. 1987. *Mirages and Miracles: The Crisis of Global Fordism*. London: New Left Books.

———. 1992. "The Regulation Approach and Capitalist Crisis: An Alternative Compromise for the 1990s." In M. Dunford and G. Kafkalas (eds.), *Cities and Regions in the New Europe*. London: Belhaven.

Lojkine, J. 1986. "From the Industrial Revolution to the Computer Revolution: First Signs of a New Combination of Material and Human Productive Forms." *Capital and Class*, Vol. 29, pp. 111–29.

Moschonas, A. 1990. "Capital and New Technologies." In *Culture and Technology*. Athens: Praxis.

———. 1993. "The Social Dimension of the New Technologies: Trends and Concerns in the EEC." In G. Liodakis (ed.), *Society, Technology and Restructuring of Production*. Athens: Papasisis.

OECD. 1986, 1989. *Flexibility in the Labor Market*. Paris.

Papadimitriou, Z. 1991. *Assessment of Prospects for Anthropocentric Production Systems in Greece: The Case of Textile and Clothing Industry*. Brussels: Com. of the EC Res. Rpt. FAST.

Parkinson, M. 1993. "Urban Economic Change in Europe: Policy Implications for the European Community." In P. Getimis and G. Kafkalas (eds.), *Urban and Regional Development in the New Europe*. Athens: URDP, TOPOS.

Potamianos, G. 1991. "The Enhancement of Local Development in the EC and the Member States: Strategies and Means of Activation of the Local Labor Markets." *TOPOS, Review of Urban and Regional Studies*, Vol. 3, pp. 119–39.

Ruggiero, V. 1987. "Turin Today: Premodern Society or Postindustrial Bazaar?" *Capital and Class*, Vol. 31, pp. 25–38.

Sabel, C. F. 1982. *Work and Politics: The Division of Labor in Industry*. London: Cambridge University Press.

Streeck, W. and P. C. Schmitter. 1991. "From National Corporatism to Transnational Pluralism: Organized Interests in the Single European Market." *Politics and Society*, Vol. 19.

Teague, P. and J. Grahl. 1992. *Industrial Relations and European Integration*. London: Lawrence.

Tonge, J. 1993. "Training and Enterprise Councils: The Privatization of Britain's Unemployment Problem?" *Capital and Class*, Vol. 51, pp. 9–16.

Toutziarakis, J. 1990. "The Flexibilitization of the Working Time and the Crisis of the Normal Labor Relation." *The Greek Review of Social Research*, Vol. 76, pp. 174–200.

Van den Berg, L. and H. A. Van Klink. 1992. "Strategic Networks as Weapons in the Competition among European Cities and Regions." *Journal of European Integration*, Vol. 15.

Wilke, M. and W. Wallace. 1990. *Subsidiarity: Approaches to Power-Sharing in the European Community*. London: RIIA Discussion Papers 27.

Wilson, W. 1991. "Democracy in the Workplace: The French Experience." *Politics and Society*, Vol. 19, pp. 439–62.

Windolf, P. 1993. "Codetermination and the Market for Corporate Control in the European Community." *Economy and Society*, Vol. 22, pp. 137–58.

Wise, M. and R. Gibb. 1993. *Single Market to Social Europe: The European Community in the 1990s*. London: Longman.

Wobbe, W. 1991. *What Are Anthropocentric Production Systems? Why Are They a Strategic Issue for Europe?* Brussels: Com. of the EC Res. Rpt. FAST 21.

12

Political European Integration: Integration Requisites

Gianni Bonvicini

As we address the issue of the political dimension of the process of European integration, we intend to limit ourselves to the consideration of the practical effects and ad hoc experiences drawn from the application of certain policies and decision-making instruments to the building of Europe, possibly avoiding any theoretical exercise.

In fact our aim is that of reporting on the variety of different options and modifications on the way toward integration. We don't know whether a European "model" of integration can be applied outside the historical and geographical boundaries of the present European Union (EU). Today the debate about the enlargement of the EU toward Eastern countries is partly creating a similar question, although in this case we depart from the assumption that "they are Europeans anyway" and sooner or later they will join the Union. But we think that in an increasingly interdependent world, some practical measures and policies could be universally applied and achieve the same results in terms of positive integration.

This is why we continue to judge the politics of European integration as the master experience in the building of new cooperative experiences in the rest of the world. What has to be rejected is an eventual attempt to "sell" the European experience as "the absolute model."

Today, in fact, Europe too is witnessing a process of deep transformation and redefinition of the old concept of integration. And, as usual in times of transformation, we are living in a state of crisis or of "Europessimism," if we prefer to adopt "Eurocratic" jargon. A clear need to adapt EU institutions has again emerged. But the strategy to be followed is far from being clear. And again we have to turn back to our past experiences. In other words, and in opposition to Fukuyama theories, "history continues," at least at the European Union's level.

THE EUROPEAN EXPERIENCE: INSTITUTIONAL PREREQUISITES

Institutions, both national and multilateral, are not simply architectural exercises, they establish the confines of their surroundings and therefore represent the point of arrival or departure of a given historical and political circumstance.

Institutions are not neutral with respect to the environment in which they operate; on the contrary, they tend to shape it with their procedures, laws, and operating ability. At the same time, the enviroment determines the suitability of existing institutions and influences the form of the new ones set up to dominate present and future events.[1]

At the beginning of the process of European Community (EC) integration, the events and the resolution of the actors at that time determined the forms and the limits of the EC institutions. Today, after almost forty-five years of activity, the common institutions and laws constitue an *acquis communautaire* that is subject to its own internal reform dynamics and which conditions future plans; at the same time, the external environment, undergoing radical change, confronts the Union with new problems and demands and influences its role and future form. The past and the future converge in demanding a different institutional arrangement for the European Union system.

As is well known, the European experience with reference to a common decision-making process has developed a rather baroque system of institutions with which to balance Union and national interests: first of all, we count on the cohabitation of different levels of executive powers distributed unequally among the European Council, the Council of Ministers and the COREPER (Committee of Permanent Representatives) in defense of the member states' interests; it is the task of the European Commission to check all this power, but as history has shown, its ability to play an influential role largely depends on the existence of other procedural mechanisms: among them, the most important is the majority voting procedure within the Council, which essentially leaves the Commission the room to create a majority in favor of its legislative initiatives.

Other important elements in the life of the Union may be found in the structure of the own resources system and in the application of the budgetary powers with respect both to EU autonomy as regards the national budgets and the function of control played by the European Parliament. Finally, the Court of Justice must be mentioned as the decisive institution in helping Union law prevail over national law.

This complex and unique system works reasonably well only if the relationships among institutions follow a balanced pattern of cooperation. At the Union level the need to reach compromises is unavoidable, if the system is to produce decisions. When one institution wants to prevail over another, the consequence is usually paralysis. This means that a long period of time and repeated negotiations are among the basic criteria for the proper functioning of the Union, as the theory of international regimes of cooperation suggests. The relative advantage of the Union with respect to other international institutions is that of having reached a high degree of institutionalisation of its legal procedures and decision-making mechanisms.

In this light Maastricht represents another step forward in the process of institutional reform begun already in the early 1980s. It is not the end point; rather, it reaffirms the dynamic character of EU institutions. They must now adapt to new internal and external factors. This time, among endogenous elements, particular emphasis should be placed on the need for the following measures: (i) completion of the single market of 1992 with a stronger convergence in the economic field (the famous macroeconomic criteria of Maastricht); (ii) strong pressure to enlarge the Union to new members before having decided about its institutional reinforcement; and, finally, on a rather new element; and (iii) creation of a clearer social and popular perception of the importance of the existence of the EU (to address the so-called democratic deficit).

Regarding exogenous factors, the most pertinent are as follows: (i) the growing role of regionalism in global affairs; (ii) the progressive U.S. disengagement from Europe; (iii) the new concept and instruments of comprehensive security; (iv) the qualitative different meaning of any future enlargement of the Union with respect to a reinforced foreign and security policy of the Twelve; and, more generally, (v) the new role that the concept of integration is bound to play in the future pan-European architecture.

SOME LESSONS DRAWN FROM THE REFORMING PROCESSES OF THE OLD COMMUNITY

During the 1980s and the beginning of the 1990s the Community witnessed an extraordinary and dynamic period of reforms. It started with the Genscher-Colombo Plan drawn up by the two foreign ministers in 1981.

At that time, the need was felt to integrate the already operating monetary system (European Monetary System—EMS) with better Community organization in the fields of foreign policy (European Political Community—EPC) and, to some extent, security policy. Institutional procedures, similar to those of the Community, were to be extended to these two sectors—which were strictly intergovernmental at the time. But the Solemn Declaration concluding the Italo-German Plan issued in Stuttgart in June 1983 was a disappointment for all: the essential points of the plan concerning more binding decision-making procedures within EPC were shelved because of the opposition of France and other partners who wanted to maintain EPC's intergovernmental character.[2]

After the Solemn Declaration of Stuttgart, pressure for reform of the Treaty of Rome intensified in view of the imminent enlargement of the Community to Spain and Portugal. All agreed that the errors made in 1973 during the first enlargement of the EC to Great Britain, Ireland, and Denmark, when demands for deepening were largely ignored, were not to be repeated.

This state of affairs was shaken by the European Parliament in 1984. Upon the initiative of Altiero Spinelli, it decided to draw up the Draft Treaty establishing the European Union. The plan set some fundamental criteria for future debate: unity of the economic, foreign, and security policy aspects of the integration process; the principle of subsidiarity as the instrument for division of powers among the Community, states and the regions; reintroduction of the majority voting system; democratic legitimation of the system.[3]

As is known, the Draft Treaty was one, perhaps the most important, element taken into consideration when the European governments undertook partial reform of the Treaty of Rome and approved the Single European Act (SEA) at the beginning of 1986.

THE "SUCCESS STORY" OF THE SINGLE EUROPEAN ACT

Identifications of some of the positive features of the SEA may be useful in view of future reforms. The very name "Single Act" can be traced back to the need to bring together under one roof the various branches of European activity, from the EMS and the EPC to such bodies as the European Council, relegated for years to an institutional limbo. Thus, it embodied the *principle of consistency* among various activities in the integration process so often called for in prior plans, such as that of Belgian Premier Tindemans in 1976 and the 1981-83 Genscher-Colombo Plan, to mention only the better known.

This principle, which is still one of the cornerstones of debate on the future of the European Union, as set down in the Maastricht Treaty (especially when foreign and security policies are seen as a part of the EU and not as independent), was,however, only incorporated into the SEA in a very elementary manner. In fact, the Single European Act did no more than register the foreign policy activities of the Twelve; it did not "communitarize" them, as it should have. This means that the decision-making procedures have not been changed, even though efforts have been made to bring them into the same framework. Consequently, the Community method applied to all matters provided for by the Treaty of Rome and to those added by the completion of the internal market in 1992; the intergovernmental method applied to all other matters, in particular, EPC.[4]

It is clear that the "communitarization" of European Union policies, both old and new, remains an open question. When we speak about "communitarization" we have in mind a combination of balanced dialogue among organs (essentially the Council, Commission, European Parliament) and regular recourse to the majority voting procedure. Maastricht represents a clear example of the difficulty of applying the concept of "communitarization" to a variety of different fields of action and common policies, in other words, the progressive passage from a functional integration in the economic field to a similar form of procedures in the Common Foreign and Security Policy (CFSP) camps.

In fact, Maastricht continues to maintain a different legal approach in the two fields, essentially leaving the CFSP in the realm of the classical intergovernmental approach (albeit with some minor concessions to the communitarian method). The risk is that of creating competitive decision-making processes in the two fields of cooperation and weakening the efficacy of the Union's external role, as has been largely shown in the case of the ex-Yugoslavia case.

Going back to our history, the real novelty of the SEA was the elimination of an old taboo: the return of the qualified majority voting procedure to the Council. Although limited, the rehabilitation of this old procedure has made the Union decision-making procedure more efficient; it has greatly speeded up the approval of directives in all matters in which it is applied.

Parallel to the reintroduction of the majority vote, the objectives and the methods for the most rapid achievement of legislative harmonization were defined more precisely. Unlike in the past, the Commission has returned to the practice of issuing rather broad directives, leaving their detailed implementation up to individual member states.

This strategy was in keeping with another fundamental principle: equivalence. If complete harmonization as set down in Article 8a of the SEA was not achieved by 1992, Article 100b provided for the application of the criterion of equivalent provisions, in the sense that provisions judged equivalent by the Commission and the Council could be considered valid in all member states during a transition period.

This was perfectly in line with another of the founding principles of the Treaty of Rome, rendered famous by its application in some cases before the Court of Justice. The principle is known as *mutual recognition.* Its constant application could greatly accelerate and simplify the harmonization process. Although application can obviously not be automatic, it nevertheless could have great potential if backed by an increasingly active and authoritative Court of Justice, the real federating element in Union law.[5]

The last interesting feature with an institutional deepening effect was the modification of the competences of the European Parliament (EP). Although limited to the so-called cooperation procedure provided for in Article 149, the results have been better than expected. In matters pertaining to some relevant articles of the SEA—mostly concerning the internal market—the EP was given the power of influencing the legislative process by amending or rejecting the Council's common position during second readings. If the Council then wishes to override the decision of the Parliament supported by the Commission, it has to vote unanimously, and that is obviously no easy matter. This first reform has helped to further develop the EP's powers in the Maastricht Treaty, through the concession of codecision competences in the legislative field (Article 189b), a kind of veto power which allows the last word in the hands of the Parliament.

In conclusion, the experience gained from the first reform of the Treaty of Rome and, subsequently, from implementation of the SEA has provided important guidelines not only for the following drafting of the Maastricht Treaty but also for the present debate on its further future reforms.

THE POLITICAL STRATEGY THAT LED TO THE SUCCESS OF THE SEA

Three strategic elements helped turn the SEA into a success story. The first was the decision taken by the European governments (i.e., the Council of Ministers and Commission) to link enlargement of the Community to its deepening. Ratification of the SEA took place at the same time as the entry into the Community of Spain and Portugal, thus avoiding a repetition of the errors made in 1973, when widening was undertaken without provisions for deepening; that is, contemporaneous reform of decision-making structures took place.[6]

Another element which contributed to the achievement of consensus in Luxembourg in 1985 was the "package deal" strategy: rather than searching for agreement on *individual* measures of policy or institutional change, discussion centered on a *set* of policies and institutional improvements. In fact, in addition to approximately 280 directives on the completion of the internal market, the Commission suggested the introduction of some procedures streamlining decision making, including provision for a majority vote on most of the matters proposed. This mix of policies and procedures turned out to be a very dynamic factor and led to the swift implementation of most directives not requiring unanimity.[7]

A third element, perhaps less apparent but no less important, was the fact that this reform sprang more from the "force" and perceptions of European society than from the goodwill of its political leaders. The 1992 deadline served as a rallying point in the economic and business worlds and, more generally, among the citizenry concerned with assessing what impact the date would have on various sectors of the economic and social life. Not even the launching of the EMS in 1978 generated the same kind of expectations and consensus in European society. Basically, the real supporters of 1992 were the people involved in business, in banking, and so on—the citizens; the politicians, on the contrary, were fearful of losing further terrain to European sovereignty.

THE PARTIAL FAILURE OF MAASTRICHT

Those positive lessons from the past were only partially reflected in the Treaty of Maastricht. A different political climate too, both internally and outside the Union, has contributed to a remarkably less convincing performance in the implementation of the Treaty itself. We are interested here in evaluating the latest events which have marked the recent history and evolution of the Maastricht Treaty.

The most important and unexpected fact with regard to Maastricht has been the collapse of public support of the Treaty, in particular, and of the concept of integration, in general. It was not just the first Danish refusal and the scarce electoral support in the French referendum which caused concern, but the general decline in the once widespread interest for the creation of an ad hoc supranational Europe. The ratification process has taken practically two years instead of one, and the revision process of the Treaty, due to happen in late 1996 (Article N), has already started (if only unofficially) before the legal implementation date.

This slow and negative evolution of the Treaty contradicts the expectations created by the Single European Act (SEA) and the fateful date of 1992 which represented a Europe able to move quickly into an era of full freedom in the basic elements of our social life (capital, labor, trade, and services). Strangely enough, in institutional terms the SEA was far less ambitious and complex than the succeeding Treaty. Nevertheless, as we have described above, it helped Europe to relaunch a process toward deeper integration, through the restoration of a few decision-making rules (among others the reactivation of the majority voting procedure within the Council of Ministers).

The recent economic crisis does not in itself sufficiently explain the collapse of public confidence in the process of integration. Its effects began to become evident only some months after the first Danish referendum. It is true that a positive economic cycle might favor the speed of those efforts which are addressed to the launching of policies of international cooperation, but this explanation does not provide a reasonable answer for those integration processes having already reached a certain level of complexity.

Other elements have to be taken into consideration: a general one is the post-1989 crisis of the concept of multilateralism and, consequently, of its mechanisms of management. What appears to be paradoxical is not just the collapse of multilateral institutions and doctrines in the Eastern half of the old bipolar world, but the lasting difficulties for Western cooperative organizations to reorient their role and objectives to the new geostrategic situation.

Moreover, this lengthy process taking place during the last decade of this century happens to be occurring in a period in which a strong tendency toward the renationalization of policies and actions of old and new states appears to be becoming the key political factor. And here again a phenomenon which has started to emerge in the East as a legitimate reaction against a forced pattern of integration has ended up penetrating into the West, affecting the policies of cooperation and the progress toward integration. The European Union itself, as the maximum expression of supranational experience, has suffered from this resurgence of nationalism, largely due to the fact that it happened to spread mainly in the core of Europe, where former historical linkages and feelings were suddenly charged with new vitality.

Add to these factors a subtle argument, supported by many politicians and intellectuals, which asserts that true democracy lies only at the national level, where parliaments and political parties better protect the rights of individuals against the technocratic bureaucracy of Brussels, so distant from the social needs of people. Through this way of reasoning, the strict linkage which actually exists between integration and democracy is hidden and appears less evident; to deny the substantial democratic character of a voluntary integration among states and people, as a way of directing and controlling the effects of international interdependence, means to threaten the very basis of one of the most relevant postwar phenomena constituted by the various forms of supranational cooperation.

The above considerations necessarily lead us to evaluate the process of complex integration, as represented by the European experience, in a more articulated manner. This must be accomplished through an assessment of various combinations of positive and negative factors, both in political and institutional terms, the prevalence of one over the other being able to determine the direction that integration can take in particular historical periods.

A NEW "OLD PRINCIPLE": SUBSIDIARITY

The *principle of subsidiarity* is mentioned for the first time in the Treaty of Maastricht, Article 3b. The wording of the text is rather generic:

In areas which do not fall within its exclusive competence, the Community shall take action, in accordance with the principle of subsidiarity, only if and in so far as the objectives of the proposed action can not be sufficiently achieved by the Member States and can therefore, by reason of the scales or effects of the proposed action, be better achieved by the Community.

Also, it does not add very much to the understanding of the traditional relationship between the national and European Union levels. Throughout the history of the Union, there has been a laborious application of different degrees of responsibilities at the two levels. In the past, others have tried to discipline the division between nation-state and the Union. The most significant effort was made by Altiero Spinelli in the drafting of the 1984 New Treaty, through the concept of exclusive and concurrent competences (Article 12).

Since European Union institutions, more than any other multilateral institutions, are the most significant product of the transition from the old form of national state to a new form of cooperative state, it is clear that the principle of subsidiarity must be applied, if possible, in the most advanced meaning of the term: the Union must be assigned all tasks whose scope and effects go beyond national boundaries. This approach should have a decentralizing or federative effect, unlike the efficiency-oriented approach, which attributes to the Union those tasks which it can best carry out, and consequently leads to centralization. The conclusion reached on this point in Maastricht was a compromise: both concepts of subsidiarity are included in Article 3b, in its reference to "reason of scale or effects of proposed action."[8]

Moreover, unlike in the past, today a real innovation, when considering the principle of subsidiarity, is represented by the presence of a new, important, and worried actor: the regions, which are fiercely fighting to participate directly in the Union decision-making process. And through the enlargement of EU competences to new fields of action (like environment), Maastricht has convinced the regions to press for their involvement. As a sign of this pressure, the Treaty, for the first time, provides for a Committee of Regions, which for the time being has only consultative powers for a limited number of common policies.

But aside from this significant political innovation, the open question remains that of addressing the real substance of the concept of subsidiarity, which includes the following:

(i) The political and institutional mechanisms which will provide clear decisions about the appropriate level for the new and old competences—in other words, how the concept should be put into practice. This is something completely missing from the new Treaty and this absence is going to create future conflicts among institutions.

(ii) The question of how to regulate the permanent contradiction between common interests and vital national interests. The latter continues to appear as strong as it was in the past, although the majority voting procedure has helped to moderate the recourse to veto power in certain fields. The resolution of this lasting contrast has, in any case, to do with the clarification of the concept of subsidiarity: only if and when a sharp distinction between the different levels of competences exists, will the preeminence of national interest give up part of its political meaning.

(iii) The application of the concept of subsidiarity to democracy and transparency. The argument that democracy works properly only at national level largely depends on the confused implementation of the division of competences between the different levels— Union, national, and regional. In this respect the European Parliament is still playing a complementary role to that of the national ones. And in Europe we are currently witnessing a pressing call by national parliaments for directly controlling the decision-making process at the European Union level. Here again the lack of clarity about the concept of subsidiarity constitutes a misleading factor in the correct application of normal Union rules. What is missing is well-structured relations between the European Parliament and the national parliaments.

THE "PERCEPTIVE FACTOR" AS A PRECONDITION TO DEVELOP THE PROCESS OF POLITICAL INTEGRATION

For too long, the process of European integration was considered a direct result of the application of the functional theory, which by definition neglects the importance of the political and sociological factors as basic elements necessary for the consolidation of the cooperative efforts made by the states. National and Union leaders have only partially posed the question of the role of public opinion in defining the direction of the process toward closer cooperation. As a result of this absence of a strategy to get public support for the integration of Europe, we have witnessed a growing negative attitude in public opinion in various countries. The Danish and French referenda on Maastricht are cases in point.

Another aspect has to be taken into consideration when we deal with the "perceptive" factor: the growing amount of legislation produced by Brussels. With the completion of the internal market and the plan for full economic union, common legislation will inevitably have to limit progressively the room for maneuver and the autonomous decision-making power of member states. As a result, the Union will become increasingly responsible to its citizens. The president of the Commission, Jacques Delors, has repeatedly stated that almost 80 percent of economic amd social legislation will be passed by the EU. This raises two main problems: the first concerns the governing capacity of the Union, with the extension of the qualified majority voting procedure to all social and economic legislation to streamline the decision-making procedure; the second regards the democratic deficit, that is, the low level of legitimacy of the present Union decision-making process. Thus the powers of control and colegislation of the European Parliament must also be increased.

There are therefore several questions that have to be settled if national and community leaders want to win public support in order to avoid isolating the process of European integration from the perceptions of people. In brief, the following topics must be taken into consideration:

(i) A clearer linkage between European electoral representation and the protection of individual interests at European Union level. It is very difficult for a European citizen to understand how much direct involvement he/she has in the political life of the Union; from this point of view, direct elections to the European Parliament have not helped to solve the problem—the solution of which largely depends on the degree of competences and power attributed to the Parliament and on the existence of EU political parties. Both of them exist at a very low level of intensity and substance.

(ii) The complete absence of a well-functioning structure for mass media at the EU level and the subsequent lack of a formative mechanism to create a common European conscience; Union topics continue to be considered as subjects for specialists.

(iii) Information coming from EU institutions is also lacking, as is attention to public opinion; both are even less prominent than they were at the beginning of the process of European integration, when we witnessed a massive effort by the European Commission to spread information about the advantages of Union activities and on the steps to be taken to attain certain positive goals. Nothing like that exists today, and this has given national media more room to interpret EU events (frequently in a critical way).

(iv) Finally, those who are in search of stability, equity, and security must be shown that the process of integration is the right answer. Thus, it is important to provide a political solution to the requests (especially those coming from the Eastern countries) to be full members of the European Union;[9] to guarantee small and weak states a reasonably equal status in the decision-making process; to guarantee the protection of human rights both within and outside the Union.

TOWARD FURTHER ENLARGEMENTS OF THE UNION

The last point leads us to consider again the question of a growing number of members inside the Union. In fact, the problem of Union enlargement has become very serious. It is no longer a matter of giving a gradual and acceptable answer to two or three small, economically weak states: applications have come from EFTA (European Free Trade Association) countries, from Mediterranean countries, and from a growing number of Eastern European countries. This could lead to a doubling of the number of Union members in only a few years.

But the applicant countries are not homogeneous and have different reasons for applying for membership: the EFTA, the next full members, were basically motivated by economic considerations and felt less committed to political and security developments inside the Union; the Eastern countries seek not only economic, but also political and security guarantees; the Mediterranean countries, situated in an area of potential conflict, are motivated by their quest for stability, as well as by economic factors, and thus desire formal linkage to Europe.

In this light, enlargement takes on a different dimension: contrary to the strategy pursued today with the EFTA countries, it calls for a new concept of the policy of widening which has to date served simplistic and pragmatic ends. From now on, it will assume a strategic character, as general political and security (as well as military) considerations can no longer be overlooked. This means that a purely mechanical adaptation of the present institutional procedures, as is being done today with EFTA countries, will not be sufficient to match the general political interets of the Union, as explained in the preceding paragraphs. There is therefore a need for new radical institutional changes.

SCENARIOS FOR THE FUTURE

As we have said before, the uncertainty and pessimism following the signing of the Treaty of Maastricht on February 7, 1992, has given rise to a process of revision. In fact, there is no doubt that governments as well as political and business leaders have begun a critical review of Maastricht. Whether the focus is on limitations or constraints, the revision process is under way.

Clearly, the course of this process will vary according to several important developments which may arise: economic recovery, a decline in currency difficulties, maintenance of a stable process of unification in Germany, and a significant stabilization of the situation in Russia, and containment of the Balkan conflict.[10]

In any case, the result of the ratification process under way will constitute a watershed. There are essentially two possible scenarios: (i) the Twelve will try to consolidate the Treaty in its present form; (ii) the text will go through a quick and sharp revision.

Scenario 1: The Consolidation of Maastricht

Under this scenario the Treaty would again be the legitimate point of reference for European Union initiatives. While a redemption would certainly not dispel doubts about the limitations and intrinsic weaknesses of the text, the revision process would probably be required to follow the foreseen time schedule and procedures. In other words, it is unlikely that the process of integration would be accelerated or that the Treaty would be superseded by the formal creation of a "hard core," such as the one around economic and monetary union. This would only be possible during the third phase (in 1997 or 1999), as foreseen by the Treaty itself. If anything, in order to facilitate convergence, the three basic criteria could be reconsidered, as not even Germany fully meet them at the moment.

As for enlargement, the process would be as foreseen by the European Council in Lisbon 1992, that is, without further hesitation and without waiting for negotiations for the revision of the Treaty planned for 1996. In other words, no further steps would be taken toward deepening without the agreement of new members. And this is rightly what has happened with the end of the negotiations for access with the four EFTA countries. The consequence is that of complicating the process of institutional revision, due to the increased number of national actors.

Defense policy will remain necessarily intergovernmental and therefore subject to initiatives of the individual states, as foreseen by the Maastricht text. The WEU (Western European Union) may have an increased role, as is already the case today, but without a specific institutional framework within the European Union, even though events are of an urgency and nature requiring increasingly complex and unitary interventions in local crises.

Thus, Maastricht would leave the main issues that had emerged with the first reading of the text unresolved:

(i) The main question, whose answer will determine everything else, pertains to the institutional framework (whether it is strengthened or not). In other words, the problem is how to deal with the following issues within the current institutional framework: the general nature of the integration process, the maintenance of a functioning and effective decision-making system, the nature of relations with other candidates for EU admission (from full membership to superassociation). If the reinforcement of institutional mechanisms will not be immediately planned, there is a real risk of not even being able to ensure the maintenance of the current institutional framework during the planned revision of Maastricht in 1996, particularly following the first initial enlargement.

(ii) The second question regards the relationship between subsidiarity and democracy. There is currently a marked political tendency to consider the principle of subsidiarity as an instrument for protecting national competences. This is based, as we have underlined above, on the equivocal assumption that the truly democratic institutions are based only at the national level. Thus, national parliaments are placed in opposition to the European Parliament and the role of the Commission is severely weakened. It is therefore necessary to clarify the politico-institutional relationship between the division of power among the various levels of government (regional levels included) and the role played by the various institutions in legitimating and guaranteeing the democratic process.

(iii) There is a similar problem with respect to the relationship between the organs foreseen by the EMU and the management of the European economy as a whole. In other words, what type of links are necessary between those institutions which are strictly economic (i.e., those foreseen by the Treaty in the chapter on EMU [European Monetary Union]) and political institutions. For example, the European Parliament is completely excluded from the EMU (the limited powers gained in other sectors are not exercised here), while it plays a certain role in overseeing Union actions in general.

(iv) Finally, the Maastricht reforms should address both foreign policy and defense aspects of the CFSP. The dominant issue in this case is also the interrelations between other policies and institutions. In this case, however, account must be taken not only of relations among the institutional mechanisms of the European Union (i.e., the progressive "communitarization" of procedures in all fields of the Union, the meaning of the so-called common actions, etc.), but also the links which must be established with related institutions such as the WEU, and completely separate institutions such as NATO, the CSCE (Conference on Security and Cooperation in Europe), and so on. In more general terms, attention must be given to the extent to which integration in the field of security and foreign policy in the near future will serve as the engine for a more accelerated process of unification.

Scenario 2: A Quick and Sharp Revision of Maastricht.

Should the first scenario fail to become reality, there will be several options to take into consideration because, as the solidarity of the Twelve crumbles, some governments and the Union organs (Council, Commission, and Parliament) will have more freedom to imagine new models of integration, provided the Single European Act remains the common basis for all countries.

Among the possible alternatives, the following are those which are politically more likely:

(i) Immediate further enlargement (beyond that already decided with the Eftans) of the Union based on the Single European Act, without recourse to early negotiations for drafting a new treaty to replace that of Maastricht. In this case enlargement could be extended to a number and kind of candidate that is far beyond the limits the "strict" Maastricht criteria would impose. The result would be very similar to the free trade area favored by Britain and Denmark. It would certainly be much simpler to give a positive response to the Visegrad countries (Poland, Czech Republic, Slovakia and Hungary) and others who would meet the minimum conditions imposed by the old Treaty. Further- more, in a context of less cohesion within the Community, there would be no obligation for Germany to serve as the focus of the new Europe. In this scenario, enlargement is thus an alternative to the former Union of the Twelve and serves as a way of reinforcing the bilateral policies of the main powers in a multilateral framework guaranteed by an EU that becomes increasingly like a traditional cooperation regime.

(ii) The process of integration is resumed on a completely different basis. In this case, the scenario is necessarily one which has been receiving increasing attention in Europe, that is, one which is centered around the idea of a "hard core." But this scenario may be subdivided into at least three suboptions:

"Hard-core Europe": a single, homogeneous nucleus of an extremely limited number of participants. The only possible group of countries which could be envisioned in this context is the Group of Five: the three Benelux countries, France, and Germany. As the original Schengen group and as an area of monetary stability, these five countries may easily constitute a markedly homogeneous nucleus. Military integration based on the Eurocorp could also become a reality in a short time. While formally a group of five, it would actually be little more than a cosmetic variation of the Franco-German duo as the main engine of a new and different process of integration. It is thus an extreme case which would be difficult to actualize for obvious political reasons, not to mention that it would be highly destabilizing for a large number of excluded countries. This option would be pursued only in the event of a serious disintegration of the Union—one in which the countries of the South would diverge not only in economic terms, but also in terms of political stability; and the countries of the North would become increasingly unwilling to commit themselves to concerted efforts toward integration. In other words, this scenario would serve to maintain the prospect of integration at least in "hard-core" Europe at a time of serious crisis at the periphery.

"Concentric Circles Europe": a broader group than the "hard core" described above, encompassing countries which, propelled toward an accelerated integration by France and Germany, have demonstrated the greatest willingness to pursue integration, both by accepting without reservation (i.e., not requesting opting-out clauses) the provisions of the Maastricht Treaty and by making domestic policy decisions on the basis of Union priorities, even at the cost of further sovereignty concessions. Natural candidates for such a coalition include Italy and Spain. In this scenario, the strongest countries in the group should set less stringent macroeconomic criteria in order to accommodate the weakest divergent countries. Priority could thus be placed on political obligations, military issues, and foreign policy, while deemphasizing monetary and economic aspects. Enlargement to include a large number of candidates would thus be possible, though they would be "placed" within the framework of the Single European

Act, as this would continue to be a legally valid treaty to which both Britain and Denmark would still adhere. This is the classic "concentric circles" proposition, in which each "circle" would be a homogeneous group of member states having equal rights and obligations.

"Ellipsis Europe": a constellation of several groups forming an ellipsis around a strong nucleus. In part, this is what was described in the preceding scenario, which essentially attributes a specific role to a strongly integrationist political nucleus—the Group of 5 plus Spain and Italy. In this scenario, the core of seven would be surrounded by various ellipses: one of countries with convergent economies (therefore excluding Italy); one of countries which would take on the responsibility of defense (this could partially coincide with WEU countries); one of countries adhering to the Schengen agreement; and so on. Though the ellipsis model is theoretically conceivable, it is difficult to envision its implementation, as it remains unclear what role the formalization of a central political nucleus would have with respect to the peripheral ellipses—particularly in the case of the one based on economic performances and criteria, which would continue to play a central role in Union life. (In fact, the EU, as it now stands, was almost entirely built on the concept of economic integration in which the major role and responsibility was attributed to those countries which best conformed to Community discipline.) It would be difficult for those countries not partaking in the economic ellipsis to interact as equals with those countries which also meet the criteria for being part of the other ellipses—unless of course the basis for integration were shifted from the economic sphere to the military and foreign policy dimension. This would require communitarization in both fields, making the latter less national and bilateral than they are today. In other words, this scenario also involves the question of having a strong political core which corresponds to an economic and military nucleus of equally strong members, as coordination and consistency between the various fields of action is of crucial importance to the international credibility of the EU and of the nucleus itself. Enlargement is also an issue in this scenario, and it is even more complex and variegated here because of the presence of different ellipses which are not necessarily linked.

In conclusion, the future of Europe will be the result of an ad hoc combination of the different criteria illustrated above (a mix of institutional procedures, application of the principle of subsidiarity, public perception of the guarantees provided by the participation in the process of integration). Different combinations will lead to completely different outcomes. To choose the appropriate strategy is an open task for politicians: the urgency is clear and the risk of fragmentation still present. Specific criteria and carefully thought-out scenarios should be consulted and used as guides to ensure the preservation of a certain degree of integration in the presence of a totally new geostrategic situation and with the aim that the Union remain a point of stability in Europe and an example of integration for the rest of the world.

NOTES

1. On this general issue, see W. Wessels, "Basic Considerations for the Institutional Debate," in "The Institutional Debate Revisited, Introductory Remarks," paper presented at the June Conference of the College of Europe on "The Institutions of the European Community after the Single European Act: The New Procedures and the Capacity to Act," Bruges, 1990.

2. F. Lay, *L'Iniziativa italo-tedesca per il rilancio dell'Unione Europea* (Padouva: Cedam, 1983).

3. European Parliament, *Draft Treaty Establishing the European Union*, Luxembourg, February 1984.

4. C. Meriano, "The Single European Act. Past, Present, Future," *The International Spectator*, No. 2, 1987, p. 89.

5. N. Ronzitti, "The Internal Market, Italian Law and the Public Administration," *The International Spectator*, No. 1, 1990, p. 3.

6. On the first enlargement of the Community, see C. Merlini and G. Bonvicini, "The Institutional Problems Arising from the Enlargement of the European Community," *The International Spectator*, No. 2, 1979, p. 103.

7. See W. Wessels, op. cit. (note 1).

8. Committee for Institutional Affairs, "The Principle of Subsidiarity," *Working Paper*, No. 83354, Rapporteur, V. Giscard D'Estaing, European Parliament, Strasbourg, April 5, 1990.

9. The Six Institute, *The Community and the Emerging European Democracies: A Joint Policy Report*, (London: Chatham House, 1991).

10. R. Aliboni, G. Bonvicini, C. Merlini, and S. Silvestri, "Three Scenarios for the Future of Europe," *The International Spectator*, No. 1, 1991, p. 4.

13

The Limits of The European Union: The Question of Enlargement

Nicholas V. Gianaris

Historically, efforts to form and enlarge economic and geopolitical unions in parts of Europe were made, for example, by city-states in ancient Greece and Rome and later in Byzantium, by the Frankish kingdom of Charlemagne (King Father of Europe), and by the Hapsburg dynasty. However, forcible unions proved to be ineffective, whereas voluntary and democratic unions helped improve European integration.

More effective alliances and unions were those of Austria, Britain, France, Prussia, and Russia (the Concert), which reduced conflicts from 1815 to 1854, and the German customs union (Zollverein), which was established in 1834 under Prussian leadership. Also, the Benelux countries (Belgium, Luxembourg, and the Netherlands) formed a regional economic group in 1944.

During the post-World War II years, formation and enlargement of European economic and political unions acquired more importance. In 1952, France, Germany (West), Italy, and the three Benelux countries created the European Coal and Steel Community (ECSC). In 1957, the European Economic Community (EEC) was formed by the above six countries (Treaty of Rome), which came into being on January 1, 1958. In 1973, the EEC was enlarged to include Britain, Denmark, and Ireland. In 1981, Greece became the tenth member and in 1986 Portugal and Spain became the eleventh and twelfth members of the EEC.

In order to avoid the historical pattern of oscillations between wars and order or chaos and stability, the EEC moved into political and other noneconomic cooperation agreements in addition to economic integration. It was renamed the European Community (EC) and is currently the European Union (EU). On January 1, 1995, Austria, Finland, and Sweden joined the EU.

The main questions to be considered here are the following: Is the EU becoming a fortress union, limiting itself to the above fifteen members, or it is expected to expand and engulf other European countries as well? Is enlargement creating more trade and investment among present and potential members, without diverting or reducing trade with other nonmember countries? Is the gradual EU enlargement to other European states working against deepening or closer cooperation among member states?

Our thesis is that the gradual enlargement of the EU creates more trade than it diverts and that the EU and similar groups may be considered as the pioneers and the catalysts of international economic and sociopolitical stability and development. They are the forerunners of global liberalization, as they open the way for cooperation among nations instead of generating isolation, protectionism, and economic and geopolitical deterioration.

TRADE CREATION AND TRADE DIVERSION

When part of the domestic production in a member country is replaced by lower-cost imports from another member country of a customs union or a common market, such as the EU, then we have the case of trade creation. When trade among members of the union increases but trade with nonmembers is reduced because lower-cost imports from nonmembers are replaced by higher-cost imports from members of the union, we have the case of trade diversion.

The expansion of the EU to other European countries is expected to create trade because part of production in some member countries will be replaced by lower-cost imports from other member countries. Moreover, as long as lower-cost imports from nonmember nations are not replaced by higher-cost imports from EU member nations significantly, trade diversion will not be extensive. Therefore, the net effect of EU enlargement, from the standpoint of welfare of the countries involved, is expected to be positive, as trade creation will be higher than trade diversion. It seems that, from the viewpoint of welfare gains of Europe, it would be beneficial for the EU and the other European countries to join and form a pan-European community from the Urals to Lisbon, because of the lower cost of production from specialization and economies of scale, cheap transportation and labor, and a huge pan-European market.

POTENTIAL NEW EU MEMBERS

EFTA and the EU

Three years after the creation of the European Economic Community, that is in 1960, the free trade area known as the European Free Trade Association

(EFTA) was formed by Austria, Britain, Denmark, Norway, Portugal, Sweden, and Switzerland. The EFTA (in Greek meaning seven) managed to implement free trade in industrial goods by 1967, but it permitted its members to retain their individual external tariffs. Such a policy leads to "trade deflection," that is, the entry of imports from outside the group into a low-tariff member of the association to avoid the high tariffs of other members of the group. Also, the EFTA was not effective enough to reduce restrictions on agricultural trade.

The EU, on the other hand, with common external tariffs and a more cohesive organization, was more successful than the EFTA. Nevertheless, free trade in industrial goods between the EU, with headquarters in Brussels, and EFTA, with headquarters in Geneva, was achieved by 1977. As mentioned previously, Britain and Denmark, as well as Ireland, joined the EU in 1973; whereas Finland, Iceland, and Liechtenstein (a tiny state of 28,000 people between Austria and Switzerland) joined the EFTA later. As a result of the dramatic economic and political changes in the former Soviet bloc countries, the EU and EFTA set up the "European Economic Space" and abolished trade and other restrictions. In order to enjoy the benefits of the Single European Market regarding free trade and movement of resources, as well as other advantages, Austria applied for EU membership in 1989, Sweden in 1991, and Finland in 1992, whereas Switzerland started negotiations toward membership in 1991. Although in a past referendum Norway voted against EU membership by 53 percent, as did Switzerland by 50.3 percent, both countries, as well as the other EFTA countries, are expected to join the EU, with which they have the largest amount of their foreign trade. Moreover, the dissolution of the Warsaw Pact and the democratization of the former Soviet bloc nations, as well as the formation of the Conference on Security and Cooperation in Europe by thirty-four nations, removed the obstacle of neutrality for Austria, Sweden, and other EFTA nations and opened the way for an early EU membership.

From an economic standpoint, the EFTA countries are at the same level or better than the advanced countries of the EU. The per capita GNP of the then EFTA countries in 1991 varied from $20,140 for Austria to $25,110 for Sweden and $33,610 for Switzerland, which was higher than the average of the EU. Moreover, inflationary rates are not much different and current account balances are comparable to those of the EU.[1]   Therefore, adjustment to the EU conditions is expected to be easy, with mutual trade and investment in the enlarged market of some 380 million people enhanced.

The economic and sociopolitical success of the EU encouraged other countries to apply for full membership or to consider joining the EU. Such countries, which must be European and have a democratic system, include not only members of the EFTA, which are at an equivalent level of development, but other European countries which are at a lower level of development than the EU, as will be explained later.[2]

It seems that the remaining EFTA countries, notably Norway and Switzerland, will join the Union in the near future, mainly because they have a similar economic and sociopolitical structure, while the largest part of their foreign transactions is with the EU. However, for other EU candidates more time of adjustment may be required. Moreover, faced with the dilemma of widening versus deepening, the EU decided at Maastricht on December 10, 1991, to subordinate negotiations for enlargement to those of closer cooperation among its members regarding the European Monetary Union (EMU) and the completion of the budgetary arrangements.

In the meantime, to help prepare the candidate countries for membership, the EU has put in place a number of agreements with the EFTA and other European countries. An important agreement with the EFTA was the European Economic Area (EEA), which gives access to the main advantages of the EU Single Market.

SOUTHERN MEDITERRANEAN APPLICANTS

Other countries on the periphery of Europe, such as Cyprus, Malta, and Turkey, want to join the Union and are in negotiations for EU membership. Cyprus signed an association agreement with the EU in 1972. Thereafter, a number of protocols have been signed, and Cypriot agricultural products, which make up 68 percent of total exports, are enjoying related benefits from the EU Mediterranean policy. Within ten years from the first protocol of 1987, tariffs are to be gradually reduced, quantitative restrictions eliminated, and commercial policies coordinated.

Cyprus, the tourist resort island of Aphrodite (the goddess of love), applied for EU membership in the summer of 1990. However, the unlawful occupation of 38 percent of Cyprus by Turkish troops presents problems for the EU membership of the whole island, including the Turkish-Cypriot minority of 18 percent.

Malta, which signed an association agreement with the EU in 1970, applied for membership in the summer of 1990, a week after Cyprus. Thereafter, the Nationalist Party and Prime Minister Edward Fenech Adami followed a pro-EU policy, a deviation from the previous pro-Libyan policy. The economy of Malta, with low inflation and unemployment (around 4 percent), a per capita GNP of $6,365 (in 1991), and 75 percent of its trade with the EU, is in a good position to join the EU, as is Cyprus.

Turkey, an associate member of the EU since 1964, applied for membership in 1987 and expects to be a member by 1997, when the association agreement expires. However, the EU Commission and the Council declared that both the EU and Turkey are not ready to negotiate enlargement. The main reasons are human rights violations, primarily against the Kurdish population, the strained relations with Greece over Cyprus, and the expected large numbers of migrant workers into Europe from a rapidly growing Turkish population. Moreover, the lower level of development of Turkey would raise budget problems for the EU concerning the Common Agricultural Policy (CAP) and the structural funds.[3]

The per capita GNP of Turkey is very low ($1,780 in 1991) compared to that of all EU members, and many years are needed to catch up with even the poorest EU members. Nevertheless, the new role of secular Turkey against fundamentalist tendencies and its expected influence on the Asian republics of the former Soviet Union (Azerbaijan, Kazakhstan, Kyrgyzstan, Tajikistan, Turkmenistan, and Uzbekistan), with common religious and cultural traditions, makes Turkey a crucial country for the geopolitical stability of the area. It seems that if Cyprus enter the EU, Turkey will have a better chance to be an EU member, assuming that it takes the necessary measures for economic and sociopolitical improvement. Already Greece has lifted its blockade and Turkey has access to the EU related financial provisions. In the meantime, Turkey should stop its military aggression against neighboring countries, take its troops out of Cyprus, and respect human rights, particularly of the Kurdish population of twelve million, according to EU principles.

EASTERN EUROPEAN COUNTRIES

Young democracies of the former COMECON countries of Eastern Europe and the Balkans, which arose after the collapse of the former Soviet Union, are interested in joining the EU. Not only Poland, Hungary, and the Czech and Slovak republics, but the Balkan countries as well (Albania, Bulgaria, Romania, and the former Yugoslav republics) want to be members of the EU. However, their per capita GNP is far lower than that of the EU countries. This means that a number of years will be needed for their adjustment in order to be ready to join the EU. In response to my letters to the EU leaders urging a speedy acceptance of all the Balkan countries to stamp out conflicts, President Mitterrand of France and Prime Minister Major of Britain emphasized the importance of my proposal to accept the Balkan countries in the EU, assuming the fulfillment of certain requirements.

All these countries are engaged in drastic economic and political reforms and in a shift from trade with the former COMECON countries toward trade with the EU, with which they currently have the largest part of their foreign trade. Recently, interim agreements (European agreements) have been signed or are under negotiations by each of these countries and the EU in order to facilitate gradual adjustment toward full membership. These agreements need to be ratified by the EU and the partner countries.

Similar desires toward EU membership were expressed by the European republics of the former Soviet Union, mainly Belarus, Moldova, and Ukraine, as well as the Baltic countries (Estonia, Latvia, and Lithuania) and, to a lesser extent, Russia, Georgia, and Armenia.

Privatizations and other reforms are used by all the European countries of the previous Soviet bloc to adjust their systems to the market economies of the EU and the West. Such reforms include the transfer of shares of state enterprises to individuals through sales in auctions or at low prices and, in some cases, free distributions.[4] Moreover, in order to increase work incentives and avoid labor disturbances, employees and workers are given shares free, or at a discount, by the companies in which they work. Similar privatizations and employee participations take place in almost all EU countries, including Britain (Thatcherism), France (popular capitalism), Germany (labor-capital management or *Mitbestimmung*), Greece, and Spain. Also, in the United States, there are more than 9,000 companies with about eleven million employees under employee stock ownership plans (ESOPs), and in Japan there is a similar system of "share economy."

The EU enlargement toward the Eastern European countries, including the Balkans and eventually Russia and other former Soviet republics, is related to the stability and growth of their economies. The instability of their currencies makes convertibility in strong currencies difficult and trade and investment with the EU and other countries problematic. In order to avoid the problems created for Germany in the 1920s, when it was left unable to trade with its neighbors, financial and other support is needed. This may take the form of a plan similar to the U.S. Marshall Plan for Western Europe after World War II or a policy of establishing currency advisement committees by the EU, similar to the currency boards of John Maynard Keynes (the father of macroeconomics) for Russia in 1918.

Like Germany and Japan, as late starters, the former Soviet bloc countries can go directly to the most advanced technology, such as fiber optics and digital communications, computers, and other innovative techniques which are bolstering entrepreneurship. A well-educated and cheapwork force, available natural resources, high expected demand for products and services, and a marketplace joined with incoming new technology are likely to lead to a high level of development, equivalent to that of the EU.

There is a high potential for growth in the former planned economies of Europe, particularly in Russia with its oil, gold, and other valuable resources. For example, only 40 percent of the 4,000 oil wells are operational and large reserves of oil and gas exist in Siberia and other areas. EU companies, such as Royal Dutch/Shell, British Petroleum, AGIP, and Statoil, along with automobile, telecommunications, and many other firms, may be considered the pioneers of EU enlargement. Moreover, the construction of the gas pipeline, transferring natural gas from Russia to EU countries, will necessitate closer economic and political cooperation of the countries involved.

Other EU firms, which are aggressively moving into the countries of the former planned economies of Europe, include Fiat SpA of Italy, investing in Poland and Russia; Volkswagen AG, Mercedes-Benz AG, and Siemens of Germany, as well as Renault and Air France in former Czechoslovakia; and in

Hungary the Tengelmann Group of Germany (together with Holland's Philips and Finland's Nokia) in retail business, the Deutsche Bundespost Telecom (in joint venture with Ameritech), the Mirror Group publishing firm of Britain, and the Heineken beer company of Holland. All these and a host of other large and small EU firms are paving the way for closer cooperation and the eventual integration of Europe.[5]

Financial institutions, such as the European Bank for Reconstruction and Development (established in Paris in 1990 to help finance the development of the former planned economies of Europe), the Banque Nationale de Paris and the Crédit Lyonnais of France, the Bank of Macedonia-Thrace of Greece and many other EU banks are establishing subsidiaries or providing loans to investors in the expected profitable ventures of Eastern and other European countries. Moreover, EU governments are subsidizing private investment in the former planned economies, as, for example, Greece is doing in Albania.

ENLARGEMENT VERSUS DEEPENING

There is skepticism regarding the movement for EU expansion and, to some extent, a setback, mainly because expansion may work against deeper integration and because of the instability and ethnic conflicts in some European nations (as, for example, in the former Yugoslav republics). However, member states of the EU and primarily Germany seem to favor both closer unity and gradual enlargement of the Union.

It seems that there is no better alternative to a European federal state from the standpoint of economies of large-scale production, market expansion, and peaceful coexistence through liquidation of chauvinism and old-fashioned nationalism. A stage-by-stage pan-European confederation, with the member states maintaining their role in internal matters, without creating a huge bureaucracy in Brussels, would be the proper policy for the creation of a "United States of Europe."

In order to make enlargement feasible and successful, the EU should accommodate other European countries which aspire to join it, as long as cohesion of the Union would not be strained by bringing in new members which might overload its budget. This means that priority should be given to countries at the same level of development and with homogeneous institutions, such as the EFTA countries. Furthermore, the admission of new members will require adaptations in the numerical proportions of the EU institutions, particularly the Commission, for effective decision making and governance of an enlarged Union.

EFFECTS OF THE MAASTRICHT TREATY

An EU monetary and political union, which seemed to delay enlargement, was introduced by the Maastricht Treaty, which was signed by the EU government heads in December 1991 and the respective ministers of finance and foreign affairs on February 7, 1992. It provides for the European Monetary Union (EMU) and the political union of the member states, with people being citizens of the European Union; inflation cannot exceed the average of the lowest three countries by 1.5 percent; the budget deficit must be no more than 3 percent of GDP a year before the commencement of EMU; and public debt cannot exceed 60 percent of GDP. Also, it provides for a common foreign and security policy and increased power for the European Parliament.[6]

After its final ratification by all EU members, the Maastricht Treaty is in force from September 1993. It aims at the establishment of a single currency (the European currency unit, or ECU) and a central bank by 1997 or by 1999 at the latest, which is a far-reaching phase of integration difficult to achieve. As soon as the finance and budgetary reforms are completed, negotiations with other candidates, for membership will begin, particularly the remaining EFTA countries and the new democracies of Eastern Europe.

To succeed in the strategy of closer integration, currently the EU concentrates on internal economic and sociopolitical matters at the neglect of enlargement. This is so because the entry of more members at this stage would complicate matters, mainly monetary and budgetary. Moreover, poorer member states (Greece, Ireland, Portugal, Spain) would object to the acceptance of other equivalent- or lower-income countries, such as those of Eastern Europe and Turkey, because of the expected shift in development assistance. However, through time, stability and growth in the candidate countries will reduce objections and open the way toward EU enlargement.

CREATION OF OTHER REGIONAL UNIONS NECESSITATES ENLARGEMENT

The formation of the North American Free Trade Agreement (NAFTA) by Canada, the United States, and Mexico, as well as the Asian-Pacific Rim (Japan and other neighboring nations), and the little-known Asia Pacific Economic Cooperation (APEC), with Australia, Canada, China, Japan, the United States and ten other Pacific countries, necessitates expansion of the EU for a tripolar world competition.

The Commonwealth of Independent States (CIS) of the former Soviet republics, although presently weak, may be strong enough to be antagonistic to the EU in the future. Expectations are, though, that some of its members, particularly the European ones, would apply for EU membership. Likewise, the obscure Union of the Black Sea nations, mainly Armenia, Bulgaria, Georgia,

Greece, Romania, and Turkey, is not expected to have much importance. This group may rather be considered as complementary to the EU.

With the expansion of the EU to gradually engulf the whole of Europe, the role of NATO, which was created to "keep the Americans in, the Russians out, and the Germans down," should be adjusted to new geopolitical conditions. Perhaps its new role will be to resist the siren song of ethnic conflicts and discourage military dictatorships in the countries of the former Soviet bloc. Nevertheless, the enlargement of NATO, parallel to that of the EU, should include not only the Eastern European nations, but Russia as well, first as partners of peace and eventually as full members.[7]

FUTURE EXPECTATIONS

The enlargement of the EU is expected to lead to large markets, technological dissemination, and economic growth, as well as a border-free and peaceful Europe. The gap between the poor and the rich countries of Europe will be reduced and ethnic and other conflicts will be stamped out. The growing interdependence of nations and the development of information science support the expansion of economic-political unions as forerunners of universal free trade and peaceful coexistence. Such trends encourage free trade enthusiasts and panegyrists and doom narrow-minded nationalists and protectionists.

The gradual expansion of the EU toward the advanced EFTA countries (Norway and Switzerland), the southern Mediterranean applicants, and eventually the low-income new democracies of the former Soviet bloc will create a pan-European union, able to compete with the NAFTA and similar regional groups, which are expected to expand as well. The radical economic and political reforms in Eastern Europe, including the Balkans, and the former Soviet Union will offer future opportunities for EU trade and investment and an improvement of all the economies involved.[8] Nevertheless, in the short run, emphasis will be given to closer monetary and fiscal cooperation of the EU members and the expansion to some countries which are close to the EU, economically and geographically. *Ceteris paribus*, enlargement to other European states will depend on the success of the EU in the process of integration.

It seems that in an enlarged EU, trade creation will occur more than trade diversion, productivity will increase, and socioeconomic inequalities will be reduced. Already, EU agreements (European agreements) with other European partners provide for the removal of tariffs and other restrictions, financial support, and technical cooperation between the Union and other candidates for membership.

Capitalism, which was born in Europe, is changing to a new popular form. This is the era of Eurocapitalism, with a drive to an enlarged market, a single currency, and a democratic system, as Aristotle, Adam Smith, and other great thinkers envisioned.

NOTES

1. For the performance of the EU countries, see Nicholas V. Gianaris, *The European Community and the United States: Economic Relations* (New York: Praeger, 1991), Chapter 4.

2. More details in Anna Michalski and Helen Wallace, *The European Community: The Challenge of Enlargement* (London: Royal Institute of International Affairs, 1992), pp. 79-112.

3. Ibid, pp. 120-29. Also, "Turkey," *The Financial Times*, May 21, 1992; and *Europe*, No. 5759, June 27, 1992, p. 7.

4. Valuable information in Jeffrey Sachs, *Capitalism in Europe after Communism* (Cambridge, MA: M.I.T. Press, 1991), Chapters 2-4.

5. Jane Perlez, "Western Ventures Helping East's Phones to Ring," *New York Times*, December 21, 1993, D5. Also, Nicholas V. Gianaris, "Helping Eastern Europe Helps the West," *New York Times*, February 8, 1990, p. A28.

6. Further review in Commission of the European Communities, *From Single Market to European Union* (Brussels: Office for Official Publications of the European Communities, 1992), pp. 13-20; and Wolfgang H. Reinicke, *Building a New Europe* (Washington, DC: The Brookings Institution, 1992), Chapter 9.

7. Additional comments in Alexei Pushkov, "Building a New NATO at Russia's Expense," *Foreign Affairs*, Vol. 73, No. 1, January 1994, pp. 173-74.

8. For reforms in Russia and other former Soviet republics, see Nicholas V. Gianaris, *The European Community, Eastern Europe and Russia: Economic and Political Changes* (Westport, CT: Praeger, 1994), Chapters 9-10; and *Contemporary Economic Systems: A Regional and Country Approach* (Westport, CT: Praeger, 1993), Chapter 9. Also, his *Modern Capitalism: Privatization, Employee Ownership, and Industrial Democracy* (Westport, CT: Praeger, 1995), Chapter 5; and *The Balkan Countries: Economic Changes and Geopolitical Dynamics* (Westport, CT: Praeger, 1996), Chapters 5-6.

REFERENCES

Commission of the European Communities. 1992. *From Single Market to European Union*. Brussels: Office for Official Publications of the European Communities.
Gianaris, Nicholas V. "Helping Eastern Europe Helps the West." *New York Times*, February 8, 1990, p. A28.
———. 1991. *The European Community and the United States: Economic Relations*. New York: Praeger.
———. 1993. *Contemporary Economic Systems: A Regional and Country Approach*. Westport, CT: Praeger.

———. 1994. *The European Community, Eastern Europe and Russia: Economic and Political Changes*. Westport, CT: Praeger.

———. 1995. *Modern Capitalism: Privatization, Employee Ownership, and Industrial Democracy*. Westport, CT: Praeger.

———. 1996. *The Balkan Countries: Economic Changes and Geopolitical Dynamics*. Westport, CT: Praeger.

International Monetary Fund (IMF). *International Financial Statistics*, various issues.

Michalski, Anna and Helen Wallace. 1992. *The European Community: The Challenge of Enlargement*. London: Royal Institute of International Affairs.

Perlez, Jane. "Western Ventures Helping East's Phone to Ring." *New York Times*, December 21, 1993, p. D5.

Pushkov, Alexei. "Building a New NATO at Russia's Expense." *Foreign Affairs*, Vol. 73, No. 1, January 1994, pp. 173-74.

Reinicke, Wolfgang H. 1992. *Building a New Europe*. Washington, DC: The Brookings Institution.

Sachs, Jeffrey. 1991. *Capitalism in Europe after Communism*. Cambridge, MA: M.I.T. Press.

World Bank. *World Development Report*. New York: Oxford University Press, for the World Bank, annual.

14

Return to Decadent Europe: Debating Europe's Security

Kostas Messas

INTRODUCTION

Contrary to expectations, stability in Europe did not appear to be the natural by-product of the end of the Cold War. It is becoming increasingly clear that it is threatened by regional conflicts due to ethnic disputes and aggressive nationalism. More and more, the EU (European Union), the United States, NATO, Russia, and the UN are preoccupied, although in varying degrees, with finding a solution to the war in former Yugoslavia, hoping to prevent it from becoming regional and/or international. Despite some minor successes toward cease fire, the war rages on.

The conflict in Yugoslavia has become the litmus test that will determine whether Europe can contain aggressive nationalism, devise ways of peacefully handling nationalist aspirations, and, ultimately, secure its own stability. Thus far, regional and international collective security bodies, such as NATO and the UN, have failed to intervene with credibility in the Yugoslav war. The EU appeared both unwilling and unable to do very much, primarily because of the varying preferences of the member states. The United States, although still the source of leadership in Western Europe's security, hoped that the Europeans would take the leadership in settling the Yugoslav crisis. Finally, Russia has been preoccupied primarily with sorting out its national interests and less with the Yugoslav conflict. The failure of these countries and organizations to act as brokers of peace, either singularly or collectively, raises serious concerns whether and to what extent they will succeed in restoring stability in Europe.

UNDERSTANDING EUROPE'S PREDICAMENT

Europe's new threat, namely aggressive nationalism, is a complex phenomenon. It contains a variety of nuances of national consciousness, national identity, geographical identification, and patriotism. In addition, it appears to mean different things to different people. Ethnic groups in Eastern Europe embrace nationalism as something positive, perhaps because it allows them to assert their identities; Western Europeans, concerned about instability in the region, consider it to be something negative. Moreover, nationalism generates both strongly positive and negative feelings within the same country. In Russia, for example, the ultranationalist fervor of Zhirinovksy and his voters is not shared equally by the reformists.

Historically, European nationalism[1] has contributed to excessive militarism and imperialism on several occasions. Major historical examples include the Napoleonic Wars, the two short Balkan Wars, and the two world wars.[2] The resurgence of heightened nationalism in Yugoslavia provides testimony to nationalism's unique capacity to persist and to acquire regional and international dimensions. Moreover, it demonstrates Europe's proneness to the destructive components of nationalism. This does not necessarily mean that Europe will follow the path of its ethnic destiny and return to the worlds of the Napoleonic, Balkan, and world wars or suffer a new epidemic of nationalist conflicts.[3] It does mean, however, that Europe must seek ways to actively address the latest wave of nationalism and extremism.

In Yugoslavia, there were nationalist movements initiated by all linguistic, religious, and cultural groups in all the republics.[4] The nationalist government in Serbia is said to have contributed to the conflict because instead of "a constructive policy of negotiation and economic development," it favored "a policy of nationalistic confrontation."[5]

Yugoslavia is not alone in possessing ethnic and national groups that desire their own independent state and/or wish to pursue nationalist-inspired foreign policies. Similar groups exist across Eastern Europe and Russia. Examples abound. The presence of ethnic Hungarians in Slovakia, estimated at 600,000, has already resulted in ethnic strife. In response to Slovak Hungarians' calls for greater political and economic rights, Slovak nationalists have responded with determined resistance.[6]

Because there are various ethnic groups residing within each other's borders, there is a possibility of ethnic strife, due to secessionist movements, in all of the former republics of the Soviet Union, including Russia. Ethnic Russians, for example, reside in all of the other former republics; strong ethnic Russian minorities exist in Estonia, Kazakhstan, Latvia, and Ukraine, where they make up 30 percent, 41 percent, 34 percent and 20 percent of their respective populations. There are fears that the high concentration of ethnic Russians in the "near abroad" may lead Russia into an "imperial temptation."[7]

The fears for a revival of imperialist Russia were intensified in December 12, 1993, when parliamentary elections resulted in a strong nationalist opposition headed by Vladimir Zhirinovsky. Zhirinovsky, in the fervor of nationalistic rhetoric, spoke "of restoring Russia to the imperial frontiers of 1900, when Russia included parts of contemporary Poland and Finland . . . [warning] that denying Russia its historical borders will only lead to war . . . [and proclaiming that] the mere acceptance of the dissolution of the Soviet Union into sovereign successor states is an act of treason."[8] Whether he proves to be "a harmless clown or an evil clown"[9] remains to be seen. Yet, for the reform-minded political leaders and intellectuals in Russia, Eastern Europe, and the West it would be dangerous to dismiss Zhirinovsky and the powerful support given to him by Russia's voters.[10]

Ukraine and Kazakhstan, both of which enjoy the status of a regional nuclear power, display the same brand of assertive nationalism and nationalist-inspired foreign policies toward Russia. In both cases, the resurgence of nationalism takes place in an environment that is characterized by political violence and a stumbling economy.[11] Hard-liners both in Ukraine and Kazakhstan view their nuclear arsenal as a source of growing self-confidence, but reformers, both within and outside, express serious concerns.

Eastern Europe is afraid of nationalist movements, potential Russian neoimperialism, and the possibility of ethnic wars throughout the former Soviet Union. These fears compelled Eastern European leaders to seek membership in NATO and the EU. Their objectives are quite clear: to benefit from NATO's security guarantees and from EU's prosperity. NATO and EU leaders, too, have been compelled to find ways of protecting their accomplishments in the areas of security and prosperity. Russia is interested in preventing internal and regional nationalist movements from endangering its political and economic reforms. The United States, as the main source of leadership in NATO, recognizes the need for a credible strategy of dealing with ethnic conflicts outside the Atlantic area. It is apparent that they are all compelled to find an antidote against the potential threats of ambitious nationalism. The question is no longer whose responsibility it is to do so, but how best can the EU, the United States, NATO, and Russia cooperate in designing and delivering it. It is increasingly clear, therefore, that (i) the main security objective in Europe is to devise a security framework which will enable Europeans to deal with regional tensions, prevent these from becoming armed conflicts, and determine under what conditions military force might be used to stop them without suffering setbacks; (ii) the EU, the United States, NATO, and Russia will have to sort out their respective commitments and interests and join forces in spelling out a security policy that will achieve Europe's security; (iii) their collective efforts will have to be expanded to secure an even greater role for the UN (United Nations) and Europe's various regional security arrangements, such as the WEU (Western European Union) and the CSCE (Conference on Security and Cooperation in Europe); (iv) they must get to the root of the problem of

Europe's tenacious nationalism by analyzing it as being primarily ethnic and linguistic in nature as opposed to territorial; and, subsequently, (v) they must identify, recognize, and protect the status of minorities.

MAJOR ACTORS

NATO

NATO outlived the Soviet threat and, contrary to some assessments, continues to be the only viable collective security system in Europe. With a new range of threats, NATO is challenged to adjust its basic mission. In the past, NATO's activities were restricted within a particular territory;[12] today, NATO is challenged to respond to growing security concerns outside the Euro-Atlantic community. The fighting in Yugoslavia is clearly outside NATO's treaty-prescribed territory. In order for NATO to work effectively in ending the Yugoslav conflict, it must expand its mandate to include Central and Eastern Europe. NATO is in effect made to "realize that the projection of stability to Central and Eastern Europe is the most important current challenge facing the Euro-Atlantic community."[13]

The issues of how best to expand NATO's mandate in out-of-territory crises and what types of political and military reforms are needed to guarantee it are actively being debated. NATO strategists promise that the new NATO will[14] (i) consist of two pillars, the United States and Europe; (ii) assist the European pillar, namely the WEU, develop into a viable partner of the United States; (iii) assist Europe's integration; (iv) seek strong institutional links with complementary European institutions, such as the North Atlantic Cooperation Council (NACC)[15] the CSCE,[16] the WEU,[17] and the Council of Europe;[18] (v) seek strong institutional links with the UN; and (vi) achieve Europe's security through cooperative arrangements based on division of labor and costs.

Meanwhile, Lithuania and afterward Poland, Bulgaria, Romania, Hungary, the Czech Republic, and Slovakia have applied for membership in NATO. Their main reasons for seeking membership include the threat of potential ethnic rivalries and the specter of Russian domination should the transition to democracy not succeed. The applicants have confronted NATO with a double challenge: first, to what extent to integrate Eastern Europe into its structures and, second, how to do so without provoking Russia. Full membership would mean providing security guarantees against the growing danger of ethnic rivalries and invariably against Russia.

Within the overall debate on stability in Europe, the reactions to the applications were mixed. For some, "the best way to preserve stability [would be] with the rapid integration of Eastern European nations into NATO."[19] Others argued that "a strong and democratic Russia [would be] the strongest guarantee of peace and stability in Europe."[20] Russian leaders reacted by saying that "they would view NATO expansion as a security threat that could spark an arms buildup."[21] NATO rejected the applications for full membership and offered, instead, the possibility of defense-related contacts through the U.S.-sponsored "Partnership for Peace" program. Participation in the program, formally endorsed at the NATO summit in Brussels, between January 10 and 11, 1994, was offered to the Eastern European countries and to Russia, as well as to the other republics of the post-Soviet Union.[22] At this point, it is unclear how far integration will go.

European Union

The process of integration within the EU (formerly known as the EC or European Community) gave its institutions valuable experience on building a framework within which nationalist aspirations are curtailed. Membership has been voluntary. Being a member state of the EU has meant to willingly accept, although at times reluctantly, some restrictions upon one's sovereignty in the name of prosperity and stability.[23]

In clear contrast to the Western European countries, ambitious nationalism in Eastern Europe was curtailed by the rigid structure of the Cold War. With the Cold War over, and with no framework in place, either political or military, within which to cooperate, Eastern European countries are subjected to the negative aspects of nationalism. The overall situation constitutes a serious barrier to the integration of the East with the West and retards the process of integration already under way in the West.[24] It is clear that integration requires a stable and secure framework.

In order to safeguard its accomplishments, it is imperative for the EU to make Europe safe for integration. It will have to consider accepting in its fold Eastern European countries interested in joining the EU. Eastern European countries have already stepped up pressure for closer ties.[25] The EU can respond favorably and demonstrate its goodwill toward Eastern European countries through increased multilateral cooperation at first and eventually through full membership. Through stronger ties, the EU can hope "to prevent the failure of the political and economic transformation in central and east European countries"[26] and, thus, help create political and economic stability in the region.

In addition to the membership option, the EU is challenged to consider military responses to the upheavals from the East. To do so, it may have to use force in a credible manner. In order to develop and maintain military credibility, it needs to develop "converging foreign and, subsequently, defense policies,"[27] institutional reforms which rest ultimately on the coordinated political and financial commitment of the member states. The EU maintained always that those achievements would be the logical outgrowth of the creation of a common political will. With new security problems in the region, the EU realizes that it no longer possesses that flexibility. It will have to keep on thrusting toward a common political will, which was painfully absent from EU's policy initiatives toward the Yugoslav conflict.

Most importantly, it will have to intensify efforts of building up the WEU, EU's military arm, from its present rudimentary stage into a fully developed military organization. This clearly requires the member states to uphold the Maastricht Treaty, which gives the WEU "a new impetus as the coordinating agent for the security policy of the European Union."[28] With the WEU, Europeans can hope to create the groundwork for a real strategic culture which will enable them, if necessary, to intervene militarily in regional crises.

The need to forge ahead with a European defense system by the Europeans has also been reinforced by a change in U.S. policy toward Europe. It is becoming increasingly clear that Americans wish for the European leaders to formulate their own post-Cold War security strategy. The reduction of the Soviet threat has revived old arguments about the perceived unevenness in the strategic situation of U.S.-European relations and on the need to pursue a foreign policy that is closer to its national interests.

That was precisely the message that President Clinton delivered to the Europeans during the NATO summit in January 1994. In his various comments about security in Europe and Eastern Europe's integration into the EU, the president appeared to be saying "that Western Europe must begin taking responsibility for a broader Europe's economic well-being, political development, and security."[29]

Is the EU ready for the new leadership challenge? European leaders, unable and unwilling to assume Europe's strategic leadership mantle, appear to be saying, "at this stage we [in Western Europe] are not up and ready to go."[30] Strong supporters of European defense by the Europeans, such as the French, question "the readiness and enthusiasm of [their] European partners for a 'European defense identity.'"[31] Lingering recession and heavy defense cutbacks are the reasons most frequently cited for this predicament. There are questions, indeed, as to whether the EU's economic resources are adequate for the EU to develop its own defense posture and to prepare Eastern European countries for full membership without suffering major economic setbacks.

The United States

With the end of the Soviet threat, many Americans, within and outside the government, hoped that the government would pay greater attention to domestic issues and conduct a foreign policy much closer to the country's national interests. Both of these were to have implications for United States' long-term relationship with Western Europe and its status as a superpower. In order to pursue a domestic agenda, such as the ambitious health care reforms, the Clinton administration has implemented heavy defense cutbacks which have also affected America's military presence in Europe.

Overall, the new direction in the U.S. policy contains the following elements: (i) a desire to benefit from the reduction of the Soviet threat by allocating funds from defense to domestic reforms; (ii) a desire to redefine the long-term relationship between the U.S. and Western Europe by asking the Europeans, and the EU in particular, to take the lead in defining Europe's security policy; (iii) a desire to reduce its contribution to the European security burden; and (iv) a recognition that because of political and economic considerations, the United States is no longer able and willing to exercise the full range of its power capabilities in the international arena.

As the initial euphoria of the communist collapse eroded, many within and outside the country warned the United States to be careful in implementing its new policy. America's prosperity and security, it has been argued, depend on long-term relationships, such as the relationship with Western Europe, and must not be overshadowed by domestic interests. The United States and the EU are each other's major trading partner and, invariably, they are mutually responsible for each other's well-being. Maintaining a peaceful and stable Europe rests primarily with the Europeans; but the United States has vested interests in the region, enough to warrant its continued, albeit redefined, participation in Europe's security matters. With the EU unable and unwilling to assume the leadership role in shaping Europe's security policy at this particular time, the prudent thing will be for the United States to continue to provide leadership in Europe's security through NATO and for the EU to carry a fairer proportion of the burden until such time when the baton of leadership in Europe's security can safely be passed on.

Russia

Internally, the Soviet Union enjoyed a relatively high degree of stability. This was accomplished primarily through the establishment of particular economic, political, and military structures. The rigidity of those structures inhibited the type of internal conflicts that were dramatically illustrated by the conflict in Yugoslavia. Externally, the Soviet Union succeeded in staving off threats from the Western Allies, thus preventing the Cold War from evolving into a hot war.

The disintegration of the Soviet Union allowed Russia to break free from the old structures and pursue a new course of economic, political, and military development. It hoped to grow economically strong and politically democratic. The disintegration of the old structures resulted instead in political violence, magnified by a resurgence of nationalism, and religious intolerance. All of these continue to inhibit the consolidation of the postcommunist institutions and to pose threats to Russian society.

Russia's predicament contributes significantly to the security dilemmas in Eastern and Western Europe. The greatest challenge that Europe faces is to discern with clarity Russia's national interests. Internal developments provide support for rival conceptions of Russia's intentions. President Yeltsin, who is genuinely committed to market and democratic reforms, supports an image of a Russia that will pursue its interests within a framework of cooperation with Europe. His archrival, radical nationalist Vladimir Zhirinovsky, supports fears of a serious ideological conflict within Russia, the possibility of the transition from authoritarian to democratic rule going bad, and of Russia becoming more hard-line in its foreign policies. He may very well turn out to be nothing more than a demagogue, but his election to the parliament with a high vote total prompted alarm in the EU, the United States, NATO, and Eastern Europe.

The problem of rival conceptions of Russia's intentions is complicated further by uncertainties surrounding the role of the military and Russia's ongoing difficulties with Ukraine. With regard to the former, it is unclear whether and to what extent the armed forces support democratization in Russia. It is feared that budget cuts, due to limited resources, may prompt members of the professional officer corps to assume control of politics in order to safeguard their institutions and corporate interests.[32] "Already there are some fears that the influence of the Russian military was beginning to turn Yeltsin to more anti-American foreign policies."[33]

With regard to Ukraine, it is uncertain what it will do. It is widely known that it fosters fierce anti-Russian sentiments and, most importantly, that it is intransigent about giving up its entire nuclear arsenal and settling peacefully its disputes over the former Soviet fleet in Crimea. As was already discussed, the EU and NATO too are eager to convince Ukraine to give up its independent nuclear arsenal. This is already a major U.S. policy goal. It is clear that the nuclear threat is not over.[34] In fact, there are serious questions about whether and to what extent the Russian government has control over its own nuclear arsenal and material. It has been strongly suggested that with organized crime on the rise in Russia nuclear terrorism is a distinctive possibility.[35]

The combined effect of these fears and uncertainties prompted Eastern European leaders to seek speedy membership in NATO. NATO, as was seen, is facing a great challenge, that is, how best to accommodate the Eastern European countries without isolating Russia and setting in motion a process that would threaten Russia's democracy, provide inadvertent support for Zhirinovsky, and complicate further Europe's search for stability. The security debate in Europe is definitely being affected by Russia's political, economic, and military choices. Conversely, Russia's success or failure with reforms and domestic and regional stability is, in part, determined by the security debate in Europe. There is perhaps no other alternative but to maintain bilateral and multilateral ties with and between the EU, NATO, the United States, and Russia as a matter of major policy at the highest levels. It is imperative, at least, that the United States and Russia, both military superpowers, maintain ties with each other and their respective allies.

CONCLUSION

The end of the Cold War failed to deliver guarantees of uninterrupted security and stability in Europe. The political vacuum that was left behind was quickly occupied by ethnic tensions. The disintegration of Yugoslavia and the ensuing civil war between the various factions in Bosnia-Herzegovina exposed Europe to the growing dangers of those tensions. Europe failed to prevent Yugoslavia's ethnic tension from degenerating into an armed conflict and, thus far, it has failed to stop the war. These important setbacks are clear signs that Europeans cannot take their stability and security for granted. It is imperative that they devise a security strategy that will spell out their security requirements and a course of action to fulfill those requirements. At this time, Europeans cannot do it alone.

It appears, however, that the end of the Cold War gave rise to unprecedented opportunities for more collective responses to security and stability. Support for those collective arrangements will have to be established through a major policy by each political actor in the region. The Europeans will have to seize the moment.

By implication, the security of the EU, NATO, Central Europe, Eastern Europe, and Russia ought to be linked and must be pursued through available collective security bodies such as the UN, NATO, WEU, and the CSCE. There are various compelling reasons that encourage such international conflict management. Collective responses (i) can help create a neutral political environment; (ii) keep in check the efforts of some actors who, in the interest of achieving their foreign policy objectives, hinder the peaceful resolution of the conflict, as may be the case, for example, with the arms-producing nations; (iii) are more suitable to multilayered preventive diplomacy, negotiation, and mediation, all of which are important approaches to conflict prevention and management, (iv) possess the possibility of delivering fair peacekeeping; (v) encourage a change in values that makes possible the "rejection of violence as a tool of power", places emphasis on mediation of disputes, and provides incentives for cooperative behavior; (vi) can be cost-effective due to the division of labor; (vii) can limit the possibility of unilateral military interventions, both small- and large-scale, by emphasizing collective use of force when force is necessary; and (viii) discourage the arms race.

In dealing with ethnic tensions and conflicts, the bodies of the collective response can be expected to respond fairly to a set of challenges, including the following: (i) to have a comprehensive understanding of the full spectrum of the crisis through a careful identification and study of the relevant ethnic groups and their histories, policies and activities; (ii) to recognize and guarantee the status of minorities and foster respect for human rights and for the existing borders; (iii) to act before the tension reaches an irreversible status quo; (iv) to develop criteria, which will be applied consistently, to determine whether and when force should be used; (v) to develop the institutional links between collective bodies, secure the political will of their members, and outline the financial commitment of the members, taking into consideration their simultaneous memberships in more than one collective body; (vi) to have an assessment of each other's military capabilities so as to avoid duplication of efforts, using NATO's standing naval forces, for example, to provide support to UN, which has not yet developed an effective naval peacekeeping component; (vii) to develop institutional arrangements that will facilitate political decision making and military command; (viii) to formulate a rationale that will spell precisely how and under whose auspices collective military action will take place; and (ix) to explore the possibility of making the UN the main agent for collective action.

Europe in general and Central and Eastern Europe in particular will not necessarily be overcome by tenacious nationalistic movements. Ethnic tensions do not necessarily have to degenerate to armed conflicts. Yugoslavia's civil war can be resolved and Yugoslavia-type conflicts can be avoided. One needs to understand that nationalist movements are not an epidemic that can be treated directly once and for all. Their cure requires protracted efforts and patience. NATO and the EU possess enough military and economic resources, which, if coordinated, could form a temporary bulwark against such ethnic conflicts. What Europe needs, instead, is a comprehensive framework of security and stability within which European unification can be realized. An achievement of that magnitude can only be accomplished through political, economic, and military cooperation among the major actors in the region.

NOTES

1. My use of "nationalism" is based on Stephen Van Evera's conceptualization that views nationalism "as a political movement having two characteristics: (1) individual members give their primary loyalty to their own ethnic or national community and (2) these ethnic or national communities desire their own independent state." See Stephen Van Evera, "Hypotheses on Nationalism and War," *International Security*, Vol. 18, No. 4, Spring 1994, p. 6.

2. Despite the proliferation of written works on nationalism, there has been very little attention paid to the association between nationalism and war. Recent exceptions include Barry R. Posen, "Nationalism, the Mass Army, and Military Power," *International Security*, Vol. 18, No. 2, Fall 1993, pp. 80-124; and Stephen Van Evera, "Hypotheses on Nationalism and War," *International Security*, Vol. 18, No. 4, Spring 1994, pp. 5-39.

3. Arguments against such realist scenarios are provided by Ernst B. Haas, "Nationalism: An Instrumental Social Construction," *Millennium: Journal of International Studies*, Vol. 22, No. 3, Winter 1993, pp. 505-45; and Richard Ned Lebow, "The Long

Peace, the End of the Cold War, and the Failure of Realism," *International Organiza-tion*, Vol. 48, No. 2, Spring 1994, pp. 249-77.

4. For a discussion of the disintegration of Yugoslavia, see Milica Z. Bookman, "War and Peace: The Divergent Breakups of Yugoslavia and Czechoslovakia," *Journal of Peace Research*, Vol. 31, No. 2, 1994, pp. 175-187.

5. Nicholas J. Miller, "Serbia Chooses Aggression," *Orbis: A Journal of World Affairs*, Vol. 38, No. 1, Winter 1994, p. 60.

6. *The Christian Science Monitor*, Friday, January 7, 1994, p. 6.

7. See, for example, William D. Jackson, "Russia after the Crisis—Imperial Temptations: Ethnics Abroad," *Orbis: A Journal of World Affairs*, Vol. 38, No. 1, Winter 1994, pp. 1-17.

8. Jacob W. Kipp, "The Zhirinovsky Threat," *Foreign Affairs*, Vol. 73, No. 3, May/June 1994, p. 77.

9. Quoted in ibid., p. 75.

10. See, for example, *The Christian Science Monitor*, Tuesday, December 14, 1993, pp. 1 and 18; Wednesday, December 15, 1993, p. 7; Tuesday, December 14, 1993, p. 22; and Thursday, March 31, 1994, p. 7.

11. In Ukraine, inflation was reported to have been over 6,500 percent in 1993. See *The Christian Science Monitor*, Tuesday, March 22, 1994, p. 19.

12. The territorial range of NATO's activities was prescribed by Article 5 of the Atlantic Treaty, which committed the member states to help each other in the event of an armed attack on any of them. See *NATO Handbook* (Brussels: NATO Information Service, 1980), p. 14.

13. "Adapting the Alliance in the Face of Great Challenges," *NATO Review*, December 1993, p. 3.

14. Based on discussions found in *Europe*, January/February 1991, pp. 13-14; *Europe*, December/January 1993-94, pp. 26-27; *NATO Review*, December 1993, entire issue and especially pages 25-33, which contain documentation establishing NATO's cooperation in peacekeeping with NACC.

15. NACC has thirty-eight participants: the members of NATO (Belgium, Canada, Denmark, France, Germany, Greece, Iceland, Italy, Luxembourg, the Netherlands, Norway, Portugal, Spain, Turkey, the UK, and the United States), plus Armenia, Azerbaijan, Belarus, Bulgaria, the Czech Republic, Estonia, Hungary, Kazakhstan, Kyrgyzstan, Latvia, Lithuania, Moldova, Poland, Romania, Russia, Slovakia, Tajikistan, Turkmenistan, Ukraine, and Uzbekistan. See *Whitaker's Almanack* (1994), pp. 768-69.

16. The CSCE has fifty-three participant states: Albania, Armenia, Austria, Azerbaijan, Belarus, Belgium, Bosnia-Herzegovina, Bulgaria, Canada, Croatia, Cyprus, the Czech Republic, Denmark, Estonia, Finland, France, Georgia, Germany, Greece, Hungary, Iceland, Ireland, Italy, Kazakhstan, Kyrgyzstan, Latvia, Liechtenstein, Lithuania, Luxembourg, Malta, Moldova, Monaco, the Netherlands, Norway, Poland, Portugal, Romania, the Russian Federation, San Marino, Slovakia, Slovenia, Spain, Sweden, Switzerland, Tajikistan, Turkey, Turkmenistan, the U.K., Ukraine, the United States, Uzbekistan, the Vatican, and Yugoslavia (in July 1992, Yugoslavia was suspended from ECSC activities). See ibid., p. 755.

17. The WEU has ten participants, mainly members of the EU: Belgium, France, Germany, Greece, Italy, Luxembourg, the Netherlands, Portugal, Spain, and the U.K. Denmark and Ireland, although members of the EU, do not yet participate in the WEU. See ibid., p. 776.

18. The Council of Europe, whose aim is to increase cooperation among its members, has thirty-one participants: Austria, Belgium, Bulgaria, Cyprus, the Czech Republic, Denmark, Estonia, Finland, France, Germany, Greece, Hungary, Iceland, Ireland, Italy, Liechtenstein, Lithuania, Luxembourg, Malta, the Netherlands, Norway, Poland, Portugal, San Marino, Slovakia, Slovenia, Spain, Sweden, Switzerland, Turkey, and the U.K. Other countries, including Albania, Belarus, Croatia, Latvia, Romania, the Russian Federation, and Ukraine, have been granted "special guest status." See ibid., p. 755.

19. *The Christian Science Monitor*, Friday, January 7, 1994, p. 6.

20. Ibid.

21. Ibid.

22. As of March 30, 1994, the Partnership for Peace framework document had been signed by Romania (January 26), Lithuania (January 27), Poland (February 2), Estonia (February 3), Hungary (February 8), Ukraine (February 8), Slovakia (February 9), Bulgaria (February 14), Latvia (February 14), Albania (February 23), Czech Republic (March 10), Moldova (March 16), Georgia (March 23), and Slovenia (March 30). See *NATO Review*, April 1994, p. 32.

23. EU's membership consists of Austria, Belgium, Britain, Denmark, Finland, France, Germany, Greece, Ireland, Italy, Luxembourg, the Netherlands, Portugal, Spain and Sweden. Associate members include Cyprus, Malta, and Turkey and from Eastern Europe Bulgaria, the Czech Republic, Hungary, Poland, Romania, and Slovakia. See *Whitaker's Almanack* (1994), p. 757.

24. The particular theoretical perspective that the integration process of the EU benefited from certain aspects of the Cold War is advanced by Peter van Ham, *The EC. Eastern Europe and European Unity: Discord. Collaboration and Integration since 1947*, (London: Pinter Publishers, 1993).

25. Bulgaria, the Czech Republic, Hungary, Poland, Romania, and Slovakia are associate members of the EU. Of these, Hungary and Poland have already submitted formal applications.

26. Heinz Kramer, "The European Community's Response to the 'New Eastern Europe,'" *Journal of Common Market Studies*, Vol. 31, No. 2, June 1993, p. 214.

27. Ian Davidson, "Building New Security Structures: View from Europe," *Europe*, January/February 1991, p. 11.

28. Davis W. Lewis, *The Road to Europe: History. Institutions and Prospects of European Integration 1945-1993* (New York: Peter Lang, 1993), p. 183.

29. Howard LaFranchi, "Clinton Asks Europe to Take the Lead, but Are Its Leaders Ready?" *The Christian Science Monitor*, Thursday, January 13, 1994, p. 7.

30. Ibid.

31. Ibid.

32. For a more extensive theoretical discussion of the factors that may induce the armed forces to intervene in politics, see Kostas Messas, "Democratization of Military Regimes: Contending Explanations," *Journal of Political and Military Sociology*, Vol. 20, No. 2, Winter 1992, pp. 243-55.

33. Peter Grier, "Russian Vote Prompts Alarm in NATO and Western Capitals," *The Christian Science Monitor*, Wednesday, December 15, 1993, p. 7.

34. For a relevant discussion, see John R. Powers and Joseph E. Muckerman, "Rethink the Nuclear Threat," *Orbis: A Journal of World Affairs*, Vol. 38, No. 1, Winter 1994, pp. 99-108.

35. For a recent account of organized crime in Russia, see Seymour M. Hersh, "The Wild East," *The Atlantic Monthly*, June 1994, pp. 61-86.

Annotated Bibliography

Adams, William, ed. 1992. *Singular Europe: Economy and Polity of the European Community after 1992*. Ann Arbor, the University of Michigan Press. This is a very good blend of various aspects of the European integration written by some of the most specialized authors in the field. Fourteen papers look at the post-1992 community in terms of the evolution of Europe during the past 20 years. Topics include issues of legitimacy, the role of the new Germany, economic and monetary union, competition policy and so on.

Aliboni, Roberto ed 1992. *Southern European Security in the 1990s*. London: Pinter Publications. This book describes the security and defense concerns of Southern Europe against the background of improved relations between the East and the West and analyzes how the prospects for stability in Southern Europe might be jeopardized if the West ignores Southern Europe by directing its attention exclusively to maintaining the climate of cooperation with the East.

Bailey, Joe, ed. 1992. *Social Europe*. Essex: Longman Group. This book provides the most comprehensive and focused set of accounts currently available to social scientists of basic formations like industrial structure, social stratification and gender, and of how societies in Western Europe compare on important issues such as education, crime and policing, health and religion. This information is set within an analysis of the profound changes taking place in all European societies, inspired both by the pressure to unite in a larger economic and political unit, and by the impulse to protect and encourage national distinctiveness. It provides a strong framework of sociological analysis of Europe and European societies in the latter part of the twentieth century.

Blis, Christopher and Jorge Braga DeMacedo, eds. 1990. *Unity with Diversity in the European Community: The Community's Southern Frontier*. New York: Cambridge University Press. Proceedings of a conference on the aspects and problems of the enlargement to include Greece, Portugal and Spain. This is a valuable volume on the relatively underdeveloped sector of the European Community.

Bottomore, Robert and J. Brym, eds. 1989. *The Capitalist Class: An International Study*. Henel Hempstead: Harvester-Wheatsheaf: New York: New York University Press. This collection contains an up-to-date profile of the ruling classes in the major capitalist countries, with important papers notably on the French, Italian, and German bourgeoisis.

Buchan, David. 1993. *Europe: The Strange Superpower*. London: Dartmouth Publ. This book argues that the European Community, despite its impressive economic success and growing regional and international importance, will be limited in how it uses its full range of political and economic powers, in large part because of the varying preferences of the member states and regional problems and prospects.

Burger, K., M. Post, DeGroot and V. Zachariasse, eds. 1991. *Agricultural Economics and Policy: International Challenges for the Nineties*. Elsevier: Amsterdam. This collective work offers a panorama of the analysis concerning the new directions of the agricultural economics and policies in different countries of the OCDE. It is a useful collection of different academic views.

Delors, Jacques. 1992. *Our Europe: The Community and National Development*. London: Verso. In this book Delors elaborates the strategy behind the Social Charter and the Delors Plan which has delivered Europe to the brink of "The European Act." Delors explains that his conception of the community arose as a response to the menacing international economic conjuncture, and outlines the role of an integrated Europe in the new world order. *Our Europe* is more than an economic and political program: it is a work of great vision which explores how we might live and act together to transform education, work, and free time.

Dinan, Desmond. 1994. *Ever Closer Union? An Introduction to the European Community*. London: Macmillan. The book is a comprehensive and interdisciplinary introduction to the history and political development of the European Community, the institutions and key policies of the European Union, and the main challenges they face today. It provides a clear overview of the extent and character of European integration since the Second World War, and serves as an ideal introductory text for all students of the European Community and the European Union.

Duke, Simon. 1991. *The New European Security Disorder*. New York: St. Martin's Press. This book offers a comprehensive overview of Europe's military and non-military security threats in the post-Cold War era, provides a critical assessment of the responses to those threats by NATO, WEI, CSCE, and the EC, and makes a strong case for Europe's defense by Europe.

Duff, Andres, John Pinder and Roy Pryce, eds. 1994. *Maastricht and Beyond: Building the European Union*. London: Routledge. This is a critical assessment of the European Union as brought into being by the Treaty of Maastricht. A team of experts provides a clear and thorough appraisal of the main provisions of the Treaty, including the three pillared structure--the European Community (including economic and monetary union), common foreign and security policy, and justice and home affairs--and discusses their implications for the future of the European Union.

Dunfor, Mick and Grigoris Kafkalas, eds. 1992. *Cities and Regions in the New Europe: The Global-Local Interplay and Spatial Development Strategies*. London: Belhaven. This volume examines how the economic and political restructuring of Europe is reflected in urban and regional development. In particular, it focuses on the impact of the globalization of economic activities and the debate about regulating frameworks. The role of Europe's major cities, regional inequalities and the idea of a Europe of the regions are specifically examined.

EC Commission. 1993. *White Paper on Growth, Competitiveness, and Employment.* An overview of the EC Commission's approach to the question of SME's potential contribution to growth, employment and competitiveness enhancement of the European economy.

Feld, Werner J. 1993. *The Future of European Security and Defense Policy.* Boulder, CO: Lynne Rienner Publications. This book discusses how changes associated with the end of the Cold War have impacted upon Europe's security and defense policy and explores the potential of NATO, the CSCE, the WEU, and EC to assist Europe, either individually or collectively, respond to new security and defense challenges and maintain peace.

Greenwood, Juliet, Jurgen R. Grote and Karsten Ronit, eds. 1992. *Organized Interests and the European Community.* London: Newbury Park. New Delhi: Sage. This collection brings together studies on how organized interests in various areas influence processes of market internationalization in Europe. It contains studies of particular sectors, business associations but also trade unions.

Hitiris, T. *European Community Economics*, second edition. 1991. New York: St. Martin's Press. Although written and published before the Maastrict Treaty, this is an excellent study of the overall problems and prospects of European integration. The author examines the objectives of the community, its successes as well as its failures, with an emphasis on policy analysis.

Holland, Martin. *European Community Integration.* London: Pinter Publishers. It presents a reappraisal of the current state of community integration. The events of 1989/90 in Eastern Europe, the continuing interest by non member states in full membership as well as the thrust for economic and political union developed by Delors, have all combined to promote a new, deeper phase of community integration despite controversy over the details and the timing. This book reexamines the broad thematic ideas of Jean Monnet and applies these to the Europe of the 1990s. The question of a federal community acts as the organized principle of the volume.

Holman, Otto. 1995. *Integrating Southern Europe.* London and New York Routledge.

Jacquemin, Alexis and André Sapir, eds. 1990. *The European Internal Makret: Trade and Competition.* New York: Oxford University Press. This is a selection of mostly previously published works that examine the impacts of economic integration on competition and welfare. It requires a good understanding of economics and, especially, international trade theory.

Kjeldahl, R. and M. Tracy, eds. 1994. *Re-nationalization of the Common Agricultural Policy?* Agricultural Policy Studies (IAE), Belgium. This collective book contains the recent orientations of the reform of the Common Agricultural Policy. The contributions in this book cover all relevant debates concerning the future of the agricultural policies in the turn of this century in Europe.

Leibfried, Stephan and Paul Pierson, eds. 1995. *European Social Policy: Between Fragmentation and Integration* Washington, DC: Brookings Institution. What is the state of "Social Europe?" What effects has the European Union's multitiered institutional structure had on the formulation and implementation of social policies? This brand-new volume provides answers to such questions and includes a chapter by Patrick Ireland on "Migration, Free Movement, and Immigrant Integration," to which he sees the European Union providing a bifurcated policy response.

Mazey, S. and J. Richardson, eds. 1993. *Lobbying in the European Community.* Oxford University Press. In this collective work, the authors analyze how various groups of interests are organized and how they coordinate their actions in order to exercise their influence in the decision making process of the European Union. It contains valuable information concerning the lobbying process in the European Union.

Meehan, Elizabeth. 1993. *Citizenship and the European Community*. London: Sage Publications. This is an interesting contribution to the debates on citizenship. It provides an incisive analysis of its meaning, and the links between civil, political and social citizenship. More specifically, it provides a clear account of the development of social rights within the European Community in three key areas: social security and assistance, participation by workers in the undertakings in which they are employed, and the equal treatment of men and women. The author critically assesses the extent to which inequalities of class, gender and ethnicity are successfully addressed by the community.

Miles, Robert and Dietrich Thränhardt, eds. 1995. *Migration and European Integration: The Dynamics of Inclusion and Exclusion*. London: Fairleigh Dickinson Univ. Press.

Moyer, H., Wayne and Timothy E. Josling. 1990. *Agricultural Policy Reform. Politics and Process in the EC and USA*. Harvester Wheatsheaf: New York. In this collective work, the authors examine the reform of the Common Agricultural Policy in comparison with the agricultural policy of the USA. This book gives a comprehensive overview of the political process of the agricultural policy reform on both sides of Atlantic.

Nugent, Neill. 1994. *The Government and Politics of the European Union*. Third Edition, London: Macmillan. The book explains the history, the institutional and decision-making framework, and the policies of the European Union. Further, it shows how the EU is both of immense importance in its own right and is also increasingly shaping the political and economic life of its member states.

Overturf, Stephen F. 1986. *The Economic Principles of European Integration*. New York: Praeger.

Petit, M., M. DeBenedictis, D. Britton, M. DeGroot, W. Henrichsmeyer and F. Icchi. 1987. *Agricultural Policy Formation in the European Community: The Birth of Milk Quotas and CAP Reform*. Elsevier: Amsterdam. This book contains a pioneer study about the agricultural policy formation in the EEC. It is an indispensable introduction to the problems related to the reform of the Common Agricultural Policy.

Piore, M. and C. Sabel. 1984. *The Second Industrial Divide*, Basic Books. This book attempts a synthesis of politics and economics in order to produce a review of the forces shaping international competition and the variety of responses to these forces. The main argument is that major changes are occurring in the structure of the world economy and that the way out of the crisis implies that industry should abandon its attachment to standardized mass production for a system of flexible specialization.

Poulantzas, Nicos. 1975. *Classes in Contemporary Capitalism*. From the French by David Fernbach. London: New Left Books. This book contains the important essay "The Internationalization of Capitalist Relations and the Nation State" which analyzes the ways in which European class formation is structured by processes of internationalization charted mainly by American capital.

Pyke, F.G. Becattini and W., eds. 1990. *Industrial District and Inter-Firms Co-Operation in Italy*, International Institute for Labour Studies, Geneva. This book

shows how a particular combination of economic, social and institutional arrangements have provided the conditions to enable small and medium-sized firms,
organized into networks of competitive and cooperative relations, to compete
successfully on both national and international markets.

Pyke, F. and W. Sengenberger, eds. 1922. *Industrial Districts and Local Economic
Regeneration*, International Institute for Labour Studies, Geneva. This book
addresses two basic questions. First, how do the experiences of the Italian industrial
districts compare with those of other countries (Canada, Cyprus, Denmark,
Germany and Spain)? And second, what are the policy interventions needed in
order to sustain existing industrial districts and to guide other regions considering
pursuing a similar strategy in the interests of local economic regeneration?

Reid, Euen and Hans Reich, eds. 1992. *Breaking the Boundaries: Migrant Workers'
Children in the EC*. Clevedon, UK: Multilingual Matters Ltd. After setting out the
historical and international context for current action on intercultural education in
the European Union—with respect to equal opportunities, anti-racist education,
bilingual education, and materials development—this book presents a systematic and
comprehensive description of fifteen projects carried out between 1986 and 1989 in
primary and secondary schools in ten European Union member states under the
auspices of the European Union. The accounts of the various policies provide useful
background information for those concerned with the second immigrant generation.

Robertson, Patrick, ed. 1992. *Reshaping Europe in the Twenty-First Century*. London:
The Macmillan Press. This is a collection of essays examining the economic and
political arguments which are advanced to support the case for European Union.
These arguments are analyzed and for the most part rejected. Alternatively, the
contributors put forward a wide-ranging plan for a European confederation which
respects individuals' freedom to pursue their economic and political interests while
bringing European countries closer together. It is argued that unity in diversity is
stronger than a potential European superstate run from Brussels.

Rootes, Chris and Howard Davis, eds. 1994. *A New Europe? Social Change and
Political Transformation*. London: UCL Press. Following the 1989 events in
Europe, it is timely to reconsider the question of convergence among European
societies. The book is a thorough examination of political transformation, and in
it leading contributors from western and eastern Europe give their views on how
European society and institutions are changing. The themes of social change, new
movements and the development of European institutions are developed within a
broad framework, and are supported by considerable empirical detail relating to the
European Community and a disaggregated eastern Europe.

Sbragia, Alberta M., ed. 1992. *Euro-Politics: Institutions and Policymaking in the
"New" European Community*. Washington, DC: The Brookings Institution. This
volume provides a good introduction to relatively recent developments in the
European Community that will be useful for scholars and students alike. By
situating the 1992 initiative and community institutions within the broader
framework of comparative politics, it opens up new perspectives on the exciting
events now taking place in Western Europe.

Sengenberger, W., G. Loveman and M. Piors, eds. 1990. *The Re-Emergence of Small
Enterprises: Industrial Restructuring in Industrialized Countries*, International
Institute for Labour Studies, Geneva. This book is based on case-studies material
from the largest market economies, and summarizes the recent developments in the

SME sector, its composition by types of firms and its status and role in the economy.

Springer, Beverly. 1994. *The European Union and Its Citizens: The Social Agenda*. Westpro, CT and London: Greenwood Press. this is a study of the relations of European institutions and the citizenry as envisioned by the Maastrict Treaty.

Tarditi, S., K. Thomson, P. Pierani, E. Croci-Angelini, eds. 1989. *Agricultural Trade Liberalisation and the European Community*. Clarendon Press: Oxford. This book contains a number of contributions written by well known specialists in the area of International Trade of Agricultural Commodities, including quantitative estimates concerning the trade liberalization impact in terms of welfare in different countries (USA, European Community, Japan).

Teague, Paul. 1989. *The European Community: The Social Dimension*. London: Kogan. This monograph contains an original analysis of European labour market policies, including the following areas: free movement of workers, cooperation between national labour market institutions, the European Social Fund, employment and labour legislation, and European collective bargaining. In each of these sections it gives a brief overview of the current extent of the community's influence, as well as an analysis of possible future developments.

Tsoukalis, Loukas. 1981. *The European Community and its Mediterranean Enlargement*. London: George Allen and Unwin.

———. 1983. *The European Community: Past, Present, and Future*. Oxford: Basil Blackwell.

Van der Pijl, Kees. 1984. *The Making of an Atlantic Ruling Class*. London: Verso. This study analyzes the alignment of North American and European ruling classes into patterns of trans-Atlantic and European integration and collusion from the beginnings of the twentieth century. It concentrates on the struggles between rival factions of capital within this larger framework.

Van Tulder, Rob and Junne Gerd. 1988. *European Multinationals in Core Technologies*. Chichester: Wiley. This book analyzes the restructuration of European capital around biotechnology and information technology clusters (core technologies). It also contains an analysis of the European Round Table of Industrialists.

Winters, Alan and Anthony Venables, editors. 1991. *European Integration: Trade and Industry*. New York: Cambridge University Press. Nine topics, in nine papers and discussions presented at a conference on the effects of the 1992 program on the international trade of the community. The papers cover external as well as internal impacts on trade, technology, factor demand, and foreign direct investment.

Wise, Mark and Richard Gibb. 1993. *Single Market to Social Market: The European Community in the 1990s*. Essex: Longman Group. This book is a topical and original investigation linking the well-known issue of a single European Market with the rather less publicized efforts to develop a common social policy for the community, showing the very important relationship that exists between them. Treatment of each is supported by specific case studies of economic and social policy in action, which will assist the reader in understanding and forming opinions about the numerous and diverse initiatives which continue to flow from EC institutions.

Wistrich, Ernest. *The United States of Europe*. This book examines the Maastrich Treaty, looks at the implications of change in Eastern Europe and the former USSR, and points the way to a federation, meaningful to its citizens, which will integrate the whole of Europe and play a significant role in world affairs. Its aim is to update and continue the debate begun in *After 1992*, with a discussion of the developments that have taken place in Europe in the meantime, and an emphasis on political issues rather than "the market."

Index

About the Editors and Contributors

GIANNI BONVICINI is Director, Istituto Affari Internazionali (IAI), Rome, and editor of *The International Spectator*, a quarterly journal of the IAI. He is a Visiting Professor of International Relations, Johns Hopkins University, Bologna Center and a columnist of various scientific publications, professional journals, and newspapers. Main publications include J. Coffey and G. Bonvicini (eds.), *The Atlantic Alliance and the Middle East* (1989); G. Bonvicini (ed.), *L'Italia nel mutato assetto dei rapporti comunitari e internazionali* (1984); G. Bonvicini (ed.), *La politica estera dell'Europa: Autonomia o dipendenza?* (1980); G. Bonvicini and S. Solari (eds.), *I partiti e le elezioni del Parlamento europeo: Intressi nazionali ed europei a confronto* (1979); G. Bonvicini and J. Sassoon (eds.), *Governare l'economia europea: Divergenze e processi integrativi* (1978); G. Bonvicini et al., *La Comunit à europea e le nascenti democrazie dell'Est*, joint policy report of six European foreign policy research institutes (1991).

ELEFTHERIOS N. BOTSAS received an M.A. and Ph.D. in economics. Currently, he is a Professor of Economics and Management, with special interests in international trade and finance, and former chairman of the Economics Department at Oakland University, Rochester, Michigan. He has published on East-West trade, trade and central planning, trade stability, international migration, and the economics of alliances. His current research interests concern the political economy of European integration.

NICHOLAS V. GIANARIS is a Professor of Economics at Fordham University. He has an LL.B., an M.A. and Ph.D. He is the author of many articles and a number of books, including *The Balkan Countries: Economic Changes and Geopolitical Dynamics* (Praeger, 1996), *Modern Capitalism: Privatization, Employee Ownership, and Industrial Democracy* (Praeger, 1995), *The European Community, Eastern Europe and Russia: Economic and Political Changes* (Praeger, 1994), *Contemporary Economic Systems* (Praeger, 1993), and *The European Community and the United States: Economic Relations* (Praeger, 1991).

OTTO HOLMAN studied Political Science at the University of Amsterdam. Senior lecturer in International Relations at the University of Amsterdam since 1983 and since 1990 Jean Monnet senior lecturer in European Integration Studies at the same University. His main fields are the political economy of European Integration and the impact of transnational class formation on processes of economic modernization and political democratization. His publications include *Integrating Southern Europe. EC expansion and the transnationalization of Spain* (1995), and Political and Economic Transformations in Central and Eastern Europe: the International Dimension (The Hague: WRR, 1995, in Dutch). He edited a special issue of the International Journal of Political Economy on European Unification in the 1990s (1992). Recent research includes the transnational dimension of regime transformation in Central and Eastern Europe and the enlargement of the European Union.

PATRICK R. IRELAND earned his Ph.D. in 1990 and is an Associate Professor at the University of Denver's Graduate School of International Studies. He has authored *The Policy Challenge of Ethnic Diversity* (1994), several book chapters, and articles on immigration in major American and European journals. His current research focuses on social and immigration policies in Germany and the EU.

KARL MAGNUS JOHANSSON is a doctoral research student. He is currently engaged in a cross-national research project on transnational parliamentary assemblies, in which he is doing research on the European Parliament and the Nordic Council, and is completing a doctoral thesis on transnational party cooperation between conservative and Christian democratic parties.

ANDREAS G. KOURVETARIS has received his M.A. in social sciences at the University of Chicago. His master's thesis was "Natural Disasters and Community Health: A Case Study of the Mississippi River Flood of 1993 in the Quad-Cities." He is working toward his Ph.D. in sociology at Columbia University. His areas of interest include medical sociology, research methods, and intergroup relations.

GEORGE A. KOURVETARIS was educated both in Greece and the United States, where he received his Ph.D. in 1969. He is currently a Professor of Sociology at Northern Illinois University. His major academic and research interests include political sociology, social theory, intergroup relations, and civil- military relations. His most recent publications include a coauthored book, *A Profile of Modern Greece* (1987), and his most recent book, *Social Thought* (1994). He has authored and coauthored over sixty articles on a range of topics including political clientelism, electoral politics, class identification, political power, political participation, civil-military relations, intergroup relations, and ethnicity. He is also the editor of the *Journal of Political and Military Sociology*, which he founded in 1973. He just completed *Political Sociology*.

JULIET LODGE (M.A., M.Phil., Ph.D., D.Litt., F.R.S.A.) is a a Professor of European Politics, Jean Monnet Professor of European Integration, Director of the Centre for European Studies at the University of England; and also Visiting Professor at the Vrieje Universitet Brussel and the Université Libre de Bruxelles. *European Woman of Europe* 1992/93, her research focuses on the European Union, EU institutions, transparency and legitimacy, judicial cooperation, and foreign affairs. Her most recent books include *The EC and the Challenge of the Future* (1993) and *The 1994 Euro-Elections* (1995).

ANTIGONE LYBERAKI is an Assistant Professor at the Department of Urban and Regional Development, Panteion University, Athens, Greece. She is working on small-scale industry, industrialization, and the implications of new technologies for industrial organization and industrial policy. She has published a number of articles and books, including *Flexible Specialization? Crisis and Restructuring in the Greek Small Firms* (1991), *The Challenge of "Small" Technological Flexibility and Institutional Rigidities* (1992), and *The Convergence that Failed to Come True: Greece EC Comparative Economic Performance during the 1980s* (1993).

NAPOLEON MARAVEYAS is an Associate Professor of Political Economy at the Agricultural University of Athens. He holds a degree in economics (1978), a D.E.A. (Diplôme d' Études Approfondies) in European integration and a Ph.D. in economics (1983). His recent major publications are: *Agricultural Policy and Economic Development in Greece* (1992), *The Process of European Integration and Greek Agriculture* (1993), and "Greek Agriculture and the Common Agricultural Policy," in *Greek Membership Evaluated* (1994). His current research interests are the Common Agricultural Policy, European rural development and policy, and political economy of European integration.

KOSTAS MESSAS is an Assistant Professor of International Studies at the Political Science Department at the Metropolitan State College of Denver. He is the author of "Democratization of Military Regimes: Contending Explanations" and has three more forthcoming articles. Dr. Messas's research interests include various aspects of civil-military relations, democratization, and European integration.

ANDREAS MOSCHONAS (M.A., Ph.D.), is an Assistant Professor in the Department of Sociology at the University of Crete, Greece, and Jean Monnet Professor of European Integration. He has published on Greece and the EU. He is currently completing a monograph, *Education and European Integration*, and does research on Euro-elections, and political parties and European integration.

VASSILIS PESMAZOGLOU studied Economics and Mathematics at Yale, U.S.A. and Development Economics at Bradford, U.K. He has worked for eight years for the Commission of the European Union and is now an Assistant Professor at the Department of Economics, University of Crete, Greece.

KEES VAN DER PIJL studied Law and Political Science at the University of Leyden. Reader in International Relations at the University of Amsterdam since 1973, and board member of the Research Centre for International Political Economy at the University of Amsterdam. His main field is transnational class formation. His publications include a study on the Marshall Plan and the European Coal and Steel Community (*An American Plan for Europe*, 1978, in Dutch), a collection of essays (*Marxism and International Politics*, 1982, in Dutch), and *The Making of an Atlantic Ruling Class* (1984). He edited a special issue of the International Journal of Political Economy on *Transnational Relations and Class Strategy* (1989), including papers by Otto Holman and Henk Overbeek. Current interests include a comprehensive study of the global unification of the capitalist class against attempts at a state–monitored world economy. In the field of the history of ideas, *The Making of International Relations Theory* (of which Dutch and German editions were published in 1992 and 1995 already), will appear in late 1996.

PHILIPPE C. SCHMITTER (Ph.D.) has been on the Stanford faculty since the fall of 1986. He taught for many years at the University of Chicago (1967–82) and held visiting appointments at the University of Brazil in Rio de Janeiro, the Institute for the Integration of Latin America in Buenos Aires, Harvard University, the Universities of Geneva, Zurich, Paris, and Mannheim, the Wissenschaftszentrum in Berlin, the Centro de Estudios Avanzados en Ciencias Sociales in Madrid, and the Institut d'Etudes Politiques de Paris. Before coming to Stanford, he spent the previous four years as a professor at the European University Institute in Florence. Schmitter has conducted research on comparative politics and regional integration in both Latin America and Western Europe, with special emphasis on the politics of organized interests. He is the co–author of *Transitions from Authoritarian Rule: Prospects for Democracy* (4 vols.) and is currently completing, *Consolidations of Democratic Rule*. At Stanford, he served as the director of the Center for European Studies from its foundation in 1986 until early 1992. He has been the recipient of numerous professional awards and fellowships, including a Guggenheim in 1978, and has been vice–president of the American Political Science Association.

WOLFGANG STREECK is a Professor of Sociology and Industrial Relations at the University of Wisconsin–Madison. He was a Senior Research Fellow at the Wissenschaftszentrum, Berlin, and held visiting appointments at the European University Institute, Florence; the University of Warwick, Bocconi University, Milan, and the Center for Advanced Studies in the Social Sciences, Madrid. In 1993–94 he was a Fellow at the Institute for Advanced Study, Berlin. Fields of interest include trade unions, business associations, industrial relations, industrial change, and European integration. Recent books include *Social Institutions and Economic Performance: Studies in Industrial Relations in Advanced Capitalist Economies* (1992), *Governing Capitalist Economies: Performance and Control of Economic Sectors* (coedited with J. Rogers Hollingsworth and Philippe C. Schmitter, 1994), *Public Interest and Market Pressures: Problems Posed by Europe 1992* (with David G. Mayes and Wolfgang Hager, 1992), *Beyond Keynesianism: The Socio-Economics of Production and Employment* (coedited with Egon Matzner, 1991, paperback edition 1994), and *New Technology and Industrial Relations* (coedited with Richard Hyman, 1988).